Sitton Spelling and Word Skills™

Sourcebook 5

Rebecca Sitton

EDUCATORS PUBLISHING SERVICE
Cambridge and Toronto

Holly Chapman
Graphic Design and Production

Donna Bernard
Illustrator

Christy Fong
Consultant

Teresa Therriault
Consultant

Mary Euretig
Consultant

 Sitton Spelling and Word Skills™, Sourcebook 5, 3rd edition

888-WE-SPELL
www.sittonspelling.com

Printed in USA

ISBN 978-1-886050-69-3

1 2 3 4 5 DBH 12 11 10 09 08

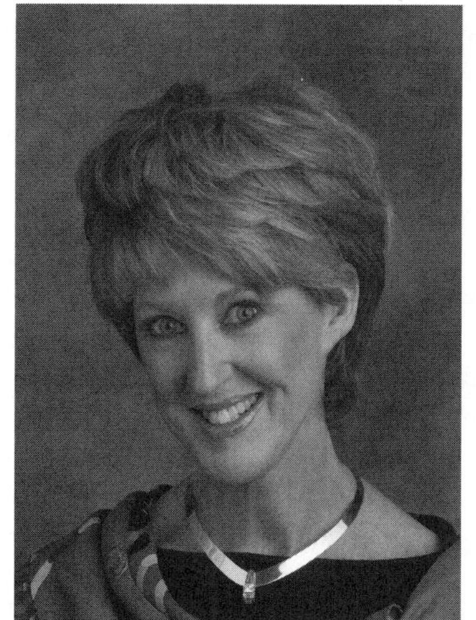

Why a new edition?

Dear Educators,

Welcome to the Third Edition!

The First Edition evolved over time as a result of educators who, like me, were dissatisfied with their spelling curriculum, and wanted to do more than fault it. Although I didn't realize it then, this was the beginning of an exciting journey of inquiry, collaboration, research, and the construction of ideas to teach students to spell where it counts—in their writing.

The Second Edition transformed the format. We were discovering not only what works, but how to organize the materials to make them easy to manage and welcoming. Teachers responded with enthusiasm! The word spread. Teachers in rural communities, as well as those in districts that are among the largest in the country, eagerly told others about their success!

What could be more inspiring than educators breaking with tradition to embrace research-based strategies to guide their students in new ways to discover the exciting complexities of words and language? It was immensely gratifying! Change was taking place in spite of the deep roots of tradition. You see, this program's methodology requires a change in thinking about spelling and word work. Yet, if nothing changes, nothing changes.

Now, in its Third Edition, refinements have been made. The optional student Practice Books are for educators who asked for better ways to engage students in follow-ups to selected Sourcebook lessons. Teachers wanted word cards for their walls and CD-ROM activities. Now they have them with two new complements to the primary levels of the Series. Teachers asked for training options, giving birth to Tutor Me for each grade, and one for parents, too.

Note another new element: Teachers said, "Rebecca, this is far more than a spelling program—it's all about words for reading, writing, speaking, thinking, and spelling. It's phonics, vocabulary, usage, literature, writing!" So, the name of the Series now reflects its integrated communications approach.

Bravo to the talented and dedicated teachers who have been so generous with their suggestions to make this new edition a stronger resource for all educators—thank you! Let's continue this journey together learning how to help children learn!

Rebecca Sitton

Table of Contents

BLACKLINE MASTERS

REFERENCES

FOR YOUR TEACHING PLEASURE...
MOTIVATIONAL SPELLING WORKSHOPS!!
888-WE-SPELL
TEACHING TIPS AND TOOLS....
VISIT
WWW.sittonspelling.com
WOW!

Let's Get Started

As you peruse your Sourcebook, you'll see it differs from a customary spelling program in which each unit opens with a word list followed by activities to prepare students for the Friday Test. The goal is to learn the words for the test. After the test, the words vanish—not only from the program, but often from the minds of students. The Sourcebook's research-based instructional design ensures that students learn to spell for writing—to spell words *forever*, not just for a test. Further, students learn to spell within the framework of a total word-skills curriculum.

Your Sourcebook has thirty-five units, each set up in the same way. Units have two main parts: *Build Skills and Word Experiences* and *Assess Words and Skills*. Each of these two parts is divided into sections that support its focus. Note the graphic organizer (see page 401).

Build Skills and Word Experiences focuses on how all words work. Students expand their knowledge of words for writing, spelling, reading, speaking, and thinking. They make discoveries about all elements of language and its correct use to form a solid word-skills foundation to complement any communications curriculum.

In Assess Words and Skills, the focus changes from *general* word work to *specific* word work. Here students get *Spelling Words*. Here students' personal Spelling Words are identified through ongoing whole-class tests—the Cloze Story Word Test (see pages 336–339) and the Sentence Dictation Test (see pages 342–345) for students who need more practice or greater challenge. Students do not prestudy the words for these tests. The words they miss become their Spelling Words, differentiated to each student's writing needs. Further, acquisition of skills is evaluated on the Skill Test in each unit.

Words tested and targeted for mastery are researched high-frequency writing words, called Core Words, and are introduced in frequency-of-use order (see Core Words List, pages 363–365). Their mastery makes writing easier for emerging writers, a foremost goal of the program. The activity options include essential communication skills to ensure that students know how to use the words they're learning to spell (see Scope and Sequence, pages 402–403).

It's not enough to teach words and skills without expecting their transfer to writing. The Priority Word expectation achieves this (see pages 330–335). Students learn "how to proofread," and then they develop a proofreading habit through clear expectations for doing so in all their everyday writing.

The Sourcebook's instructional model is research based. For example, the words targeted for mastery are researched high-use writing words differentiated to each student's needs. Teachers select from a menu of activity options that reflect researched best practices. Their range of topics and difficulty allows teachers to customize instruction for diverse learners. Students are guided to discover essential skills through inquiry and analysis. Careful recycling of all words and skills achieves high density exposure for mastery. Research clearly validates each of these elements for achieving confident spellers and language users.

Is review necessary before getting started?

Begin with Unit 1 regardless of the students' backgrounds or the time of year. All words and skills from the previous levels are reintroduced in this level; therefore, no review is necessary—the program automatically provides review.

What is the first step for commencing?

The first step is to acquaint yourself with the program. Peruse the Table of Contents for an overview of teaching support options. Then look at the first unit. Read the Teaching Notes on the page numbers indicated below each unit section.

The get-acquainted CD-ROM training, Tutor-Me (see page 407), introduces you to your Sourcebook. For more in-depth training, you can contact Egger Publishing, Inc. for a Sourcebook Consultant to provide on-site staff development, or you can attend a training seminar (check the web site for schedules: www.sittonspelling.com).

Acquaint parents with the program. Send home the INTRODUCING SPELLING BLACKLINE MASTER, page 372. This is the first parent communication among several to develop parent-child partnerships. Use the Tutor Me Training Parent Introduction for additional support (see page 407).

Then begin. Don't hesitate. Don't worry about making mistakes. Soon your teaching will become a comfortable routine.

Are the student books necessary or optional?

If you use the student Practice Books (see page 389), the correlated activities are indicated on the ⟨pencil icon⟩ under the headline opening each unit's two main parts: *Build Skills and Word Experiences* and *Assess Words and Skills*. These student materials are optional.

Are there supplementary materials for the Level 5 Sourcebook?

The Spell Check is fifth graders' favorite spelling reference, and *Word-Wise Sourcebook Three* extends the Level 5 Sourcebook skills and concepts to laugh-aloud rhymes for learning some of the most challenging language elements (see page 407).

What materials are necessary to teach the program?

Yet, all you really need to use this program is your Sourcebook. No part of it is consumable. Its high flexibility will serve you well over time as students, as well as your language materials, change. Your Sourcebook accommodates change, but to achieve success through its methodology, you, too, must change. Relinquish the "word list-Friday test" paradigm and acquire the Sourcebook thinking that resurrects researched skill-based instruction, common sense, and expectations for spelling in writing.

What if questions arise?

As you transition into this approach, enjoy it! If questions arise, please call. We're eager to help you make *every child a speller*!

Toll-Free: 888-WE-SPELL

www.sittonspelling.com

Build Skills and Word Experiences

• Send home the INTRODUCING SPELLING BLACKLINE MASTER, page 372.

Use Student Practice Pages 1–2 to follow up instruction for:
Activity 1A • Activity 1B

Build Visual Skills

Do the Word Preview, a visual warm-up activity, with all students.
Use Core Words **music** (501), **buy** (502), **window** (503), **mark** (504), **heat** (505).

Teaching Notes, page 316

Build Spelling and Language Skills

Choose from among these quick tasks to customize instruction
for all or selected students.

Teaching Notes, page 319

It left a mark on his jacket.

(discuss possible options for expansion)

Window comes from one word that means "wind" and an other that means "eye." We by windows to keep an eye on the wind. We also use them too keep heat in when its cold outside

(*another, buy, to, it's,* final period)

heat, meeting, anything, study, reading, bumblebee, teacher, sheet, suddenly, daydream, energy, weekend, weaver, carefully

(demonstrate sorting: e.g., /ē/ spelling pattern; number of syllables; does/doesn't have a suffix; is/isn't a compound)

car, mark, carve, ______

(words with *ar* and each word has one more letter)

I wanted to buy the one in the window, but ______.

Words that illustrate types of music

(e.g., rock, classical, jazz, pop)

Teaching Notes, page 325

Build Basic Concepts

Choose from among these skill-building activities to customize instruction
for all or selected students.

concept one	Short vowel sounds are usually spelled with one vowel. Long vowel sounds are usually spelled with two vowels.

phonics, word analysis, writing words, sorting words, compound words, proofreading

1A Select students to write on the chalkboard: *heat, chain, scream, twine, beast*. To reinforce Concept One, ask student pairs to make these long vowel words into short vowel words (remove a vowel).

Next, review that a compound word is a combination of two or more words. Dictate these compounds for students to write: *cattail, pancake, sunshine, treetop, weekend, frostbite*. Write the words on the chalkboard, or have a student do so, for students to self-check. Then have students rewrite the word parts of each compound, sorting them by long/short vowel sound, noting the number of vowel letters. Next, challenge some students to find and write more compound words for which at least one word part has a short or long vowel sound. Ask these students to present their compounds to the class for further reinforcement of the concept.

Challenge students to substitute one homophone set for the underlined words.
<u>So long</u>! I'm going <u>via</u> bus to a store <u>near</u> the park to <u>purchase</u> new shoes.
(Bye! I'm going by bus to a store by the park to buy new shoes.)

phonics, more words, spelling word patterns

1B Organize students into small groups to write words with the long vowel sound you call out—*a, e, i, o, u*. Limit each word find to two minutes. Use students' words to begin a class chart for each long vowel to review their most frequent spelling patterns (/ā/: *a, ai, ay, a*-consonant-*e*; /ē/: *e, ea, ee, y*; /ī/: *i, igh, ind, y, i*-consonant-*e*; /ō/: *o, oa, ow, old, o*-consonant-*e*; /yü/: *u, ew, ue, u*-consonant-*e*). Label columns and include a column for unexpected spellings called "other."

Over time, have students find more words to round out the collection for each spelling pattern. Note that long vowel sounds are often spelled with two vowels.

concept two	Frequent spelling patterns for /k/ are *c, k, ch, ck,* and *qu.*

phonics, more words, spelling word patterns, word analysis

2A Select a student to write *mark* and *music* on the chalkboard. Compare the ending sound and letter. Ask students to brainstorm /k/ words. Guide them to discover that /k/ is spelled most often with *c, k, ch,* and *ck,* and *qu* spells /kw/. Further, *ke* often signals a long vowel sound at the end of a word, and *x* can spell /ks/. Challenge capable students to discover less frequent spellings, such as those indicated in Did You Know? on page 3.

Have students write 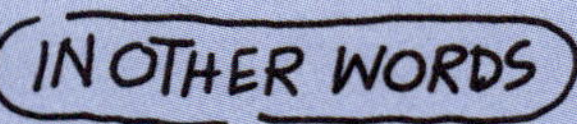: If you can't stand the heat, get out of the kitchen.

Build Skillful Writers

Use these interrelated language learnings for all or selected students.

Teaching Notes, page 328

Skillful writers must be on the lookout for a specific set of words—those that end in *ic*. Use *ic/ics*-ending words (Word Mysteries and Histories, this unit) to have students explore these spelling and language idiosyncrasies:

- The *ly* suffix usually becomes *ally*: *specifically, athletically, basically* (an exception is *publicly*).
- A *k* is added before suffixes beginning with *e, i,* or *y*: *frolicked, picnicking, panicky*.
- Some *ics*-ending nouns look plural, but are treated as singular: *mathematics, politics*. These words use a singular verb, such as *is*.

Letter sounds are written inside //. The sound at the end of music is /k/. The letter *c* spells /k/ almost 75% of the time, followed by *k/ke* occurring about 13% of the time. Other frequent spellings are *ck* (black), *ch* (echo), and less often *kk* (Hanukkah) and *cc* (occupy). The letter *q* is usually followed by *u* and spells /kw/ in words except some of foreign origin in which *qu* spells /k/—*unique* (French); *mosquito* (Spanish). The letter *x* can spell /ks/, as in *extra*.

Build Assessment Readiness

Use these at-school and at-home exercises to prepare all students for the Skill Test.

Teaching Notes, page 329

at-school   Introduce Teaching Poster 1 and discuss the proofreading pointers and marks. Then have students complete a copy of PERSONAL POSTER 1 BLACKLINE MASTER, page 367, adding the words that are personally challenging for them to spell—their "bad guys." Have students save their Personal Poster to use as a proofreading reference.

Skill to be tested:
visual skills

at-home   Send home a copy of TAKE-HOME TASK 1 BLACKLINE MASTER, page 4, with each student to encourage parent-child partnerships.

Skill to be tested:
visual skills

Build Proofreading Skills

Track students' ability to meet a minimum competency for spelling and proofreading within selected samples of their everyday writing.

Teaching Notes, page 330

- Send home papers for proofreading and a copy of the IDEAS FOR PROOFREADING BLACKLINE MASTER, page 373.

Dear Parents,

Here is your child's first Take-Home Task. It is a visual skill-building lesson to help your child develop the skills necessary for accurate proofreading. Learning to spell is important—we work toward this goal daily at school—but proofreading is just as important. The classroom is your child's rehearsal for real-world spelling, where careful proofreading and spelling in writing is expected.

First, have some fun practicing visual skills with your child. Ask your child to picture and write the details of something familiar, such as the face of an often-used clock, the TV set, the front of the refrigerator. You do the same thing. After the details are recalled and written independently (of course, without looking), then check it out together. We often look at something daily, but don't really see it. Help your child learn that when proofreading, s/he must not just look at, but actually see everything on the page—in detail.

The next activity engages your child in a spelling and proofreading activity that uses a format comparable to many standardized spelling tests—really proofreading tests. Ask your child to read the directions and then explain to you what is expected. Have your child complete the exercise. Then review each row together.

Circle the word in each row that is spelled right.

musick	musik	music	mussic
brot	bruoght	broght	brought
carefully	carefuly	carfuly	carefilly
enything	enytheng	anything	anythin
redy	ready	reedy	readdy
thot	thuoght	thought	thoght
beautiful	beautifull	bautiful	beoutiful
insted	innsted	insteed	instead
sudenly	suddenlly	suddenly	suddently
hapened	happened	hapenned	happenned

There's more! Have your child look at the circled words for a few moments. Then turn the paper over. Ask your child to recall and write the words. Last, have your child turn the paper over to self-check each word with the word in the exercise.

Thanks, parents! Every child a speller!

Assess Words and Skills

- Spelling Words (words missed on tests) are recorded in the Spelling Notebook.
- Use Proof It, Practice Page 3, for proofreading/editing practice.

Teaching Notes, page 336

Assess Spelling Progress

Give this Cloze Story Word Test of Core Words within the frequencies 1–505 to all students. Words students miss are their Spelling Words.

THE CLOZE STORY WORD TEST

Students do not prestudy the words. Provide students with a copy of REVIEW 1 BLACKLINE MASTER, page 8. Tell students that this story will get them thinking about a common snack food that became popular partly as the result of an insect!

Read the entire story aloud, including the test words. Then read it again slowly as students write the missing words.

Planting Peanuts

   (1) Years ago, the most (2) important crop in the South was threatened. (3) There were vast (4) fields of cotton lost to the boll weevil. This insect left (5) its (6) mark as it ate (7) through entire crops. George Washington Carver, a scientist, knew (8) hundreds of uses for peanuts. He (9) told farmers to grow peanuts, but they didn't (10) buy his idea. So, he invited them for a fine day of (11) music and lunch, (12) later telling them that (13) everything they ate was made from peanuts! Many quickly changed (14) their minds, grew peanuts, and grew prosperous! (15) Which state do you think planted so many peanuts that (16) it's leading in the production of peanuts today?

   You can plant your (17) own peanuts outside in (18) warm climates or (19) inside by a (20) window that gets (21) heat from the sun. Use this technique. Crack the shells of a few raw peanuts (not roasted), cover the peanuts with dirt, and (22) water them. Stalks grow from each flower into the soil, producing the peanut pods. After (23) they're grown, you can dig up the pods, roast them, and serve peanuts to your (24) friends!

Words tested:
there (37), which (41), their (42), its (76), water (90), through (102), own (163), important (195), year(s) (225), it's (253), told (255), later (288), inside (321), hundred(s) (374), warm (412), everything (432), field(s) (472), friend(s) (498), music (501), buy (502), window (503), mark (504), heat (505), *they're (1010)

*The testing of they're (1010) is included to help students differentiate among the there/their/they're homophones.

AFTER THE CLOZE STORY WORD TEST

1. Have students research which state produces the most peanuts. Then have them write and share their answer. Conclude that Georgia produces far more peanuts than any other state. Challenge students to research products made from the peanut.

research, writing

2. Have students record the words they missed on the test in their Spelling Notebook (see page 338) for at-school study, and on a copy of the WORDS TO LEARN BLACKLINE MASTER, page 375, for at-home study. Send home the completed WORDS TO LEARN personal study list with a copy of the IDEAS FOR WORD STUDY BLACKLINE MASTER, page 374.

recording words for personal study list

Assess Skill Application

Give this assessment of spelling and related skills to all students.
The REVIEW 1 BLACKLINE MASTER is on page 9.

Teaching Notes, page 339

 **THE SKILL TEST**

Skill tested:
visual skills

Circle the word in each row that is spelled right.

1.	windew	wendow	whendow	(window)
2.	(everything)	evrything	everytheng	evryting
3.	yourseff	(yourself)	yourselve	yourselff
4.	(question)	qestion	quesion	queastion
5.	betwean	bettween	beatween	(between)
6.	somer	(summer)	sumer	sommer
7.	hete	heet	(heat)	heate
8.	chek	(check)	checke	cheke

Note the ability of each student to use visual skills to proofread familiar words.

Assess Proofreading Application

Give this assessment of spelling and related skills to all students.
The REVIEW 1 BLACKLINE MASTER is on page 9.

Teaching Notes, page 341

 **THE PROOFREADING TEST**

If an underlined word in each line is incorrect, write it correctly in the space.

the Orchestra

The musik of an orchestra is made up of four kinds	The
of instruments. Thay are the strings, woodwinds,	music
brass, and percussion. The instruments our grouped	They
into families bye the sounds the instruments make.	are
The stings include instruments that have strings. One	by
example is a violin. The lagest stringed instrument is	strings
the bass. Than there are the woodwinds, which make	largest
music when air is blown though them. A flute is one	Then
kind of woodwind. The brass famly includes the	through
instruments made of brass, such as a trumpet. finaly,	family
their are percussion instruments that make music	Finally
when they are hit. A dum and a triangle are examples	there
of theese instruments in an orchestra.	drum
	these

If an orchestra had only one kind of instrument, how would it change the sound of the music?

Note the ability of each student to proofread for spelling and capitalization errors.

Extend Spelling Assessment

Give this in-context assessment of Core Words within the frequencies 1–505 to students who need more practice or challenge.

Teaching Notes, page 342

Words tested:
the (1), of (2), and (3), to (5), in (6), was (13), on (14), be (21), from (23), I (24), one (28), had (29), we (36), there (37), so (57), who (77), my (80), long (91), our (109), take(ing) (135), line (161), world (191), want(ed) (193), almost (216), best (246), young (256), sun (257), hear (260), toward (275), money (279), move(d) (290), group (295), stood (373), hundred (374), outside (420), everyone('s) (430), rock (489), friend (498), music (501), buy (502), window (503), mark (504), heat (505)

Extra words: chance, reached, slowly, sunburned, tickets, Tuesday, we'd, woman

THE SENTENCE DICTATION TEST

Students do not prestudy the words. Provide students with writing paper and pencil. Have students write the sentences as they are dictated.

1. My friend and I stood outside in the long line to buy our tickets.
2. We moved slowly toward the young woman in the window who was taking everyone's money.
3. The heat from the sun had almost reached the one hundred mark, so there was the chance we'd be sunburned.
4. On Tuesday we wanted to hear the music of the best rock group in the world!

AFTER THE SENTENCE DICTATION TEST

1. Have students hypothesize which rock group the friends were going to see. Then give reasons why they think the group is the best. Challenge some students to create an advertising piece that announces the rock group's performance. Then have them present their work to the class.

2. Have students record the words they missed on the test in their Spelling Notebook (see page 345) for at-school study, and on a copy of the WORDS TO LEARN BLACKLINE MASTER, page 375, for at-home study. Send home the completed WORDS TO LEARN personal study list with a copy of the IDEAS FOR WORD STUDY BLACKLINE MASTER, page 374.

hypothesizing, writing an explanation, writing an advertisement

recording words for personal study list

The words a student misses on the Cloze Story Word Test or the Sentence Dictation Test become a student's personal study list. These words are a student's <u>Spelling Words</u> for this unit. Subsequent tests automatically retest each student's words.

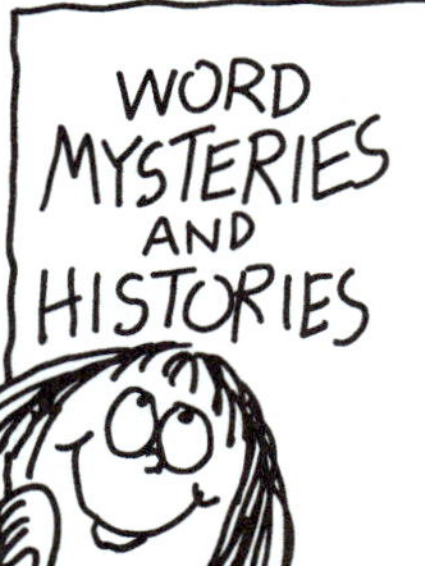

WORD MYSTERIES AND HISTORIES

Greek myths, or tales, are the origin of *panic* and *music*. The god Pan harassed people—the fright he caused was called panic. Muses, the nine Greek goddesses of song and other arts, became the origin of music.
- Have students write more words that end in *ic* (e.g., basic, picnic, mimic, traffic, athletic, logic, arctic, metric). Save words for Build Skillful Writers, this unit.
- Ask students to explore Greek myths—then retell a myth to the class.
- The Greek root *therm* means "heat." Have students explain in writing how *therm* contributes to the meaning of a word containing the root (e.g., thermometer, thermos, thermostat).

— Word Test —

Planting Peanuts

(1) _______________ ago, the most (2) _______________ crop in the south was

threatened. (3) _______________ were vast (4) _______________ of cotton lost to

the boll weevil. This insect left (5) _______________ (6) _______________ as it ate

(7) _______________ entire crops. George Washington Carver, a scientist, knew

(8) _______________ of uses for peanuts. He (9) _______________ farmers to grow

peanuts, but they didn't (10) _______________ his idea. So, he invited them for a fine

day of (11) _______________ and lunch, (12) _______________ telling them that

(13) _______________ they ate was made from peanuts! Many quickly changed

(14) _______________ minds, grew peanuts, and grew prosperous! (15) _______________

state do you think planted so many peanuts that (16) _______________ leading in

the production of peanuts today?

You can plant your (17) _______________ peanuts outside in (18) _______________

climates or (19) _______________ by a (20) _______________ that gets

(21) _______________ from the sun. Use this technique. Crack the shells of a few raw

peanuts (not roasted), cover the peanuts with dirt, and (22) _______________

them. Stalks grow from each flower into the soil, producing the peanut pods. After

(23) _______________ grown, you can dig up the pods, roast them, and serve

peanuts to your (24) _______________!

Skill Test

Circle the word in each row that is spelled right.

1.	windew	wendow	whendow	window
2.	everything	evrything	everytheng	evryting
3.	yourseff	yourself	yourselve	yourselff
4.	question	qestion	quesion	queastion
5.	betwean	bettween	beatween	between
6.	somer	summer	sumer	sommer
7.	hete	heet	heat	heate
8.	chek	check	checke	cheke

Proofreading Test

If an underlined word in each line is incorrect, write it correctly in the space.

the Orchestra _______________________

The musik of an orchestra is made up of four kinds _______________________

of instruments. Thay are the strings, woodwinds, _______________________

brass, and percussion. The instruments our grouped _______________________

into families bye the sounds the instruments make. _______________________

The stings include instruments that have strings. One _______________________

example is a violin. The lagest stringed instrument is _______________________

the bass. Than there are the woodwinds, which make _______________________

music when air is blown though them. A flute is one _______________________

kind of woodwind. The brass famly includes the _______________________

instruments made of brass, such as a trumpet. finaly, _______________________

their are percussion instruments that make music _______________________

when they are hit. A dum and a triangle are examples _______________________

of theese instruments in an orchestra. _______________________

If an orchestra had only one kind of instrument, how would it change the sound of the music?

Build Skills and Word Experiences

Build Visual Skills

Do the Word Preview, a visual warm-up activity, with all students.
Use Core Words **grew** (506), **listen** (507), **ask** (508), **single** (509), **clear** (510).

Teaching Notes, page 316

Build Spelling and Language Skills

Choose from among these quick tasks to customize instruction
for all or selected students.

Teaching Notes, page 319

The water was clear.

(discuss possible options for expansion)

We grew still when we saw the cubs We did'nt make a singel sound as we listened to see if the mother bear was close. She was! Bill aksed us to clear out quickly without panicing.

(period at end of first sentence, *didn't*, *single*, *asked*, *panicking*)

kind, nickname, Kentucky, ask, picnic, music, Alaska, clearly, Oklahoma, bookstore, attic, hockey, Kansas

(demonstrate sorting: e.g., /k/ spelling pattern; is/isn't a noun; is/isn't a state name)

ask/tell, listen/talk, clear/cloudy, _______ /______

(antonyms)

There wasn't a single cloud in the sky, so I _______.

Synonyms for *ask*

(e.g., inquire, question)

Build Basic Concepts

Choose from among these skill-building activities to customize instruction for all or selected students.

Teaching Notes, page 325

| **concept one** | A prefix is a letter or letters added to the beginning of a word. A suffix is a letter or letters added to the end of a word. |

1A Select a student to write *clear* and *unclear* on the chalkboard. Discuss how the addition of the prefix changes the meaning of the base word. Identify a prefix as a word part that may be added to the beginning of some words to alter meaning.

prefix/suffix practice, vocabulary development, nouns/verbs, spelling rules, writing words

Demonstrate adding *ed* to *ask* to make *asked*. Identify *ed* as a suffix, a word part that may be added to the end of some words. Most often its purpose is to change the part of speech of the base word (an exception is the *less* suffix). Discuss the verb *clear* and the noun *clearance*.

To add a prefix or a suffix to a base word, begin with the spelling of the base word. Then decide how to make the addition.
- For a prefix: Never change the spelling of the base word—just add the prefix.
- For a suffix: The spelling of the base word may change for the addition of some suffixes.

Introduce Teaching Poster 2 and have students complete a copy of PERSONAL POSTER 2 BLACKLINE MASTER, page 368. There are minimal exceptions to the rules on the Teaching Poster. Exceptions worth noting are—

For Rule 2:
- Some words retain the silent *e* before a suffix beginning with a vowel to maintain pronunciation (e.g., mileage, acreage, or words ending in ce/ge—noticeable, changeable) or to prevent them from being confused with other words (e.g., dyeing).
- Some words drop the silent *e* before a suffix beginning with a consonant (ninth, truly, wholly, judgment, argument).

For Rule 3:
- The consonants *w*, *x*, and *y* are never doubled (newest, fixing, played).

Heighten students' awareness of silent consonants, a significant contributor to spelling errors.
- Challenge students to collect words with silent t (e.g., listen, often, castle, wrestle, whistle, trestle, fasten, glisten, soften, mortgage).
- Challenge students to collect more words with silent consonants, such as b (doubt), k (knot), w (wrench), l (talk).
(These activities provide a head start for silent letter lessons—the first appears in Unit 4.)

Teaching Notes, page 328

Build Skillful Writers

Use these interrelated language learnings for all or selected students.

Singular is a form of *single*, meaning "one." Its opposite, *plural*, means "more than one." Most nouns have a singular and plural form. Have students provide examples to demonstrate that—

- Singular subjects need singular verbs.
- Plural subjects need plural verbs.

Some nouns look plural and have no singular form, but need a singular verb (e.g., mathematics, politics, phonics, news, checkers). Often these are *ics*-ending words (Build Skillful Writers, page 3). Other nouns look plural and have no singular form, but need a plural verb. Provide clues for students to identify *scissors, trousers, pliers, tongs, pants, mumps*. Dictionary entries list singular forms, but a plural may be given if the plural form is other than the addition of an *s*. Its spelling follows the abbreviation for plural— *pl*. Challenge students to verify this with examples of dictionary entries for plural forms.

Teaching Notes, page 329

Build Assessment Readiness

Use these at-school and at-home exercises to prepare all students for the Skill Test.

Skill to be tested:
short/long vowels

at-school Select a student to write *tap* and *tape* on the chalkboard. Identify the short/long vowel sounds. Remind students that long vowel words are often spelled with two vowels, while short vowel words usually have one vowel. Post Teaching Poster 2. Add the *ing* suffix to *tap/tape* and have students indicate which rule on Teaching Poster 2 applies (*tapping*—Rule 3, *taping*—Rule 2). Then have students write these words with the *ing* suffix and sort them by vowel sound: *hop/hope, pin/pine, grip/gripe, wag/wage, mop/mope.*

Later, write the sorts on the chalkboard, or have a student do so, for students to self-check. Discuss the meaning of unfamiliar words. Last, reverse the process—have students write the base word for each of the ing word forms.

Skill to be tested:
short/long vowels

at-home Send home a copy of TAKE-HOME TASK 2 BLACKLINE MASTER, page 13, with each student to encourage parent-child partnerships.

Teaching Notes, page 330

Build Proofreading Skills

Track students' ability to meet a minimum competency for spelling and proofreading within selected samples of their everyday writing.

- Send home papers for proofreading and a copy of the IDEAS FOR PROOFREADING BLACKLINE MASTER, page 373.

Dear Parents,

This is your child's second Take-Home Task. These activities will be sent home routinely for you to do together. You're on your child's spelling team!

This exercise develops vocabulary and thinking skills. Further, it reviews long and short vowel sounds. At school we're reviewing how these sounds are most often spelled. Begin by having your child read the directions and explain to you what is expected. Guide your child through the activity, letting your child do as much as possible without your help.

Read the words in each row. Circle the two synonyms—the words with similar meanings.

grinning	smiling	smelling
tacking	taking	nailing
gripping	clasping	griping
hopping	hoping	wishing
gabbing	grabbing	chatting
tracing	racing	rushing
dining	eating	spinning
sobbing	diving	weeping
draping	dropping	spilling
tapping	taping	knocking

On another sheet of paper, have your child write the base word for the words in the activity—the word without the ing suffix.

Next, ask your child to sort the base words into two columns—one for short vowel words, one for long vowel words.

How many vowel letters are there in the long vowel words?

How many vowel letters are there in the short vowel words?

Thanks, parents! Together, we're helping your child develop an understanding of our language and its spelling. Every child a speller!

Assess Words and Skills

- Spelling Words (words missed on tests) are recorded in the Spelling Notebook.
- Use Proof It, Practice Page 6, for proofreading/editing practice.

WORD TEST

Teaching Notes, page 336

Assess Spelling Progress

Give this Cloze Story Word Test of Core Words within the frequencies 1–510 to all students. Words students miss are their Spelling Words.

THE CLOZE STORY WORD TEST

Students do not prestudy the words. Provide students with a copy of REVIEW 2 BLACKLINE MASTER, page 17. Tell students that this story describes a game.

Read the entire story aloud, including the test words. Then read it again slowly as students write the missing words.

Words tested:
there (37), their (42), first (74), its (76), most (99), write(ten) (108), does (128), together (187), sure (251), it's (253), several (263), face(s) (291), group(s) (295), among (345), surface (393), follow (428), build (487), check (493), grew (506), listen (507), ask (508), single (509), clear (510), *they're (1010)

*The testing of they're (1010) is included to help students differentiate among the there/their/they're homophones.

Trivia Insanity

WORD TEST

This is a trivia game. (1) <u>It's</u> played in (2) <u>groups</u>, or teams. Each team gets a Trivia Insanity Sheet with (3) <u>several</u> questions. (4) <u>They're</u> read aloud by the Trivia Master, your teacher. Team members (5) <u>listen</u> and (6) <u>follow</u> along. Teams may (7) <u>ask</u> a (8) <u>single</u> question about each item to be (9) <u>sure</u> they are (10) <u>clear</u> about (11) <u>its</u> meaning. Next, teams work (12) <u>together</u> to (13) <u>build</u> answers. References can be used. Teams submit a (14) <u>written</u> answer on (15) <u>their</u> Insanity Sheet for each question so that the Master can (16) <u>check</u> for accuracy. The (17) <u>first</u> team to have the correct answer for an item wins for that item. The object is to be the team with the (18) <u>most</u> "wins" when the ending bell sounds!

(19) <u>There</u> are many examples of great trivia questions. What (20) <u>does</u> the "zip" in ZIP Code stand for? Which (21) <u>faces</u> are carved on the (22) <u>surface</u> of Mount Rushmore? Which story character (23) <u>grew</u> a long nose when he told a lie? Now, you write trivia questions with answers. The Master may select some game items from (24) <u>among</u> those you write.

AFTER THE CLOZE STORY WORD TEST

research, writing questions and answers

1. Have students research and write answers to the story trivia questions. Conclude that ZIP stands for Zoning Improvement Plan; the faces on Mount Rushmore are George Washington, Thomas Jefferson, Abraham Lincoln, Theodore Roosevelt; the one with the long nose was Pinocchio. Next, ask students to write their own trivia questions/answers for a Trivia Insanity game. Ask them to state sources for all answers. Then prepare the Trivia Insanity Sheet and play!

recording words for personal study list

2. Have students record the words they missed on the test in their Spelling Notebook (see page 338) for at-school study, and on a copy of the WORDS TO LEARN BLACKLINE MASTER, page 375, for at-home study.

Assess Skill Application

Give this assessment of spelling and related skills to all students.
The REVIEW 2 BLACKLINE MASTER is on page 18.

Teaching Notes, page 339

 **THE SKILL TEST**

Sort the words.

tapping, dive, pin, race, grabbing, hoping, pine, smelling, run, heating, sweeping,
hop, nail, stripe, dropping

Short Vowel Words	Long Vowel Words
tapping	dive
pin	race
grabbing	hoping
smelling	pine
run	heating
hop	sweeping
dropping	nail
	stripe

Skill tested:
visual skills

Note the ability of each student to sort words by short/long vowel sound.

Assess Proofreading Application

Give this assessment of spelling and related skills to all students.
The REVIEW 2 BLACKLINE MASTER is on page 18.

Teaching Notes, page 341

THE PROOFREADING TEST

If the underlined word in each line is incorrect, write it
correctly in the space.

You <u>know</u> that instruments in an orchestra are
organized into four families, or groups. <u>their</u> is   There
also a system <u>too</u> organize library books. You may   to
keep <u>you're</u> clothes in drawers in a certain way.   your
When we sort things, <u>we're</u> classifying them.
Things can be classified in different <u>way</u>. When you   ways
go to the grocery store, the foods that <u>our</u> alike   are
are grouped <u>bye</u> sections. Potatoes, frozen french   by
fries, and potato chips are all made <u>from</u> potatoes,
but they are <u>fond</u> in different places in the store.   found
One is with fresh fruit and vegetables, one is <u>kapt</u> in   kept
the freezer section, and one with the <u>snak</u> foods.   snack

Why do you suppose that foods that contain potatoes are not found together at
the grocery store?

Note the ability of each student to proofread for spelling and capitalization errors.

Teaching Notes, page 342

Words tested:
the (1), a (4), to (5), in (6), is (7), you (8), that (9), he (11), for (12), this (22), I (24), or (26), had (29), there (37), can (38), an (39), each (47), about (48), up (50), my (80), little (92), very (93), after (94), words (95), through (102), every (151), read (165), always (183), often (186), story (237), hear (260), usually (278), half (297), plants (300), remember (315), problem (422), carefully (427), sky (467), hour (480), grew (506), listen(s) (507), ask(s) (508), single (509), clear (510)

Extra words: afternoon, brother, child, dinner, tale

writing a description/explanation

recording words for personal study list

Extend Spelling Assessment

Give this in-context assessment of Core Words within the frequencies 1–510 to students who need more practice or challenge.

THE SENTENCE DICTATION TEST

Students do not prestudy the words. Provide students with writing paper and pencil. Have students write the sentences as they are dictated.

1. I usually read to my little brother for half an hour each afternoon or after dinner.
2. He always listens very carefully to every single word read.
3. There is a story about a plant that grew clear up through the sky that he often asks to hear.
4. Can you remember the problem the child in this tale had?

AFTER THE SENTENCE DICTATION TEST

1. Have students describe in writing the story problem and its solution. There are many versions of the classic "Jack and the Beanstalk" story.

2. Have students record the words they missed on the test in their Spelling Notebook (see page 345) for at-school study, and on a copy of the WORDS TO LEARN BLACKLINE MASTER, page 375, for at-home study.

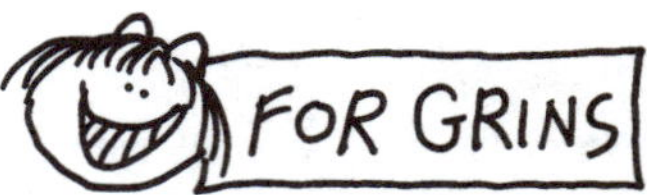

If rhyming words are a "dingle jingle," what is a one-tile roof? A single shingle!

Have students use the letters in *listen* to make words. Choices may include: isle, its, lets, line, list, nest, silent, ten, tile.

Have students write 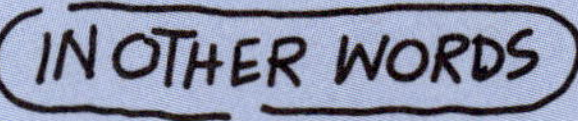 : "The less you talk, the more you're listened to." Abigail Van Buren

Knowing the meaning of common prefixes and roots helps to unlock the mystery of word meanings. Have students brainstorm
- words with the *mon/mono* prefix meaning single, or one (e.g., monarch, monopoly, monotone).
- words with a *bi* prefix to discover it means two (e.g., biweekly, bicuspid, bifocals, bilingual, bicycle, biplane).
- more words with number prefixes (e.g., uni/one—uniform, du/two—dual, tri/three—triangle, quad/four—quadruplets, pent/five—pentagon, dec/ten—decade, cent/hundred—century).

Guide students to discover the meaning of the Greek root *bio* (life—e.g., biology, biography).

Word Test

Trivia Insanity

This is a trivia game. (1) ________________ played in (2) ________________, or teams. Each team gets a Trivia Insanity Sheet with (3) ________________ questions.

(4) ________________ read aloud by the Trivia Master, your teacher. Team members

(5) ________________ and (6) ________________ along. Teams may (7) ________________

a (8) ________________ question about each item to be (9) ________________ they

are (10) ________________ about (11) ________________ meaning. Next, teams work

(12) ________________ to (13) ________________ answers. References can be used.

Teams submit a (14) ________________ answer on (15) ________________ Insanity

Sheet for each question so that the Master can (16) ________________ for

accuracy. The (17) ________________ team to have the correct answer for an item

wins for that item. The object is to be the team with the (18) ________________

"wins" when the ending bell sounds!

(19) ________________ are many examples of great trivia questions. What

(20) ________________ the "zip" in ZIP Code stand for? Which (21) ________________

are carved on the (22) ________________ of Mount Rushmore? Which story

character (23) ________________ a long nose when he told a lie? Now, you write

trivia questions with answers. The Master may select some game items from

(24) ________________ those you write.

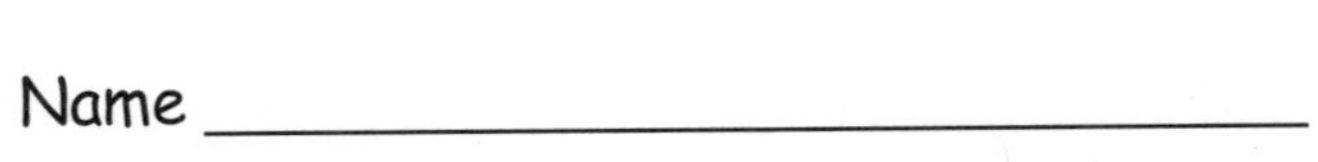

Skill Test

Sort the words.

tapping, dive, pin, race, grabbing, hoping, pine, smelling, run, heating, sweeping, hop, nail, stripe, dropping

<u>Short Vowel Words</u>

____
____
____
____
____
____
____
____

<u>Long Vowel Words</u>

____
____
____
____
____
____
____
____

Proofreading Test

If the underlined word in each line is incorrect, write it correctly in the space.

You <u>know</u> that instruments in an orchestra are

organized into four families, or groups. <u>their</u> is ___________________

also a system <u>too</u> organize library books. You may ___________________

keep <u>you're</u> clothes in drawers in a certain way. ___________________

When we sort things, <u>we're</u> classifying them. ___________________

Things can be classified in different <u>way</u>. When you ___________________

go to the grocery store, the foods that <u>our</u> alike ___________________

are grouped <u>bye</u> sections. Potatoes, frozen french ___________________

fries, and potato chips are all made <u>from</u> potatoes, ___________________

but they are <u>fond</u> in different places in the store. ___________________

One is with fresh fruit and vegetables, one is <u>kapt</u> in ___________________

the freezer section, and one with the <u>snak</u> foods. ___________________

Why do you suppose that foods that contain potatoes are not found together at the grocery store?

Build Skills and Word Experiences

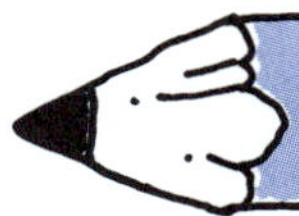

Use Student Practice Pages 7–8 to follow up instruction for:
Activities 1A, 1B • Build Skillful Writers, Test Ready

Build Visual Skills

Do the Word Preview, a visual warm-up activity, with all students.
Use Core Words **energy** (511), **week** (512), **explain** (513), **lost** (514), **spring** (515).

Teaching Notes, page 316

Build Spelling and Language Skills

Choose from among these quick tasks to customize instruction
for all or selected students.

Teaching Notes, page 319

She had to explain it.

(discuss possible options for expansion)

Last spring, me and my friend took a bicycle trips for a week I can't explane how we got lost one day, but we did. We used all are energy to get back on track.

(*my friend and I, trip*, period after *week*, *explain, our*)

weekly, yellow, boyhood, employees, you'll, plywood, alley, yearbook, honeybees, gloomy, sleepily, storyteller

(demonstrate sorting: e.g., location of *y* in word; does/doesn't have a suffix; contains *ee/ll/oo*; is/isn't a compound)

week, century, year, _______

(measures of time)

Energy is available from many sources. For example, _______.

Words that rhyme with *spring*

(e.g., bring, ring, sting)

Teaching Notes, page 325

Build Basic Concepts

Choose from among these skill-building activities to customize instruction
for all or selected students.

> **concept one**   Frequent spelling patterns for /j/ are *j*, *ge*, *gi*, and *gy*.

word analysis, phonics, spelling word patterns, writing words, sorting words

1A Select a student to write *single* and *energy* on the chalkboard. Ask students to contrast the sound of *g* (/g/, /j/). Point out that the *g* in *single* is called the *hard g* and the *g* in *energy* is called the *soft g*. Ask students to identify another letter that often spells /j/ (j). Organize students into small groups to brainstorm words that contain *soft g*. Make a cumulative list on the chalkboard (e.g., page, large, judge, gentle, gym, region, imagine, edge). Next, have students sort the words by the letter following *g* to discover that *g* spells /j/ when followed by *e*, *i*, or *y*—the *dge* variant of *ge* is also common. (Words are reused in Activities 1B and 1C, this unit.)

phonics, spelling word patterns, spelling rules, writing an explanation

1B Begin with a bank of *ge/dge* words (Activity 1A, this unit) and ask students to make additions until there is a generous list. Then ask students to determine when *dge* spells /j/ and when *ge* spells /j/. Help students discover that when /j/ follows a short vowel, *dge* is usually used. Otherwise, *ge* is usually used. (Words are reused in Activity 1C, this unit.) Have students explain in writing what they learned about the *dge/ge* spelling pattern.

dge	*ge*
edge	cage
dodge	change
judge	charge
ledge	huge
ridge	strange
bridge	page
hedge	stooge
lodge	stage

visual skill building, writing words, proofreading, spelling game

1C Conceal the /j/ words students collected (Activities 1A and 1B, this unit). Ask them to recall and write the words from memory. Then reveal the /j/ words for students to self-check. Demonstrate making a bingo board by folding an 8½" x 11" sheet of paper into sixteen boxes (four folds). Have students create a bingo board and randomly write one /j/ word from the collection in each box. Then play bingo! Ask students to trace each word with a colored pen as it is called out. Play until several winners emerge.

A /j/ is spelled most often with *g*—nearly 70% of the time. It is called the soft sound of *g*, as in *energy*. Often the soft *g* is followed by *e*, *i*, or *y*. The letter *j* spells /j/ less often—about 20% of the time. A *g* also spells the hard sound of *g*, as in *single*.

Have students write **(IN OTHER WORDS)**: Heads I win, tails you lose.

Build Skillful Writers

Use these interrelated language learnings for all or selected students.

Teaching Notes, page 328

Have students collect and sort past tense verb forms to discover that:

- Regular verbs add *ed*—*explain/explained*.
- Some verbs are irregular verbs—*win/won, grow/grew*. Many irregular verbs use a *t* ending—*lose/lost*. For some, either a *t* ending or an *ed* ending is correct, but *ed* is usually preferred—*dreamed/dreamt, spilled/spilt, burned/burnt, smelled/smelt, leaped/leapt*.
- Some verbs are correct in more than one form—*spring/sprang* or *sprung, shine/shined* or *shone, sweat/sweat* or *sweated, swim/swam* or *swum, wake/woke* or *waked, hang/hung* or *hanged, shrink/shrank* or *shrunk, dive/dived* or *dove*.
- Some verbs use the same present and past tense form—*set, put, shut, split, spread, cut, shed, let*.

Provide students with word cards (use the WORD CARD BLACKLINE MASTER, **page 384**). Have students write the present tense form of a verb on one side and the past tense form(s) on the other. Then they flash the present tense to a partner to write the past tense, or vice-versa.

Build Assessment Readiness

Use these at-school and at-home exercises to prepare all students for the Skill Test.

Teaching Notes, page 329

at-school Write *regular* and *irregular* on the chalkboard to show how the *ir* prefix alters the meaning of a word.

A regular verb is one for which *ed* is added to the end to make the past tense—ask students for examples. An irregular verb is one for which the past tense is made by action other than adding *ed*—ask students for examples.

Skill to be tested:
regular/irregular verb forms

at-home Send home a copy of TAKE-HOME TASK 3 BLACKLINE MASTER, **page 22**, with each student to encourage parent-child partnerships.

Skill to be tested:
regular/irregular verb forms

Build Proofreading Skills

Track students' ability to meet a minimum competency for spelling and proofreading within selected samples of their everyday writing.

Teaching Notes, page 330

- Send home papers for proofreading and a copy of the IDEAS FOR PROOFREADING BLACKLINE MASTER, **page 373**.

Name_______________________________

Dear Parents,

This Take-Home Task gives your child experience with regular and irregular verb forms. Regular verbs add ed to make the past tense, while irregular verbs do not. This activity also helps your child develop vocabulary and the ability to use analogous thinking.

Begin by having your child read the directions and explain to you what is expected. Guide your child through the activity, letting your child do as much as possible without your help. For each analogy, discuss the word relationships.

An analogy expresses a relationship between words. In this analogy, get and gets are related in the same way as write and writes are related.

Complete the analogies. First, discover the relationship between the first two words. Then add a word to make the relationship between the second two words the same as between the first two.

lose : lost :: buy : b_____________________________

grew : blew :: grow : b_____________________________

give : gave :: write : w_____________________________

remembered : forgot :: ended : b_____________________________

shut : closed :: spoke : t_____________________________

hide : hid :: think : t_____________________________

stood : sat :: lost : f_____________________________

let : let :: put : p_____________________________

leaped : jumped :: ran : j_____________________________

mean : meant :: kneel : k_____________________________

keep: kept :: weep : w_____________________________

selected : chose :: argued : f_____________________________

hear : heard :: explain : e_____________________________

eat : ate :: catch : c_____________________________

There's more! On the back of this paper, have your child sort the analogy answer words—regular verbs and irregular verbs. Every child a speller!

Assess Words and Skills

- Spelling Words (words missed on tests) are recorded in the Spelling Notebook.
- Use Proof It, Practice Page 9, for proofreading/editing practice.

Teaching Notes, page 336

Assess Spelling Progress

Give this Cloze Story Word Test of Core Words within the frequencies 1–515 to all students. Words students miss are their Spelling Words.

THE CLOZE STORY WORD TEST

Students do not prestudy the words. Provide students with a copy of REVIEW 3 BLACKLINE MASTER, page 26. Tell students that this story is a thinking game with clues to help students determine the names of certain states.

Read the entire story aloud, including the test words. Then read it again slowly as students write the missing words.

What's in a Name?

(1) <u>Every</u> state has (2) <u>its</u> own (3) <u>special</u> name. A state's name can (4) <u>usually</u> be traced to a (5) <u>certain</u> origin. Only a few derivations have been (6) <u>lost</u> in history. The Papago Indian word arizonac, meaning (7) "<u>little</u> (8) <u>spring</u>," was the name origin of the 48th state to gain its statehood. (9) <u>English</u> King George II was the namesake of the (10) <u>beautiful</u> Peach State. The last name of (11) <u>another</u> famous "George" names a state in the northwest (12) <u>area</u> of the (13) <u>United States</u> that puts much (14) <u>energy</u> into producing lumber and apples. You can (15) <u>explain</u> one state's name by combining words from the French (16) <u>language</u> for green mountain. (17) <u>It's</u> the top maple syrup producer in this (18) <u>country</u>. (19) <u>There's</u> a Spanish word meaning "feast of flowers" that names our Sunshine State, a state in which a (20) <u>week</u> never passes (21) <u>without</u> the sun shining (22) <u>upon</u> it. The Lone Star State was named for an Indian word meaning (23) "<u>friends</u>." The name of our fourth largest state was derived from the Spanish word for mountainous. How (24) <u>easy</u> will it be for you to name these states? Give it a try.

Words tested:
there('s) (37), its (76), little (92), another (121), every (151), without (204), country (228), it's (253), usually (278), upon (286), United States (305), English (350), certain (353), special (361), area (384), beautiful (429), easy (459), friend(s) (498), language (499), energy (511), week (512), explain (513), lost (514), spring (515)

AFTER THE CLOZE STORY WORD TEST

1. Note that *arizonac* became Arizona; the Peach State is Georgia; Washington was named for George Washington; Vermont is named from a combination of the French words for green mountain; the Sunshine State is Florida; the Lone Star State is Texas; and Montana is named for the Spanish word for mountainous. Can students determine the origin of their own state's name?

research, writing, word origins

2. Have students record the words they missed on the test in their Spelling Notebook (see page 338) for at-school study, and on a copy of the WORDS TO LEARN BLACKLINE MASTER, page 375, for at-home study.

recording words for personal study list

Teaching Notes, page 339

Assess Skill Application

Give this assessment of spelling and related skills to all students.
The REVIEW 3 BLACKLINE MASTER is on page 27.

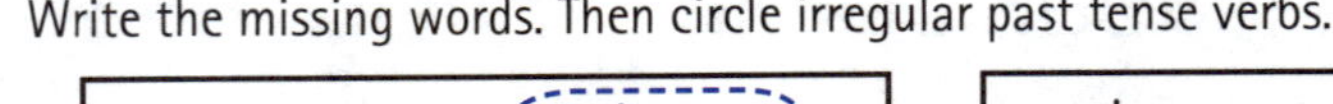

THE SKILL TEST

Skill tested:
regular/irregular verb forms

Write the missing words. Then circle irregular past tense verbs.

lose	*lost*	change	changed
write	wrote	picture	pictured
explain	explained	build	*built*
come	*came*	listen	listened
begin	*began*	think	*thought*
hear	*heard*	tell	*told*
keep	*kept*	mark	marked
ask	asked	buy	*bought*

Note the ability of each student to identify and spell regular and irregular verbs.

Teaching Notes, page 341

Assess Proofreading Application

Give this assessment of spelling and related skills to all students.
The REVIEW 3 BLACKLINE MASTER is on page 27.

THE PROOFREADING TEST

Circle the correct word to complete each line.

Plants and animals are __________. Plants usually make   *different*   diferent   diffrent

their __________ food, but animals do not. Animals   owne   *own*   owen

can usually move __________ around, however, plants   *themselves*   selves   themselfs

cannot. Based on distinctions __________ plants and   between   betwen   *between*

animals, such as these, scientists classify __________   liveing   *living*   lifing

things into groups called kingdoms. __________ a   *There's*   Theirs   They're

plant kingdom and __________ animal kingdom.   a   *an*   A

Within these __________ kingdoms, we can classify   to   *two*   too

things into smaller groups. For __________, we can   *example*   exampel   exampil

place all flowering plants into one __________ class   lardge   *large*   larg

and all nonflowering plants into __________.   other   annother   *another*

What are other ways plants and animals can be classified into smaller groups?

Note the ability of each student to proofread for spelling errors.

Extend Spelling Assessment

Give this in-context assessment of Core Words within the frequencies 1–515 to students who need more practice or challenge.

Teaching Notes, page 342

THE SENTENCE DICTATION TEST

Students do not prestudy the words. Provide students with writing paper and pencil. Have students write the sentences as they are dictated.

> Students do not study the test words before the Cloze Story Word Test or the Sentence Dictation Test. If they prestudy these words, the tests assess short-term memory rather than long-term mastery.

1. The teacher asked me to explain exactly how I lost my English paper and book report.
2. All my energy went toward carefully writing and proofreading both of them last week.
3. Now they're gone and I simply have no idea what could have happened to either of them.
4. I hope an idea will soon spring into my mind to tell me where these assignments can be found.

AFTER THE SENTENCE DICTATION TEST

1. Have students describe in writing a time they lost something, and then found it. Have them explain their process for finding the lost item.

writing a description, writing an explanation

2. Have students record the words they missed on the test in their Spelling Notebook (see page 345) for at-school study, and on a copy of the WORDS TO LEARN BLACKLINE MASTER, page 375, for at-home study.

recording words for personal study list

Mythology is the source for the names of the days of the week. Sunday is named for the day of the sun. Monday is named for the moon, or wife of the sun. Wednesday comes from the god Woden, the father of Tyr, from which we get Tuesday. Woden's wife Frigg is the source for Friday. Thursday originated with the god Thor, son of Woden and Frigg. The source for Saturday's name is Saturn.
- Ask students to write the names of the week and their abbreviations.
- Challenge students to research and write the origin of the names of the months.

Words tested: the (1), of (2), and (3), to (5), be (21), I (24), have (25), what (32), all (33), can (38), an (39), will (46), how (49), them (52), these (58), into (61), could (70), no (71), now (78), my (80), where (98), write(ing) (108), me (110), went (143), tell (147), found (152), last (166), both (180), asked (188), soon (236), paper (241), toward (275), book (307), idea (331), English (350), either (409), gone (413), mind (419), carefully (427), simple(y) (455), happened (481), energy (511), week (512), explain (513), lost (514), spring (515), *they're (1010)

*The testing of they're (1010) is included to help students differentiate among the there/their/they're homophones.

Extra words: assignments, exactly, hope, proofreading, report, teacher

Word Test

What's in a Name?

(1) _________________ state has (2) _________________ own (3) _________________

name. A state's name can (4) _________________ be traced to a (5) _________________

origin. Only a few derivations have been (6) _________________ in history. The Papago

Indian word arizonac, meaning "(7) _________________ (8) _________________," was

the name origin of the 48th state to gain its statehood. (9) _________________

King George II was the namesake of the (10) _________________ Peach State.

The last name of (11) _________________ famous "George" names a state in the

northwest (12) _________________ of the (13) _________________ that

puts much (14) _________________ into producing lumber and apples. You can

(15) _________________ one state's name by combining words from the French

(16) _________________ for green mountain. (17) _________________ the top maple

syrup producer in this (18) _________________. (19) _________________ a Spanish

word meaning "feast of flowers" that names our Sunshine State, a state in which

a (20) _________________ never passes (21) _________________ the sun shining

(22) _________________ it. The Lone Star State was named for an Indian word

meaning (23) "_________________." The name of our fourth largest state was derived

from the Spanish word for mountainous. How (24) _________________ will it be for

you to name these states? Give it a try.

Skill Test

Write the missing words. Then circle irregular past tense verbs.

lose	
	wrote
explain	
	came
begin	
	heard
keep	
	asked

change	
	pictured
build	
	listened
think	
	told
mark	
	bought

Proofreading Test

Circle the correct word to complete each line.

Plants and animals are ____________. Plants usually make	different	diferent	diffrent
their ____________ food, but animals do not. Animals	owne	own	owen
can usually move ____________ around, however, plants	themselves	selves	themselfs
cannot. Based on distinctions ____________ plants and	between	betwen	between
animals, such as these, scientists classify ____________	liveing	living	lifing
things into groups called kingdoms. ____________ a	There's	Theirs	They'res
plant kingdom and ____________ animal kingdom.	a	an	A
Within these ____________ kingdoms, we can classify	to	two	too
things into smaller groups. For ____________, we can	example	exampel	exampil
place all flowering plants into one ____________ class	lardge	large	larg
and all nonflowering plants into ____________.	other	annother	another

What are other ways plants and animals can be classified into smaller groups?

Build Skills and Word Experiences

Use Student Practice Pages 10–11 to follow up instruction for:
Activity 1A • Build Skillful Writers

Build Visual Skills

Do the Word Preview, a visual warm-up activity, with all students.
Use Core Words **travel** (516), **wrote** (517), **farm** (518), **circle** (519), **whose** (520).

Teaching Notes, page 316

Build Spelling and Language Skills

Choose from among these quick tasks to customize instruction
for all or selected students.

Teaching Notes, page 319

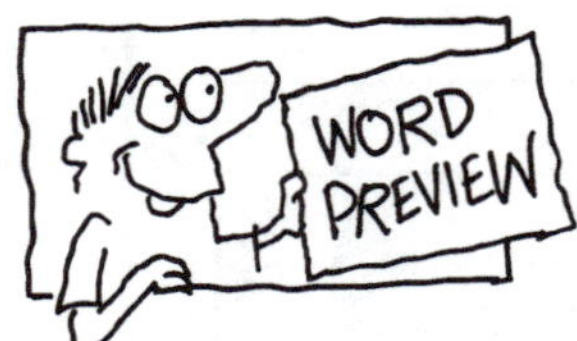

They sat in a circle.

(discuss possible options for expansion)

When I traveled to our fram in the country, I saw several fields that was plowed in circles. I asked who's idea that was. Dad said its becuse of the new watering system

(*farm, were, whose, it's, because,* final period)

wrote, circle, fasten, whose, picture, because, listen, wrinkle, often, someone

(demonstrate sorting: e.g., by silent letter *w/e/t*; number of syllables; number of letters)

travel, circle, pencil, ______

(words that end with /əl/)

The storm made travel to the farm impossible, so we ______.

Words with silent *w*

(e.g., sword, two, wrote)

Build Basic Concepts

Choose from among these skill-building activities to customize instruction for all or selected students.

Teaching Notes, page 325

concept one — Some sounds are spelled more than one way.

1A Organize students into small groups for a brisk two-minute brainstorm for /s/ words. Make a cumulative list on the chalkboard. Then have students sort the words by spelling pattern to discover that /s/ is most frequently spelled *s*, *ss*, *sc*, and *c*. Further, note that *se* can spell /s/ at the end of a word, as in *horse*; and *x* can spell /ks/, as in *extra*. Remind students that earlier they learned that *c* can also spell /k/ (Activity 2A, page 2). Then reengage groups for another brisk brainstorm for /k/ words spelled with *c*. Make a cumulative list on the chalkboard to note that /k/ is most frequently spelled *c*.

phonics, spelling word patterns, sorting words, more words

Conclude that *c* can spell both /s/ and /k/. (Save word banks for Activity 1B, this unit.)

1B Ask students what they can tell you about *c* in *circle*. Review that *c* can spell both /s/ (the soft c) and /k/ (the hard c). Begin with the collection of /s/ words spelled with *c* (Activity 1A, this unit), have students add more words, and then sort the words by the second letter. Conclude that when *c* spells /s/, it is usually followed by *e*, *i*, or *y*. Repeat the activity with the collection of /k/ words spelled with c (Activity 1A, this unit) to discover that when *c* spells /k/, it is usually followed by *a*, *o*, *u*, *l*, or *r*.

phonics, spelling word patterns, sorting words, writing words, art

Next, using art paper, have students make colorful word wheels—circles from which spokes radiate. On one word wheel students write *soft c* in the circle's center and on the spokes write words that illustrate *c* spelling /s/, and on another they write *hard c* and words that illustrate *c* spelling /k/. Post the wheels on a bulletin board.

The letter *c* spells /s/ when followed by *e*, *i*, or *y* and spells /k/ when followed by *a*, *o*, *u*, *l*, or *r*. Our *c* is extra baggage—every sound that *c* spells can be spelled with another letter. Have students verify this.

The words *circle* and *circus* originated from the Greek *kirkos*, meaning "a ring." The circus often features shows in "rings," as in the "three-ring circus." Further, the Latin *circulus*, meaning "little circle," influenced words we use in English.
- Challenge students to explain in writing how the origin of *circle* contributes to the meaning of related words (e.g., circulate, circular, circulation, circuit, circumference, circa, circumvent).
- Ask students to speculate why a boxing "ring" is square.

Teaching Notes, page 328

Build Skillful Writers

Use these interrelated language learnings for all or selected students.

Write on the chalkboard or on a chart for students to read chorally:

> What's a careful speller to do?
> Some words are easy to misconstrue!
> Whose and who's, and loose and lose,
> We're and were, and wear and where,
> Theirs and there's, and there, their, and they're.
> Its and it's, and to, two, and too,
> Your and you're, and thought, though, and through.
> What's a careful speller to do?
> Learn these words or errors ensue!

Ask students why homophones, or words that often sound like homophones, can create spelling challenges. Further, have students scrutinize other look-alike words which may be misconstrued—*finely/finally, later/latter, are/our, choose/chose, loose/lose, weather/whether, quit/quiet/quite, moral/morale, then/than, final/finale, farther/further, wear/where, dinner/diner, dairy/diary, lightening/lightning, desert/dessert, were/we're, formally/formerly, angle/angel, advice/advise, picture/pitcher*. Have students write the rhyme and decorate it with words that they think may be the easiest to misconstrue.

Teaching Notes, page 329

Skill to be tested:
silent consonants—w, t, b, k, l

Build Assessment Readiness

Use these at-school and at-home exercises to prepare all students for the Skill Test.

at-school Ask students why silent letters can cause spelling problems. Review final silent *e* (wrote, whose, circle, single). Explore silent consonants: *w* (wrote), *t* (listen), *b* (comb), *k* (knot), and *l* (talk). Use collections of words initiated earlier (*Did You Know?* on page 11) and expand them on ongoing charts to create a growing resource of silent-consonant words as students discover them.

Skill to be tested:
silent consonants—w, t, b, k, l

at-home Send home a copy of TAKE-HOME TASK 4 BLACKLINE MASTER, page 31, with each student to encourage parent-child partnerships.

Teaching Notes, page 330

Build Proofreading Skills

Track students' ability to meet a minimum competency for spelling and proofreading within selected samples of their everyday writing.

- Send home papers for proofreading and a copy of the IDEAS FOR PROOFREADING BLACKLINE MASTER, page 373.

Dear Parents,

Here is an activity to help your child become familiar with the spelling challenges of silent letters. This exercise provides practice identifying the silent consonants w, t, b, k, and l. Words with these silent letters are incorporated in proverbs or expressions you'll enjoy discussing with your child.

Begin by having your child read the directions and explain to you what is expected. Then guide your child in the identification of the silent-consonant words and the interpretation of the proverbs and sayings in which they appear.

Circle the words with a silent w, t, b, k, or l. Then add them to the lists below.

1. The pen is mightier than the sword.
2. He's a wolf in lamb's clothing.
3. Two wrongs don't make a right.
4. A good beginning is half the battle.
5. Don't fasten the barn door after the horses are stolen.
6. Knowledge is power.
7. A soft answer turns away wrath.
8. Talk is cheap.
9. Whose bread I eat, his song I sing.
10. Don't build castles in the air.
11. You have to learn to crawl before you can walk.
12. The glass is either half empty or half full.
13. It takes one to know one.
14. The best laid plans often go awry.
15. It's not worth the paper it is written on.

w: wren, wreck, wrote, wrench, wrinkle, wrap, wrist, wreath, whole, who

____

t: trestle, soften, glisten, mortgage, whistle, listen, hasten

____

b: comb, thumb, crumb, bomb, plumber, dumb, numb, doubt, limb, climb

____

k: kneel, knot, knife, knock, knee, knight, knit, knew, knuckle, knack

____

l: salmon, balm, calf, calves, balk, could, should, would

____

- Spelling Words (words missed on tests) are recorded in the Spelling Notebook.
- Use Proof It, Practice Page 12, for proofreading/editing practice.

WORD TEST

Teaching Notes, page 336

Assess Spelling Progress

Give this Cloze Story Word Test of Core Words within the frequencies 1–520 to all students. Words students miss are their Spelling Words.

 **THE CLOZE STORY WORD TEST**

Students do not prestudy the words. Provide students with a copy of REVIEW 4 BLACKLINE MASTER, page 35. Tell students that this story is another guessing game. There are clues to determine the identity of a well-known poet.

Read the entire story aloud, including the test words. Then read it again slowly as students write the missing words.

Words tested:
there('s) (37), their (42), then (53), than (73), who('s) (77), often (186), answer(s) (265), I'm (284), perhaps (352), notice (379), that's (390), beautiful (429), watch (436), friend(s) (498), music (501), single (509), explain (513), travel (516), wrote (517), farm (518), circle (519), whose (520), *they're (1010)

*The testing of they're (1010) is included to help students differentiate among the there/their/they're homophones.

> WORD TEST
>
> *Guess Again*
>
> (1) <u>I'm</u> thinking of a poet. Can you guess (2) <u>who's</u> on my mind? This poet is one (3) <u>whose</u> poems will have you laughing, thinking, and rereading them (4) <u>often</u>. (5) <u>They're</u> fun! He (6) <u>wrote</u> one poem about a homework machine. Just put in your homework, drop in a (7) <u>single</u> dime, (8) <u>watch</u> your paper (9) <u>circle</u> through the machine and out the other end—all done! Wait. You'll (10) <u>notice</u> a few wrong (11) <u>answers</u>! (12) <u>There</u> is another poem about seven kids. If they had a rock and roll band, they'd (13) <u>travel</u> all over the land! (14) <u>Perhaps</u> you'd like to be in (15) <u>their</u> lively (16) <u>music</u> group. Silly Geraldine, featured in one of his poems, is down on the (17) <u>farm</u> making milkshakes in a way (18) <u>that's</u> sure to trouble the poor cow! (19) <u>There's</u> a (20) <u>beautiful</u> idea in "How Many, How Much." If you're eager to have more good days (21) <u>than</u> bad and a lot of fine (22) <u>friends</u>, (23) <u>then</u> this poem will (24) <u>explain</u> how. Read these and other poems in this poet's book *A Light in the Attic*. Choose a favorite and tell why it's the best.

 **AFTER THE CLOZE STORY WORD TEST**

relating to poetry, writing reasons

1. Have students use the story clues to write the name of the poet (Shel Silverstein). Have *A Light in the Attic*, *Where the Sidewalk Ends*, and *Falling Up* available for students. Ask students to name their favorite poem from among those Shel Silverstein has written and give reasons why they think it's the best. Ask students to read their favorite poem orally. The poems indicated in the story are "The Homework Machine," "Rock 'N' Roll Band," "Shaking," and "How Many, How Much."

recording words for personal study list

2. Have students record the words they missed on the test in their Spelling Notebook (see page 338) for at-school study, and on a copy of the WORDS TO LEARN BLACKLINE MASTER, page 375, for at-home study.

Assess Skill Application

Give this assessment of spelling and related skills to all students.
The REVIEW 4 BLACKLINE MASTER is on page 36.

Teaching Notes, page 339

THE SKILL TEST

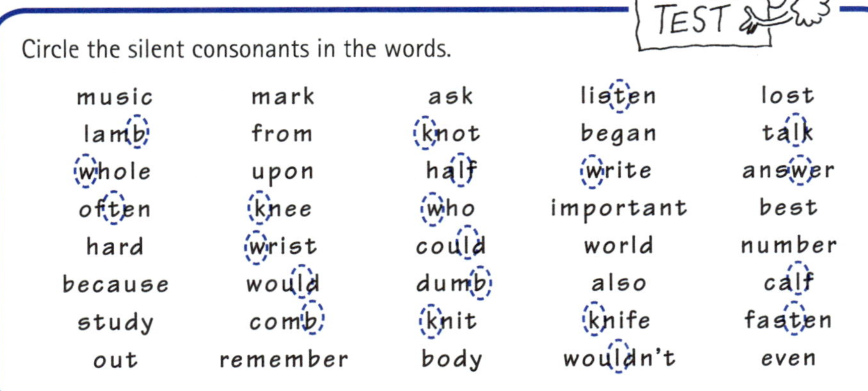

Circle the silent consonants in the words.

music	mark	ask	listen	lost
lamb	from	knot	began	talk
whole	upon	half	write	answer
often	knee	who	important	best
hard	wrist	could	world	number
because	would	dumb	also	calf
study	comb	knit	knife	fasten
out	remember	body	wouldn't	even

Skill tested:
silent consonants—w, t, b, k, l

Note the ability of each student to identify silent consonants *w, t, b, k,* and *l.*

Assess Proofreading Application

Give this assessment of spelling and related skills to all students.
The REVIEW 4 BLACKLINE MASTER is on page 36.

Teaching Notes, page 341

THE PROOFREADING TEST

Proofread for one spelling, capitalization, or punctuation error
in the underlined parts. Circle errors. Write the correction in the space.

Classifying <u>Living things</u>
We classify <u>thing to make them</u> easier to work with
and understand. <u>You no that plants</u> and animals
form two kingdoms into <u>wich living things are</u> sorted.
<u>once the microscope</u> was invented—which helped us
<u>lern more about</u> living things—new classifications
<u>became necessary,</u> Scientists found out that fungi
were <u>different enogh from plants</u> to be placed in a
separate kingdom. The protist kingdom <u>was farmed</u>
for creatures that had <u>both plant and anmal</u> features.
Bacteria and algae <u>become the fifth</u> kingdom called
monerans. <u>These our the simplest</u> living things of all.

Things
things
know
which
Once
learn
.
enough
formed
animal
became
are

What do you think is the likelihood that more kingdoms will be necessary in the
future? Why?

Note the ability of each student to proofread for spelling, capitalization, and
punctuation errors.

Teaching Notes, page 342

Words tested:
of (2), and (3), a (4), in (6), you (8), that (9), he('ll) (11), was (13), with (17), his (18), be (21), this (22), by (27), there('s) (37), do (45), him (67), time (69), long (91), very (93), called (96), know (100), back (103), write(ing) (108), man('s) (111), day (114), why (136), name (155), always (183), important (195), life (208), paper (241), remember(ed) (315), ago (322), close (328), person (367), beautiful (429), everyone (430), friend(s) (498), explain (513), travel (516), wrote (517), farm (518), circle (519), whose (520)

Extra words: describe, mansion, Monticello, please

Extend Spelling Assessment

Give this in-context assessment of Core Words within the frequencies 1–520 to students who need more practice or challenge.

 **THE SENTENCE DICTATION TEST**

Students do not prestudy the words. Provide students with writing paper and pencil. Have students write the sentences as they are dictated.

1. Do you know whose beautiful farm mansion was called Monticello?

2. There's a very important paper that this person wrote long ago with his circle of close friends.

3. Please name him and explain in writing why he'll always be remembered by everyone.

4. Travel back in time and describe in writing a day in this man's life.

 **AFTER THE SENTENCE DICTATION TEST**

research, writing, speculating

1. Have students research and write why Thomas Jefferson will always be remembered. Then have them write about a day in his life on his Monticello farm.

Thomas Jefferson, the third US President, was a man of accomplishment. He was author of the Declaration of Independence and founder of the University of Virginia. An avid gardner and farmer, he invented a plow. Further, he developed the swivel chair and spherical sundial. He studied architecture and built a plantation home he called Monticello, the c pronounced /ch/, from Italian. Jefferson spoke Italian. His Virginia home-site, still beautiful today, was built on a little hill—monticello means "little mountain" in Italian. Jefferson, born April 13, 1743, passed away on the 50th anniversary of American independence, July 4, 1826.

recording words for personal study list

2. Have students record the words they missed on the test in their Spelling Notebook (see page 345) for at-school study, and on a copy of the WORDS TO LEARN BLACKLINE MASTER, page 375, for at-home study.

Have students redefine in rhyme:
• arithmetic anger (math wrath!)
• a plumber's tool from France (French wrench!)
• circular hill (round mound!)

— Word Test —

Guess Again

(1) _________________ thinking of a poet. Can you guess (2) _________________ on my

mind? This poet is one (3) _________________ poems will have you laughing, thinking,

and rereading them (4) _________________. (5) _________________ fun! He

(6) _________________ one poem about a homework machine. Just put in your

homework, drop in a (7) _________________ dime, (8) _________________ your paper

(9) _________________ through the machine and out the other end—all done! Wait.

You'll (10) _________________ a few wrong (11) _________________! (12) _________________

is another poem about seven kids. If they had a rock and roll band, they'd

(13) _________________ all over the land! (14) _________________ you'd like to be in

(15) _________________ lively (16) _________________ group. Silly Geraldine, featured in

one of his poems, is down on the (17) _________________ making milkshakes in a way

(18) _________________ sure to trouble the poor cow! (19) _________________ a

(20) _________________ idea in "How Many, How Much." If you're eager to have more

good days (21) _________________ bad and a lot of fine (22) _________________,

(23) _________________ this poem will (24) _________________ how. Read these and

other poems in this poet's book *A Light in the Attic.* Choose a favorite and tell why

it's the best.

REVIEW 4

Skill Test

Circle the silent consonants in the words.

music	mark	ask	listen	lost
lamb	from	knot	began	talk
whole	upon	half	write	answer
often	knee	who	important	best
hard	wrist	could	world	number
because	would	dumb	also	calf
study	comb	knit	knife	fasten
out	remember	body	wouldn't	even

Proofreading Test

Proofread for one spelling, capitalization, or punctuation error in the underlined parts. Circle errors. Write the correction in the space.

Classifying Living things

We classify thing to make them easier to work with

and understand. You no that plants and animals

form two kingdoms into wich living things are sorted.

once the microscope was invented—which helped us

lern more about living things—new classifications

became necessary, Scientists found out that fungi

were different enogh from plants to be placed in a

separate kingdom. The protist kingdom was farmed

for creatures that had both plant and anmal features.

Bacteria and algae become the fifth kingdom called

monerans. These our the simplest living things of all.

____

____

____

____

____

____

____

____

____

____

What do you think is the likelihood that more kingdoms will be necessary in the future? Why?

Build Skills and Word Experiences

Use Student Practice Pages 13–14 to follow up instruction for:
Activity 1A • Test Ready

Build Visual Skills

Do the Word Preview, a visual warm-up activity, with all students.
Use Core Words **correct** (521), **bed** (522), **measure** (523), **straight** (524), **base** (525).

Teaching Notes, page 316

Build Spelling and Language Skills

Choose from among these quick tasks to customize instruction
for all or selected students.

Teaching Notes, page 319

STRETCH IT

They didn't measure it.

(discuss possible options for expansion)

FIX IT

Suddenly, the ball flew over Jacks head. In the meantime, Matt traveled straight to frist base and than circled around to home plate. Everything he did was corect, Its hard to measur the team's joy.

(*Jack's, first, then, correct,* period instead of comma, *It's, measure*)

SORT IT

straight, bakery, payment, stairway, brainstorm, birthday, papers, bricklayer, skyscraper, painter, stadium, pathway

(demonstrate sorting: e.g., /ā/ spelling pattern; beginning letter; suffix/no suffix; is/isn't a compound)

ADD IT

measure, future, feature, _______

(words that end with *ure*)

FINISH IT

Kristin and her friends stood at the base of the mountain. They _______.

FIND IT

Words that describe units of measure

(e.g., inch, gallon, pound, minute)

Teaching Notes, page 325

Build Basic Concepts

Choose from among these skill-building activities to customize instruction for all or selected students.

concept one	A prefix is a letter or letters added to the beginning of a word. A suffix is a letter or letters added to the end of a word.

suffix practice, writing words, sorting words, spelling rules, proofreading

1A Dictate to students: *begin*, *box*, *measure*, *write*, *explain*, *enjoy*, *forget*, *watch*, *say*. Post Teaching Poster 2. Tell students they will add suffixes to the words. Guide students through the strategy:

- Ask students for the first step (check the spelling of the base word). Write the words on the chalkboard, or have a student do so, for self-checking.
- Ask students for the second step (decide how to make the suffix addition by sorting the words by their endings). Have students sort the words.
- Ask students for the third step (add the suffix). Students add the *ing* and *s* suffixes to each base word.
- Ask students for the last step (proofread). Next, write the words on the chalkboard, or have a student do so, for discussion and proofreading.

Have students repeat the process independently adding the *ed* suffix to *circle*, *listen*, *march*, *ask*, *study*, and *shop*. Then they write more ed-ending words that illustrate the rules on Teaching Poster 2.

suffix practice, writing words, vocabulary development, oral reporting

1B Post Teaching Poster 2. Review the process for adding a suffix to a base word (Activity 1A, above). Organize students into small groups. Provide each group with chart paper and a marking pen. Ask each group to select a different suffix. Then they find and write words with their suffix. Next, each group presents their chart to the class for proofreading and discussion.

prefix practice, choral reading, predicting spelling, more words

1C Ask students to explain why adding a prefix is less complex than adding a suffix (the spelling of the base word never changes with the addition of a prefix, but it may change with the addition of a suffix). Introduce Teaching Poster 3. Have students read the rhyme chorally and discuss the word examples. Ask students how the addition of a prefix influences a base word (alters meaning). Brainstorm more words that illustrate each prefix and write them on the chalkboard as students predict the spelling. Have students complete a copy of PERSONAL POSTER 3 BLACKLINE MASTER, page 369, using this word bank for assistance.

Prefixes and suffixes are affixes. A prefix is affixed before the word, a suffix, after the word. Ask students how the word parts of a prefix create its meaning. *Suf* is a form of the *sub* prefix meaning "below, beneath, lesser." *Sub* becomes *suf* before words beginning with f, *suc* before c, *sug* before g, *sum* before m, *sup* before p, *sur* before r—and may change to *sus* before c, p, and t.

- Challenge students to find words that illustrate the *sub* prefix and its variants.

Build Skillful Writers

Use these interrelated language learnings for all or selected students.

Teaching Notes, page 328

Review the rhyme from Build Skillful Writers, page 30. The words most often misspelled or misused are homophones—words that sound alike but have different spellings and meanings. Topping the list are *there/their/they're* and their cousins *there's/theirs*. Ranking second are *to/too/two*. Also often incorrect in writing are *its/it's* and *your/you're*.

Have students make word cards for these words (use the WORD CARD BLACKLINE MASTER, page 384). Then have students write sentences that use these words, read their sentences to the class, and have students respond by holding up the correct word card. (Word cards are reused in Activity 1C, page 92.)

Build Assessment Readiness

Use these at-school and at-home exercises to prepare all students for the Skill Test.

Teaching Notes, page 329

at-school Set up five classroom stations, each with chart paper. Write a frequent /k/ spelling pattern on each chart: *c, k, ck, ch, qu*. Divide students into five groups. Give each group a different color marking pen. Position each group at a chart station. Ask students to note the /k/ spelling pattern on their chart and use their colored pen to write words that contain the pattern. Time the session (about two minutes) and then tell students to move, carousel fashion, to the next station to contribute to that chart. Continue until each group has been to each station. Then have students read and proofread the words on each chart, noting the contribution of each group signaled by their color marking pen. Point out that *c* is the most frequent spelling pattern for /k/. Point out that *qu* most often spells /kw/, *x* spells /ks/, and *ke* is often a signal at the end of a word for a long vowel spelling. Further, reinforce the less frequent /k/ options: *cc* (occasion), *kk* (Hanukkah), *que* (antique), and *ic*-ending words (music).

Skill to be tested:
/k/ spelling patterns

at-home Send home a copy of TAKE-HOME TASK 5 BLACKLINE MASTER, page 40, with each student to encourage parent-child partnerships.

Skill to be tested:
/k/ spelling patterns

Build Proofreading Skills

Track students' ability to meet a minimum competency for spelling and proofreading within selected samples of their everyday writing.

Teaching Notes, page 330

- Send home papers for proofreading and a copy of the IDEAS FOR PROOFREADING BLACKLINE MASTER, page 373.

Name _______________________________

Dear Parents,

The centerpiece of this vocabulary-building activity is words that contain the sound heard at the beginning of 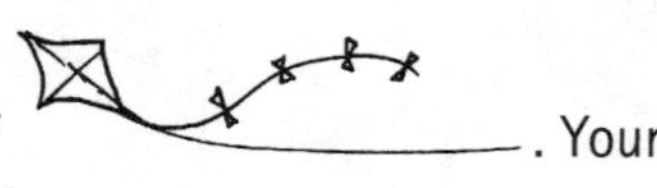 . Your child is learning the most frequent spelling patterns for this sound.

Begin by having your child read the directions and explain to you what is expected. Guide your child through the activity, letting your child do as much as possible without your help. Take special care to discuss the meaning of unfamiliar words.

Draw a line to connect words in columns 1 and 2 that have similar meanings.

1	2
pail	same
equal	monarch
superior	choral
leader	bucket
canoe	excellent
musical	kayak
funny	in order
shake	stream
brook	comical
unkind	call
chronological	quarter
one-fourth	quake
sorting	compassionless
commandment	riot
beckon	rule
curtsy	classifying
ruckus	bow
explain	correct
accurate	amount
quiz	clarify
battle	frightened
quantity	combat
stir	test
panicked	inquire
four	mix
ache	increase
ask	pain
add	mimicking
coat	quad
copying	collapse
quarrel	training
fall	cloak
rest	argue
schooling	relax

Point out to your child that the ___________ sound is most frequently spelled with a c, but other frequent spelling patterns include k/ke, ck, ch, and q. When c spells this sound, it is usually followed by a, o, u, l, or r. Note that q is most often followed by u and spells the kw sound, and x can spell the ks sound.

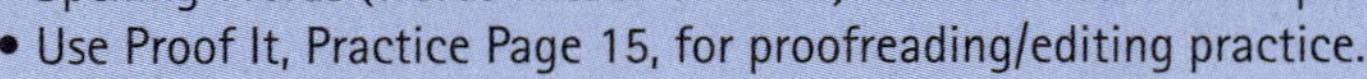

- Spelling Words (words missed on tests) are recorded in the Spelling Notebook.
- Use Proof It, Practice Page 15, for proofreading/editing practice.

Assess Spelling Progress

Teaching Notes, page 336

Give this Cloze Story Word Test of Core Words within the frequencies 1–525 to all students. Words students miss are their Spelling Words.

THE CLOZE STORY WORD TEST

Students do not prestudy the words. Provide students with a copy of REVIEW 5 BLACKLINE MASTER, page 44. Tell students that this story will teach them something peculiar about a common animal.

Read the entire story aloud, including the test words. Then read it again slowly as students write the missing words.

Sleep Like a Horse

You may have (1) <u>heard</u> someone say "work like a horse," but what about "sleep like a horse"? Have you (2) <u>noticed</u> horses standing (3) <u>straight</u> up, yet appearing to be (4) <u>sound</u> asleep? Are they (5) <u>really</u> sleeping? Would it be more (6) <u>correct</u> to say that (7) <u>they're</u> resting with closed eyes? (8) <u>There's</u> evidence that these (9) <u>animals</u> do sleep standing up, (10) <u>although</u> they may also sleep lying down, perhaps in a (11) <u>bed</u> of straw. It may be hard to (12) <u>measure</u>, but it would seem that horses would sleep better on the (13) <u>ground</u> than in a standing position. We might (14) <u>base</u> that opinion on our own experience, (15) <u>because</u> we know it takes (16) <u>energy</u> to stand. If we dozed off, (17) <u>we'd</u> fall. However, horses (18) <u>usually</u> do sleep standing up, and it's not the (19) <u>least</u> bit difficult for them to do. Horses have a unique (20) <u>system</u> of interlocking bones and ligaments. (21) <u>They're</u> able to lock (22) <u>their</u> legs upright allowing the leg muscles to relax (23) <u>completely</u>. How might things be (24) <u>different</u> if our own legs could do this same special thing?

Words tested:
we('d) (36), there('s) (37), their (42), because (127), different (139), sound (175), heard (262), usually (278), ground (311), really (313), complete(ly) (365), notice(d) (379), animals (418), system (434), although (450), least (478), energy (511), correct (521), bed (522), measure (523), straight (524), base (525), *they're (1010)

*The testing of they're (1010) is included to help students differentiate among the there/their/they're homophones.

AFTER THE CLOZE STORY WORD TEST

1. Have students write and share their answer to the question at the end of the story. Discuss "work like a horse." Then have students describe what might be meant by the newly coined phrase "sleep like a horse."

speculating, writing

2. Have students record the words they missed on the test in their Spelling Notebook (see page 338) for at-school study, and on a copy of the WORDS TO LEARN BLACKLINE MASTER, page 375, for at-home study.

recording words for personal study list

Assess Skill Application

Give this assessment of spelling and related skills to all students.
The REVIEW 5 BLACKLINE MASTER is on page 45.

Teaching Notes, page 339

THE SKILL TEST

Skill tested:
/k/ spelling patterns

Circle the letter or letters that make the spelling
pattern for the sound you hear at the beginning of ✦.

special	black	bank
explained	fixed	question
music	change	school
next	circle	which
clearly	square	church
sixteenth	could	because
crashing	once	second
sentence	track	chorus

Note the ability of each student to identify /k/ and its most frequent spelling patterns.

Assess Proofreading Application

Give this assessment of spelling and related skills to all students.
The REVIEW 5 BLACKLINE MASTER is on page 45.

Teaching Notes, page 341

THE PROOFREADING TEST

If the underlined word in each line is incorrect, write it
correctly in the space.

Things are measured so that we can describe <u>then</u>.   them
We can measure matter. Matter is <u>anything</u> that takes
up <u>spase</u>, such as water or marbles. If you filled one   space
<u>cups</u> to the top with water and another with marbles,   cup
the marbles would weigh more. That <u>meens</u> the marbles   means
have more matter <u>then</u> the water. Matter is measured   than
by weight. Length is something else we <u>offen</u> measure.   often
Length is the <u>distence</u> from one point to another, but it   distance
isn't always in a <u>straght</u> line. We frequently measure time.   straight
Matter, or mass, is measured in one <u>weigh</u>, length is   way
measured in another way, and time has <u>its</u> own units of
measure. All the measures can be <u>writen</u> in numbers   written
to compare, <u>explane</u>, and discuss them more easily.   explain

To measure speed, which units are used—matter, length, or time? Give reasons for
your answer.

Note the ability of each student to proofread for spelling errors.

Extend Spelling Assessment

Give this in-context assessment of Core Words within the frequencies 1–525 to students who need more practice or challenge.

Teaching Notes, page 342

THE SENTENCE DICTATION TEST

Students do not prestudy the words. Provide students with writing paper and pencil. Have students write the sentences as they are dictated.

1. My friend and his mother built a special bed for their little puppy.
2. They were careful to measure and write down the correct numbers before they began their work.
3. They wanted straight sides, a square base, and no top.
4. List everything the two of them probably used to build this box for their new pet.

Words tested:

the (1), of (2), and (3), a (4), to (5), for (12), his (18), they (19), this (22), were (34), their (42), them (52), two (65), no (71), my (80), down (84), use(d) (88), little (92), new (107), write (108), number(s) (145), want(ed) (193), side(s) (203), began (215), mother (226), top (269), before (332), built (360), special (361), list (372), probably (383), box (388), everything (432), build (487), friend (498), correct (521), bed (522), measure (523), straight (524), base (525)

Extra words: careful, pet, puppy, square

AFTER THE SENTENCE DICTATION TEST

1. Ask students to research the materials and tools necessary to build the puppy's box and determine their possible sources. Students list this information—materials, tools, sources. Then have them pair up to evaluate content for completeness and accuracy. They check spelling. As a class, make a cumulative list.

research, writing a list, evaluating, proofreading

2. Have students record the words they missed on the test in their Spelling Notebook (see page 345) for at-school study, and on a copy of the WORDS TO LEARN BLACKLINE MASTER, page 375, for at-home study.

recording words for personal study list

We expect /ā/ to be spelled *ai* (straight), *ay* (today), or *a*-consonant-*e* (base). We don't expect /ā/ to be spelled *ea* (great); therefore, *great* is a Surprise Word. Create an ongoing collection of Surprise Words, words with irregular spellings.

The word *measure* comes to the English language from *meter*, meaning "measure" from the Greek word *metron*, the Latin word *metrum*, and the French word *metre*.

- Have students explain in writing how *meter* contributes to the meaning of a word containing the word part (e.g., thermometer—Word Mysteries and Histories, page 7— diameter, kilometer, barometer, perimeter, speedometer).
- Challenge students to find the length of one meter (about 39.37 in).

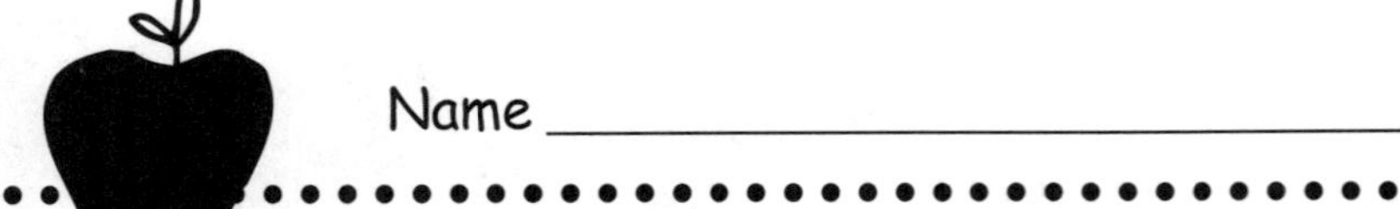

Name ___________________________________

— Word Test —

Sleep Like a Horse

You may have (1) ___________________ someone say "work like a horse," but what

about "sleep like a horse"? Have you (2) ___________________ horses standing

(3) ___________________ up, yet appearing to be (4) ___________________ asleep? Are

they (5) ___________________ sleeping? Would it be more (6) ___________________ to say

that (7) ___________________ resting with closed eyes? (8) ___________________ evidence

that these (9) ___________________ do sleep standing up, (10) ___________________ they

may also sleep lying down, perhaps in a (11) ___________________ of straw. It may

be hard to (12) ___________________, but it would seem that horses would sleep

better on the (13) ___________________ than in a standing position. We might

(14) ___________________ that opinion on our own experience, (15) ___________________

we know it takes (16) ___________________ to stand. If we dozed off, (17) ___________________

fall. However, horses (18) ___________________ do sleep standing up, and it's not

the (19) ___________________ bit difficult for them to do. Horses have a unique

(20) ___________________ of interlocking bones and ligaments. (21) ___________________

able to lock (22) ___________________ legs upright allowing the leg muscles to relax

(23) ___________________. How might things be (24) ___________________ if our own legs

could do this same special thing?

45

Skill Test

Circle the letter or letters that make the spelling pattern for the sound you hear at the beginning of

special	black	bank
explained	fixed	question
music	change	school
next	circle	which
clearly	square	church
sixteenth	could	because
crashing	once	second
sentence	track	chorus

Proofreading Test

If the underlined word in each line is incorrect, write it correctly in the space.

Things are measured so that we can describe <u>then</u>. _______________________

We can measure matter. Matter is <u>anything</u> that takes _______________________

up <u>spase</u>, such as water or marbles. If you filled one _______________________

<u>cups</u> to the top with water and another with marbles, _______________________

the marbles would weigh more. That <u>meens</u> the marbles _______________________

have more matter <u>then</u> the water. Matter is measured _______________________

by weight. Length is something else we <u>offen</u> measure. _______________________

Length is the <u>distence</u> from one point to another, but it _______________________

isn't always in a <u>straght</u> line. We frequently measure time. _______________________

Matter, or mass, is measured in one <u>weigh</u>, length is _______________________

measured in another way, and time has <u>its</u> own units of _______________________

measure. All the measures can be <u>writen</u> in numbers _______________________

to compare, <u>explane</u>, and discuss them more easily. _______________________

To measure speed, which units are used—matter, length, or time? Give reasons for your answer.

Build Skills and Word Experiences

Use Student Practice Pages 16–17 to follow up instruction for:
Activity 2A • Test Ready

Build Visual Skills

Do the Word Preview, a visual warm-up activity, with all students.
Use Core Words **mountain** (526), **caught** (527), **hair** (528), **bird** (529), **wood** (530).

Teaching Notes, page 316

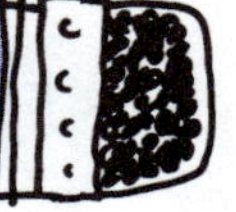

Build Spelling and Language Skills

Choose from among these quick tasks to customize instruction
for all or selected students.

Teaching Notes, page 319

It made my hair stand on end.

Some birds are finded in the woods and others are common in high mountain areas Some people have cot and tagged birds too measured the distance thay travel.

(*found*, period after *areas*, *caught*, *to*, *measure*, *they*)

mountain, I'll, caught, unexcused, bottom, hair, bird, wood, summary, guessed, beginning, ferry

(e.g., is/isn't a homophone; does/doesn't have double letters; number of syllables)

caught/cot; hair/hare; wood/would; _______/______

(homophones)

We caught a glimpse of its back as it disappeared down the mountain. We were so ___

Names of kinds of birds

(e.g., robin, eagle, hawk)

Build Basic Concepts

Choose from among these skill-building activities to customize instruction for all or selected students.

Teaching Notes, page 325

---

concept one | Frequent spelling patterns for /o/ are *o*, *al*, *au*, and *ow*.

1A Label the top boxes of the Ten-Box Reusable Chart (see page 396): *o, al, au, aw, Surprise*. Engage students in small groups to collect words to illustrate each spelling pattern. Conclude—

- *o* spells /o/ most often (lost)
- when *a* is followed by *l*, it usually spells /o/ (always)
- *au* is a frequent spelling pattern initially (August) and medially (caught)
- *aw* occurs initially (awful), medially (yawn), but most often terminally (saw)
- *a* spells /o/ rarely, so it's an unexpected Surprise Word spelling (father)

phonics, spelling word patterns, sorting words, more words

Use this word collection to play bingo (Activity 1C, page 20) and other games (see page 390), and as a source for words to which students can add prefixes and suffixes.

---

concept two | Spelling patterns for /ou/ are *ou* and *ow*.

2A Select a student to write *mountain town* on the chalkboard. Underline the /ou/ spelling patterns (*ou* and *ow*). Tell students that these spelling patterns consistently spell /ou/. Remind students that *ow* can also spell /ō/ (window), and *ou* can spell many sounds—it is the most erratic vowel pattern—a rough, tough group of words to spell! Write this rhyme for students to read chorally.

phonics, spelling word patterns, choral reading, writing a rhyme, more words, creating a book

Have students begin a book to collect Rough Toughie *ou* spellings (e.g., your, brought, through, could, enough, dough). Have them copy the rhyme as their opening page.

2B Remind students that /ou/ is spelled *ou* or *ow*, but *ou* and *ow* can spell other sounds. Then make large letter cards for the chalk tray or a pocket chart: *a, d, i, m, n, n, o, t, u, w*. Have students make a personal set of letters (use the LETTER CARD BLACKLINE MASTER, page 385). Together make *mountain*. Then have students continue making words: *mound—noun—now— town—wound—down—dawn—daunt—aunt—auto—donut—omit—admit—amount— mount*—and back to *mountain*. Confirm the spelling of each word with the large letter cards. Discuss the meaning of unfamiliar words. Later, have students work in pairs to make more words with their letters. Have them write the words as they make them.

phonics, spelling word patterns, making words, vocabulary development

Teaching Notes, page 328

Build Skillful Writers

Use these interrelated language learnings for all or selected students.

An apostrophe can cause a spelling catastrophe! To avoid a catastrophe, tell students that an apostrophe always has a purpose. An apostrophe—

- takes the place of a letter or letters in a contraction (Build Skillful Writers, page 93), or
- signals ownership, or possession.

Write these phrases on the chalkboard and guide students to an understanding of each:

birds nest—(birds—a flock, nest—a verb; birds = plural of bird)
bird's nest—(a nest belonging to one bird; bird's = singular possessive)
birds' nest—(a nest belonging to more than one bird; birds' = plural possessive)

Then have students apply what they learned to explain in writing the differences among: *farmers plow, farmer's plow, farmers' plow.*

This symbol—ə—is a schwa, a German word that refers to a sound in some unstressed syllables when the vowel letter(s) is obscured. For example, the *ain* of *mountain* is unstressed, the vowel letters are anonymous, and are so noted by a ə. This presents a spelling challenge that some languages do not incur—Spanish and German vowels in unstressed syllables remain clear making them easier to spell.

Teaching Notes, page 329

Build Assessment Readiness

Use these at-school and at-home exercises to prepare all students for the Skill Test.

Skill to be tested:
there, their, they're

at-school Have students find and write examples of *there, their, they're* in print material. Provide students with their word cards for *there/their/they're* (Build Skillful Writers, page 39). Then have students read one of their examples to the class to respond with the correct word card.

Skill to be tested:
there, their, they're

at-home Send home a copy of TAKE-HOME TASK 6 BLACKLINE MASTER, **page 49**, with each student to encourage parent-child partnerships.

Teaching Notes, page 330

Build Proofreading Skills

Track students' ability to meet a minimum competency for spelling and proofreading within selected samples of their everyday writing.

- Send home papers for proofreading and a copy of the IDEAS FOR PROOFREADING BLACKLINE MASTER, **page 373**.

Name ___________________________________

Dear Parents,

Topping the list of the most misspelled or misused words in the English language are there, their, and they're. This activity provides practice with these troublemakers. Guide your child through the story, monitoring the word choices to ensure their accuracy. Always discuss why a word is the correct one. Then work out the story puzzle together.

Read the story and fill in the blanks with there, their, or they're. Then solve the puzzle.

Bess and Tim Chang waited for _________________ bus. The twins were on

_________________ way to the snowy mountain to ski with _________________

friends. They were eager to get _________________. Then they saw Joe and Eric

walking to the bus stop with _________________ ski gear. "_________________

the best skiers on the hill!" said Bess to Tim. "I wish I could ski as well as

_________________ skiing." Tim replied, "_________________ good skiers, but

_________________ also good in math." The boys were in _________________

older brother Dan's math class. _________________ math grades were at the top

of _________________ class.

Just as the boys got to the bus stop, _________________ bus arrived. The

four of them put _________________ equipment in the ski rack and boarded.

_________________ were four seats in the back. As they were sitting down, Joe

asked the twins, "Are _________________ only two of you going to the mountain

today? Will any of your brothers and sisters be _________________?" Bess told

Joe, "The others aren't skiing today because _________________ doing other

things." Then Joe asked, "How many Chang kids are _________________ in the

family?" "Well," grinned Tim, "_________________ are several of us. I have as

many brothers as sisters." "And I have twice as many brothers as sisters," added

Bess. "Are _________________ enough clues for you to figure out how many of

us _________________ are?" asked Tim. "Sure, _________________ great clues!"

said Joe. How many kids are in the Chang Family?

Ponder the solution with your child. Then check your answer (upside down below).

There are seven Chang children—four brothers and three sisters.

Assess Words and Skills

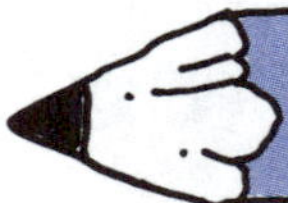

- Spelling Words (words missed on tests) are recorded in the Spelling Notebook.
- Use Proof It, Practice Page 18, for proofreading/editing practice.

Teaching Notes, page 336

Assess Spelling Progress

Give this Cloze Story Word Test of Core Words within the frequencies 1–530 to all students. Words students miss are their Spelling Words.

 THE CLOZE STORY WORD TEST

Students do not prestudy the words. Provide students with a copy of Review 6 Blackline Master, page 53. Tell students that this story asks them to do some creative thinking.

Read the entire story aloud, including the test words. Then read it again slowly as students write the missing words.

Words tested:
their (42), than (73), its (76), only (85), through (102), work (124), thought (179), sure (251), morning (283), later (288), course (317), early(ier) (324), able (346), perhaps (352), beautiful (429), watch(ed) (436), happened (481), explain (513), straight (524), mountain(s) (526), caught (527), hair (528), bird (529), wood (530)

> ### Quinn's Clever Idea
>
>
>
> The wind was whipping (1) <u>through</u> Quinn's (2) <u>hair</u> as he flew his (3) <u>beautiful</u> kite. (4) <u>Earlier</u>, he nearly lost the kite. It got (5) <u>caught</u> in the (6) <u>wood</u> branches of a tree, but he was (7) <u>able</u> to climb and set it free. He is a keen climber and can scale tall (8) <u>mountains</u> and buildings. What he wanted more (9) <u>than</u> anything was to climb the church spire, but of (10) <u>course</u> the archbishops would never allow it. (11) <u>Perhaps</u> he would climb it at night. No, that wouldn't (12) <u>work</u>. It would (13) <u>only</u> cause trouble. Then, as he (14) <u>watched</u> his kite flying high in the sky like a (15) <u>bird</u>, he had a fine idea. He would get the archbishops to ask him to climb the spire in broad daylight! (16) <u>Later</u>, on his way home, he stopped by the church. Yes, he (17) <u>thought</u>, I shall climb (18) <u>straight</u> to (19) <u>its</u> top tomorrow. When Quinn hurried to the church the next (20) <u>morning</u>, it (21) <u>happened</u>—his wish came true! (22) <u>Sure</u> enough, the archbishops invited Quinn to ascend (23) <u>their</u> spire! A huge crowd of admirers gathered as Quinn scaled the steeple. (24) <u>Explain</u> Quinn's clever plan.

 AFTER THE CLOZE STORY WORD TEST

reasoning, writing an explanation

1. Have students write and share their answer to the story request. Conclude that on Quinn's way home, he tangled his kite high on the church spire. Of course, the archbishops were pleased the next morning when Quinn offered to remove the kite from the church top. The archbishops immediately invited him to do so, unknowingly granting Quinn his wish.

recording words for personal study list

2. Have students record the words they missed on the test in their Spelling Notebook (see page 338) for at-school study, and on a copy of the Words to Learn Blackline Master, page 375, for at-home study.

Assess Skill Application

Give this assessment of spelling and related skills to all students.
The REVIEW 6 BLACKLINE MASTER is on page 54.

Teaching Notes, page 339

THE SKILL TEST

Read the story and fill in the blanks with **there**, **their**, or **they're**.

Would ___there___ be anything that would frighten scary monsters? What might make ___their___ eyes close tightly and ___their___ bodies shake in fright? Perhaps ___they're___ not afraid of another big animal, but ___they're___ frightened by bright light or loud noise. ___There___ may be many things that would scare them and cause ___their___ bodies to shiver that wouldn't scare us. ___There___ are differences of opinion about what is scary.

Skill tested:
there, their, they're

Note the ability of each student to discriminate among *there*, *their*, and *they're*.

Assess Proofreading Application

Give this assessment of spelling and related skills to all students.
The REVIEW 6 BLACKLINE MASTER is on page 54.

Teaching Notes, page 341

THE PROOFREADING TEST

Proofread for one spelling, capitalization, or punctuation error in the underlined parts. Circle errors. Write corrections in the spaces.

The United States is big, <u>but when it is maesured</u> and comparisons are made, it looks much <u>smaller. All of north</u> America, of <u>wich the United States</u> is a part, covers only about 16% <u>of erath. Asia</u> is much larger and takes in about 30% of the <u>worlds land. The highest</u> mountain range is also in Asia, the Himalayas. <u>Of coarse, the</u> loftiest mountain, Mt. <u>Everest, is their. It towers</u> just above 29,000 feet, while <u>the hiest point in North</u> America is just over 20,000 <u>feet. That's Mt</u> McKinley. It's tall, but it does not rank <u>amung the ten tallest</u> peaks in the world. The longest river <u>is the Nile It</u> stretches over 4,100 miles. The length of the Mississippi <u>and it's main</u> tributaries is only about <u>3,700 mile</u> in comparison.

measured	
North	
which	
Earth	
world's	
course	
there	
highest	
Mt.	
among	
.	
its	
miles	

How does your state or province compare with other states or provinces when various measures are made?

Note the ability of each student to proofread for spelling, capitalization, and punctuation errors.

Book Tie-In

Steve Jenkins introduces middle-grade readers to the history, geography, climate, culture, and excitement of Mt. Everest in *The Top of the World: Climbing Mt. Everest*. The full-color adventure into mountain climbing received a Boston Globe and a Horn Book Award.

Teaching Notes, page 342

Words tested:

the (1), of (2), and (3), a (4), to (5), in (6), for (12), on (14), from (23), I (24), by (27), were (34), we (36), there (37), each (47), them (52), my (80), over (82), use(ing) (88), water (90), our (109), day (114), away (140), went (143), every (151), whole (259), city (273), car(s) (282), morning (283), body (285), family (287), fish (299), living (301), fire (356), kept (378), river (394), instead (408), listen(ed) (507), clear (510), week (512), spring (515), travel(ing) (516), mountain(s) (526), caught (527), hair (528), bird(s) (529), wood (530)

Extra words: busy, camping, clean, cooked, dinner, sing, streets

writing

recording words for personal study list

Extend Spelling Assessment

Give this in-context assessment of Core Words within the frequencies 1–530 to students who need more practice or challenge.

THE SENTENCE DICTATION TEST

Students do not prestudy the words. Provide students with writing paper and pencil. Have students write the sentences as they are dictated.

1. Our whole family went camping in the mountains for a week away from city living.
2. Every day we were there, we caught fish from the river and cooked them for dinner over a wood fire.
3. I kept my hair and body clean using clear spring water during our outing.
4. Each morning we listened to birds sing instead of cars traveling by on busy streets.

AFTER THE SENTENCE DICTATION TEST

1. Have students write a brochure advertising the campground this family visited. Tell students to help persuade campers to visit by writing vivid, enticing descriptions of the lifestyle they'll enjoy on this outing.

2. Have students record the words they missed on the test in their Spelling Notebook (see page 345) for at-school study, and on a copy of the WORDS TO LEARN BLACKLINE MASTER, page 375, for at-home study.

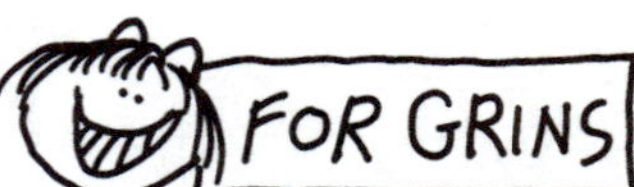

- What's a stove designed for high altitudes? A mountain range!
- If a bird complaint is a "hawk squawk," what's a bird frown? An owl scowl!

Most cultures have been concerned about hair. The Greeks valued long hair. The Greek word *kometes* meant "wearing long hair," from which *comet* aptly gets its name. *Shampoo* was a word coined by English hairdressers from the Hindu *champo*, meaning "to massage or knead." American John Breck, who concocted serums for his baldness, eventually produced the first shampoos.

- Have students research and report on the array of hair products available today.
- Have students speculate why hair can be a fashion statement in our and other cultures.

— Word Test —

Quinn's Clever Idea

The wind was whipping (1) _________________ Quinn's (2) _________________ as he

flew his (3) _________________ kite. (4) _________________, he nearly lost the kite. It

got (5) _________________ in the (6) _________________ branches of a tree, but he

was (7) _________________ to climb and set it free. He is a keen climber and can scale

tall (8) _________________ and buildings. What he wanted more (9) _________________

anything was to climb the church spire, but of (10) _________________ the

archbishops would never allow it. (11) _________________ he would climb it at night.

No, that wouldn't (12) _________________. It would (13) _________________ cause

trouble. Then, as he (14) _________________ his kite flying high in the sky like a

(15) _________________, he had a fine idea. He would get the archbishops to ask

him to climb the spire in broad daylight! (16) _________________, on his way

home, he stopped by the church. Yes, he (17) _________________, I shall climb

(18) _________________ to (19) _________________ top tomorrow. When Quinn hurried

to the church the next (20) _________________, it (21) _________________—his wish

came true! (22) _________________ enough, the archbishops invited Quinn to ascend

(23) _________________ spire! A huge crowd of admirers gathered as Quinn scaled

the steeple. (24) _________________ Quinn's clever plan.

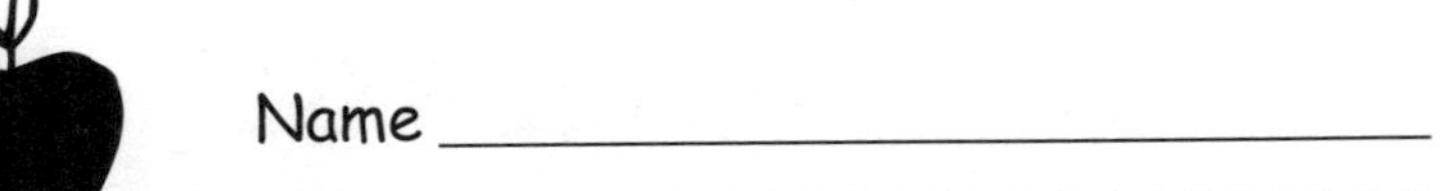

Name _________________________

Skill Test

Read the story and fill in the blanks with **there**, **their**, or **they're**.

Would _________________ be anything that would frighten scary monsters?

What might make _________________ eyes close tightly and _________________

bodies shake in fright? Perhaps _________________ not afraid of another

big animal, but _________________ frightened by bright light or loud noise.

_________________ may be many things that would scare them and cause

_________________ bodies to shiver that wouldn't scare us. _________________

are differences of opinion about what is scary.

Proofreading Test

Proofread for one spelling, capitalization, or punctuation error in the underlined parts. Circle errors. Write corrections in the spaces.

The United States is big, <u>but when it is maesured</u> and   _________________

comparisons are made, it looks much <u>smaller. All of north</u>   _________________

America, of <u>wich the United States</u> is a part, covers only   _________________

about 16% <u>of erath. Asia</u> is much larger and takes in   _________________

about 30% of the <u>worlds land. The highest</u> mountain range   _________________

is also in Asia, the Himalayas. <u>Of coarse, the</u> loftiest   _________________

mountain, Mt. <u>Everest, is their. It towers</u> just above 29,000   _________________

feet, while <u>the hiest point in North</u> America is just over   _________________

20,000 <u>feet. That's Mt</u> McKinley. It's tall, but it does not   _________________

rank <u>amung the ten tallest</u> peaks in the world. The longest   _________________

river <u>is the Nile It</u> stretches over 4,100 miles. The length   _________________

of the Mississippi <u>and it's main</u> tributaries is only about   _________________

<u>3,700 mile</u> in comparison.   _________________

How does your state or province compare with other states or provinces when various measures are made?

Use Student Practice Pages 19–20 to follow up instruction for:
Activities 1A and 1B • Build Skillful Writers

Build Visual Skills

Do the Word Preview, a visual warm-up activity, with all students.
Use Core Words **color** (531), **war** (532), **fly** (533), **yourself** (534), **seem** (535).

Teaching Notes, page 316

Build Spelling and Language Skills

Choose from among these quick tasks to customize instruction
for all or selected students.

Teaching Notes, page 319

STRETCH IT It couldn't fly.

FIX IT The beautiful colors of are american flag always fly weather were at war or piece. You may fined yourself watching the flag at a ball game.

(our, American, whether, we're, peace, find)

SORT IT flying, delightful, reapply, midnight, insightful, kindness, bicycle, enlighten, stylish, rewinding

(e.g., /ī/ spelling pattern; has prefix/suffix/both; number of syllables)

ADD IT war, warm, award, warden, ______

(words that contain war)

FINISH IT If I could fly anywhere in North America, it would be ______.

FIND IT Words that are homophones

(e.g., seem/seam)

Teaching Notes, page 325

Build Basic Concepts

Choose from among these skill-building activities to customize instruction for all or selected students.

| concept one | A suffix is a letter or letters added to the end of a word. |

suffix practice, word analysis, choral reading, writing a rhyme, more words, proofreading

1A Select students to write *color* and its other word forms on the chalkboard: *colors, colored, coloring, colorless, colorful*. Note the one *l* in the *ful* suffix—the word *full* has two *l*'s, the suffix *ful* has one. Write this rhyme on the chalkboard or on a chart for students to read chorally.

> **One "l" Will Do**
> Something a careful speller must do,
> Is learn when a word has one l or two.
> Surely you know that until ends in one.
> U-n-t-i-—write one l and you're done!
> An extra l is an unwanted guest.
> More is not better—less is the best.
> It's the same with the suffix ful, my friend.
> A careful speller writes one l at the end.
> F-u-l—just one l. Now quit 'cause you're through!
> Don't ever write two l's when one l will do!

Have students copy the rhyme. Then they proofread it with a partner. Below the rhyme, have students list words that end with the *ful* suffix—remind students to be careful to write one *l*! (Words are reused in Activity 1B, below.)

suffix practice, word analysis, spelling rules, writing words, proofreading

1B Have students scrutinize their *ful*-suffix words (Activity 1A, above) for those to which the *ly* suffix can be added (e.g., careful/carefully, colorful/colorfully, hopeful/hopefully, cheerful/cheerfully). Note that the *ly* suffix is just added to the *ful* ending—both *l*'s are retained. The same principle applies to any word ending in *l*—the *ly* is just added. Have students apply this *ly* rule to—*final/finally, usual/usually, natural/naturally, total/totally, equal/equally*. Next, have students fold writing paper to make two vertical columns. In the first column they write a word ending in *l* to which the *ly* suffix can be added. In the second column they write the word with the *ly* suffix. Then students share/proofread their list with a partner.

Have students write 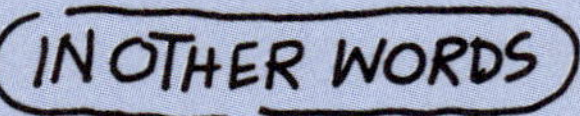

: "Whenever you do a thing never known but to yourself, ask yourself how you would act were all the world looking, and carefully act accordingly." Thomas Jefferson

The saying "to fly off the handle" originated in frontier days when many tools had wooden handles, such as an ax. When the tools were exposed to weather, the wooden handles often separated from the metal upon reuse. Especially when an ax blade flew off its handle, everyone nearby was endangered. A violent temper was equally dangerous, thus the expression.

• Have students write the meaning of "to fly off the handle."

Build Skillful Writers

Use these interrelated language learnings for all or selected students.

Teaching Notes, page 328

An apostrophe always has a purpose (Build Skillful Writers, page 48). One use is to signal ownership, or possession. However, possessive pronouns never have an apostrophe. Have students take turns writing the possessive pronouns on the chalkboard (my, mine, his, her, hers, their, theirs, our, ours, your, yours, its, whose). Then position some students at the chalkboard as others write at their desks as you dictate this paragraph. Identify and differentiate the words with *s*, *'s*, and *s'*, and discuss why *its* and *theirs* have no apostrophe.

> When the batter's bat hit the ball, its trip to center field began. A fielder's job is to catch the batter's flies. The fielders ran for the batter's fly ball, hoping it would soon be theirs. The players in the players' dugout stood to watch.

Then have students write a story ending.

Build Assessment Readiness

Use these at-school and at-home exercises to prepare all students for the Skill Test.

Teaching Notes, page 329

at-school   Revisit *Snowflake Bentley*, the 1999 Caldecott Medal winner, and the distinctive woodcut illustrations Mary Azarian fashioned to complement the story (two excellent information sources on Azarian and her art are *The Reading Teacher*, Vol. 53, No. 4, Dec. 1999/Jan. 2000, and *The Horn Book Magazine*, July/August 1999). Then help students discriminate between compound words and two-syllable words, particularly those with a suffix (e.g., snowflake, snowing). Introduce compound equations to verify that each part of a compound is a complete word (e.g., your + self = yourself). Provide students with clues to identify compound words for students to write equations. Choices may include *snowflake, woodcut, bookmark, farmhouse, baseball, bedtime, hairdo, birdbath, driftwood, wartime, butterfly, windowsill,* and *weekend*. Then have students write compound word clues to play again later.

Skill to be tested: compound words

at-home   Send home a copy of Take-Home Task 7 Blackline Master, page 58, with each student to encourage parent-child partnerships.

Skill to be tested: compound words

Build Proofreading Skills

Track students' ability to meet a minimum competency for spelling and proofreading within selected samples of their everyday writing.

Teaching Notes, page 330

- Send home papers for proofreading and a copy of the Ideas for Proofreading Blackline Master, page 373.

Name ___________________________________

Dear Parents,

In these activities, you can help your child identify and spell compound words—words made up of two or more words. Have your child read the directions to the first activity and explain to you what is expected. Guide your child through the activity. Listen and discuss your child's explanations. Then proceed with the other activities in the same way.

1. Circle the compound words. Underline the word parts. Explain why they are compound words, while the others are not.

colorful	weekly	basement	springtime
myself	bluebird	correcting	Sunday
newspaper	housefly	basketball	applesauce
listening	noticeable	anything	useful
careless	yourself	friendly	golden

2. Write compound words using the clues. Underline the word parts.

ring for an ear _______________________   day of birth _______________________

home for a bird _______________________   a boat that sails _______________________

drops of rain _______________________   board for skating _______________________

measuring stick _______________________   pain in the head _______________________

falling water _______________________   after midday _______________________

3. Make compound words using the word parts.

proof	foot	place
score	earth	print
birth	down	ball
ground	shield	waste
quake	card	read
basket	touch	wind

____

____

____

____

____

- Spelling Words (words missed on tests) are recorded in the Spelling Notebook.
- Use Proof It, Practice Page 21, for proofreading/editing practice.

WORD TEST

Assess Spelling Progress

Teaching Notes, page 336

Give this Cloze Story Word Test of Core Words within the frequencies 1–535 to all students. Words students miss are their Spelling Words.

THE CLOZE STORY WORD TEST

Students do not prestudy the words. Provide students with a copy of REVIEW 7 BLACKLINE MASTER, page 62. Tell students that this is a story about monsters from ancient to modern times.

Read the entire story aloud, including the test words. Then read it again slowly as students write the missing words.

> ### Monster Mysteries
>
> Monsters (1) <u>seem</u> to fascinate people. Lore from long ago, as well as from modern times, describes monsters. They're large and strangely put (2) <u>together</u>, any (3) <u>color</u>, some (4) <u>fly</u>, some have (5) <u>hair</u>, and all are frightening. Ancient legends present the ongoing (6) <u>war</u> (7) <u>against</u> the griffin, a half-lion and half-eagle. Bigfoot, a jumbo woolly creature, is (8) <u>said</u> to exist today in the northwest (9) <u>woods</u> of the (10) <u>United States</u>. The enormous Loch Ness monster supposedly lurks at the (11) <u>bottom</u> of a lake in Scotland. Can the sightings of these monsters be (12) <u>explained</u>? If not, why would people keep (13) <u>their</u> legends alive? Do you believe in them (14) <u>yourself</u>?
>
> (15) <u>Often</u> scientists and others doubt the existence of these odd (16) <u>animals</u>, however, some reports have (17) <u>turned</u> out to be (18) <u>correct</u>. It took over a (19) <u>hundred</u> years before the accounts of a huge sea creature, our giant squid, were confirmed. The Komodo lizard was (20) <u>finally</u> documented in 1912. This creature (21) <u>measures</u> twelve feet long and is sizable (22) <u>enough</u> to eat a buffalo! Before then, it was (23) <u>thought</u> to be only a legend, (24) <u>although</u> now we know it's real.

Words tested:
their (42), said (43), thought (179), often (186), together (187), enough (209), against (268), turned (270), United States (305), hundred (374), finally (414), animals (418), although (450), bottom (492), explain(ed) (513), correct (521), measure(s) (523), hair (528), wood(s) (530), color (531), war (532), fly (533), yourself (534), seem (535)

AFTER THE CLOZE STORY WORD TEST

1. Ask students to tell in writing whether they believe the current tales about Bigfoot and the Loch Ness monster. Then have students research the monsters to form opinions on their existence. Speculate why monster legends continue to thrive throughout history.

research, speculating, writing

2. Have students record the words they missed on the test in their Spelling Notebook (see page 338) for at-school study, and on a copy of the WORDS TO LEARN BLACKLINE MASTER, page 375, for at-home study.

recording words for personal study list

Assess Skill Application

Give this assessment of spelling and related skills to all students.
The REVIEW 7 BLACKLINE MASTER is on page 63.

Teaching Notes, page 339

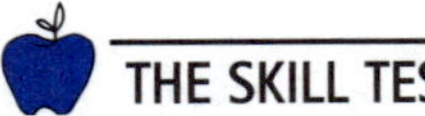 THE SKILL TEST

Skill tested:
compound words

Combine to make compound words:

bird	your	color	house	self
board	ful	ment	fly	ing
sun	use	my	shine	bath
farm	clear	lost	sail	boat
full	ly	set	skate	er

yourself, myself, birdbath, sailboat, boathouse, birdhouse, skateboard,
sunset, sunshine, farmhouse, housefly

Note the ability of each student to make compound words.

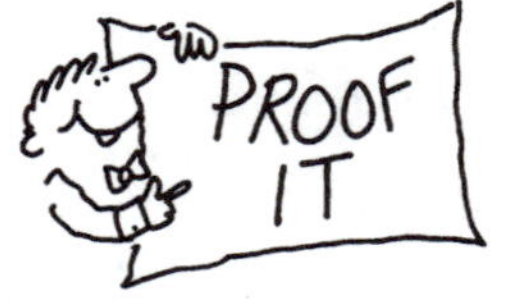

Assess Proofreading Application

Give this assessment of spelling and related skills to all students.
The REVIEW 7 BLACKLINE MASTER is on page 63.

Teaching Notes, page 341

 THE PROOFREADING TEST

Circle the correct word to complete each line.

__________ are particular tools to measure different things.	Therre	(There)	Their
To measure yourself, what might you use? __________, decide	Frist	Furst	(First)
what you wish to measure __________ yourself. To measure	abaut	(about)	abote
your age, you're measuring time. __________ likely you'd use	(It's)	Its	its
years, months, and even days and __________. To measure	Minutes	minits	(minutes)
your height, __________ is being measured. A yardstick or	(distance)	distanse	distents
measuring tape would work. Of __________, if you wanted to	caorse	corse	(course)
measure your temperature, eyesight, __________, or	wait	waite	(weight)
strength, other devices would be used. A __________ could	thermeter	(thermometer)	themometer
determine your temperature in units called __________,	degreez	degreets	(degrees)
which are expressed in numbers by using __________ the	(either)	ether	ethere
Fahrenheit or Celsius scale. There are __________ things to	meny	manny	(many)
measure and __________ different ways to measure each one.	(usually)	usualy	useully

Do you think that everything about you could be measured, or are there some things that couldn't be
measured? Why?

Note the ability of each student to proofread for spelling errors.

Extend Spelling Assessment

Give this in-context assessment of Core Words within the frequencies 1–535 to students who need more practice or challenge.

Teaching Notes, page 342

THE SENTENCE DICTATION TEST

Students do not prestudy the words. Provide students with writing paper and pencil. Have students write the sentences as they are dictated.

1. Most posters seem to explain an idea very well through words, pictures, and color.
2. I'm sure you've seen some really great examples for yourself.
3. They may point out the importance of the war against drugs or wild gangs.
4. One might show a beautiful city you can fly to for fun, warm weather, and great food.

Words tested:

the (1), of (2), and (3), a (4), to (5), you('ve) (8), for (12), they (19), or (26), one (28), can (38), an (39), out (51), some (56), may (89), very (93), words (95), most (99), through (102), well (132), great (146), might (173), show (184), food (198), picture(s) (232), sure (251), example(s) (261), against (268), point (272), city (273), seen (280), I'm (284), really (313), idea (331), warm (412), beautiful (429), wild (463), weather (464), explain (513), color (531), war (532), fly (533), yourself (534), seem (535)

Extra words: drugs, fun, gangs, importance, posters

AFTER THE SENTENCE DICTATION TEST

1. Have students create a poster with a message.

creating a poster

2. Have students record the words they missed on the test in their Spelling Notebook (see page 345) for at-school study, and on a copy of the WORDS TO LEARN BLACKLINE MASTER, page 375, for at-home study.

recording words for personal study list

All Core Words, beginning with word number one (the), are recycled extensively through the Cloze Story Word Test and Sentence Dictation Test. This provides ongoing maintenance for lifetime mastery of important words. Words students miss become their Spelling Words—differentiated to their specific needs. If parents want a list of the Core Words for which mastery is the goal for Level 5, send home the Core Words list, page 363–365. The Words to Learn sheet signals for parents the specific words their child has not yet mastered that need practice.

REVIEW 7

Name _______________________________

Monster Mysteries

Monsters (1) _________________ to fascinate people. Lore from long ago, as well as from modern times, describes monsters. They're large and strangely put (2) _________________, any (3) _________________, some (4) _________________, some have (5) _________________, and all are frightening. Ancient legends present the ongoing (6) _________________ (7) _________________ the griffin, a half-lion and half-eagle. Bigfoot, a jumbo woolly creature, is (8) _________________ to exist today in the northwest (9) _________________ of the (10) _________________. The enormous Loch Ness monster supposedly lurks at the (11) _________________ of a lake in Scotland. Can the sightings of these monsters be (12) _________________? If not, why would people keep (13) _________________ legends alive? Do you believe in them (14) _________________?

(15) _________________ scientists and others doubt the existence of these odd (16) _________________, however, some reports have (17) _________________ out to be (18) _________________. It took over a (19) _________________ years before the accounts of a huge sea creature, our giant squid, were confirmed. The Komodo lizard was (20) _________________ documented in 1912. This creature (21) _________________ twelve feet long and is sizable (22) _________________ to eat a buffalo! Before then, it was (23) _________________ to be only a legend, (24) _________________ now we know it's real.

Skill Test

Combine to make compound words:

bird	your	color	house	self
board	ful	ment	fly	ing
sun	use	my	shine	bath
farm	clear	lost	sail	boat
full	ly	set	skate	er

____

____

____

____

Proofreading Test

Circle the correct word to complete each line.

________ are particular tools to measure different things.	Therre	There	Their
To measure yourself, what might you use? ________, decide	Frist	Furst	First
what you wish to measure ________ yourself. To measure	abaut	about	abote
your age, you're measuring time. ________ likely you'd use	It's	Its	its
years, months, and even days and ________. To measure	Minutes	minits	minutes
your height, ________ is being measured. A yardstick or	distance	distanse	distents
measuring tape would work. Of ________, if you wanted to	caorse	corse	course
measure your temperature, eyesight, ________, or	wait	waite	weight
strength, other devices would be used. A ________ could	thermeter	thermometer	themometer
determine your temperature in units called ________,	degreez	degreets	degrees
which are expressed in numbers by using ________ the	either	ether	ethere
Fahrenheit or Celsius scale. There are ________ things to	meny	manny	many
measure and ________ different ways to measure each one.	usually	usualy	useully

Do you think that everything about you could be measured, or are there some things that couldn't be measured? Why?

Build Skills and Word Experiences

Use Student Practice Pages 22–23 to follow up instruction for:
Find It • Activity 1A

Build Visual Skills

Do the Word Preview, a visual warm-up activity, with all students.
Use Core Words **thus** (536), **square** (537), **moment** (538), **teacher** (539), **happy** (540).

Teaching Notes, page 316

Build Spelling and Language Skills

Choose from among these quick tasks to customize instruction
for all or selected students.

Teaching Notes, page 319

STRETCH IT

He ate his meal on a square plate.

FIX IT

Four squared is sixteen. Our math teacher, Mr Brown, was happy the moment are class finely understood that idea. Thus, he ordered a treat for us from a place on oak street.

(*Mr., our, finally, Oak Street*)

SORT IT

teachers, teeth, sheriff, thumb, peaches, shoulder, children, radish, grandfather, cheek, sandwiches, cherries

(e.g., food/people/body parts; contains *ch/sh/th*; is/isn't plural; number of syllables)

ADD IT

square, circle, triangle, ______

(shapes)

FINISH IT

The game wasn't going our way, thus ______

FIND IT

Words to which the suffix *ness* can be added

(e.g., happy/happiness, kind/kindness)

The Exercise Express can be used as "sponge activities" to "soak up" students' free time between assignments, or they can be homework. On occasion, you may wish to assign a different Exercise Express activity to student teams to do and present orally to the class; or teams can complete the same activity and compare results.

Build Basic Concepts

Choose from among these skill-building activities to customize instruction for all or selected students.

Teaching Notes, page 325

concept one	A prefix is a letter or letters added to the beginning of a word. A suffix is a letter or letters added to the end of a word.

1A Post Teaching Poster 2. Ask students how a suffix is added to words that end in consonant *y*. Have students demonstrate with *try* and *happy*. Note that *happily* is the result of the addition of the *ly* suffix to *happy*. Have students find and write more words that follow this pattern (e.g., angrily, heavily, easily, ordinarily, readily, primarily, luckily, momentarily, busily).

suffix practice, plural practice, spelling rules, writing words

Next, ask students how a suffix is added to words that end in silent *e*. Have students demonstrate with *measure* and *square*. Note that to add the *able* suffix to *measure*, the *e* is dropped before its addition. Alert students that for the addition of *able* to some words ending in silent *e*, the *e* is not dropped. The silent *e* is retained when it is preceded by /j/ spelled with the "soft g" (e.g., changeable, manageable, knowledgeable) or /s/ spelled with the "soft c" (e.g., noticeable, serviceable, replaceable).

Then ask students how the *s/es* suffix is added to words that end in *s*, *sh*, *ch*, *x*, and *z*. Have students demonstrate with *thermos*, *miss*, *dash*, *beach*, *fox*, and *buzz*. Alert students that some *o*-ending words also add *es* to form the plural (e.g., potatoes).

1B Write on the chalkboard: *I'm not happy*. Ask students to change *not happy* to a word with a prefix (unhappy). Review Teaching Poster 3 to reinforce that *un* is one prefix that can be added to a base word to make it mean "the opposite." Have students fold paper to make two columns. Dictate these words for students to write in the first column: *friendly, noticed, happily, clear, explained, common, certain, opened, able*. In the second column they add a prefix to make the word mean the opposite. Then have students add more words in both columns (save words for Test Ready, page 84).

prefix practice, vocabulary development, writing words

Have students write 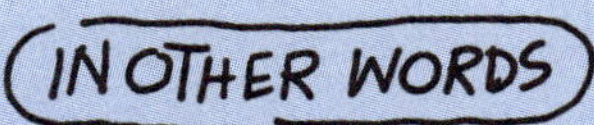

: You can't fit a round peg in a square hole.

"Happiness comes from within, not from without." Benjamin Franklin

The plurals of *o*-ending nouns are an annoyance. Nouns that end in *o* preceded by a vowel usually add *s* (e.g., radios). Nouns that end in *o* preceded by a consonant usually add *es* (e.g., potatoes), yet others add *s* (e.g., memos), and still others may add either *s* or *es*, with one preferred (e.g., mottoes/mottos). Usually words of Spanish or Portuguese origin add *s* (e.g., ponchos) and musical terms, which are invariably of Italian origin, add *s* (e.g., pianos).

Teaching Notes, page 328

Build Skillful Writers

Use these interrelated language learnings for all or selected students.

Guide students to discover the spelling of the most common suffixes that mean "one who."

Introduce *er*, the most frequently used pattern.

    teach/teacher   *listen/listener*   *farm/farmer*   *build/builder*

Then introduce *ar* and *or*.

    act/actor   *visit/visitor*   *beg/beggar*   *lie/liar*

Have students collect more examples of verbs that become nouns meaning "one who" with the addition of *er*, *or*, or *ar*. Students may discover that these suffixes may also mean "something that," for inanimate objects (e.g., refrigerator, toaster).

Challenge students to explore more suffixes that mean "one who." Students may discover: *assistant, librarian, payee, student, waitress, cashier, lawyer, chauffeur, technologist.*

Teaching Notes, page 329

Skill to be tested:
/s/ spelling patterns—s, ss, sc, ce, ci, cy

Build Assessment Readiness

Use these at-school and at-home exercises to prepare all students for the Skill Test.

at-school Review that most often *s* spells /s/, but *ce/ci/cy*, *ss*, and *sc* can spell /s/. Further, *x* can spell /ks/ and *se* can spell /s/ at the end of a word. But remind students that sometimes *s* spells /z/ (e.g., was) and when combined with *h* spells /sh/ (e.g., ship). Have students take turns writing words on the chalkboard that illustrate one of the /s/ spelling patterns. Then underline the letter(s) spelling /s/. Next, conceal the words. Have students write the words they can recall, sorted by spelling pattern. Then reveal the words for students to self-check.

Skill to be tested:
/s/ spelling patterns—s, ss, sc, ce, ci, cy

at-home Send home a copy of Take-Home Task 8 Blackline Master, page 67, with each student to encourage parent-child partnerships.

Teaching Notes, page 330

Build Proofreading Skills

Track students' ability to meet a minimum competency for spelling and proofreading within selected samples of their everyday writing.

- Send home papers for proofreading and a copy of the Ideas for Proofreading Blackline Master, page 373.

Name ___________________________

Dear Parents,

In this activity, you can work with your child to reinforce the patterns for spelling the sound heard at the beginning of  —s, ss, sc, ce, ci, cy. Further, an x can spell the ks sound, as in extra. You can also help your child build vocabulary skills. This lesson focuses on antonyms—words that have opposite meanings. As you have done before, begin by having your child read the directions and explain to you what is expected. Let your child do as much as possible without your help as the two of you proceed through the lesson.

Write an antonym that contains the sound you hear at the beginning of the sun. Then circle the letter(s) that spell this sound.

Not a monarchy, but a _d_ __ _m_ __ __ __ __ __ _y_

Not the country, but the __ __ _t_ __

Not uncles, but __ __ _n_ __ __

Not a square, but a __ __ _r_ __ __ __

Not failure, but _s_ _u_ __ __ __ __ __

Not include, but _e_ __ __ __ __ __ _e_

Not the whole pie, but just one _p_ __ __ __ __

Not the bottom of the ocean, but the __ __ __ _f_ __ __ __

Not a nephew, but a _n_ __ __ __ __

Not an actor, but an __ __ __ _r_ _e_ __ __

Not the employee, but the _b_ __ __ __

Not simple, but _c_ __ _m_ __ _l_ __ __

Not colorful, but _c_ __ _l_ __ __ __ _e_ __ __

Not addition, but __ __ _b_ __ __ __ __ __ __ __ __

Not the prince, but the __ __ __ _n_ __ __ __ __

Not the base of the mountain, but the __ __ _m_ _m_ __ __

Not yourself, but __ _y_ __ __ __ __

Not bland food, but __ _p_ _i_ __ __

Not unknown, but _f_ __ __ __ __ __

Not ascend the stairs, but __ __ __ __ __ _n_ __

Not war, but __ __ __ _c_ __

Not a sunrise, but a __ __ _n_ __ __ __

Not children, but _a_ __ __ __ __ __

Not the whites of the eggs, but the __ __ __ _k_ __

Assess Words and Skills

- Spelling Words (words missed on tests) are recorded in the Spelling Notebook.
- Use Proof It, Practice Page 24, for proofreading/editing practice.

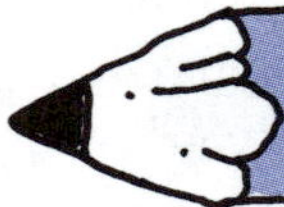

Teaching Notes, page 336

Assess Spelling Progress

Give this Cloze Story Word Test of Core Words within the frequencies 1–540 to all students. Words students miss are their Spelling Words.

THE CLOZE STORY WORD TEST

Students do not prestudy the words. Provide students with a copy of REVIEW 8 BLACKLINE MASTER, page 71. Tell students that this is a story about winning.

Read the entire story aloud, including the test words. Then read it again slowly as students write the missing words.

Go for the Gold!

Winning an Olympic gold medal is a unique honor. Yet, even with much talent and a fine (1) <u>teacher</u>, most of us will have to be (2) <u>happy</u> with less than the "gold." Wait! What about the four-man bobsled? You could be on the bobsled team! All (3) <u>you'd</u> have to do is ride (4) <u>along</u>! Well, (5) <u>there's</u> more to a sled victory than that. The difference (6) <u>between</u> a medal and no medal is less than one (7) <u>second</u>. (8) <u>Thus</u>, you must find ways to (9) <u>travel</u> a (10) <u>moment</u> faster than everyone (11) <u>else</u>. There are three (12) <u>areas</u> to study. (13) <u>First</u>, the push. Strength is (14) <u>important</u>, but so is agility (15) <u>because</u> you do have to get into the sled. Next, the sled. Design (16) <u>yourself</u> a sled that moves (17) <u>across</u> the (18) <u>surface</u> of the ice like a rocket moves (19) <u>through</u> air—nothing (20) <u>square</u> and clumsy. (21) <u>Finally</u>, steering. You must be an engineering genius. Not (22) <u>too</u> high on the curves or you'll have farther to go! Knowing the difficulty of a bobsled win, is there (23) <u>another</u> event that offers you a chance for (24) <u>possible</u> victory? Choose one sport and state your winning strategies.

Words tested:
you('d) (8), there('s) (37), first (74), through (102), too (112), another (121), because (127), between (154), along (171), important (195), second (235), across (247), area(s) (384), surface (393), finally (414), possible (452), else (485), travel (516), yourself (534), thus (536), square (537), moment (538), teacher (539), happy (540)

AFTER THE CLOZE STORY WORD TEST

speculating, writing

1. Discuss the different sports featured in the summer and winter Olympics. Then have students speculate in writing which sport they might choose to win their "gold" and the strategies they'd use for success. Have students share their speculations and strategies. Then discuss "victory" in terms of being any athlete who even qualifies for participation in the coveted Olympic Games!

recording words for personal study list

2. Have students record the words they missed on the test in their Spelling Notebook (see page 338) for at-school study, and on a copy of the WORDS TO LEARN BLACKLINE MASTER, page 375, for at-home study.

Assess Skill Application

Give this assessment of spelling and related skills to all students.
The REVIEW 8 BLACKLINE MASTER is on page 72.

Teaching Notes, page 339

THE SKILL TEST

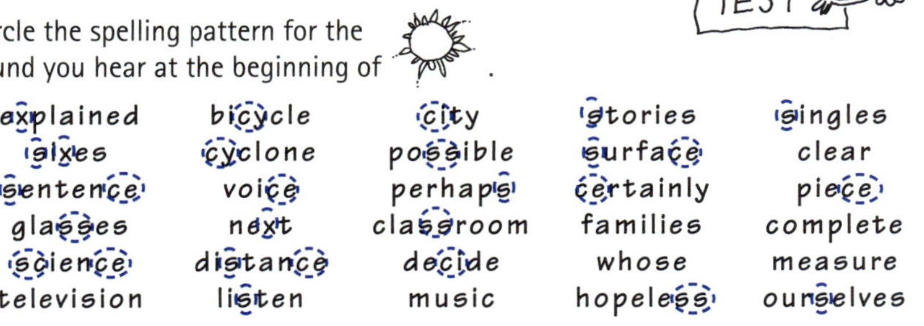

Skill tested:
/s/ spelling patterns—s, ss, sc, ce, ci, cy

Note the ability of each student to identify the most frequent spelling patterns for
/s/—*s, ss, sc, ce, ci,* cy; and to identify that *x* can spell /ks/.

Assess Proofreading Application

Give this assessment of spelling and related skills to all students.
The REVIEW 8 BLACKLINE MASTER is on page 72.

Teaching Notes, page 341

THE PROOFREADING TEST

If the underlined word in each line is incorrect, write it
correctly in the space.

A rectangle is any four-sided <u>figure</u>, or shape. A square
is a rectangle, but a triangle <u>isnt</u>. A triangle has only
three sides. A square is a <u>spechial</u> kind of rectangle. It
has four equal sides and four <u>write</u> angles. A circle is a
shape that has no angles, but a <u>singel</u> curved line that's
an equal distance from a <u>point</u> in its center. The distance
<u>arond</u> the outside of a circle is called the circumference.
<u>however,</u> this same distance is called the perimeter
<u>wen</u> the shape is a square. One way to determine the
perimeter of a square <u>ore</u> the circumference of a circle is
to place a <u>piece</u> of string along the edge of each shape.
Then you mark the end. Next, you <u>mesure</u> the distance
of the string from <u>its</u> end to the mark on a ruler.

Is there another way to determine the perimeter of a square or the circumference
of a circle?

	isn't
	special
	right
	single
	around
	However
	when
	or
	measure

Note the ability of each student to proofread for spelling and capitalization errors.

Teaching Notes, page 342

Words tested:
the (1), of (2), a (4), to (5), you (8), at (20), or (26), there (37), your (40), them (52), into (61), make (72), over (82), use (88), may (89), just (97), write (108), right (116), give (159), often (186), want (193), let('s) (230), paper (241), across (247), money (279), cut (293), front (318), special (361), either (409), heavy (426), carefully (427), beautiful (429), friend (498), circle (519), straight (524), color(ed) (531), yourself (534), thus (536), square (537), moment (538), teacher (539), happy (540)

Extra words: card(s), cost, greeting, lot, note, pens

Extend Spelling Assessment

Give this in-context assessment of Core Words within the frequencies 1–540 to students who need more practice or challenge.

 ## THE SENTENCE DICTATION TEST

Students do not prestudy the words. Provide students with writing paper and pencil. Have students write the sentences as they are dictated.

1. Greeting cards often cost a lot of money, thus you may want to make them yourself.
2. Let's just cut heavy paper into either a square or a circle.
3. Over there are colored pens you can use to carefully write a happy note straight across the front.
4. At the right moment, give your beautiful card to a special friend or a teacher.

 ## AFTER THE SENTENCE DICTATION TEST

writing, art

1. Have students create a greeting card to give to someone special. Remind students that they should first develop a clear main idea for their message. Then they select words and art appropriate for the recipient of their greeting.

recording words for personal study list

2. Have students record the words they missed on the test in their Spelling Notebook (see page 345) for at-school study, and on a copy of the WORDS TO LEARN BLACKLINE MASTER, page 375, for at-home study.

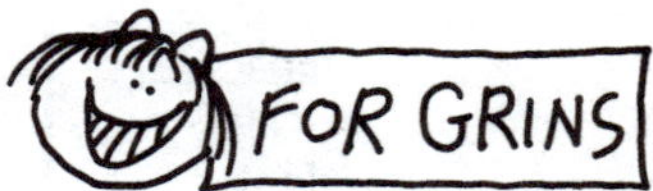

If unusual twins are a "rare pair," what is a rectangular rabbit? A square hare!

WORD MYSTERIES AND HISTORIES

The word mosquito comes from the Spanish word for fly—mosca and ito/ita, or "little one." Mosquito, then, means "little fly."

• Ask students to check the plural of this o-ending noun.

Word Test

Go for the Gold!

Winning an Olympic gold medal is a unique honor. Yet, even with much talent and a

fine (1) ________________, most of us will have to be (2) ________________ with

less than the "gold." Wait! What about the four-man bobsled? You could be on the

bobsled team! All (3) ________________ have to do is ride (4) ________________!

Well, (5) ________________ more to a sled victory than that. The difference

(6) ________________ a medal and no medal is less than one (7) ________________.

(8) ________________, you must find ways to (9) ________________ a

(10) ________________ faster than everyone (11) ________________. There are

three (12) ________________ to study. (13) ________________, the push. Strength

is (14) ________________, but so is agility (15) ________________ you do have

to get into the sled. Next, the sled. Design (16) ________________ a sled that

moves (17) ________________ the (18) ________________ of the ice like a rocket

moves (19) ________________ air—nothing (20) ________________ and clumsy.

(21) ________________, steering. You must be an engineering genius. Not

(22) ________________ high on the curves or you'll have farther to go! Knowing

the difficulty of a bobsled win, is there (23) ________________ event that offers

you a chance for (24) ________________ victory? Choose one sport and state

your winning strategies.

Skill Test

Circle the spelling pattern for the sound you hear at the beginning of ☀.

explained	bicycle	city	stories	singles
sixes	cyclone	possible	surface	clear
sentence	voice	perhaps	certainly	piece
glasses	next	classroom	families	complete
science	distance	decide	whose	measure
television	listen	music	hopeless	ourselves

Proofreading Test

If the underlined word in each line is incorrect, write it correctly in the space.

A rectangle is any four-sided <u>figure</u>, or shape. A square   _______________

is a rectangle, but a triangle <u>isnt</u>. A triangle has only   _______________

three sides. A square is a <u>spechial</u> kind of rectangle. It   _______________

has four equal sides and four <u>write</u> angles. A circle is a   _______________

shape that has no angles, but a <u>singel</u> curved line that's   _______________

an equal distance from a <u>point</u> in its center. The distance   _______________

<u>arond</u> the outside of a circle is called the circumference.   _______________

<u>however</u>, this same distance is called the perimeter   _______________

<u>wen</u> the shape is a square. One way to determine the   _______________

perimeter of a square <u>ore</u> the circumference of a circle is   _______________

to place a <u>piece</u> of string along the edge of each shape.   _______________

Then you mark the end. Next, you <u>mesure</u> the distance   _______________

of the string from <u>its</u> end to the mark on a ruler.   _______________

Is there another way to determine the perimeter of a square or the circumference of a circle?

Build Skills and Word Experiences

Use Student Practice Pages 25–26 to follow up instruction for:
Activity 1A • Test Ready

Build Visual Skills

Do the Word Preview, a visual warm-up activity, with all students.
Use Core Words **bright** (541), **sent** (542), **present** (543), **plan** (544), **rather** (545).

Teaching Notes, page 316

Build Spelling and Language Skills

Choose from among these quick tasks to customize instruction
for all or selected students.

Teaching Notes, page 319

They sent a present.

Our present plan is to paint the hallway with wild, bright color
rather then brown or white. We have all ready send for the paint
and will begin the moment it comes. Whose going to help us

(*colors*, *than*, *already*, *sent*, *Who's*, question mark)

rather, dollar, alligator, inventor, prettier, beaver, sailor, deeper, cougar, faster, jogger,
rooster, beggar

(e.g., ends in *ar/er/or*; vowel-*r* ending is part of base word/suffix meaning one who/suffix meaning more;
does/doesn't contain double letters; is/isn't an animal word)

bright, brighter, brightest; clear, clearer, clearest; _______

(words that are comparisons)

One thing that I plan to do is _______

Words that double the final letter before adding *ed* or *ing*

Have students write 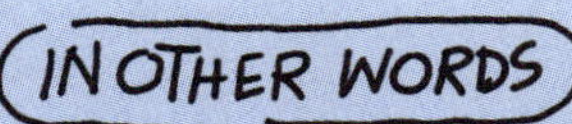 : "Plan your day, then work your plan."
Norman Vincent Peale

Teaching Notes, page 325

Build Basic Concepts

Choose from among these skill-building activities to customize instruction
for all or selected students.

concept one — Some words are spelled with consonant digraphs.

phonics, word analysis, more words, sorting words, parts of speech

1A Select students to write on the chalkboard: *camp/champ, sort/short, ten/then, were/where, pony/phony*. Note that when *h* follows *c, s, t, w,* or *p* the combination stands for a new sound. Have students brainstorm words that contain each digraph at the beginning, middle, and end of the word. Help students discover that words do not end with *wh*.

ch at the beginning	ch in the middle	ch at the end
chain	teacher	peach
chalk	branches	touch
chair	kitchen	coach
checkers	poncho	porch
chew	purchase	march
choice	rancher	rich
charge	exchange	sandwich
chapter	attached	switch

Challenge some students to sort the words by nouns, verbs, and words that can be both.

concept two — Some words are spelled with consonant blends.

phonics, writing word clues, reading

2A Review digraphs (Activity 1A) to point out that these adjacent consonants make one sound. But sometimes adjacent consonants make separate sounds that blend together. Write *present* on the chalkboard to point out how the separate sounds *pr* and *nt* are easier to spell when you listen to the sound of each of the letters. Have students write words with consonant blends, write clues for the words, and read the clues for their classmates to identify and write.

phonics, homographs, writing sentences, vocabulary development

2B Write on the chalkboard: *content, desert, object, present, record*. Have students identify the consonant blends (nt, rt, ct, pr, rd). Help students discover that these words can be pronounced in two ways, and each pronunciation has a different meaning. They are homographs (homographs are one focus of Teaching Poster 5, introduced in Unit 13). Have students use the homographs in oral and written sentences.

Have students write 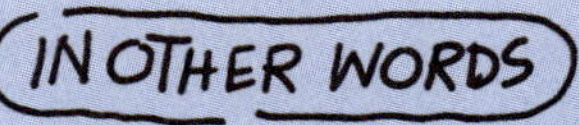

: "The present day is the critical day, because each day presents itself with the potential for being significant. Every day is life's present to you." Ralph Waldo Emerson

Build Skillful Writers

Use these interrelated language learnings for all or selected students.

Teaching Notes, page 328

Dictionaries show the correct spelling, meaning, and pronunciation of a word. Explore a dictionary pronunciation key, highlighting these word groups—

- Homographs (see Activity 2B, this unit) are words that have more than one pronunciation and meaning (e.g., present).
- Some words have more than one correct pronunciation (e.g., tomato, roof, aunt).
- Some mispronounced words result in their misspelling (e.g., government, library, February, sophomore, chocolate, surprise, pumpkin, probably, literature, asked, hundred, *candidate). Have students check their pronunciation in a dictionary. [*See Word Mysteries and Histories, page 79.]

Make three accordion class books (see page 394) to highlight each word group. Have students include a page for each word that shows its pronunciation, its meaning, and a sentence that uses the word.

Build Assessment Readiness

Use these at-school and at-home exercises to prepare all students for the Skill Test.

Teaching Notes, page 329

at-school Review *er*, the most common spelling pattern for the suffix meaning "one who" or "something that" (Build Skillful Writers, page 66). Then remind students that *er* can mean "more" (e.g., bright/brighter). Post Teaching Poster 2 to guide students through the suffix addition process.

Skill to be tested:
er suffix

Dictate these words for students to add the *er* suffix: *heavy, race, ship, rich, present, white, teach, listen, travel, plan, mow*. Later, write the words on the chalkboard, or have a student do so, for self-checking. Then have students sort the words by the meaning of the suffix: *one who/something that* or *more*. Next, students find and write more words for each category.

at-home Send home a copy of Take-Home Task 9 Blackline Master, page 76, with each student to encourage parent-child partnerships.

Skill to be tested:
er suffix

Build Proofreading Skills

Track students' ability to meet a minimum competency for spelling and proofreading within selected samples of their everyday writing.

Teaching Notes, page 330

- Send home papers for proofreading and a copy of the Ideas for Proofreading Blackline Master, page 373.

Name _______________________________

Dear Parents,

Your child's word experiences, vocabulary, and spelling skills expand as your child masters how to add suffixes to words. This activity focuses on the addition of the er suffix, meaning one who (build/builder) or more (bright/brighter). The centerpiece for this practice is another analogy activity, a powerful exercise to help your child learn to think about words and their properties.

Have your child read and explain the directions to you. Then work together to complete the exercise. Take the time to discuss each analogy—ask your child why the answer is appropriate to ensure understanding. In fact, you and your child may wish to write more analogy exercises once you complete this Take-Home Task. The ability to write word analogies demonstrates a thorough understanding of them.

Complete the analogies using a word with the er suffix.

cut : scissors :: farm : f ___ ___ ___ ___ ___

circle : square :: blacker : w ___ ___ ___ ___ ___

walked : strolled :: shinier : b ___ ___ ___ ___ ___ ___ ___

starting : stopping :: lower : h ___ ___ ___ ___ ___

middle : center :: thinner : s ___ ___ ___ ___ ___ ___ ___

question : answer :: sooner : l ___ ___ ___ ___

correct : right :: instructor : t ___ ___ ___ ___ ___ ___

furnace : warmer :: sugar : s ___ ___ ___ ___ ___ ___

simple : easy :: neater : t ___ ___ ___ ___ ___

schooner : canoe :: runner : j ___ ___ ___ ___ ___

north : south :: older : y ___ ___ ___ ___ ___ ___

hike : hiker :: employ : e ___ ___ ___ ___ ___ ___ ___

sweeping : sweeper :: boxing : b ___ ___ ___ ___

build : construct :: chef : b ___ ___ ___ ___

Next, have your child write each of the analogy answer words on the back of this paper sorted by meaning: one who or more. Thanks parents—every child a speller!

Assess Words and Skills

- Spelling Words (words missed on tests) are recorded in the Spelling Notebook.
- Use Proof It, Practice Page 27, for proofreading/editing practice.

Assess Spelling Progress

Teaching Notes, page 336

Give this Cloze Story Word Test of Core Words within the frequencies 1–545 to all students. Words students miss are their Spelling Words.

THE CLOZE STORY WORD TEST

Students do not prestudy the words. Provide students with a copy of Review 9 Blackline Master, page 80. Tell students that this is a story about dams. Dams are built in a unique way for good reason.

Read the entire story aloud, including the test words. Then read it again slowly as students write the missing words.

> ### Devising a Dam
>
>
>
> Dams have helped (1) <u>people</u> use water as a resource (2) <u>since</u> ancient times. Dams harness water for such things as irrigation, flood control, water storage, conservation, and power. The water power (3) <u>they're</u> able to produce is (4) <u>important</u>. Water is (5) <u>sent</u> through gigantic turbines to generate electrical (6) <u>energy</u>. Grand Coulee Dam on the Columbia (7) <u>River</u> is one of the greatest power producers in the (8) <u>world</u>. (9) <u>It's</u> made of concrete and, like other (10) <u>strong</u> dams, the convex side is by the water source. The dam curves, or bows, in a half (11) <u>circle</u> (12) <u>toward</u> the water. Engineers always (13) <u>plan</u> the construction of a dam in this way for a (14) <u>simple</u> reason. Why does the convex side of the dam need to be next to the water source (15) <u>rather</u> than (16) <u>its</u> concave side? Why don't they (17) <u>build</u> dams (18) <u>straight</u> (19) <u>across</u> the water supply? Please (20) <u>present</u> a (21) <u>bright</u> explanation for why dams are (22) <u>built</u> this way. Explain your answer by drawing a (23) <u>picture</u> to make your idea (24) <u>clear</u>.

Words tested:

its (76), people (79), world (191), important (195), picture (232), since (238), across (247), it's (253), toward (275), built (360), strong (381), river (394), simple (455), build (487), clear (510), energy (511), circle (519), straight (524), bright (541), sent (542), present (543), plan (544), rather (545), *they're (1010)

*The testing of they're (1010) is included to help students differentiate among the there/their/they're homophones.

AFTER THE CLOZE STORY WORD TEST

1. Have students locate Grand Coulee Dam on a map. Discuss convex/concave. Have students write and draw their explanation. Conclude that concrete dams are built with the convex side toward the water to make them stronger. Concrete may crack. If this happened, the concrete could break if the dam's construction had its concave side against the water source, and the concrete would be forced outward. With convex construction, the water source would force the concrete inward through compression, averting a break.

reasoning, writing, art

2. Have students record the words they missed on the test in their Spelling Notebook (see page 338) for at-school study, and on a copy of the Words to Learn Blackline Master, page 375, for at-home study.

recording words for personal study list

Teaching Notes, page 339

Assess Skill Application

Give this assessment of spelling and related skills to all students.
The REVIEW 9 BLACKLINE MASTER is on page 81.

🍎 THE SKILL TEST

Skill tested:
er suffix

Add the **er** suffix. Then write the meaning of the suffix.

plan	planner	one who	catch	catcher	one who
listen	listener	one who	blue	bluer	more
bright	brighter	more	clear	clearer	more
buy	buyer	one who	run	runner	one who
write	writer	one who	happy	happier	more
fly	flier	one who	farm	farmer	one who
straight	straighter	more	friendly	friendlier	more
box	boxer	one who	teach	teacher	one who

Note the ability of each student to write words with the *er* suffix and to identify the meaning of the suffix.

Teaching Notes, page 341

Assess Proofreading Application

Give this assessment of spelling and related skills to all students.
The REVIEW 9 BLACKLINE MASTER is on page 81.

🍎 THE PROOFREADING TEST

If any underlined word or words in each line are incorrect,
write the correction(s) in the space.

We know about shapes, such as <u>circles and squares</u>, and
we know about <u>the different</u> angles and curves of the lines
that make these shapes. Have you ever <u>thougt about</u> a   <u>thought</u>
melody <u>having a shape</u>? Melodies have shapes made of
lines going up and down that <u>you can pickture</u>. The shape   <u>picture</u>
of "Row, Row, Row Your Boat" begins with a <u>straght line</u>.   <u>straight</u>
<u>then it goes</u> up and comes back down. In longer songs,   <u>Then</u>
if you <u>listen carfully</u>, you may hear a melody repeat   <u>carefully</u>
itself. Sometimes when it repeats, the <u>melody is a littel</u>   <u>little</u>
higher or lower. The Star-Spangled Banner <u>has a very</u>
dramatic shape that suits <u>its' grand mesage</u>. The lines   <u>its, message</u>
of its melody go up high, bursting into the sky, <u>and than</u>   <u>then</u>
swoop down <u>agin like a soaring</u> eagle.   <u>again</u>

Think of a song you know, write the song's words, and then under the words draw
the lines formed by its melody.

Note the ability of each student to proofread for spelling and/or capitalization errors.

Extend Spelling Assessment

Give this in-context assessment of Core Words within the frequencies 1–545 to students who need more practice or challenge.

Teaching Notes, page 342

THE SENTENCE DICTATION TEST

Students do not prestudy the words. Provide students with writing paper and pencil. Have students write the sentences as they are dictated.

1. Tomorrow I'll present my written book report to my English teacher.
2. There's a chance I'll write it on bright blue paper rather than plain white.
3. Mrs. Brown plans to carefully check my work and listen as I explain it to her.
4. If it's in good form, then it will be sent to the library for other children to read.

Words tested:
the (1), and (3), a (4), to (5), in (6), it (10), for (12), on (14), as (16), be (21), I (24), there('s) (37), if (44), will (46), then (53), other (60), her (64), than (73), my (80), good (106), write (108), work (124), read (165), form (197), children (200), white (239), paper (241), it's (253), book (307), I'll (325), English (350), blue (407), carefully (427), check (493), listen (507), explain (513), teacher (539), bright (541), sent (542), present (543), plan(s) (544), rather (545)

Extra words: Brown, chance, library, Mrs., plain, report, tomorrow, written

AFTER THE SENTENCE DICTATION TEST

1. Have students write a brief book report on a recent fictional reading. Have them suggest another ending to the story in their report.

writing a book report

2. Have students record the words they missed on the test in their Spelling Notebook (see page 345) for at-school study, and on a copy of the WORDS TO LEARN BLACKLINE MASTER, page 375, for at-home study.

recording words for personal study list

Dictate this tongue-twister for students to write and say: There's no need to light a night-light on a slightly light night like tonight's night.

• Challenge students to write more sentences for dictation to twist their classmates' tongues.

WORD MYSTERIES AND HISTORIES

Long ago, Romans running for a public office wanted to make a good impression on the voters. To do so, they wore spotless, white robes when they gave speeches. The Latin word *candidatus* means "one who dresses in white," thus they became known as candidates. *Candidate* is often mispronounced and, as a result, often misspelled. (See Build Skillful Writers, page 75).

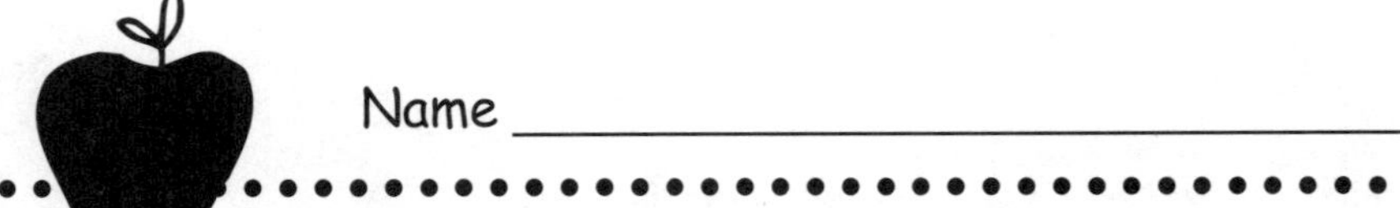

Name ______________________________

— Word Test —

Devising a Dam

Dams have helped (1) ________________ use water as a resource (2) ________________

ancient times. Dams harness water for such things as irrigation, flood control,

water storage, conservation, and power. The water power (3) ________________

able to produce is (4) ________________. Water is (5) ________________ through

gigantic turbines to generate electrical (6) ________________. Grand Coulee Dam

on the Columbia (7) ________________ is one of the greatest power producers in

the (8) ________________. (9) ________________ made of concrete and, like other

(10) ________________ dams, the convex side is by the water source. The dam

curves, or bows, in a half (11) ________________ (12) ________________ the water.

Engineers always (13) ________________ the construction of a dam in this way for

a (14) ________________ reason. Why does the convex side of the dam need to be

next to the water source (15) ________________ than (16) ________________

concave side? Why don't they (17) ________________ dams (18) ________________

(19) ________________ the water supply? Please (20) ________________ a

(21) ________________ explanation for why dams are (22) ________________ this

way. Explain your answer by drawing a (23) ________________ to make your idea

(24) ________________.

Skill Test

Add the **er** suffix. Then write the meaning of the suffix.

plan	_______	_______	catch	_______	_______
listen	_______	_______	blue	_______	_______
bright	_______	_______	clear	_______	_______
buy	_______	_______	run	_______	_______
write	_______	_______	happy	_______	_______
fly	_______	_______	farm	_______	_______
straight	_______	_______	friendly	_______	_______
box	_______	_______	teach	_______	_______

Proofreading Test

If any underlined word or words in each line are incorrect, write the correction(s) in the space.

We know about shapes, such as <u>circles and squares</u>, and ________________

we know about <u>the different</u> angles and curves of the lines ________________

that make these shapes. Have you ever <u>thougt about</u> a ________________

melody <u>having a shape</u>? Melodies have shapes made of ________________

lines going up and down that <u>you can pickture</u>. The shape ________________

of "Row, Row, Row Your Boat" begins with a <u>straght line</u>. ________________

<u>then it goes</u> up and comes back down. In longer songs, ________________

if you <u>listen carfully</u>, you may hear a melody repeat ________________

itself. Sometimes when it repeats, the <u>melody is a littel</u> ________________

higher or lower. The Star-Spangled Banner <u>has a very</u> ________________

dramatic shape that suits <u>its' grand mesage</u>. The lines ________________

of its melody go up high, bursting into the sky, <u>and than</u> ________________

swoop down <u>agin like a soaring</u> eagle. ________________

Think of a song you know, write the song's words, and then under the words draw the lines formed by its melody.

Build Skills and Word Experiences

Use Student Practice Pages 28–29 to follow up instruction for:
Activity 1A • Test Ready

Build Visual Skills

Do the Word Preview, a visual warm-up activity, with all students.
Use Core Words **length** (546), **speed** (547), **machine** (548), **information** (549), **except** (550).

Teaching Notes, page 316

Build Spelling and Language Skills

Choose from among these quick tasks to customize instruction
for all or selected students.

Teaching Notes, page 319

He had information for them.

Are new washing mashine came with helpful information. It told
about the lenth of the wash cycles and the speed of the spin cycle.
it explained everything accept who's job it is to washing the clothes!

(Our, machine, length, It, except, whose, wash)

except, scientist, recital, cereal, exciting, muscle, peace, circled, graceful, scene

(e.g., /s/ spelling pattern; is/is't a homophone; does/doesn't have a suffix; number of syllables)

length, though, ghost, _______

(each word begins with the last two letters of the previous word)

A machine that is useful to me is _______

Words that can be both nouns and verbs

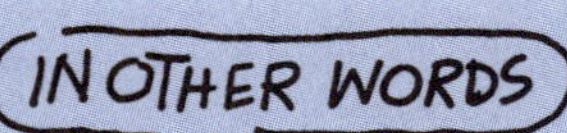
Have students write : "There is more to life than increasing
its speed." Mahatma Gandhi

Build Basic Concepts

Choose from among these skill-building activities to customize instruction for all or selected students.

Teaching Notes, page 325

| concept one | Homophones are words that sound the same but have different spellings and meanings. |

1A Ask students to write a definition of a homophone and explain why it is important for a writer to use homophones correctly. (Homophones are a focus of Teaching Poster 5, introduced in Unit 13.) Ask students which information source to consult for the meaning of a homophone (see Build Skillful Writers, this unit). Note homophones on students' Spell Check card (see page 389) and the sentences that confirm their meanings. Contrast *except* and *accept* and have students write the words in sentences. Provide time for students to read their sentences to the class for the class to respond with the correct homophone. Then have students create a personal book that lists homophones, each written in a context sentence to confirm meaning.

homophones, vocabulary development, writing a definition/explanation, writing homophone context sentences, creating a book

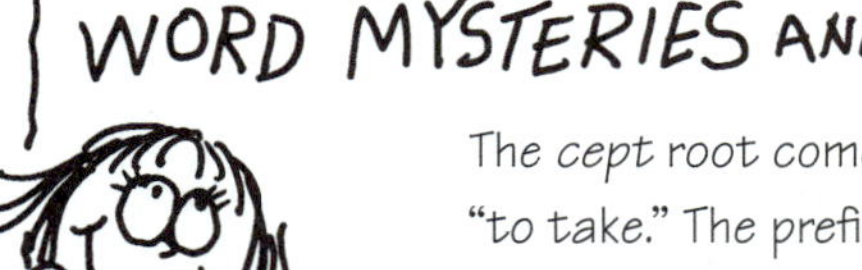

WORD MYSTERIES AND HISTORIES

The *cept* root comes from the Latin *capere*, meaning "to take." The prefix *ex* means "out," thus *except* means "to take out." The prefix *ad* or *ac* means "to" or "toward," thus *accept* means "to take toward."

1B Have students write: *We come to school every day, except weekends*. Then write the sentence on the chalkboard, or have a student do so, for self-checking. Contrast *except/accept*. Then have students write *exception* and *exceptional*. Discuss meanings. Have students find and write more words to which *ion/tion/sion* can be added and discern different actions for the addition of this suffix group (e.g., ion—compete/competition; sion—divide/division; ation—inform/information; ition—compete/competition). Then use students' word examples to begin charts for the ongoing collection of spelling patterns for the addition of this suffix family.

homophones, suffix practice, more words, word analysis, spelling word patterns, proofreading

Have students redefine in rhyme: story forecast (fiction prediction!)

Teaching Notes, page 328

Build Skillful Writers

Use these interrelated language learnings for all or selected students.

Skillful writers verify their information. Explore information in a webbing activity connecting it to related topics for study. Write *information* in a circle on the chalkboard. Radiating from the circle have students write information sources (e.g., dictionary, thesaurus, telephone book, Internet, almanac, atlas). Assign student groups to research the information each source provides.

Challenge some students to investigate information sources within books (e.g., table of contents, glossary, index, appendix) and report to the class the function of each.

Conclude with a game in which questions are posed and students use information sources to extract the answers, reporting their answer and its source. For example:
- the length of a mile in feet (5,280 feet)
- the speed animals run (The cheetah is the fastest land animal, reaching speeds of seventy miles an hour.)
- another word for machine (e.g., motor, engine, generator, turbine)
- the closest service to get a package sent for next-day delivery

Teaching Notes, page 329

Skill to be tested:
prefixes re, ex, sub, dis, un, non

Build Assessment Readiness

Use these at-school and at-home exercises to prepare all students for the Skill Test.

at-school Note that a prefix alters the meaning of a base word but not its spelling. Post Teaching Poster 3. Review three of the prefixes that mean *not/opposite of*: *un* (use words from Activity 1B, page 65), *dis* (disappear), *non* (nonstop). Have students brainstorm more words with these prefixes (e.g., unclear, unplanned, undo; disagree, discolored, dislike; nonfiction, nonsense, nonprofit).

Discuss the prefixes *re* (again), *sub* (below, lesser), *ex* (out, down). Have students brainstorm more words with these prefixes (e.g., restart, relive, replay; subdivide, subheading, subconscious; exchange, expel, exhale).

Skill to be tested:
prefixes re, ex, sub, dis, un, non

at-home Send home a copy of TAKE-HOME TASK 10 BLACKLINE MASTER, page 85, with each student to encourage parent-child partnerships.

Teaching Notes, page 330

Build Proofreading Skills

Track students' ability to meet a minimum competency for spelling and proofreading within selected samples of their everyday writing.

- Send home papers for proofreading and a copy of the IDEAS FOR PROOFREADING BLACKLINE MASTER, page 373.

Name ___________________________

Dear Parents,

This activity focuses on the addition of prefixes. Review with your child two important items about the addition of prefixes to a base word or root:

- The purpose of a prefix is to alter the meaning of the base word or root.
- The addition of a prefix never changes the spelling of the base word or root.

Explore these prefixes with your child:

un	not/opposite of	sub	below/lesser
dis	not/opposite of	ex	out/down
non	not/opposite of	re	again

As before, have your child read and explain the directions. Then guide your child through the activity, taking care to discuss unfamiliar words.

Add a prefix (un, dis, non, sub, ex, re) to the word or word part to make it mean nearly the same thing as a phrase in the opposite column. Then write the letter of that phrase in the blank following the word.

________marine	________	(a)	organize again
________common	________	(b)	build again
________arrange	________	(c)	go in again
________satisfied	________	(d)	look at again
________port	________	(e)	not sure
________view	________	(f)	not ordinary
________pel	________	(g)	not equivalent
________normal	________	(h)	not proceed
________it	________	(i)	not liked
________construct	________	(j)	not happy
________fiction	________	(k)	not seen
________cel	________	(l)	transportation below ground
________certain	________	(m)	boat for underwater travel
________continue	________	(n)	less than standard
________way	________	(o)	change out
________equal	________	(p)	go out
________enter	________	(q)	ship out
________liked	________	(r)	throw out
________change	________	(s)	outshine
________appeared	________	(t)	not make-believe

Assess Words and Skills

- Spelling Words (words missed on tests) are recorded in the Spelling Notebook.
- Use Proof It, Practice Page 30, for proofreading/editing practice.

Teaching Notes, page 336

Assess Spelling Progress

Give this Cloze Story Word Test of Core Words within the frequencies 1–550 to all students. Words students miss are their Spelling Words.

 **THE CLOZE STORY WORD TEST**

Students do not prestudy the words. Provide students with a copy of REVIEW 10 BLACKLINE MASTER, page 89. Tell students that this story asks them to do some serious thinking.

Read the entire story aloud, including the test words. Then read it again slowly as students write the missing words.

Words tested:
there (37), who('s) (77), little (92), asked (188), young (256), stop(ped) (396), girl (405), finally (414), problem (422), possible (452), explain (513), caught (527), yourself (534), seem(ed) (535), moment (538), teacher (539), bright (541), rather (545), length (546), speed (547), machine (548), information (549), except (550), *they're (1010)

*The testing of they're (1010) is included to help students differentiate among the there/their/they're homophones.

Who Is Anna?

A mother with her (1) <u>little</u> daughter, Anna, came to visit her son's (2) <u>teacher</u> at school for a conference. First, the mother (3) <u>stopped</u> by the school office where the secretary greeted her with a (4) <u>bright</u> smile. It was a busy office. While the FAX (5) <u>machine</u> fed out (6) <u>information</u> with great (7) <u>speed</u>, the secretary and the mother talked. (8) <u>Finally</u>, it was decided that Anna would stay in the office (9) <u>rather</u> than accompany her mother to the classroom. The child (10) <u>seemed</u> to accept this without a (11) <u>problem</u>. As the mother left to walk the (12) <u>length</u> of the school hall to her son's classroom, the secretary said to Anna, "I'd like to talk with you, Anna, (13) <u>except</u> I'm working. (14) <u>There</u> are books on the table. Help (15) <u>yourself</u>. (16) <u>They're</u> good ones." At that (17) <u>moment</u>, the principal opened his door and looked into the office. (18) <u>Young</u> Anna (19) <u>caught</u> his eye. (20) "<u>Who's</u> that?" he (21) <u>asked</u> the school secretary. The secretary replied, "That (22) <u>girl</u> is my daughter." How could that be (23) <u>possible</u>? You (24) <u>explain</u>.

 **AFTER THE CLOZE STORY WORD TEST**

reasoning, writing

1. Have students write and share a possible solutioin to the story problem. Students may resolve that Anna is the daughter of the lady, just as the story indicates, and the school secretary is her father. Most students won't consider the school's secretarial position one a male would fill, hence providing an opportunity to discuss male/female employment equality. Further most students' experiences void the possibility of two female caregivers in a family, another opportunity for discussion in selected situations.

recording words for personal study list

2. Have students record the words they missed on the test in their Spelling Notebook (see page 338) for at-school study, and on a copy of the WORDS TO LEARN BLACKLINE MASTER, page 375, for at-home study.

Assess Skill Application

Give this assessment of spelling and related skills to all students.
The Review 10 Blackline Master is on page 90.

Teaching Notes, page 339

THE SKILL TEST

The purpose of a prefix is to change the __meaning__ of the base word or root.

The addition of a prefix never changes the __spelling__ of the base word or root.

Add a prefix: re, ex, sub, dis, un, or non.

__non__ fiction	__sub__ way	__re__ build
__un__ kind	__dis__ continue	__un__ sure
__ex__ change	__re__ use	__re__ construct

Skill tested:
prefixes re, ex, sub, dis, un, non

Note the ability of each student to add the prefixes *re*, *ex*, *sub*, *dis*, *un*, and *non* to base words and to understand that the addition of the prefix never changes the spelling of the base word, but does alter its meaning.

Assess Proofreading Application

Give this assessment of spelling and related skills to all students.
The Review 10 Blackline Master is on page 90.

Teaching Notes, page 341

THE PROOFREADING TEST

Proofread for one spelling, capitalization, or punctuation error in the underlined parts. Circle errors. Write corrections in the spaces.

A melody is a <u>peice of music's</u> notes, or sound. Some people may call it the <u>tune. You no that</u> the notes may go high and low, creating <u>a shape to the melody The</u> rhythm is the <u>leangth of time</u> each note is played, or sounded. When music <u>is writen, the</u> melody and the rhythm are created. These creators may be called composers<u>. One of our</u> greatest composers was Wolfgang <u>amadeus Mozart. He</u> lived in Austria and composed music about the <u>time Americka was founded. he</u> composed a kind of music called classical music. Some of his work was in the <u>form of operas, wich</u> are musical plays in which the characters <u>sing rather then</u> talk. <u>He also wrotte</u> symphonies. They are grand musical compositions played <u>by many insterments</u> in an orchestra.

__piece__
__know__
__.__
__length__
__written__
__.__
__Amadeus__
__America__
__He__
__which__
__than__
__wrote__
__instruments__

How do you think today's composers compare to Mozart?

Note the ability of each student to proofread for errors.

Teaching Notes, page 342

Extend Spelling Assessment

Give this in-context assessment of Core Words within the frequencies
1–550 to students who need more practice or challenge.

THE SENTENCE DICTATION TEST

Students do not prestudy the words. Provide students with writing paper and pencil.
Have students write the sentences as they are dictated.

1. One simple way to stay strong and healthy is to work out through fast walking on an exercise machine.

2. The machine tells the walkers information about the speed they're going.

3. It also measures the correct length of their travel in miles.

4. My friend and I always use it every night, except on weekends.

Words tested:
the (1), of (2), and (3), to (5), in (6), is (7), it (10), on (14), I (24), one (28), an (39), their (42), about (48), out (51), my (80), way (86), use (88), through (102), also (119), work (124), tell(s) (147), every (151), always (183), going (192), night (231), fast (376), strong (381), simple (455), walked(ing)(ers) (468), stay (473), friend (498), travel (516), correct (521), measure(s) (523), length (546), speed (547), machine (548), information (549), except (550), *they're (1010)

*The testing of they're (1010) is included to help students differentiate among the there/their/they're homophones.

Extra words: exercise, healthy, miles, weekends

WORD MYSTERIES AND HISTORIES

In England, a traveler may be wished "good speed" before leaving, meaning "have a good trip." The word *speed* entered Old English through the German word *spedan* meaning "do well" or "succeed." This original meaning of *speed* is the intent of the English saying.

AFTER THE SENTENCE DICTATION TEST

writing

1. Have students write a persuasive advertisement for an exercise machine.

recording words for personal study list

2. Have students record the words they missed on the test in their Spelling Notebook (see page 345) for at-school study, and on a copy of the WORDS TO LEARN BLACKLINE MASTER, page 375, for at-home study.

The most frequent spelling pattern for /sh/ is *ti*, as in *information*, spelling /sh/ about 53% of the time. About 25% of the time *sh* spells /sh/, as in *wish*. Other /sh/ spelling patterns include *ce* (ocean), *ci* (special), *ss* (pressure), *si* (mission), *sci* (conscious), and *sch* (fuschia), and *ch* in words with a French origin (machine). The least common spelling pattern for /sh/ is a single *s*, as in *sugar* and *sure*, the only two words and their word forms that spell /sh/.

• Ask students to explore the spelling pattern for /sh/. Create a chart for the collection of students' /sh/ words to reuse in Unit 12.

Word Test

Who Is Anna?

A mother with her (1) _______________ daughter, Anna, came to visit her son's

(2) _______________ at school for a conference. First, the mother (3) _______________

by the school office where the secretary greeted her with a (4) _______________

smile. It was a busy office. While the FAX (5) _______________ fed out

(6) _______________ with great (7) _______________, the secretary and the

mother talked. (8) _______________, it was decided that Anna would stay in the

office (9) _______________ than accompany her mother to the classroom. The child

(10) _______________ to accept this without a (11) _______________. As the mother

left to walk the (12) _______________ of the school hall to her son's classroom, the

secretary said to Anna, "I'd like to talk with you, Anna, (13) _______________ I'm

working. (14) _______________ are books on the table. Help (15) _______________.

(16) _______________ good ones." At that (17) _______________, the principal

opened his door and looked into the office. (18) _______________ Anna

(19) _______________ his eye. (20) "_______________ that?" he (21) _______________

the school secretary. The secretary replied, "That (22) _______________ is my

daughter." How could that be (23) _______________? You (24) _______________.

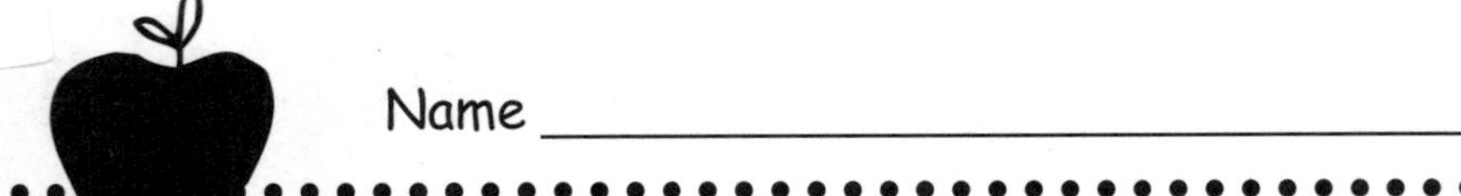

Name _______________________________

Skill Test

The purpose of a prefix is to change the _______________________ of the base word or root.

The addition of a prefix never changes the _______________________ of the base word or root.

Add a prefix: re, ex, sub, dis, un, or non.

_____fiction   _____way   _____build

_____kind   _____continue   _____sure

_____change   _____use   _____construct

Proofreading Test

Proofread for one spelling, capitalization, or punctuation error in the underlined parts. Circle errors. Write corrections in the spaces.

A melody is a <u>peice of music's</u> notes, or sound. Some people   _______________

may call it the <u>tune. You no that</u> the notes may go high   _______________

and low, creating <u>a shape to the melody The</u> rhythm is the   _______________

<u>leangth of time</u> each note is played, or sounded. When music   _______________

<u>is writen, the</u> melody and the rhythm are created. These   _______________

creators may be called composers, <u>One of our</u> greatest   _______________

composers was Wolfgang <u>amadeus Mozart. He</u> lived in   _______________

Austria and composed music about the <u>time Americka was</u>   _______________

<u>founded. he</u> composed a kind of music called classical   _______________

music. Some of his work was in the <u>form of operas, wich</u>   _______________

are musical plays in which the characters <u>sing rather then</u>   _______________

talk. <u>He also wrotte</u> symphonies. They are grand musical   _______________

compositions played <u>by many insterments</u> in an orchestra.   _______________

How do you think today's composers compare to Mozart?

Build Skills and Word Experiences

Use Student Practice Pages 31–32 to follow up instruction for:
Activity 1B • Test Ready

Build Visual Skills

Do the Word Preview, a visual warm-up activity, with all students.
Use Core Words **figure** (551), **you're** (552), **free** (553), **fell** (554), **suppose** (555).

Teaching Notes, page 316

Build Spelling and Language Skills

Choose from among these quick tasks to customize instruction
for all or selected students.

Teaching Notes, page 319

The tree fell.

The glass figure on Kims table fell when she was cleaning? It did'nt
break, becuse Kim caught it as it sailed threw the air. Your correct if
you think Kim was happy about that!

(*Kim's*, period instead of question mark, *didn't*, *because*, *through*, *You're*)

**carefree, please, yesterday, airplane, chest, someplace, freckle, mystery, grapefruit,
compliment, stairway, friendly**

(e.g., contains consonant blend *fr/pl/st*; is/isn't a compound; ends in *e/t/y*; number of syllables)

free meal, free ride, free spirit, _______

(phrases that begin with *free*)

The saying "The best things in life are free" refers to things like _______.

Words with double letters

Teaching Notes, page 325

Build Basic Concepts

Choose from among these skill-building activities to customize instruction for all or selected students.

concept one	A contraction is a combination of two or more words with an apostrophe replacing a letter or letters.

vocabulary development, contractions, homographs, writing an explanation

1A Discuss the meanings and pronunciations of the homograph *contract* (e.g., agreement, pact, deal, promise; deflate, shrink, collapse). Ask students when contracts might be used (e.g., treaty, purchase paid in installments). Write *you are* on the chalkboard. Then contract the words to *you're*. Change *contract* to *contraction*. Have students explain in writing why *contraction* is a suitable term for this word group.

contractions, homophones, apostrophe practice, writing words, carousel activity

1B Ask students what we call words like *you're* (contraction, homophone). Discuss contractions and the role of the apostrophe. Review "What's a Careful Speller to Do?" (Build Skillful Writers, page 30) and have students identify the rhyme's contractions (who's, we're, they're, there's, it's). Have students write the longer form of each on the chalkboard. Then prepare for a carousel activity (see Test Ready, page 39). Label four charts: *not*; *shall/will*; *would/had, are, am, us*; *have, is/has*. Follow up by posting the completed charts and asking students to identify the homophone contractions. (Charts are reused in Build Skillful Writers and At-School, this unit.)

Ask students to recall another role of an apostrophe. Guide students through a discussion of possessives—singular possessives (e.g., our cat's toy) and plural possessives (e.g., our cats' toy).

There are over 2000 sets of homophones in the English language. Homophones are prominent among the most misspelled or misused words (Build Skillful Writers, page 39). The homophone contractions pose the biggest challenge, such as *there's/theirs*, *your/you're*, *its/it's*, and *who's/whose*.

contractions, homophones, writing words

1C Introduce Teaching Poster 4. Discuss the Commonsense Strategies. Have students complete a copy of PERSONAL POSTER 4 BLACKLINE MASTER, page 370. Have students make word cards for the words on the poster (reuse the starter set from Build Skillful Writers, page 39). Say sentences that use these words and students respond with the correct word card. Later, have students write sentences that use these words to read to the class. The class responds by holding up the appropriate word card. (Note: *it's* can mean *it is* or *it has*.)

Students have an additional reference for these homophone contractions on their Spell Check card (see page 389). Encourage students to use the context sentences for the often-confused words on their Spell Check to clarify meaning and usage.

Build Skillful Writers

Use these interrelated language learnings for all or selected students.

Teaching Notes, page 328

Skillful writers are familiar with the use of contractions—

- Contractions usually comprise a shortened form of two words—one word is a verb, the other word is *not* or is a subject: *You're (You are) here. Bob's (Bob is) here.* Discuss the difference: *Bob's car/Bob's here.*
- Contractions may comprise a shortened form of three or more words, such as *o'clock—of the clock.*
- Some contractions are antiquated: *'twas—it was, 'tis—it is, shan't—shall not*
- Some contractions are considered inappropriate in writing: *could've, should've, would've, might've, must've, it'd, that'd, there'd, this'd, what'd, where'd, that'll, there'll, this'll, when'll, where'll, that're, there're, when're, where're, why're, that've, there've, why've, when's, why's.*

Build Assessment Readiness

Use these at-school and at-home exercises to prepare all students for the Skill Test.

Teaching Notes, page 329

at-school   An apostrophe always has a purpose: to take the place of a letter or letters in a contraction; or to signal ownership, or possession (Build Skillful Writers, page 48).

Skill to be tested: the apostrophe

Have students use print material to find and write examples of words that require an apostrophe. Ask students to sort their examples by:

- contractions (an ' signals an omitted letter or letters)
- singular possessives (an *'s* signals a singular possessive noun)
- plural possessives (an *s'* signals a plural possessive noun—exceptions are plurals that do not end in s, and thus use *'s*, such as *men/men's*)

Have students apply what they know by writing sentences that use an apostrophe in a contraction, a singular possessive, and a plural possessive.

at-home   Send home a copy of Take-Home Task 11 Blackline Master, page 94, with each student to encourage parent-child partnerships.

Skill to be tested: the apostrophe

Build Proofreading Skills

Track students' ability to meet a minimum competency for spelling and proofreading within selected samples of their everyday writing.

Teaching Notes, page 330

- Send home papers for proofreading and a copy of the Ideas for Proofreading Blackline Master, page 373.

Dear Parents,

In this activity you can guide your child to a greater understanding of apostrophe use. Help your child recall that an apostrophe always has a purpose. It is a signal.

- An apostrophe is used to signal that a letter or letters have been omitted in a contraction.

  who + is = who's (the apostrophe signals that i has been omitted)
- An apostrophe is used to signal possession, or ownership.

  boy's bikes (the apostrophe signals that the bikes belong to a boy—singular possessive)

  boys' bikes (the apostrophe signals that the bikes belong to the boys—plural possessive)

Then provide guidance as your child completes the word charts.

Write the missing contractions.

	are	have	will	is
you	you're			
not		haven't		
they			they'll	
she				
we				

Why does a contraction have an apostrophe?

____

Write the missing nouns.

singular	singular possessive	plural	plural possessive
bear	bear's	bears	bears'
		mothers	
boy			
		snakes	
turtle			

Why does a possessive have an apostrophe?

____

Read the phrase on the left. Add the apostrophe to the phrase on the right, if needed.

- three bears had some honey   bears honey
- more than one snake in the grass   snakes in the grass
- our team had a victory   teams victory

Assess Words and Skills

- Spelling Words (words missed on tests) are recorded in the Spelling Notebook.
- Use Proof It, Practice Page 33, for proofreading/editing practice.

Assess Spelling Progress

Teaching Notes, page 336

Give this Cloze Story Word Test of Core Words within the frequencies 1–555 to all students. Words students miss are their Spelling Words.

THE CLOZE STORY WORD TEST

Students do not prestudy the words. Provide students with a copy of Review 11 Blackline Master, page 98. Tell students that this story is a guessing game with several clues.

Read the entire story aloud, including the test words. Then read it again slowly as students write the missing words.

A Favorite Beverage

What do you (1) <u>suppose</u> is the most popular beverage on this (2) <u>Earth</u>—that is, after (3) <u>common</u> water? It was discovered long ago by a Chinese emperor, Shen Nung. Over the years, (4) <u>its</u> popularity grew (5) <u>until</u> people (6) <u>often</u> drank it daily. (7) <u>There</u> are many who still do today. (8) <u>It's</u> not (9) <u>free</u>, but it is quite inexpensive. However, (10) <u>during</u> times past, it was so prized that it was occasionally used in place of (11) <u>money</u>, especially in Europe and Asia. Of course, (12) <u>you're</u> familiar with the historical incident in which 342 chests of it (13) <u>fell</u> into Boston Harbor.

Are you still trying to (14) <u>figure</u> out the (15) <u>answer</u>? Here's more (16) <u>information</u>. This drink is (17) <u>usually</u> brewed in (18) <u>special</u> kettles or pots. People can drink it hot, or it can be a cold drink. Most people, (19) <u>except</u> those who may add sugar, cream, or lemon, drink it straight. It comes in (20) <u>several</u> flavors, or kinds. It is estimated that over 855 billion (21) <u>single</u> cups of it are consumed (22) <u>every</u> year. (23) <u>That's</u> a lot! By now you have (24) <u>surely</u> guessed this beverage. What is it?

Words tested:
there (37), its (76), every (151), often (186), until (196), earth (220), during (248), sure(ly) (251), it's (253), several (263), answer (265), usually (278), money (279), special (361), that's (390), common (395), single (509), information (549), except (550), figure (551), you're (552), free (553), fell (554), suppose (555)

AFTER THE CLOZE STORY WORD TEST

1. Have students identify the beverage, and then explain how each of the story clues supports their answer. Then have students share their answer. Conclude that the beverage is tea.

reasoning

2. Have students record the words they missed on the test in their Spelling Notebook (see page 338) for at-school study, and on a copy of the Words to Learn Blackline Master, page 375, for at-home study.

recording words for personal study list

Assess Skill Application

Give this assessment of spelling and related skills to all students.
The Review 11 Blackline Master is on page 99.

Teaching Notes, page 339

 **THE SKILL TEST**

Skill tested:
the apostrophe

An apostrophe always has a purpose.

One purpose for an apostrophe is
to take the place of a letter or letters in a contraction .

Examples: _________ answers will vary _________

Another purpose for an apostrophe is
to signal ownership, or possession .

Examples: _________ answers will vary _________

Note the ability of each student to state two purposes for an apostrophe—to take the place of an omitted letter or letters in a contraction and to show possession—and to provide examples of each.

Assess Proofreading Application

Give this assessment of spelling and related skills to all students.
The Review 11 Blackline Master is on page 99.

Teaching Notes, page 341

 **THE PROOFREADING TEST**

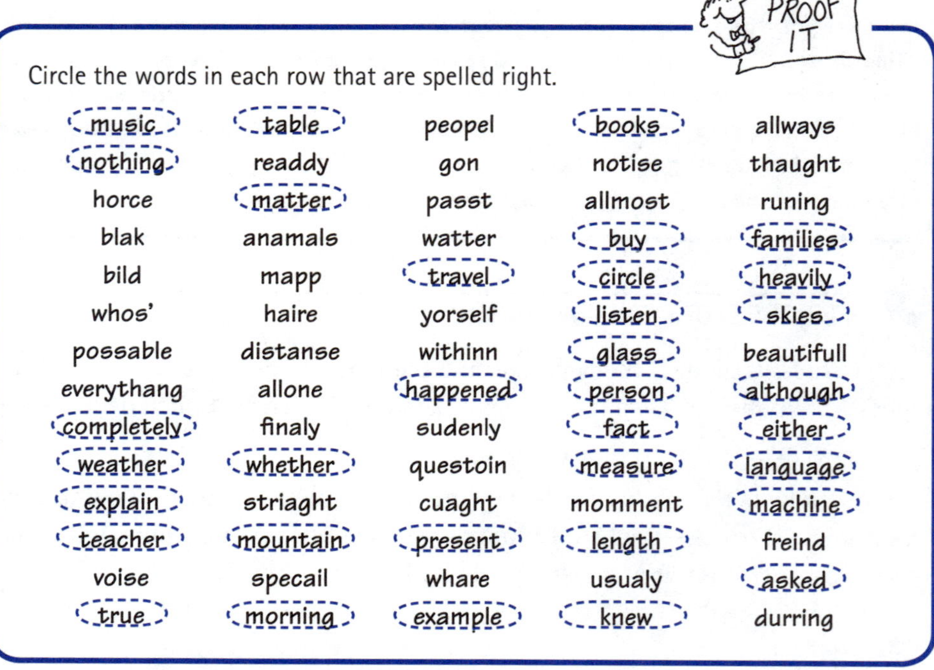

Note the ability of each student to proofread for spelling errors.

Extend Spelling Assessment

Give this in-context assessment of Core Words within the frequencies 1–555 to students who need more practice or challenge.

Teaching Notes, page 342

 **THE SENTENCE DICTATION TEST**

Students do not prestudy the words. Provide students with writing paper and pencil. Have students write the sentences as they are dictated.

1. What if students missed five straight school days and suddenly fell behind in their work?
2. Figure out the length of time you're usually in class for that number of days.
3. Would your teachers say you're to make up the assignments during your free time?
4. I suppose that's fair, however, you might discover that it's rather difficult to do.

Words tested:

the (1), of (2), and (3), to (5), in (6), you (8), that (9), for (12), I (24), what (32), your (40), their (42), if (44), do (45), up (50), out (51), would (59), time (69), make (72), day(s) (114), work (124), number (145), say (149), might (173), school (194), during (248), however (250), it's (253), five (276), usually (278), behind (342), that's (390), class (391), suddenly (458), miss(ed) (465), straight (524), teacher(s) (539), rather (545), length (546), figure (551), you're (552), free (553), fell (554), suppose (555)

Extra words: assignments, difficult, discover, fair, students

 **AFTER THE SENTENCE DICTATION TEST**

1. Have students figure out the number of hours they're in class for five days. Then have them estimate the number of hours they watch or listen to television in five days. Next, have them contrast the two and explain why this time apportionment is good or bad.

analyzing, writing an explanation

2. Have students record the words they missed on the test in their Spelling Notebook (see page 345) for at-school study, and on a copy of the WORDS TO LEARN BLACKLINE MASTER, page 375, for at-home study.

recording words for personal study list

Dictate this tongue-twister for students to write and say: Three free fruit floats.

• Challenge students to write more sentences for dictation to twist their classmates' tongues.

Word Test

A Favorite Beverage

What do you (1) ________________ is the most popular beverage on this

(2) ________________—that is, after (3) ________________ water? It was discovered

long ago by a Chinese emperor, Shen Nung. Over the years, (4) ________________

popularity grew (5) ________________ people (6) ________________ drank it daily.

(7) ________________ are many who still do today. (8) ________________ not

(9) ________________, but it is quite inexpensive. However, (10) ________________ times

past, it was so prized that it was occasionally used in place of (11) ________________,

especially in Europe and Asia. Of course, (12) ________________ familiar with the

historical incident in which 342 chests of it (13) ________________ into Boston Harbor.

Are you still trying to (14) ________________ out the (15) ________________?

Here's more (16) ________________. This drink is (17) ________________ brewed in

(18) ________________ kettles or pots. People can drink it hot, or it can be a cold drink.

Most people, (19) ________________ those who may add sugar, cream, or lemon, drink it

straight. It comes in (20) ________________ flavors, or kinds. It is estimated that over

855 billion (21) ________________ cups of it are consumed (22) ________________ year.

(23) ________________ a lot! By now you have (24) ________________ guessed this

beverage. What is it?

REVIEW 11

Skill Test

An apostrophe always has a purpose.

One purpose for an apostrophe is ________________________________

____.

Examples: ____

Another purpose for an apostrophe is ___________________________

____.

Examples: ____

Proofreading Test

Circle the words in each row that are spelled right.

music	table	peopel	books	allways
nothing	readdy	gon	notise	thaught
horce	matter	passt	allmost	runing
blak	anamals	watter	buy	families
bild	mapp	travel	circle	heavily
whos'	haire	yorself	listen	skies
possable	distanse	withinn	glass	beautifull
everythang	allone	happened	person	although
completely	finaly	sudenly	fact	either
weather	whether	questoin	measure	language
explain	striaght	cuaght	momment	machine
teacher	mountain	present	length	freind
voise	specail	whare	usualy	asked
true	morning	example	knew	durring

Use Student Practice Pages 34–35 to follow up instruction for:
Activity 1B • Build Skillful Writers

Build Visual Skills

Do the Word Preview, a visual warm-up activity, with all students.
Use Core Words **natural** (556), **ocean** (557), **government** (558), **baby** (559), **grass** (560).

Teaching Notes, page 316

Build Spelling and Language Skills

Choose from among these quick tasks to customize instruction
for all or selected students.

Teaching Notes, page 319

It came in off the ocean.

You might've heard that turtles are animals born in sandy rather than grass nests. After they are born, they naturaly head to the ocaen or some body of water. Are govenment cares about turtle's safety.

(*might have, grassy, naturally, ocean, Our, government, turtles'*)

government, weigh, begin, giraffe, assign, finger, page, daughter, arrange, organize, fight, energy

(e.g., sound of *g*; is a verb/noun/both; number of syllables)

grass, green, grind, ______
(five-letter words beginning with *gr*)

Some natural resources that we have are ______.

Words that are made plural by adding *es*

Build Basic Concepts

Choose from among these skill-building activities to customize instruction for all or selected students.

Teaching Notes, page 325

> An /ē/ or /ī/ at the end of a word is usually spelled *y*.

1A Ask students what letter usually spells /ē/ or /ī/ at the end of a word (y). Help students recall that *ay* is a frequent /ā/ spelling pattern. Label three charts: /ē/, /ī/, /ā/. Have students brainstorm /ē/, /ī/ and /ā/-ending words for the charts. (Charts are reused in Activity 1B, this unit.) Note that *ey* is a fairly frequent /ē/ pattern (e.g., valley, trolley, hockey). However, *ey* is a surprise spelling for /ā/, as in *they*. Have students chant—

phonics, word analysis, spelling word patterns, irregular spellings, chanting a rhyme, more words

> There is no *a* in *they*!
> There is no *a* in *they*!
> Just write *the*—then add *y*.
> It's as easy as huckleberry pie!

Further, students will discover that *ie* occurs with some regularity for /ē/ and /ī/ (e.g., pie, prairie).

1B Have students select *y*-ending words (Activity 1A, this unit) and sort them: consonant-*y* and vowel-*y*. Next, have students select from among these words to write words with the *s/es* suffix (baby/babies, fly/flies, play/plays). Then have students write what they observed with the addition of *s* (consonant-*y* ending words change *y* to *i* and add *es*, vowel-*y* ending words add *s*). Revisit the rhyme introduced in Level 4 to reinforce this concept—

sorting words, word analysis, suffix practice, spelling rules, writing an explanation, chanting/writing a rhyme

> For words that end in consonant-*y*   But if a vowel comes before the *y*,
> That you would like to multiply,   Here's the rule that you'll apply.
> Forget the math and just do this—   Just write the word and then add *s*.
> Change *y* to *i* and add *es*!   Can you do it? Yes! Yes! Yes!

Have students write the rhyme and decorate each stanza with word examples.

1C Provide clues for students to identify a synonym for *trip* that ends in *ey* (journey). Have students make *trip* and *journey* plural (add s). Then have students explain why the *y* in *journey* is not changed to *i* and *es* added (because *journey* ends in vowel-*y*, not consonant-*y*). Introduce students to *The Wanderer*, by Sharon Creech. This 2001 Newbery Honor Book is the story of thirteen-year-old Sophie's journey across the Atlantic Ocean in which she makes many personal discoveries. Encourage students to read/report on this award-winning story.

relating to literature, synonyms, suffix practice, reading, writing a book report

Have students redefine in rhyme:
- twitching fowl (jerky turkey)
- rabbit cash (bunny money)
- happy streetcar (jolly trolley)

Teaching Notes, page 328

Build Skillful Writers

Use these interrelated language learnings for all or selected students.

Skillful writers often make comparisons. To compare two things, the *er* suffix is used or *more* (or *less*). These are called comparatives.

> *The three billy goats thought the other field was grassier than theirs.*

To compare three or more things, the *est* suffix is used or *most* (or *least*). These are called superlatives.

> *The biggest goat quickly went across the bridge first to check it out.*

- Usually short words take the *er/est* suffixes, while longer words use *more* (or *less*) and *most* (or *least*).

    bigger/biggest   more immense/most immense

- When a word ends in *ly, ful, ous, ive, less,* or *able, more* (or *less*) and *most* (or *least*) are used.

    quickly   more quickly   most quickly

- Some words do not follow the usual comparison patterns.

    good   better   best

- Some words have no comparative or superlative form.

    first   ~~firster~~   ~~firstest~~

Have students find and write more examples of each comparison. Then introduce the use of superlatives in hyperbole, a figure of speech that employs exaggeration (e.g., It's the most beautiful day on the face of the Earth!).

Teaching Notes, page 329

Build Assessment Readiness

Use these at-school and at-home exercises to prepare all students for the Skill Test.

Skill to be tested:
contractions

at-school   Have small groups of students brainstorm contractions from memory. Time the session (about four minutes). Then make a cumulative list of contractions on the chalkboard, sorted by *not, shall/will, have, would/had, are, is/has, am, us.* After listing all the contractions that can be recalled, reuse Personal Poster 4 for students to check the contractions listed on the chalkboard against those on their poster to ensure a complete list.

Skill to be tested:
contractions

at-home   Send home a copy of TAKE-HOME TASK 12 BLACKLINE MASTER, page 103, with each student to encourage parent-child partnerships.

Teaching Notes, page 330

Build Proofreading Skills

Track students' ability to meet a minimum competency for spelling and proofreading within selected samples of their everyday writing.

- Send home papers for proofreading and a copy of the IDEAS FOR PROOFREADING BLACKLINE MASTER, page 373.

Dear Parents,

The focus of this story activity is contractions. Help your child learn to identify contractions and their longer forms, and to spell them. This activity also encourages reasoning skills.

Read the story and answer the question. Then underline the story contractions, list them on another sheet of paper, and write their longer forms.

Mr. Bailey owned a small business he'd started long ago. He didn't like to leave his business, but this summer that wasn't possible. His mother, who'd lived in a big home overlooking the Pacific Ocean for many years, hadn't been well. She'd asked him to help her move to a smaller place and get the big house sold. She couldn't do it herself. So, Mr. Bailey decided to move his family to the ocean community for the summer, and they'd all work together to get the job done.

Millie, who'd worked for Mr. Bailey since the business began, said, "I'll mind the store while you're away. Don't worry. We're a team. There's no reason for concern. You mustn't neglect your mother." Mr. Bailey had confidence in Millie. She'd send him the bills that came in the mail, and he'd take care of that part of the business over the summer.

Mr. Bailey couldn't believe how much his mother had accumulated over the years. "We'll have a garage sale. Let's sell some of this," he told his family. "You'll all help, won't you?" Indeed, they'd all pitch in!

Mr. Bailey and the family got so busy that time passed very quickly. He thought, "It's strange I've not received any bills from Millie. Where's my mail? I'd better check to see if there's a problem." When Mr. Bailey called Millie, she said, "I'm unable to get inside the mailbox, because you've got the mailbox key." So, Mr. Bailey said, "Sure thing! I'm going to mail it to you today! That'll solve the problem!"

Did Mr. Bailey solve the problem? What's your thought on this?

____

____

____

____

Assess Words and Skills

- Spelling Words (words missed on tests) are recorded in the Spelling Notebook.
- Use Proof It, Practice Page 36, for proofreading/editing practice.

Teaching Notes, page 336

Assess Spelling Progress

Give this Cloze Story Word Test of Core Words within the frequencies 1–560 to all students. Words students miss are their Spelling Words.

THE CLOZE STORY WORD TEST

Students do not prestudy the words. Provide students with a copy of REVIEW 12 BLACKLINE MASTER, page 107. Tell students that this is a story about definitions for geographical words.

Read the entire story aloud, including the test words. Then read it again slowly as students write the missing words.

Words tested:
there (37), then (53), than (73), its (76), because (127), thought (179), let('s) (230), it's (253), example (261), body (285), group (295), piece (392), instead (408), fact (445), quite (447), although (450), size (462), correct (521), suppose (555), natural (556), ocean (557), government (558), baby (559), grass (560)

> ### Island or Continent?
>
> An island is defined as a (1) <u>piece</u> of land surrounded by a (2) <u>body</u> of water. Right? If this is accurate, (3) <u>ocean</u> completely surrounds the land mass of North, Central, and South America. So (4) <u>then</u>, are the Americas an island? This would be a (5) <u>natural</u> assumption, but it is not (6) <u>quite</u> (7) <u>correct</u>. With islands, (8) <u>size</u> makes a difference. An island is (9) <u>any</u> land smaller (10) <u>than</u> a continent that is surrounded by water. In (11) <u>fact</u>, a big island isn't an island, (12) <u>it's</u> a continent or (13) <u>group</u> of continents. Likewise, a (14) <u>baby</u> island is not an island, but an islet or isle. And when it comes to defining continents, politics and (15) <u>government</u> must be regarded. Sometimes politics overrides geography. For (16) <u>example</u>, Europe and Asia seem to be one continent, (17) <u>although</u> they are (18) <u>thought</u> of (19) <u>instead</u> as two. (20) <u>There</u> are seven continents in all. Is Greenland one of them? Find it on a map. Is it an island, or (21) <u>because</u> it is fairly large, is it a continent? Do you (22) <u>suppose</u> the land is green as (23) <u>grass</u>, as the name suggests? (24) <u>Let's</u> find out.

AFTER THE CLOZE STORY WORD TEST

reasoning, writing

1. Have students write and share their answers to the story questions. Conclude that the seven continents are North America, South America, Europe, Asia, Africa, Australia, and Antarctica. Greenland is the world's largest island and is considered part of North America. Ice covers four-fifths of Greenland. It never was a green land, but was named so by Eric the Red, perhaps in an attempt to attract settlers.

recording words for personal study list

2. Have students record the words they missed on the test in their Spelling Notebook (see page 338) for at-school study, and on a copy of the WORDS TO LEARN BLACKLINE MASTER, page 375, for at-home study.

Assess Skill Application

Give this assessment of spelling and related skills to all students.
The REVIEW 12 BLACKLINE MASTER is on page 108.

Teaching Notes, page 339

THE SKILL TEST

Write 15 contractions by combining these words.

we   not   have   would   are   they   will   I   who   is   there   it   you

__________ __________ __________ __________ __________
__________ __________ (answers will vary) __________ __________
__________ __________ __________ __________ __________

Skill tested: contractions

Write the longer forms of these contractions.

let's	let us	I'm	I am	where's	where is
don't	do not	she'd	she would/had	here's	here is
hasn't	has not	that's	that is	he'll	he will/shall

Note the ability of each student to write contractions from base words and base words
from contractions.

Assess Proofreading Application

Give this assessment of spelling and related skills to all students.
The REVIEW 12 BLACKLINE MASTER is on page 108.

Teaching Notes, page 341

THE PROOFREADING TEST

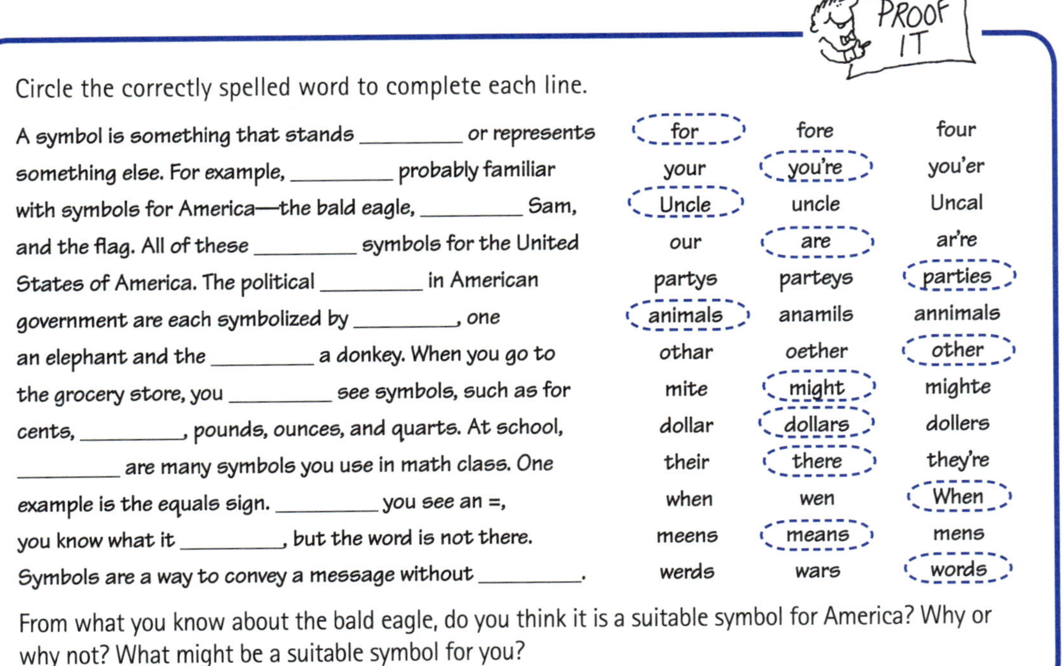

Circle the correctly spelled word to complete each line.

A symbol is something that stands __________ or represents
something else. For example, __________ probably familiar
with symbols for America—the bald eagle, __________ Sam,
and the flag. All of these __________ symbols for the United
States of America. The political __________ in American
government are each symbolized by __________, one
an elephant and the __________ a donkey. When you go to
the grocery store, you __________ see symbols, such as for
cents, __________, pounds, ounces, and quarts. At school,
__________ are many symbols you use in math class. One
example is the equals sign. __________ you see an =,
you know what it __________, but the word is not there.
Symbols are a way to convey a message without __________.

(for)	fore	four
your	(you're)	you'er
(Uncle)	uncle	Uncal
our	(are)	ar're
partys	parteys	(parties)
(animals)	anamils	annimals
othar	oether	(other)
mite	(might)	mighte
dollar	(dollars)	dollers
their	(there)	they're
when	wen	(When)
meens	(means)	mens
werds	wars	(words)

From what you know about the bald eagle, do you think it is a suitable symbol for America? Why or
why not? What might be a suitable symbol for you?

Note the ability of each student to proofread for spelling and capitalization errors.

Teaching Notes, page 342

Words tested:
the (1), and (3), a (4), to (5), in (6), is (7), you (8), that (9), for (12), as (16), from (23), not (30), but (31), there('s) (37), your (40), some (56), has (62), like (66), make (72), its (76), people (79), made (81), good (106), right (116), place (131), such (133), keep (199), let('s) (230), it's (253), example (261), against (268), usually (278), cut (293), fish (299), remember (315), cannot (343), among (345), probably (383), river (394), power(s) (421), leaves (460), natural (556), ocean (557), government (558), baby (559), grass (560), *they're (1010)
*The testing of they're (1010) is included to help students differentiate among the there/their/they're homophones.

Extra words: catch, law(s), material, reasons, rules

writing

recording words for personal study list

Extend Spelling Assessment

Give this in-context assessment of Core Words within the frequencies 1–560 to students who need more practice or challenge.

 **THE SENTENCE DICTATION TEST**

Students do not prestudy the words. Provide students with writing paper and pencil. Have students write the sentences as they are dictated.

1. Among the powers a government has is the right to make laws for its people.
2. For example, there's a law that you cannot catch and keep baby fish from the ocean.
3. It's probably against the rules to place your cut material, such as grass and leaves, in the river.
4. It's natural not to like some laws, but let's remember they're usually made for good reasons.

 **AFTER THE SENTENCE DICTATION TEST**

1. Have students write a rule or law they do not like. Then ask them to explain the rationale given for why the rule or law should be observed. Then ask them to give reasons why this rationale is faulty or sound.

2. Have students record the words they missed on the test in their Spelling Notebook (see page 345) for at-school study, and on a copy of the WORDS TO LEARN BLACKLINE MASTER, page 375, for at-home study.

Dictate this tongue-twister for students to write and say: Rubber baby buggy bumpers
• Challenge students to write more sentences for dictation to twist their classmates' tongues.

WORD MYSTERIES AND HISTORIES

The Greek *cracy* means "form of government." Have students define and use in sentences: democracy, autocracy, aristocracy, plutocracy, bureaucracy.

— Word Test —

Island or Continent?

An island is defined as a (1) ________________ of land surrounded by a

(2) ________________ of water. Right? If this is accurate, (3) ________________

completely surrounds the land mass of North, Central, and South America. So

(4) ________________, are the Americas an island? This would be a (5) ________________

assumption, but it is not (6) ________________ (7) ________________. With

islands, (8) ________________ makes a difference. An island is (9) ________________

land smaller (10) ________________ a continent that is surrounded by water. In

(11) ________________, a big island isn't an island, (12) ________________ a

continent or (13) ________________ of continents. Likewise, a (14) ________________

island is not an island, but an islet or isle. And when it comes to defining

continents, politics and (15) ________________ must be regarded. Sometimes

politics overrides geography. For (16) ________________, Europe and Asia seem to

be one continent, (17) ________________ they are (18) ________________ of

(19) ________________ as two. (20) ________________ are seven continents in all. Is

Greenland one of them? Find it on a map. Is it an island, or (21) ________________ it

is fairly large, is it a continent? Do you (22) ________________ the land is green as

(23) ________________, as the name suggests? (24) ________________ find out.

Name ________________________________

Write 15 contractions by combining these words.

we   not   have   would   are   they   will   I   who   is   there   it   you

________   ________   ________   ________   ________

________   ________   ________   ________   ________

________   ________   ________   ________   ________

Write the longer forms of these contractions.

let's ________________   I'm ________________   where's ________________

don't ________________   she'd ________________   here's ________________

hasn't ________________   that's ________________   he'll ________________

Circle the correctly spelled word to complete each line.

A symbol is something that stands ________ or represents	for	fore	four
something else. For example, ________ probably familiar	your	you're	you'er
with symbols for America—the bald eagle, ________ Sam,	Uncle	uncle	Uncal
and the flag. All of these ________ symbols for the United	our	are	ar're
States of America. The political ________ in American	partys	parteys	parties
government are each symbolized by ________, one	animals	anamils	annimals
an elephant and the ________ a donkey. When you go to	othar	oether	other
the grocery store, you ________ see symbols, such as for	mite	might	mighte
cents, ________, pounds, ounces, and quarts. At school,	dollar	dollars	dollers
________ are many symbols you use in math class. One	their	there	they're
example is the equals sign. ________ you see an =,	when	wen	When
you know what it ________, but the word is not there.	meens	means	mens
Symbols are a way to convey a message without ________.	werds	wars	words

From what you know about the bald eagle, do you think it is a suitable symbol for America? Why or why not? What might be a suitable symbol for you?

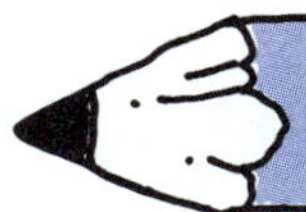
Use Student Practice Pages 37–38 to follow up instruction for:
Activity 1B • Build Skillful Writers

Build Visual Skills

Do the Word Preview, a visual warm-up activity, with all students.
Use Core Words **plane** (561), **street** (562), **couldn't** (563), **reason** (564), **difference** (565).

Teaching Notes, page 316

Build Spelling and Language Skills

Choose from among these quick tasks to customize instruction
for all or selected students.

Teaching Notes, page 319

They saw the plane.

The reason we hurry was to catch a plane We could'nt be late. We moved quickly threw the city streets, because we knew the differance a few minutes would make. There was no time to loose!

(*hurried*, period after *plane*, *couldn't*, *through*, *difference*, *lose*)

couldn't, minute, it's, street, does, who's, present, what's, plane, you're, content, they're

(e.g., is/isn't a contraction; is a homophone/homograph/neither; ends in *e/s/t*)

plane, plate, slate, ______

(change one letter to make a new word)

The difference between a prefix and a suffix is ______.

Kinds of planes and other flying objects

(e.g., jet, helicopter, spaceship)

Teaching Notes, page 325

Build Basic Concepts

Choose from among these skill-building activities to customize instruction
for all or selected students.

concept one	Homophones are words that sound the same but have different spellings and meanings. Homographs are words that have the same spelling, different meanings, and may have different pronunciations.

homophones, homographs,
writing words, proofreading,
vocabulary development, choral
reading

1A Select a student to write *plane* and *present* on the chalkboard.
Identify *plane* as a homophone and *present* as a homograph. Ask
students to define homophones and homographs. Organize students into
small groups and have them brainstorm examples.

Introduce Teaching Poster 5. Have students read the rhymes chorally. Then have
students check and proofread their lists against words on the chart. Discuss meanings
of unfamiliar homophones and homographs on the poster and the pronunciation of the
homographs. Next, have students complete a copy of PERSONAL POSTER 5 BLACKLINE MASTER,
page 371, to use over time as a personal homophone reference.

homophones, vocabulary
development, class book

1B Post Teaching Poster 5. Tell students that most homophone sets are a pair, but
some are a trio. Identify and discuss the trios on Teaching Poster 5. Then challenge
students to identify the other two homophones when you provide one from these
trio sets: *heal, I'll, vain, seas, pedal, air, burro, carrot, crews, flew, praise, rays, teas.*
Discuss the meanings of unfamiliar words. Then challenge students to make a personal
book of the homophone trios—one set to a page, written in sentences and illustrated.
Further, students may wish to add these homophones to their Personal Poster 5.

homophones, homographs,
making words, vocabulary
development, more words

1C Write *bass* on the chalkboard. Identify *bass* as a homograph and a
homophone. Discuss its different meanings and pronunciations. Then
select a student to write its homophone on the chalkboard (base).
Next, prepare for a letter-card activity (see Activity 2B, page 47) using
a, b, d, e, e, l, r, s, s, and *t.* Together make *desert.* Then have students continue making
words: *deter—later—laser—leader—lead—led—red—read—relate—elated—belated—
debate—baste—base—bass—erase—berate—beast—beard—bread—drab—dress—
dessert*—and back to *desert.* Ask students to identify homophones and homographs as
words are made. Later, have students work in pairs to make more words with their letter
cards. Have them write the words as they make them and identify the homophones/
homographs.

Have students write 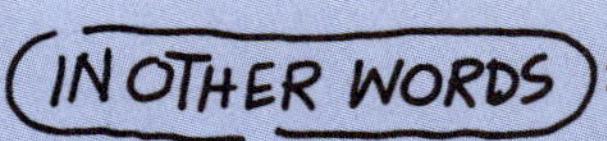: "It's the little things you do that make you
different. That makes all the difference—the
difference between winning and losing in
life and on the court." Kareem Abdul-Jabbar

Build Skillful Writers

Use these interrelated language learnings for all or selected students.

Teaching Notes, page 328

Tell students that working with homophones and homographs may make them think they're "hearing double" and "seeing double." Ask students to explain which is which. Then help students unclutter their writing with words that produce "double trouble"— the words say the same thing. Ask students to unclutter these phrases and explain why they're "double trouble."

separate out	unexpected surprise	right beside
free gift	return again	small in size
square in shape	end result	actual facts
flat plateau	urban cities	final outcome
extra additions	rock back and forth	continue on
usual customs	over and done with	untrue lie
sum total	the reason is because	exact same

Later, have students proofread papers with partners for "double trouble" phrases.

Build Assessment Readiness

Use these at-school and at-home exercises to prepare all students for the Skill Test.

Teaching Notes, page 329

at-school   The first step in conquering homophones is to learn to identify them. Next, students must learn their difference in meaning. Then they must learn to spell them. Dictate these sentences for students to write. Then have them underline the homophones. After each sentence, write the homophones on the chalkboard for discussion and for students to self-check.

Skill to be tested:
homophones

- *It's time you're* saying *bye,* because *night* is almost *here.*
- *You* must *accept* that *your* friends should *be* on *their way* home.
- The *weather* is *so* cold; *I* hope everyone *wore* warm *clothes.*
- Will they *choose to* go home along the *main road or through* the park?

Next, have students write the partners of these homophones in sentences.

at-home   Send home a copy of TAKE-HOME TASK 13 BLACKLINE MASTER, page 112, with each student to encourage parent-child partnerships.

Skill to be tested:
homophones

Build Proofreading Skills

Track students' ability to meet a minimum competency for spelling and proofreading within selected samples of their everyday writing.

Teaching Notes, page 330

- Send home papers for proofreading and a copy of the IDEAS FOR PROOFREADING BLACKLINE MASTER, page 373.

Dear Parents,

Homophones are among writers' biggest challenges. These are words that sound the same, or nearly the same, but have different spellings and meanings. One set of homophones you've already presented to your child for practice in an earlier Take-Home Task is there/their/they're. In this crossword puzzle, many more homophone sets are practiced. Work with your child to complete the puzzle. Over time, help your child reinforce the meaning and spelling of these and other homophones.

Write the homophone of the clue word.

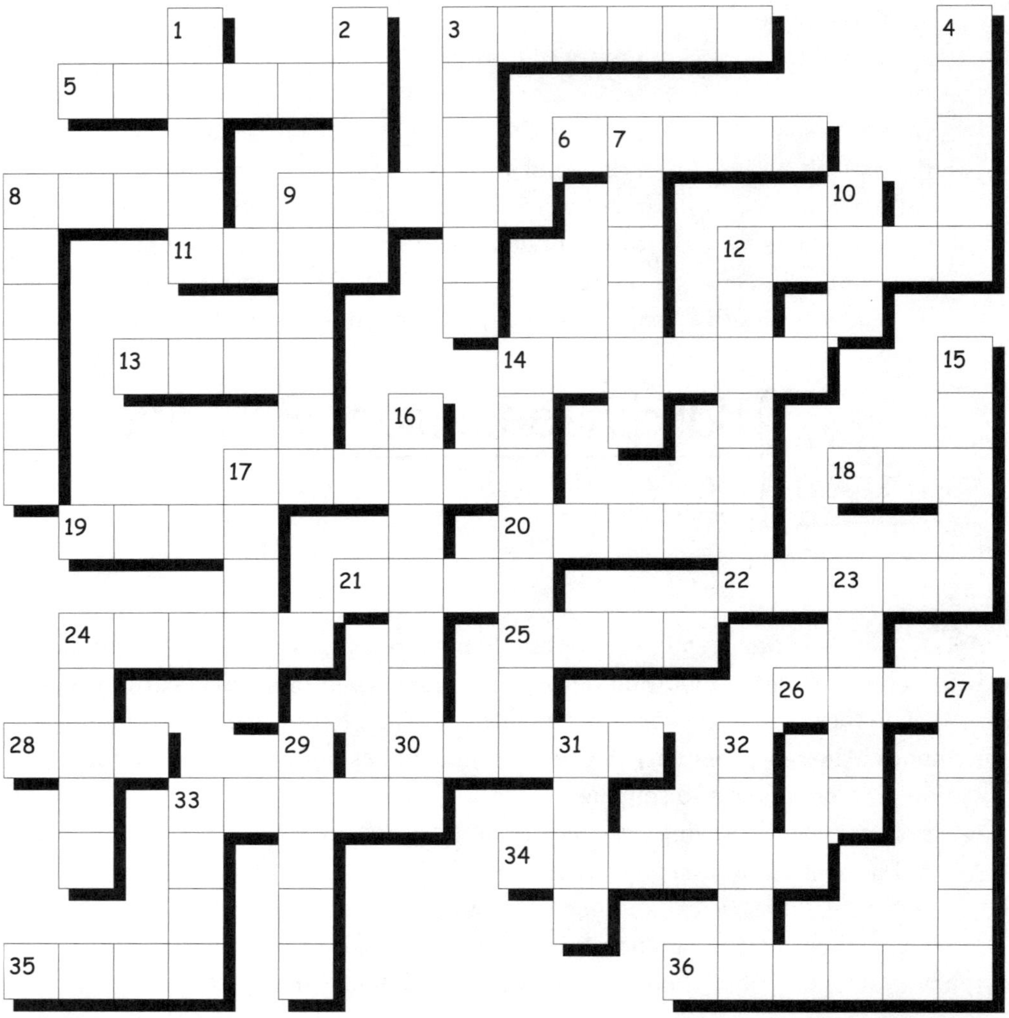

ACROSS		DOWN	
3. cot	20. sees	1. leader	17. great
5. wait	21. tied	2. steal	23. right
6. hole	22. road	3. coarse	24. who's
8. sum	24. waist	4. bored	27. thrown
9. fairy	25. knows	7. horse	29. paced
11. role	26. missed	8. side	31. week
12. wood	28. one	9. flour	32. their
13. blue	30. choose	10. bye	33. where
14. past	33. we've	12. weather	
17. Greece	34. band	14. presents	
18. sun	35. you're	15. mind	
19. our	36. petal	16. patients	

Assess Words and Skills

- Spelling Words (words missed on tests) are recorded in the Spelling Notebook.
- Use Proof It, Practice Page 39, for proofreading/editing practice.

Teaching Notes, page 336

Assess Spelling Progress

Give this Cloze Story Word Test of Core Words within the frequencies 1–565 to all students. Words students miss are their Spelling Words.

THE CLOZE STORY WORD TEST

Students do not prestudy the words. Provide students with a copy of REVIEW 13 BLACKLINE MASTER, page 116. Tell students that this story is a riddle.

Read the entire story aloud, including the test words. Then read it again slowly as students write the missing words.

Riddling

Riddles are fun! People have been riddling (1) <u>since</u> time began (2) <u>until</u> the present. It's (3) <u>always</u> fun to ask a riddle that no one can (4) <u>answer</u>. It's even more fun if (5) <u>you're</u> able to solve a riddle that no one (6) <u>else</u> can (7) <u>figure</u> out! Here's a riddle with letter clues that will (8) <u>surely</u> test (9) <u>your</u> ability to (10) <u>reason</u>. (11) <u>Carefully</u> think through the (12) <u>information</u> and you'll have the (13) <u>simple</u> solution.

Remove all my letters, I (14) <u>couldn't</u> complain,
Send them away in a (15) <u>plane</u> or a train.
Drop a letter or two somewhere down the (16) <u>street</u>,
The (17) <u>difference</u> is none—my name stays (18) <u>complete</u>.
My letters are (19) <u>something</u> I don't ever reclaim,
(20) <u>Because</u> when they're gone, my name's the same.
So, who am I? You decide.

Then write (21) <u>another</u> "Who am I?" riddle for (22) <u>friends</u> of (23) <u>yours</u> to solve that cause them to use (24) <u>their</u> brain.

Words tested:
your(s) (40), their (42), another (121), because (127), something (178), always (183), until (196), since (238), sure(ly) (251), answer (265), complete (365), carefully (427), simple (455), else (485), friend(s) (498), information (549), figure (551), you're (552), plane (561), street (562), couldn't (563), reason (564), difference (565)

AFTER THE CLOZE STORY WORD TEST

1. Have students write their answer and their own "Who am I?" riddle. Discuss the different meanings of letter. Have students share their answer to the riddle. Conclude that the answer is the mail carrier. Then have students exchange their "Who am I?" riddles so solutions can be formulated and shared. Compile the riddles into a class book with answers in the back.

reasoning skills, multiple meanings, writing riddles, class book

2. Have students record the words they missed on the test in their Spelling Notebook (see page 338) for at-school study, and on a copy of the WORDS TO LEARN BLACKLINE MASTER, page 375, for at-home study.

recording words for personal study list

Teaching Notes, page 339

Assess Skill Application

Give this assessment of spelling and related skills to all students.
The REVIEW 13 BLACKLINE MASTER is on page 117.

 **THE SKILL TEST**

Skill tested:
homophones

Circle the homophone(s) in each row. Then write the partner(s) on the line below.

theirs	ever	strait	weak	buy
there's		straight	week	by, bye
write	hare	war	seem	fly
right, rite	hair	wore	seam	
square	accept	you're	wood	spring
	except	your	would	
plain	let's	cent	present	length
plane	lets	sent, scent		

Note the ability of each student to identify and spell homophones.

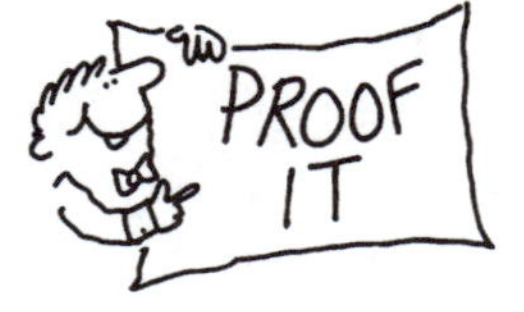

Teaching Notes, page 341

Assess Proofreading Application

Give this assessment of spelling and related skills to all students.
The REVIEW 13 BLACKLINE MASTER is on page 117.

 **THE PROOFREADING TEST**

If the underlined word or words in each line are incorrect, write the correction(s) in the space.

Symbols <u>are one example</u> of a communication shortcut.
<u>You lerned</u> that symbols can send a message. The symbol
stands for the real thing, such as a <u>country's flag</u> can stand
for the country <u>itself. their</u> is another communication
shortcut you know—contractions. <u>They make it possable</u> to
say <u>something qicker</u>. A contraction stands for the words
from which it was made. <u>In fact, the littel</u> apostrophe in a
contraction is another example of a symbol. <u>It's a symbol</u>
that stands for the <u>mising letters</u> in the contraction. In
couldn't, the <u>marke</u> that's called an apostrophe stands for
the omitted letters in <u>could not. Of coarse</u>, an apostrophe can
be used with another intent. <u>It can meen</u> "belonging to." In
Carrie's shoes, the apostrophe sends a <u>message of possession</u>.

learned

There
possible
quicker
little

missing
mark
course
mean

Explain the difference between the intent of the apostrophe in "Carrie's shoes" and in "Carrie's happy."

Note the ability of each student to proofread for spelling and capitalization errors.

Extend Spelling Assessment

Give this in-context assessment of Core Words within the frequencies 1–565 to students who need more practice or challenge.

Teaching Notes, page 342

THE SENTENCE DICTATION TEST

Students do not prestudy the words. Provide students with writing paper and pencil. Have students write the sentences as they are dictated.

1. Planes should use airport runways when they're on the ground, rather than a city street.

2. There couldn't be much difference between the two when it comes to surface, size, and length.

3. However, there are always a lot of other things that figure into such a choice.

4. Give several reasons why a pilot may have problems traveling along a busy boulevard in a plane.

Words tested:

the (1), of (2), and (3), a (4), to (5), in (6), that (9), it (10), on (14), are (15), be (21), have (25), when (35), there (37), other (60), into (61), two (65), than (73), use (88), may (89), much (104), come(s) (123), such (133), why (136), between (154), should (156), give (159), along (171), always (183), however (250), thing(s) (258), several (263), city (273), ground (311), surface (393), problem(s) (422), size (462), travel(ing) (516), rather (545), length (546), figure (551), plane(s) (561), street (562), couldn't (563), reason(s) (564), difference (565), *they're (1010)

*The testing of they're (1010) is included to help students differentiate among the there/their/they're homophones.

Extra words: airport, boulevard, busy, choice, lot, pilot, runways

AFTER THE SENTENCE DICTATION TEST

1. Students can have some fun answering this! For example, ask students to consider whether the pilot should be mindful of traffic signals, pedestrian crossings, or permits for oversized vehicles. Would the pilot get a traffic ticket?

2. Have students record the words they missed on the test in their Spelling Notebook (see page 345) for at-school study, and on a copy of the WORDS TO LEARN BLACKLINE MASTER, page 375, for at-home study.

> Have students brainstorm synonyms for street (e.g., avenue, road, boulevard, lane, court, alley). Then encourage students to read Tomie de Paola's *26 Fairmount Avenue*, a 2000 Newbery Honor Book describing a family's move into their new home in Meriden, Connecticut. Follow up with students writing a real or make-believe adventure story about moving into a new house.

speculating, writing

recording words for personal study list

> Systematic recycling of skills—from level to level and within each level—builds students' insights as they study their Spelling Words. Each student's Spelling Words may be different—their list is differentiated. Students examine their Spelling Words for phonetic patterns, prefixes, suffixes, silent letters, double letters—all the strategies they're learning in the Build Skill and Word Experiences lessons. These insights help students become discriminating observers of words to make them better spellers.

— Word Test —

Riddling

Riddles are fun! People have been riddling (1) ________________ time began

(2) ________________ the present. It's (3) ________________ fun to ask a riddle

that no one can (4) ________________. It's even more fun if (5) ________________

able to solve a riddle that no one (6) ________________ can (7) ________________

out! Here's a riddle with letter clues that will (8) ________________ test

(9) ________________ ability to (10) ________________. (11) ________________ think

through the (12) ________________ and you'll have the (13) ________________

solution.

Remove all my letters, I (14) ________________ complain,

Send them away in a (15) ________________ or a train.

Drop a letter or two somewhere down the (16) ________________,

The (17) ________________ is none—my name stays (18) ________________.

My letters are (19) ________________ I don't ever reclaim,

(20) ________________ when they're gone, my name's the same.

So, who am I? You decide.

Then write (21) ________________ "Who am I?" riddle for (22) ________________ of

(23) ________________ to solve that cause them to use (24) ________________

brain.

Skill Test

Circle the homophone(s) in each row. Then write the partner(s) on the line below.

theirs	ever	strait	weak	buy

write	hare	war	seem	fly

square	accept	you're	wood	spring

plain	let's	cent	present	length

Proofreading Test

If the underlined word or words in each line are incorrect, write the correction(s) in the space.

Symbols <u>are one example</u> of a communication shortcut.   ____________

<u>You lerned</u> that symbols can send a message. The symbol   ____________

stands for the real thing, such as a <u>country's flag</u> can stand   ____________

for the country <u>itself. their</u> is another communication   ____________

shortcut you know—contractions. <u>They make it possable</u> to   ____________

say <u>something qicker</u>. A contraction stands for the words   ____________

from which it was made. <u>In fact, the littel</u> apostrophe in a   ____________

contraction is another example of a symbol. <u>It's a symbol</u>   ____________

that stands for the <u>mising letters</u> in the contraction. In   ____________

couldn't, the <u>marke that's called</u> an apostrophe stands for   ____________

the omitted letters in <u>*could not*</u>. Of coarse, an apostrophe can   ____________

be used with another intent. <u>It can meen</u> "belonging to." In   ____________

Carrie's shoes, the apostrophe sends a <u>message of possession</u>.   ____________

Explain the difference between the intent of the apostrophe in "Carrie's shoes" and in "Carrie's happy."

Use Student Practice Pages 40–41 to follow up instruction for:
Activities 1A and 1B • Build Skillful Writers

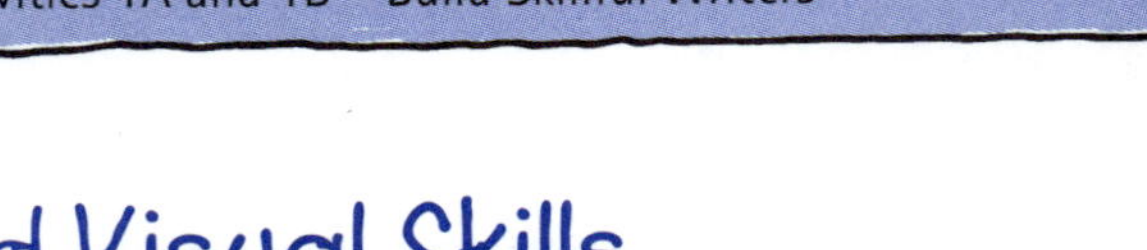

Build Visual Skills

Do the Word Preview, a visual warm-up activity, with all students.
Use Core Words **maybe** (566), **history** (567), **mouth** (568), **middle** (569), **step** (570).

Teaching Notes, page 316

Build Spelling and Language Skills

Choose from among these quick tasks to customize instruction
for all or selected students.

Teaching Notes, page 319

He was caught in the middle.

It was the middl of the day when Pat Sandy and Mike returned again to
the mouth of the cave. May be this time they would learn more about it's
history then they did before.

(*middle*, series commas, omit *again*, *Maybe*, *its*, *than*)

middle, travel, single, settle, model, total, missile, several,
terrible, musical, snorkel, tunnel

(e.g., ends in *al/el/le*; begins with *m/s/t*; does/doesn't have double letters)

accept, bear, caught, due, ______

(homophones in alphabetical order)

When someone says, "Watch your step," it means ______.

Compound words that contain /e/

(e.g., stepladder, weekend)

Build Basic Concepts

Choose from among these skill-building activities to customize instruction for all or selected students.

Teaching Notes, page 325

concept one	Double letters stand for one sound.

1A Select a student to write *middle* on the chalkboard. Note the double letters. One letter is heard, but a writer must remember to write two letters. Have students brainstorm words with one, two, and three sets of double letters (e.g., difference, cannot, common; address, accidentally, occurring; Mississippi, committee, bookkeeper.)

phonics, more words, visual skills

1B Post Teaching Poster 2. Write on the chalkboard *plan*, *begin*, and *travel*. Have students add the *er* suffix and identify the rule that applies (Rule 3: planner, beginner, traveler). Help students differentiate between the stressed second syllable in begin that requires doubling the *n* before the addition of the suffix and the unstressed second syllable in travel that does not require doubling the consonant before the addition of the suffix.

suffix practice, writing words, sorting words

Ask students to sort these words by the syllable that is stressed: *occur, listen, omit, regret, level, control, reason.* Conclude that *listen, reason,* and *level* are words with stress on the first syllable, while the others have stress on the second syllable. Next, have students add *ed* to the words, explaining which words double the final consonant and which do not. Then have students find and write more two-syllable words that end in one consonant and one vowel, sort them by the syllable with the stress, and then add a suffix beginning with a vowel.

1C Post Teaching Poster 2. Have students demonstrate their knowledge of the rules for suffix additions by applying the rules to nonsense words—not real words. Write nonsense words on the chalkboard and ask students to identify the rule that applies for the suffix you ask them to add.

suffix practice, spelling rules

When students can apply the suffix rules to nonsense words, they have developed the confidence to do so to real words rather than relying on memorization to spell them. Later, have students reverse the process and return the nonsense words with the suffixes to their base form, using the rules that apply.

The idiom "don't look a gift horse in the mouth" originated from this: You can often tell the age of a horse by looking inside its mouth at its teeth. When a horse is a gift, it's improper to quickly examine its mouth to see if it's old. Moreover, one shouldn't examine any gift too closely for defects.

Teaching Notes, page 328

Build Skillful Writers

Use these interrelated language learnings for all or selected students.

Skillful writers are careful not to misuse words. Ask students to research the difference between *historic* and *historical*. Conclude that if something has a significant place in history, it's historic; but if something has to do with the subject of history, it's historical. Other words to explore include:

- *less/fewe*r (use *fewer* if the items can be counted; use *less* if the items cannot be counted)
- *between/among* (use *between* with two objects; use *among* with three or more objects)
- *probable/possible* (*probable* means likely; *possible* means doable, but not necessarily likely)
- *each other/one another* (use *each other* for two; use *one another* for two or more)
- *farther/further* (use *farther* when referring to physical distance; use *further* to refer to a greater extent or degree)
- *set/sit* (*set* is to place something, while *sit* is to be seated)
- *lay/lie* (*lay* is to place something, while *lie* is to recline)

You may wish to select one of these sets of often misused words per day to discuss. Then have students write a sentence using one of the words, substituting a blank for the word. Next, they read their sentence aloud for the class to fill in.

Teaching Notes, page 329

Skill to be tested:
ou and *ow* spelling patterns

Build Assessment Readiness

Use these at-school and at-home exercises to prepare all students for the Skill Test.

at-school Ask students if the *ou* and *ow* vowel patterns in *mouth*, *swallow*, and *flowerpot* are expected or unexpected (expected). Reinforce that *ou* and *ow* consistently spell /ou/, that *ow* is an expected spelling pattern for /ō/, but *ou* is the most deviant vowel combination, spelling more sounds than any other. Revisit the "Rough Toughies" rhyme and words (Activity 2A, page 47). Have students work in small groups to add words to this collection, as well as brainstorm /ou/ words that reflect expected *ou* and *ow* spellings, and *ow* spellings for /ō/.

Skill to be tested:
ou and *ow* spelling patterns

at-home Send home a copy of TAKE-HOME TASK 14 BLACKLINE MASTER, page 121, with each student to encourage parent-child partnerships.

Teaching Notes, page 330

Build Proofreading Skills

Track students' ability to meet a minimum competency for spelling and proofreading within selected samples of their everyday writing.

- Send home papers for proofreading and a copy of the IDEAS FOR PROOFREADING BLACKLINE MASTER, page 373.

Name______________________________

Dear Parents,

Your child is learning that the vowel sound in house is spelled ou and ow. Yet, both ou and ow can spell other sounds. The ow is a frequent spelling pattern for long o, as in know. The ou can spell many other sounds—in fact, it has the most variants of all the vowel spelling patterns. We call these tricky ou spellings the "Rough Toughies." In this vocabulary development activity, ou and ow spellings are highlighted. Guide your child through the lesson. Look up unfamiliar words together. Then help your child sort the words.

Circle the two words in each row that are most closely related in meaning. Then on another sheet of paper, sort the ou and ow spellings into three groups—those that spell the vowel sound in house, those that spell the vowel sound in know, and those that are part of the "Rough Toughies" collection of tricky ou spellings.

journey	trip	joyous
mouth	famous	entrance
cautious	careful	doubtful
path	boulevard	street
bayou	lowlands	river
you're	you are	your
allow	bounce	rebound
own	town	borough
announce	crowd	pronounce
course	route	around
enough	bountiful	narrow
though	tough	however
snowfall	mountain	mound
young	youthful	grown
pillow	cushion	couch
courageous	rough	rigorous
throw	pounce	hurl
poultry	proud	chicken
brought	took	bought
thoughtless	throughout	everywhere

Assess Words and Skills

- Spelling Words (words missed on tests) are recorded in the Spelling Notebook.
- Use Proof It, Practice Page 42, for proofreading/editing practice.

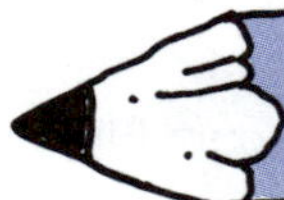

Teaching Notes, page 336

Assess Spelling Progress

Give this Cloze Story Word Test of Core Words within the frequencies 1–570 to all students. Words students miss are their Spelling Words.

THE CLOZE STORY WORD TEST

Students do not prestudy the words. Provide students with a copy of REVIEW 14 BLACKLINE MASTER, page 125. Tell students that this story tells about the history of words.

Read the entire story aloud, including the test words. Then read it again slowly as students write the missing words.

Solving Word Mysteries

(1) <u>Let's</u> explore how words originate! We'll (2) <u>step</u> back in time to explore the origins of a few (3) <u>English</u> words. As our (4) <u>language</u> grew, words were borrowed from many sources. The (5) <u>middle</u> of the word companion comes from the Latin for bread, or panis. A companion, or (6) <u>friend</u>, is someone with whom (7) <u>you're</u> to share (8) <u>your</u> bread. It (9) <u>may be</u> that the (10) <u>different</u> spellings of flower and flour may cause (11) <u>people</u> a (12) <u>problem</u>. Flower means "the best part." At (13) <u>first</u> there was only one spelling. Then the "best part of a grain" was changed to flour. (14) <u>Maybe</u> the (15) <u>reason</u> for this change was to be (16) <u>sure</u> spelling wasn't (17) <u>too</u> easy! When our (18) <u>mouth</u> says radar, it's short for "radio detection and ranging." Astronaut comes from two Greek words: astron for star and nautes for sailor, or "star sailor." (19) <u>However</u>, in Russia, an astronaut is someone (20) <u>who's</u> called a cosmonaut from the Greek kosmos meaning universe, thus "universe sailor." Now, you be a detective (21) <u>whose</u> task it is to solve the mystery and (22) <u>history</u> of a word. (23) <u>There's</u> a lot of (24) <u>information</u> on this subject.

Words tested:
be (21), there('s) (37), your (40), first (74), who('s) (77), people (79), may (89), too (112), different (139), let('s) (230), however (250), sure (251), English (350), problem (422), friend (498), language (499), whose (520), information (549), you're (552), reason (564), maybe (566), history (567), mouth (568), middle (569), step (570)

AFTER THE CLOZE STORY WORD TEST

word origins, research, class book

1. Have students research and write about the origin of an English word. Then have students share their word histories. Compile the results into a class book of word origins.

recording words for personal study list

2. Have students record the words they missed on the test in their Spelling Notebook (see page 338) for at-school study, and on a copy of the WORDS TO LEARN BLACKLINE MASTER, page 375, for at-home study.

Assess Skill Application

Give this assessment of spelling and related skills to all students.
The REVIEW 14 BLACKLINE MASTER is on page 126.

Teaching Notes, page 339

THE SKILL TEST

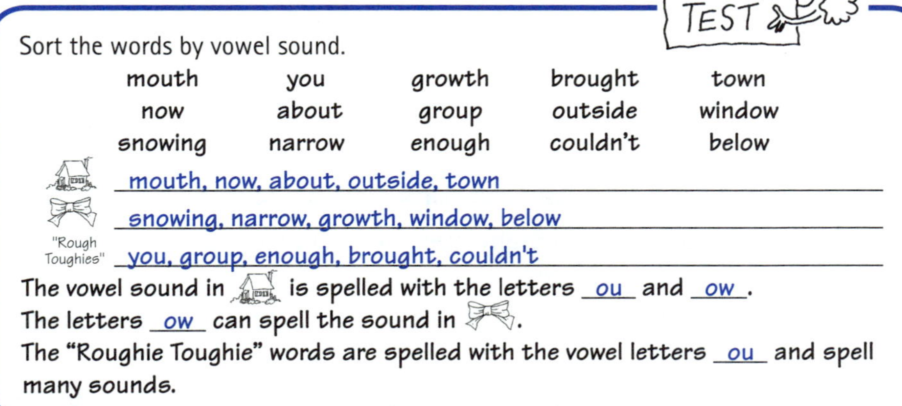

Note the ability of each student to identify words with the *ou* and *ow* spelling patterns and to identify the sounds they spell.

Assess Proofreading Application

Give this assessment of spelling and related skills to all students.
The REVIEW 14 BLACKLINE MASTER is on page 126.

Teaching Notes, page 341

THE PROOFREADING TEST

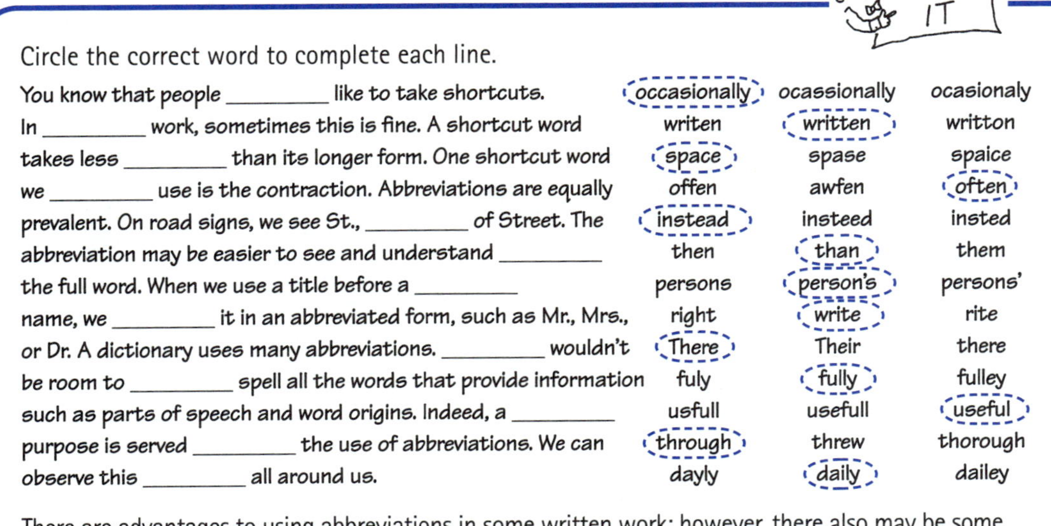

Note the ability of each student to proofread for errors.

Teaching Notes, page 342

Words tested:
the (1), of (2), and (3), a (4), to (5), for (12), with (17), at (20), be (21), I (24), one (28), all (33), there (37), up (50), some (56), my (80), only (85), water(ing) (90), just (97), began (215), got (219), soon (236), during (248), whole (259), half (297), eat (303), order (309), really (313), ready (357), class (391), instead (408), suddenly (458), friend(s) (498), explain (513), seem (535), couldn't (563), reason (564), maybe (566), history (567), mouth (568), middle (569), step (570)

Extra words: counter, hungry, I'd, lunch, sandwich

Extend Spelling Assessment

Give this in-context assessment of Core Words within the frequencies 1–570 to students who need more practice or challenge.

 **THE SENTENCE DICTATION TEST**

Students do not prestudy the words. Provide students with writing paper and pencil. Have students write the sentences as they are dictated.

1. My mouth began watering during the middle of history class.
2. I suddenly got really hungry for some reason I just couldn't seem to explain.
3. Soon I'd be there at the lunch counter with my friends, all ready to step up and order.
4. Maybe I'd eat a whole sandwich instead of only half of one.

 **AFTER THE SENTENCE DICTATION TEST**

writing a description

1. Have students describe their favorite sandwich in a way that would make anyone's mouth water. Related to word histories, note that sandwich came from the Earl of Sandwich who often asked for roast beef between two slices of bread. This became known as the "sandwich." Words such as this are called eponyms, words that originated from the name of a person or place. For example, the word Levis came from Levi Strauss and saxophone from Adolphe Sax. Ask students to investigate how Strauss's and Sax's names became eponyms.

recording words for personal study list

2. Have students record the words they missed on the test in their Spelling Notebook (see page 345) for at-school study, and on a copy of the WORDS TO LEARN BLACKLINE MASTER, page 375, for at-home study.

Have students write 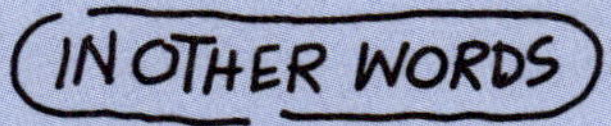

: "That's one small step for man, one giant leap for mankind." Neil Armstrong, U.S. astronaut, as he took his first steps on the moon July 20, 1969

• Challenge some students to make a time line of space exploration milestones since this historic event.

Have students redefine in rhyme: sufficiently hard—*tough enough*!

Word Test

Solving Word Mysteries

(1) ________________ explore how words originate! We'll (2) ________________

back in time to explore the origins of a few (3) ________________ words. As our

(4) ________________ grew, words were borrowed from many sources. The

(5) ________________ of the word companion comes from the Latin for bread,

or panis. A companion, or (6) ________________, is someone with whom

(7) ________________ to share (8) ________________ bread. It (9) ________________

that the (10) ________________ spellings of flower and flour may cause

(11) ________________ a (12) ________________. Flower means "the best part."

At (13) ________________ there was only one spelling. Then the "best part of a

grain" was changed to flour. (14) ________________ the (15) ________________ for

this change was to be (16) ________________ spelling wasn't (17) ________________

easy! When our (18) ________________ says radar, it's short for "radio detection

and ranging." Astronaut comes from two Greek words: astron for star and

nautes for sailor, or "star sailor." (19) ________________, in Russia, an astronaut is

someone (20) ________________ called a cosmonaut from the Greek kosmos meaning

universe, thus "universe sailor." Now, you be a detective (21) ________________ task it is

to solve the mystery and (22) ________________ of a word. (23) ________________

a lot of (24) ________________ on this subject.

Sort the words by vowel sound.

mouth	you	growth	brought	town
now	about	group	outside	window
snowing	narrow	enough	couldn't	below

"Rough Toughies"

____

____

____

The vowel sound in ___ is spelled with the letters _________ and _________.

The letters _________ can spell the sound in ___ .

The "Roughie Toughie" words are spelled with the vowel letters _________ and spell many sounds.

Circle the correctly spelled word to complete each line.

You know that people _________ like to take shortcuts.	occasionally	ocassionally	ocasionaly
In _________ work, sometimes this is fine. A shortcut word	writen	written	writton
takes less _________ than its longer form. One shortcut word	space	spase	spaice
we _________ use is the contraction. Abbreviations are equally	offen	awfen	often
prevalent. On road signs, we see St., _________ of Street. The	instead	insteed	insted
abbreviation may be easier to see and understand _________	then	than	them
the full word. When we use a title before a _________	persons	person's	persons'
name, we _________ it in an abbreviated form, such as Mr., Mrs.,	right	write	rite
or Dr. A dictionary uses many abbreviations. _________ wouldn't	There	Their	there
be room to _________ spell all the words that provide information	fuly	fully	fulley
such as parts of speech and word origins. Indeed, a _________	usfull	usefull	useful
purpose is served _________ the use of abbreviations. We can	through	threw	thorough
observe this _________ all around us.	dayly	daily	dailey

There are advantages to using abbreviations in some written work; however, there also may be some disadvantages. What do you suppose the disadvantages might be?

Build Skills and Word Experiences

Use Student Practice Pages 43–44 to follow up instruction for:
Activity 2A

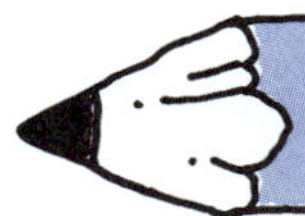

Build Visual Skills

Do the Word Preview, a visual warm-up activity, with all students.
Use Core Words **child** (571), **strange** (572), **wish** (573), **soil** (574), **human** (575).

Teaching Notes, page 316

Build Spelling and Language Skills

Choose from among these quick tasks to customize instruction
for all or selected students.

Teaching Notes, page 319

The child wished for one.

After it rains, a friends of mine walks in the midle of the deep water
and soils his shoes and socks. Its fun for a humane to do. However, his
Mother thinks its wrong and wishs he would stay clean.

(*friend, middle, It's, human, mother, it's, wishes*)

wish, child, eyelash, beach, birthday, tooth, armchair, theater, seashell

(e.g., contains *ch/sh/th*; how plural is formed; is/isn't a compound)

human/child, goat/kid, bear/cub, ______ /______

(names given adults and their young)

If a genie in a bottle granted me one wish, I would ask for ______.

Words that end in one vowel and one consonant that have stress on
the first syllable and those that have stress on the second syllable)

(e.g., *human*—stress on first syllable, *begin*—stress on second syllable)

Have students redefine in rhyme dirt work—*soil toil*!

Teaching Notes, page 325

Build Basic Concepts

Choose from among these skill-building activities to customize instruction for all or selected students.

| **concept one** | Spelling patterns for /oi/ are *oi* and *oy*. |

phonics, spelling word patterns, speculating, writing an explanation

1A Activities such as this one promote "spelling logic" rather than memory to spell words. Ask students to brainstorm words with the vowel sound in *soil*. Then have students sort the words by the vowel pattern to discover that two spellings emerge—*oi* and *oy*. The majority of the words are spelled *oi*, yet if the sound comes at the end of a word, it is spelled *oy* (e.g., cowboy, toy, annoy, destroy, decoy, convoy, soy, enjoy). Challenge students to predict this vowel spelling pattern in an unfamiliar word, such as *employment*. Ask students to speculate, write their answer, and explain their choice. Conclude that because *ment* is a suffix, the base word is *employ* and *oy* is the spelling pattern used for /oi/ terminally.

The most frequent spelling pattern for /oi/ is *oi*, spelling /oi/ about 62% of the time, while *oy* occurs just over 30% of the time. Both patterns occur initially (e.g., oil, oyster) and medially (e.g., avoid, loyal), but only the *oy* consistently spells /oi/ terminally.

| **concept two** | Unstressed syllables in words obscure the vowel sound for spelling. |

phonics, word analysis, dictionary practice, spelling word patterns

2A Write on the chalkboard: *human, lemon, raisin, children, fortune, certain, nation.* Ask students how the words are alike (two syllables, stress on first syllable, end in /ən/). Note that these words end with an unstressed syllable, or soft syllable, in which the vowel sound is the same blurred sound, but is spelled with different letters. Introduce the schwa (/ə/) that stands for this unstressed sound in a dictionary. Write cloze-letter /ən/-ending words on the chalkboard or dictate the words to students to check the unstressed vowel spelling. Choices may include *excepti_n, Afric_n, gard_n, librari_n, chick_n, muff_n, champi_n, fright_n, fount_n, drag_n.*

Expand the lesson to /əl/, as in *people* (*le, al, el*—the *le* is most prevalent), and /ər/, as in *after* (*er, or, ar*—the *er* occurs about 75 % of the time, followed by *or*, then *ar*, and finally *ur*, an infrequent pattern occurring in only a few words, such as *murmur*). Note that /ər/ is also formed by unstressed *ure*-ending words (e.g., adventure) and /əl/ by the *ful* suffix (e.g., careful). Have students find and write /ər/ and /əl/ words and sort them by their spelling pattern.

Build Skillful Writers

Use these interrelated language learnings for all or selected students.

Teaching Notes, page 328

Skillful writers become "wordsmiths" learning about words and their proper use. Discuss the difference in meaning and use of the look-alike words *human* (having to do with human beings) and *humane* (kind, sympathetic). Ask students to advance as wordsmiths by resolving the following:

- Why would a humanitarian promote recycling?
- What topics does a student studying the humanities learn?
- What values might a humanist have?
- What is an example of something that is not humanly possible?
- How do some cartoons humanize characters?
- How can human nature result in both good and bad behavior?
- What is humankind?
- What does a human relations specialist do?
- What takes place in the human resources department of a company?
- Why would you go to the Humane Society?

Build Assessment Readiness

Use these at-school and at-home exercises to prepare all students for the Skill Test.

Teaching Notes, page 329

at-school Review digraphs *ch, sh, th, wh,* and *ph* (Activity 1A, page 74). Then prepare for a carousel activity (see Test Ready, page 39) using five charts, each labeled with a digraph. Divide charts into two parts: *begins with, ends with*. After the activity, assign a chart to each group to proofread and present to the class. Conclude that no words end with *wh*. Next, each group selects one word on their chart to begin a word chain on the back of the chart. To make a word chain, students change, add, or remove one letter at a time to make a new word. Time the session (about two minutes). Later, make word chains in which two letters are changed, added, or removed at a time.

Skill to be tested:
digraphs ch, sh, th, wh, ph

at-home Send home a copy of Take-Home Task 15 Blackline Master, page 130, with each student to encourage parent-child partnerships.

Skill to be tested:
digraphs ch, sh, th, wh, ph

Build Proofreading Skills

Track students' ability to meet a minimum competency for spelling and proofreading within selected samples of their everyday writing.

Teaching Notes, page 330

- Send home papers for proofreading and a copy of the Ideas for Proofreading Blackline Master, page 373.

Name ____

Dear Parents,

Your child knows that when h follows c, s, t, w, or p, the combination spells a new sound. This activity features words with these letter pairs. As your child completes the activity, vocabulary and spelling skills are reinforced. It provides a productive pastime.

Fill in the blanks to complete the words. Notice each word already has one letter showing.

1. speak softly   ___ ___ ___ ( ) ___ ___ r

2. fake   ( ) h ___ ___ ___

3. opposite of stale   ___ r ( ) ___ ___

4. a meal at noon   ( ) u ___ ___ ___

5. opposite of adults   ___ ___ i ( ) ___ ___

6. after second   ___ ___ ( ) d

7. send a rocket   l ___ ___ ( )

8. group of sentences   ___ ___ r ( ) ___ ___ ___ ___

9. a high shrill sound   ___ ___ ( ) t ___ ___

10. hope for   w ___ ( ) ___

11. a trout is this   ( ) ___ ___ h

12. finished   ___ ___ r ___ ( ) ___ ___

13. 1/12 of a foot   ___ ( ) c ___

Print the circled letters below to form a sentence.

___ ___ ___ ___ ___ ___ ___ ___ / ___ ___ / ___ ___ ___ !

Assess Words and Skills

- Spelling Words (words missed on tests) are recorded in the Spelling Notebook.
- Use Proof It, Practice Page 45, for proofreading/editing practice.

Assess Spelling Progress

Give this Cloze Story Word Test of Core Words within the frequencies 1–575 to all students. Words students miss are their Spelling Words.

Teaching Notes, page 336

THE CLOZE STORY WORD TEST

Students do not prestudy the words. Provide students with a copy of REVIEW 15 BLACKLINE MASTER, page 134. Tell students that this story's topic is America's national sport.

Read the entire story aloud, including the test words. Then read it again slowly as students write the missing words.

Let's Play Baseball

If it's (1) <u>either</u> spring or summer, a baseball or softball game is usually in progress. Many (2) <u>human</u> beings have at (3) <u>least</u> heard of the sports and for many (4) <u>Americans</u>, a favorite fair (5) <u>weather</u> pastime is to attend a game or play in one. Most kids (6) <u>learn</u> to play the sport. They dream of the moment when they slide (7) <u>across</u> first base and, as the (8) <u>soil</u> settles, they (9) <u>suddenly</u> hear the word "safe!" echoing through the air. Wow! Now, how to get to second is the (10) <u>single</u> thought on (11) <u>their</u> minds. (12) <u>Who's</u> at bat? It's the (13) <u>wish</u> of every (14) <u>child</u> to be the player (15) <u>whose</u> hit into center (16) <u>field</u> is the one that (17) <u>lets</u> him or her win the game for the team!

Well, (18) <u>during</u> the Mudville nine's famous game, they were behind 4 to 2 in the last inning. Flynn was on second, Blake on third, and (19) <u>there</u> were (20) <u>already</u> two outs. Oh, how they needed a (21) <u>strong</u> batter! A (22) <u>strange</u>, loud roar rose from the crowd as the next player was (23) <u>all ready</u> to bat. What (24) <u>happened</u>? You write the big ending!

Words tested:

all (33), there (37), their (42), who('s) (77), let(s) (230), across (247), during (248), learn (271), American(s) (319), ready (357), strong (381), either (409), already (411), suddenly (458), weather (464), field (472), least (478), happened (481), single (509), whose (520), child (571), strange (572), wish (573), soil (574), human (575)

AFTER THE CLOZE STORY WORD TEST

1. Have students write and share their story endings. Then read to the class "Casey at the Bat," the well-known poem of the Mudville nine's famous game by Ernest Lawrence Thayer (1863-1940) that appeared in the San Francisco Examiner on June 3, 1888. The poem has been a favorite ever since.

writing a story ending, relating to literature

2. Have students record the words they missed on the test in their Spelling Notebook (see page 338) for at-school study, and on a copy of the WORDS TO LEARN BLACKLINE MASTER, page 375, for at-home study.

recording words for personal study list

Assess Skill Application

Give this assessment of spelling and related skills to all students.
The REVIEW 15 BLACKLINE MASTER is on page 135.

Teaching Notes, page 339

 **THE SKILL TEST**

Skill tested:
digraphs ch, sh, th, wh, ph

Write words that:
begin with ch ___(answers will vary)___
begin with ph ___________________
begin with sh ___________________
begin with th ___________________
begin with wh ___________________
end with ch ___________________
end with ph ___________________
end with sh ___________________
end with th ___________________
end with wh ______none______

Note the ability of each student to identify and spell words that begin and end with digraphs
ch, *sh*, *th*, *wh*, and *ph*. (Note: students should recognize that *wh* does not end words.)

Assess Proofreading Application

Give this assessment of spelling and related skills to all students.
The REVIEW 15 BLACKLINE MASTER is on page 135.

Teaching Notes, page 341

 **THE PROOFREADING TEST**

Proofread for one spelling, capitalization, or punctuation error
in the underlined parts. Circle errors. Write the correction in the space.

You know that when the letter h <u>folows some consonant</u>   follows
letters, a new sound is formed <u>unlike the sounds of eithere</u>   either
of the two letters. The two-letter <u>sound maybe called</u> a   may be
digraph. Yet, in <u>many word when two</u> consonants are   words
together, both of them retain <u>there sound and they</u> are   their
blended <u>together. the're called</u> blends. Some words   They're
behave in a similar <u>way. Fore example,</u> the word behave   For
is a combination of be and have, <u>but the knew word</u> has a   new
<u>meaning all it's own.</u> Motel is a blended word made up of   its
motor and hotel, and the meaning <u>is a mixture of the two</u>   .
Some <u>pepole call these blends,</u> but Lewis Carroll in his   people
story "Through the Looking Glass" <u>called then</u> portmanteau   them
<u>when he invented slithy bye</u> combining *lithe* and *slimy*.   by

Why would portmanteau words be examples of shortcut words? Make a portmanteau
word.

Note the ability of each student to proofread for spelling errors.

Extend Spelling Assessment

Give this in-context assessment of Core Words within the frequencies 1–575 to students who need more practice or challenge.

Teaching Notes, page 342

THE SENTENCE DICTATION TEST

Students do not prestudy the words. Provide students with writing paper and pencil. Have students write the sentences as they are dictated.

1. Every single human being I have ever known likes to wish and dream.
2. A mother and father might wish that their child could explain the strange soil mark on the new kitchen carpet.
3. Maybe a teacher would wish for a special machine that could correct math papers.
4. It may be that you're wishing for something, too.

Words tested:
the (1), and (3), a (4), to (5), that (9), it (10), for (12), on (14), be(ing) (21), I (24), have (25), their (42), would (59), like(s) (66), could (70), may (89), new (107), too (112), every (151), might (173), something (178), mother (226), father (229), ever (240), paper(s) (241), special (361), mark (504), single (509), explain (513), correct (521), teacher (539), machine (548), you're (552), maybe (566), child (571), strange (572), wish(ing) (573), soil (574), human (575)

Extra words: carpet, dream, kitchen, known, math

AFTER THE SENTENCE DICTATION TEST

1. Have students describe in writing one change at their school they wish would come to be. Then ask them to speculate how things might be different if the wish came true.

writing a description, speculating

2. Have students record the words they missed on the test in their Spelling Notebook (see page 345) for at-school study, and on a copy of the WORDS TO LEARN BLACKLINE MASTER, page 375, for at-home study.

recording words for personal study list

Dictate this tongue-twister for students to write and say:
Which rich wicked witch wished the wicked wish?

- Challenge students to write more sentences for dictation to twist their classmates' tongues.

WORD MYSTERIES AND HISTORIES

The Old English word *child* has had several spellings and plural forms. Its earliest spelling was *cild* and had no separate plural form, like *deer* today. Yet, many early English nouns formed the plural with the suffix *ru*, so *cildru* commenced, later to become *cilder*, then *childer*. Other English nouns formed the plural with the suffix *an* (which became *en*), so the plural of *childer* evolved into *childeren*, then shortened to *children*.

- The *en* suffix remains in current spellings, but is not limited to a plural form. Have students brainstorm words with the *en* suffix (e.g., awaken, driven, given, taken, flatten).
- The *en* prefix means "in" or "make." Have students brainstorm words with the *en* prefix (e.g., enrich, enliven, enforce, enlarge, ensure, enjoy).

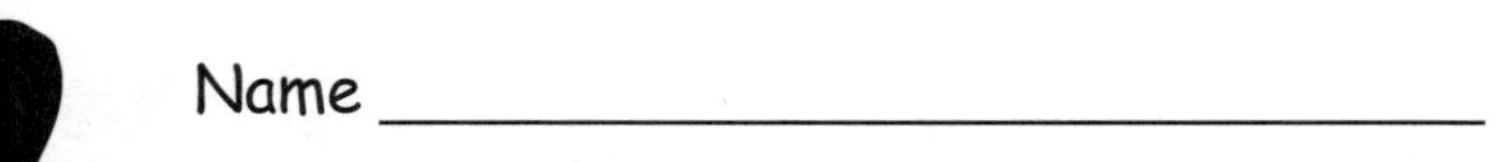

Word Test

Let's Play Baseball

If it's (1) _________________ spring or summer, a baseball or softball game is usually

in progress. Every (2) _________________ being has at (3) _________________

heard of the sports and for many (4) _________________ , a favorite fair

(5) _________________ pastime is to attend a game or play in one. Most kids

(6) _________________ to play the sport. They dream of the moment when they slide

(7) _________________ first base and, as the (8) _________________ settles, they

(9) _________________ hear the word "safe!" echoing through the air. Wow! Now, how

to get to second is the (10) _________________ thought on (11) _________________

minds. (12) _________________ at bat? It's the (13) _________________ of every

(14) _________________ to be the player (15) _________________ hit into center

(16) _________________ is the one that (17) _________________ him or her win the

game for the team!

Well, (18) _________________ the Mudville nine's famous game, they were behind 4 to

2 in the last inning. Flynn was on second, Blake on third, and (19) _________________

were (20) _________________ two outs. Oh, how they needed a (21) _________________

batter! A (22) _________________ , loud roar rose from the crowd as the next player

was (23) _________________ to bat. What (24) _________________ ? You write the big

ending!

Skill Test

Write words that:

begin with ch ___________________________________

begin with ph ___________________________________

begin with sh ___________________________________

begin with th ___________________________________

begin with wh ___________________________________

end with ch ___________________________________

end with ph ___________________________________

end with sh ___________________________________

end with th ___________________________________

end with wh ___________________________________

Proofreading Test

Proofread for one spelling, capitalization, or punctuation error in the underlined parts. Circle errors. Write the correction in the space.

You know that when the letter h <u>folows some consonant</u> ___________________

letters, a new sound is formed <u>unlike the sounds of eithere</u> ___________________

of the two letters. The two-letter <u>sound maybe called</u> a ___________________

digraph. Yet, in <u>many word when two</u> consonants are ___________________

together, both of them retain <u>there sound and they</u> are ___________________

blended <u>together. the're called</u> blends. Some words ___________________

behave in a similar <u>way. Fore example,</u> the word behave ___________________

is a combination of be and have, <u>but the knew word</u> has a ___________________

<u>meaning all it's own.</u> Motel is a blended word made up of ___________________

motor and hotel, and the meaning is a <u>mixture of the two</u> ___________________

Some <u>pepole call these blends,</u> but Lewis Carroll in his ___________________

story "Through the Looking Glass" <u>called then</u> portmanteau ___________________

<u>when he invented slithy bye</u> combining lithe and slimy. ___________________

Why would portmanteau words be examples of shortcut words? Make a portmanteau word.

Build Skills and Word Experiences

Use Student Practice Pages 46–47 to follow up instruction for:
Activity 1A • Activity 1C

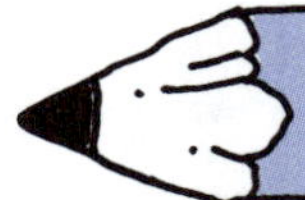

Build Visual Skills

Do the Word Preview, a visual warm-up activity, with all students.
Use Core Words **trip** (576), **woman** (577), **eye** (578), **milk** (579), **choose** (580).

Teaching Notes, page 316

Build Spelling and Language Skills

Choose from among these quick tasks to customize instruction
for all or selected students.

Teaching Notes, page 319

The milk spilled.

For this job, they will chose a women who has a good eye for color. On her first trip, she will travel by plane to buy rug for the libary in the new bilding.

(*choose, woman, rugs, library, building*)

choosing, brook, afternoon, cookies, proofreading, food, good-byes, cartoons, storybooks, looking, goose, moonlighting

(e.g., sound *oo* spells; number of syllables; ends with *ing* suffix/*s* suffix/no suffix; is/isn't a compound)

eye, treat, noun, label, _______

(words that begin and end with the same letter)

If I had to make a choice, it would be difficult for me to choose between _______.

(Note: *Between* calls for two options; *among* calls for more than two.)

Words end with /ən/

(e.g., woman)

Build Basic Concepts

Choose from among these skill–building activities to customize instruction for all or selected students.

Teaching Notes, page 325

| **concept one** | Most nouns have a singular and a plural form. |

1A Ask students to explore ways words can be made plural. Guide students to conclude:

plural practice, more words, spelling rules

1. Most nouns form the plural with the addition of s—*eye/eyes*.
2. Nouns ending in *s*, *sh*, *ch*, *x*, *z*, and some *o*-ending words are made plural by adding *es*—*class/classes*, *wish/wishes*, *peach/peaches*, *box/boxes*, *waltz/waltzes*, *potato/potatoes*.
3. Nouns ending in consonant-*y* are made plural by changing the *y* to *i* before adding *es*—*history/histories*, *activity/activities*.
4. Nouns ending in *f* or *fe* are often made plural by changing the *f* or *fe* to *v* and adding *es*—*wolf/wolves*, *life/lives*.
5. Some nouns are plural with no change—*sheep*, *deer*.
6. Some nouns are made plural with a new base word—*child/children*, *tooth/teeth*.

Use large sticky notes to label the top boxes of the Ten-Box Reusable chart (page 396) with five ways to make words plural, other than adding *s*. Have students find examples for each. They write the words on small sticky notes and place them in the appropriate box on the chart. Later, remove and distribute the words to students to write the singular forms. Then have students return their words to the chart. (Save the chart for Activity 1B, this unit, and At School, page 147.)

1B Select twenty words from the chart to dictate to students that represent the five plural rules 2-6 (Activity 1A, this unit). Then have students take turns writing the words on the chalkboard for self-checking. Next, have students create a bingo board (see Activity 1C, page 20) using sixteen of the words. Then play bingo!

writing words, spelling game, proofreading

1C Write on the chalkboard: *baby*, *baby's*, *babies*, *babies'*. Ask students to explain the difference. Conclude that *baby* is singular, *baby's* is singular possessive, *babies* is plural, and *babies'* is plural possessive.

plural practice, usage, possessives, writing words, spelling rules, more words

Repeat with *woman*, *woman's*, *women*, *women's*. Note that to make a plural noun that ends in s possessive, add an apostrophe after the *s* (e.g., *babies'*). If the plural noun does not end in *s*, add *'s* (e.g., *women's*).

Ask students to fold paper lengthwise to make four columns labeled *singular*, *singular possessive*, *plural*, *plural possessive*. Then have students work in pairs to write examples.

Have students write (*IN OTHER WORDS*): "Be careful of the wind you choose."
Avi, The True Confessions of Charlotte Doyle

Teaching Notes, page 328

Build Skillful Writers

Use these interrelated language learnings for all or selected students.

Review that singular nouns need a singular verb and plural nouns need a plural verb. Now provide experiences with nouns that mean a group of things and can be singular or plural (e.g., total, majority, number, couple). If the writer means the noun as a whole, the verb should be singular. If the writer means all the individuals of the group, the verb should be plural.

- *The total is ten.*
  Hint: When *the* comes before the noun, the verb is usually singular.
- *A total of ten are going.*
  Hint: When *a* comes before the noun and if *of* follows it, the verb is usually plural.

The words *all*, *any*, and *none* can be singular or plural. If the writer means *all/any/none of it*, the verb should be singular. If the writer means *all/any/none of them*, the verb should be plural.

Have students write sentences that use singular/plural meanings for these words.

Teaching Notes, page 329

Skill to be tested:
consonant blends

Build Assessment Readiness

Use these at-school and at-home exercises to prepare all students for the Skill Test.

at-school Have students fold writing paper into four boxes front and back (two folds) and label each box with one consonant blend: *str, spr, thr, scr, bl, sm, fr, sn*. Then have them write words in the boxes that contain the blends. Remind students how each letter of the blend can be heard and spelled.

Organize students into small groups to single out words that fit criteria, such as: words that are homophones, antonyms, compounds, nouns, verbs; words that have short vowels, long vowels, soft-syllable endings, suffixes.

Skill to be tested:
consonant blends

at-home Send home a copy of TAKE-HOME TASK 16 BLACKLINE MASTER, page 139, with each student to encourage parent-child partnerships.

Teaching Notes, page 330

Build Proofreading Skills

Track students' ability to meet a minimum competency for spelling and proofreading within selected samples of their everyday writing.

- Send home papers for proofreading and a copy of the IDEAS FOR PROOFREADING BLACKLINE MASTER, page 373.

Name _______________________

Dear Parents,

Here is another opportunity to work with your child to develop reasoning and vocabulary skills through analogies. In this activity, the focus is words with consonant blends. Your child is learning that consonant blends are easy to spell, because each letter in the blend maintains its own sound.

tap   t<u>r</u>ap   <u>s</u>trap   <u>s</u>traps

For each analogy, have your child discover the relationship between the first two words. Then think of a word that contains a consonant blend to make the relationship between the second two words the same as between the first two.

Complete the analogies using a word that begins with one of these consonant blends: scr, spr, str, thr.

mark : marker :: spread : ____ ____ ____ ____ ____ ____ ____ ____

taught : caught :: length : ____ ____ ____ ____ ____ ____ ____ ____

grass : lawn :: toss : ____ ____ ____ ____ ____

wouldn't : couldn't :: green : ____ ____ ____ ____ ____ ____

farm : ranch :: boulevard : ____ ____ ____ ____ ____ ____

boil : soil :: goat : ____ ____ ____ ____ ____ ____

nail : hammer :: screw : ____ ____ ____ ____ ____ ____ ____ ____ ____ ____

whirlwind : breeze :: downpour : ____ ____ ____ ____ ____ ____ ____

fifteen : five :: nine : ____ ____ ____ ____ ____

clarify : explain :: yelling : ____ ____ ____ ____ ____ ____ ____ ____

mountain : fountain :: change : ____ ____ ____ ____ ____ ____

lost : found :: autumn : ____ ____ ____ ____ ____ ____

rope : string :: string : ____ ____ ____ ____ ____ ____

ocean : sea :: river : ____ ____ ____ ____ ____ ____

glue : sticks :: thorns : ____ ____ ____ ____ ____ ____ ____

flower : rose :: tree : ____ ____ ____ ____ ____

man : woman :: curved : ____ ____ ____ ____ ____ ____ ____ ____

accept : except :: threw : ____ ____ ____ ____ ____ ____ ____

brother : mother :: fly : ____ ____ ____ ____

broom : sweep :: brush : ____ ____ ____ ____ ____

There's more! Ask your child to find and write more words with the consonant blends!

Assess Words and Skills

• Spelling Words (words missed on tests) are recorded in the Spelling Notebook.
• Use Proof It, Practice Page 48, for proofreading/editing practice.

WORD TEST

Teaching Notes, page 336

Assess Spelling Progress

Give this Cloze Story Word Test of Core Words within the frequencies 1–580 to all students. Words students miss are their Spelling Words.

THE CLOZE STORY WORD TEST

Students do not prestudy the words. Provide students with a copy of REVIEW 16 BLACKLINE MASTER, page 143. Tell students that this story's topic is one of America's favorite board games.

Read the entire story aloud, including the test words. Then read it again slowly as students write the missing words.

Game Time!

Get your (1) <u>milk</u> and cookies. (2) <u>Choose</u> your (3) <u>colored</u> marker and place it on the first (4) <u>square</u>. Count your paper (5) <u>money</u>. Roll the dice and get (6) <u>all ready</u> for your (7) <u>trip</u> around the game board. What will you purchase? Start with homes on Baltic and Pacific Avenues and go on to hotels at Boardwalk and Park Place! Oh, you have your (8) <u>eye</u> on some railroad property, (9) <u>too</u>! (10) <u>Buy</u> now! You can never own (11) <u>too</u> much! (12) <u>Remember</u>, you'll get another (13) <u>beautiful</u> bankroll when you pass "GO." (14) <u>There's</u> more income when your friends land on your estates, except you pay when you land on (15) <u>theirs</u>. It's fun, but don't (16) <u>draw</u> the card that sends you (17) <u>straight</u> to jail! This is a game that every (18) <u>woman</u>, man, and (19) <u>child</u> can enjoy, yet Parker Brothers, who copyrighted the game in 1935, was (20) <u>quite</u> surprised it (21) <u>caught</u> on. Then they said interest (22) <u>couldn't</u> last. Over sixty years (23) <u>later</u>, the game is tied for first in popularity. What is this popular activity, and what other old game ranks first (24) <u>along</u> with it?

Words tested:

all (33), there('s) (37), their(s) (42), too (112), along (171), money (279), later (288), remember (315), draw (338), ready (357), beautiful (429), quite (447), buy (502), straight (524), caught (527), color(ed) (531), square (537), couldn't (563), child (571), trip (576), woman (577), eye (578), milk (579), choose (580)

AFTER THE CLOZE STORY WORD TEST

hypothesizing, writing

1. Have students answer the story question and hypothesize in writing why this game continues to maintain its popularity. Then have students share their answers. Conclude that the game described is Monopoly and the other game that has enjoyed equal longtime popularity is Scrabble. Parcheesi places second. Challenge students to speculate which currently popular game will withstand the test of time. Students should write their answer with reasons for their opinion.

recording words for personal study list

2. Have students record the words they missed on the test in their Spelling Notebook (see page 338) for at-school study, and on a copy of the WORDS TO LEARN BLACKLINE MASTER, page 375, for at-home study.

Assess Skill Application

Give this assessment of spelling and related skills to all students.
The Review 16 Blackline Master is on page 144.

Teaching Notes, page 339

THE SKILL TEST

Words with consonant blends are easy to spell, because
<u>each letter in the blend maintains its own sound.</u>
Spell words beginning with consonant blends. (answers will vary)
scr_________________   str_________________   spr_________________
pr_________________   pl_________________   dr_________________
Add consonant blends to spell words. (answers will vary)
_________________ock   _________________and   _________________in
_________________ash   _________________amp   _________________ay
Spell words that end with consonant blends.
not last, but fi<u>rst_________________</u>   not water, but m<u>ilk_________________</u>
not spoons, but f<u>orks_________________</u>   not teacher, but s<u>tudent_________________</u>

Skill tested:
consonant blends

Note the ability of each student to spell words with consonant blends.

Assess Proofreading Application

Give this assessment of spelling and related skills to all students.
The Review 16 Blackline Master is on page 144.

Teaching Notes, page 341

THE PROOFREADING TEST

If any of the underlined words in each line are incorrect,
write the correction in the space.

A contraction and a blended <u>word have more then</u> one
<u>thing incommon.</u> Both are shortcut words. Both are
usually made from <u>too longer words.</u> The word plane
is also a shortcut word, <u>but theirs a very</u> important
<u>difference between</u> plane and the other two. It's not
made by combining two words, <u>but it originates form</u>
a <u>singel word.</u> Plane is a clipped form of airplane. It's
<u>likley that you use many</u> clipped words in your daily
conversation. <u>Hear are examples:</u> lunch, bike, phone,
flu, champ, fridge, gas, gym, and fax. <u>Moste of the time</u>
the <u>clipped word is speled</u> with the same letters as
its base word, but not for fax. <u>Naturaly, it's far easier</u>
to use the clipped <u>words, thus they're</u> popularity.

	than
	in common
	two
	there's
	from
	single
	likely
	Here
	Most
	spelled
	Naturally
	their

Write the longer forms of the clipped words in the story. Then brainstorm more
clipped words.

Note the ability of each student to proofread for spelling and capitalization errors.

Teaching Notes, page 342

Words tested:
the (1), of (2), and (3), a (4), to (5), that (9), are (15), as (16), be (21), all (33), an (39), your (40), their (42), then (53), two (65), make (72), may (89), good (106), man (111), such (133), take (135), great (146), every (151), should (156), food(s) (198), let('s) (230), try (254), thing(s) (258), example(s) (261), body (285), eat (303), ready (357), list (372), strong (381), themselves (443), possible (452), build (487), caught (527), child (571), trip (576), woman (577), eye (578), milk (579), choose (580)

Extra words: apples, fresh, fruit, healthy, lot, snacks, store

creating lists, writing an explanation

recording words for personal study list

Extend Spelling Assessment

Give this in-context assessment of Core Words within the frequencies 1–580 to students who need more practice or challenge.

 ## THE SENTENCE DICTATION TEST

Students do not prestudy the words. Provide students with writing paper and pencil. Have students write the sentences as they are dictated.

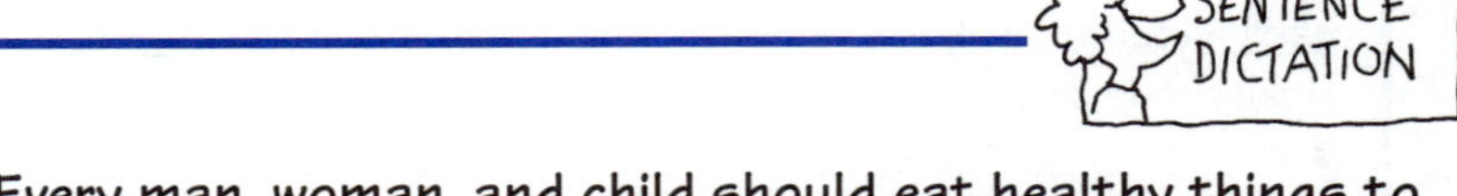

1. Every man, woman, and child should eat healthy things to build their body and make themselves as strong as possible.

2. Two great examples are milk and a lot of fresh fruit, such as apples.

3. Let's take a trip to the food store to choose good snacks that are all ready to eat.

4. Then make a list of the foods that caught your eye that may be great to try.

 ## AFTER THE SENTENCE DICTATION TEST

1. Have students create a list of healthful foods that would taste good for a snack after school. Then have them list poor choices and tell why they're not healthy.

2. Have students record the words they missed on the test in their Spelling Notebook (see page 345) for at-school study, and on a copy of the WORDS TO LEARN BLACKLINE MASTER, page 375, for at-home study.

Eye is a palindrome—a word that is spelled the same way forward and backward. Have students find and write more palindromes (e.g., noon, peep, level, kayak, repaper, rotator, mom, dad, did, madam). There are also palindrome sentences: Was it a car or a cat I saw? Step on no pets.

WORD MYSTERIES AND HISTORIES

The roots ocu/opt mean "eye." Some words relating to eye care may be easily confused.

- ophthalmologist—medical doctor for eyes; examines eyes for eyeglasses
- oculist—an ophthalmologist specializing in diseases of the eye
- optometrist—examiner of eyes for eyeglasses
- optician—makes or sells eyeglasses

Word Test

Game Time!

Get your (1) _________________ and cookies. (2) _________________ your

(3) _________________ marker and place it on the first (4) _________________.

Count your paper (5) _________________. Roll the dice and get (6) _________________

for your (7) _________________ around the game board. What will you purchase?

Start with homes on Baltic and Pacific Avenues and go on to hotels at Boardwalk

and Park Place! Oh, you have your (8) _________________ on some railroad

property, (9) _________________! (10) _________________ now! You can never

own (11) _________________ much! (12) _________________, you'll get another

(13) _________________ bankroll when you pass "GO." (14) _________________ more

income when your friends land on your estates, except you pay when you land on

(15) _________________. It's fun, but don't (16) _________________ the card that

sends you (17) _________________ to jail! Every man, (18) _________________, and

(19) _________________ enjoys this game, yet Parker Brothers, who copyrighted

the game in 1935, was (20) _________________ surprised it (21) _________________

on. Then they said interest (22) _________________ last. Over sixty years

(23) _________________, the game is tied for first in popularity. What is this

popular activity, and what other old game ranks first (24) _________________

with it?

Name _______________________________

REVIEW 16

Skill Test

Words with consonant blends are easy to spell, because _______________________

____

Spell words beginning with consonant blends.

scr_______________________   str_______________________   spr_______________________

pr_______________________   pl_______________________   dr_______________________

Add consonant blends to spell words.

_______________________ock   _______________________and   _______________________in

_______________________ash   _______________________amp   _______________________ay

Spell words that end with consonant blends.

not last, but f_______________________   not water, but m_______________________

not spoons, but f_______________________   not teacher, but s_______________________

Proofreading Test

If any of the underlined words in each line are incorrect, write the correction in the space.

A contraction and a blended <u>word have more then</u> one   _______________________

<u>thing incommon</u>. Both are shortcut words. Both are   _______________________

usually made from <u>too longer words</u>. The word plane   _______________________

is also a shortcut word, <u>but theirs a very</u> important   _______________________

<u>difference between</u> plane and the other two. It's not   _______________________

made by combining two words, <u>but it originates form</u>   _______________________

a <u>singel word</u>. Plane is a clipped form of airplane. It's   _______________________

<u>likley that you use many</u> clipped words in your daily   _______________________

conversation. <u>Hear are examples</u>: lunch, bike, phone,   _______________________

flu, champ, fridge, gas, gym, and fax. <u>Moste of the time</u>   _______________________

the <u>clipped word is speled</u> with the same letters as   _______________________

its base word, but not for fax. <u>Naturaly, it's far easier</u>   _______________________

to use the clipped <u>words, thus they're</u> popularity.   _______________________

Write the longer forms of the clipped words in the story. Then brainstorm more clipped words.

Build Skills and Word Experiences

Use Student Practice Pages 49–50 to follow up instruction for:
Activity 1B • Build Skillful Writers

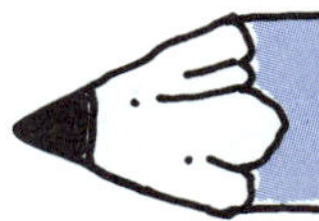

Build Visual Skills

Do the Word Preview, a visual warm-up activity, with all students.
Use Core Words **north** (581), **seven** (582), **famous** (583), **late** (584), **pay** (585).

Teaching Notes, page 316

Build Spelling and Language Skills

Choose from among these quick tasks to customize instruction
for all or selected students.

Teaching Notes, page 319

They were at the north end.

Sandy was famos for turning her books in to late Sometimes she would check out seven book's at a time. Her overdue fines we're never small in size.

(*famous*, *too*, period, *books*, *were*, omit *in size*)

infamous, soup, recount, double, cougars, dismount, grouped, doubtfully, enough

(e.g., sound *ou* spells; number of syllables; contains prefix/suffix/neither)

natural, naturally, final, finally, total, _______

(*l*-ending words to which *ly* can be added)

A famous person I would like to meet is _______.

Words to which the prefix *re*, *un*, or *dis* can be added

Teaching Notes, page 325

Build Basic Concepts

Choose from among these skill-building activities to customize instruction
for all or selected students.

| concept one | A vowel followed by *r* stands for a new sound. |

phonics, spelling word patterns, compounds, writing words, more words

 **1A** Write on the chalkboard: *gem/germ, bid/bird, bun/burn*. Point out that:

- When *r* follows a vowel, the vowel sound changes.
- The most common spelling patterns for /er/ are *er*, *ir*, and *ur*.
- When /er/ follows *w*, the spelling is often *or* (e.g., world, word, worst).
- Less frequent spelling patterns for /er/ are *ear* (e.g., earth) and *ere* (e.g., weren't).

Have students brainstorm /er/ words. Then they make compound words from their /er/ word bank (e.g., birthday, earthquake, sweatshirt, turtleneck, whirlpool, nursemaid).

phonics, spelling word patterns, antonyms, vocabulary development, writing words, word analysis, proofreading

1B Write *northern* and *boredom* on the chalkboard. Ask students how these words are alike (/or/). Point out that:

- The two most frequent patterns for /or/ are *or/ore*.
- When /or/ follows *w*, the spelling is often *ar* (e.g., warm, warp, warn).
- Less frequent /or/ spelling patterns are *oor*, *oar*, and *our* (e.g., door, floor; board, roar; your, four).

Have students fold writing paper to make two vertical columns. Dictate these words for students to write in the first column. Then they write the /or/ antonym in the second column.

after (before)	against (for)	evening (morning)
less (more)	tall (short)	backward (forward)
south (north)	unusual (ordinary)	unimportant (important)
casual (formal)	import (export)	disorganized (organized)

Have students proofread their words and sort them by spelling pattern: *or* or *ore*.

phonics, spelling word patterns, making words, vocabulary development

1C Write *shot* and *short* on the chalkboard to note that when *r* follows a vowel, the vowel sound changes. Prepare for a letter-card activity (see Activity 2B, page 47) using *a, e, h, n, o, r, r, s, t,* and *u*. Together make *north*. Then have students continue making words: *nurse—nature—earth—hers—horse—hornet—hunter—hurt—turns—torn—snort—snore—shore—shorten—ornate—another—other—outer—return—resort—sort—senator—tenor—thorn*—and back to *north*. As words are made, point out the /or/ and /er/ spelling patterns.

Later have students work in pairs to make more words with their letters. Have them write the words as they make them.

Build Skillful Writers

Use these interrelated language learnings for all or selected students.

Teaching Notes, page 328

Students have been exploring shortcut words, such as contractions (e.g., you're), clipped words (e.g., bike), blends (e.g., brunch), symbols (e.g., $), acronyms (e.g., ZIP code), initializations (e.g., CIA), and abbreviations (e.g., No.), in Units 11–17. Frequent shortcuts for writers are abbreviations, thus their inclusion on students' Spell Check cards. Examine those included on the cards. Then expand the list to make a class book of abbreviations. Assign abbreviation categories (e.g., time—minutes, days; numerical amounts—quart, pound; titles—doctor, reverend; places—mountain, road; parts of speech—noun, verb; establishments—company, hospital; other—pages, examples) to research groups. Decide on format, binding, and cover. Place the completed reference in the school or classroom library.

Build Assessment Readiness

Use these at-school and at-home exercises to prepare all students for the Skill Test.

Teaching Notes, page 329

at-school Ask students to list ways words can be made plural. Then post the Ten-Box Reusable Chart (Activity 1A, page 137) for students to self-check. Remind students that most words are made plural by adding *s*. Divide students into two teams for Spelling Baseball. Identify four "bases" in the classroom. Players take turns pitching a word (drawn from the Ten-Box sticky notes) to the batter on the opposing team. If the batter spells the word correctly and reattaches it in the right category on the chart, the batter proceeds to first base. Players continue moving around the bases and score one point upon crossing home plate. A missed word sends the other team to bat. The team with the most points at the end wins!

Skill to be tested:
plurals

at-home Send home a copy of TAKE-HOME TASK 17 BLACKLINE MASTER, page 148, with each student to encourage parent-child partnerships.

Skill to be tested:
plurals

Build Proofreading Skills

Track students' ability to meet a minimum competency for spelling and proofreading within selected samples of their everyday writing.

Teaching Notes, page 330

- Send home papers for proofreading and a copy of the IDEAS FOR PROOFREADING BLACKLINE MASTER, page 373.

Name ______________________________

Dear Parents,

At school your child is learning ways a noun can be made plural. For most nouns, an s is added. But not always. Here are other ways to make a noun plural.

- Nouns ending in s, sh, ch, x, z, and some o-ending nouns are made plural by adding es—class/classes.
- Nouns ending in consonant-y are made plural by changing the y to i before adding es—history/histories.
- Nouns ending in f or fe are often made plural by changing the f or fe to v and adding es—wolf/wolves.
- Some nouns are plural with no change—deer.
- Some nouns are made plural with a new base word—mouse/mice.

Use the clues to complete the crossword puzzle.

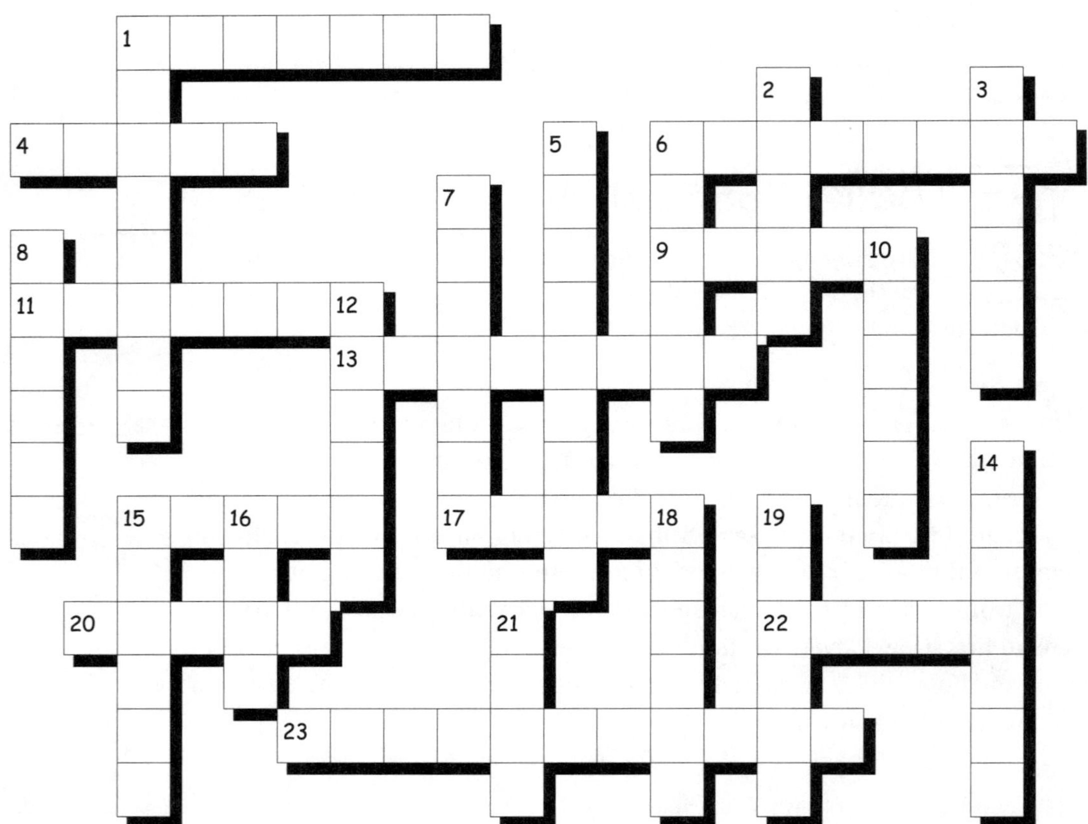

ACROSS

1. pals, buddies
4. opposite of men
6. not adults
9. you chew with these
11. bears, dogs, cats belong in this category
13. synonyms for photographs
15. more than one goose
17. more than one sheep
20. you pack things in these when you move
22. after "fives"
23. start off as caterpillars

DOWN

1. moms, dads, brothers, sisters make up these
2. some people say cats have nine of these
3. they drop from trees in the fall
5. more than one century
6. more than one city
7. noon meals
8. infants
10. more than one half, two ___ make a whole
12. they are in between words in a sentence
14. Mom uses these to read
15. bunches of people (rhymes with troops)
16. see with these
18. more than one person
19. you make these when you blow out birthday candles
21. you walk on two of them

Assess Words and Skills

- Spelling Words (words missed on tests) are recorded in the Spelling Notebook.
- Use Proof It, Practice Page 51, for proofreading/editing practice.

Assess Spelling Progress

Give this Cloze Story Word Test of Core Words within the frequencies 1–585 to all students. Words students miss are their Spelling Words.

Teaching Notes, page 336

THE CLOZE STORY WORD TEST

Students do not prestudy the words. Provide students with a copy of Review 17 Blackline Master, page 152. Tell students that this story asks them to evaluate changes in education from pioneer days to today.

Read the entire story aloud, including the test words. Then read it again slowly as students write the missing words.

Schools Then and Now

(1) There's a big (2) difference between education in (3) early America and schools today. In the (4) past, (5) children weren't required to attend school. In fact, in the (6) north, schools (7) often closed during the cold winter months and all schools (8) always closed for summer. (9) Instead of school, kids worked from sunup (10) until (11) late at night helping (12) their families on the farm or in business. Kids who went to school (13) learned to read and write, (14) perhaps with the (15) famous New England Primer that they memorized by copying each page in perfect penmanship. Students memorized math "timetables" and (16) important dates in (17) history. Elocution, or (18) correct speech and (19) language, required students to recite tongue twisters (20) carefully, such as "(21) Seven senseless sisters sleep." Indeed, all students had to (22) pay attention at school and do a lot of homework. Then schools changed. (23) They're different now. What (24) reasons contributed to the changes? Why do you think this turnabout was good or bad?

Words tested:
there('s) (37), their (42), always (183), often (186), important (195), until (196), children (200), early (324), learned (326), perhaps (352), past (403), instead (408), carefully (427), language (499), correct (521), reason(s) (564), difference (565), history (567), north (581), seven (582), famous (583), late (584), pay (585), *they're (1010)

*The testing of they're (1010) is included to help students differentiate among the there/their/they're homophones.

AFTER THE CLOZE STORY WORD TEST

1. Have students write and share their answers to the story questions. Discuss the answers. Lead students to consider: Why did all schools close in summer? Why have problem-solving tasks taken the place of memorization? Why were laws passed for school attendance? What services do schools offer today that they didn't provide in the past? Next, ask students to predict future changes for schools.

evaluating, predicting, writing

2. Have students record the words they missed on the test in their Spelling Notebook (see page 338) for at-school study, and on a copy of the Words to Learn Blackline Master, page 375, for at-home study.

recording words for personal study list

Teaching Notes, page 339

Assess Skill Application

Give this assessment of spelling and related skills to all students.
The Review 17 Blackline Master is on page 153.

 **THE SKILL TEST**

Skill tested:
plurals

Write a plural word in each box that follows the rule.

add s				
add es				
change y to i and add es				
change f or fe to v and add es				
change form				
no change				

(answers will vary)

Note the ability of each student to spell words that illustrate the plural rules.

Teaching Notes, page 341

Assess Proofreading Application

Give this assessment of spelling and related skills to all students.
The Review 17 Blackline Master is on page 153.

 **THE PROOFREADING TEST**

Proofread for one spelling, capitalization, or punctuation error
in the underlined parts. Circle errors. Write the corrections in the spaces.

You have learned that writters may use shortcuts   writers
for writing some wards or phrases. Occasionally,   words
a writer may use a contraction, blinded word,   blended
abbreviation, clipped word, or symbol in they're   their
writing rather then the longer form. These short-   than
cuts are fine accept for very formal pieces of   except
written work Another communication shortcut   .
is an acronym, a word usually made from the frist   first
letter of a Series of other words. ZIP code is made   series
from zone improvement plann, and the origin of the   plan
word radar is radio detecting and ranging. Onse in   Once
a while initials are a shortcat, such as BLT for the   shortcut
famus bacon, lettuce, and tomato sandwich.   famous

Would the initials of your classmates be an efficient shortcut for purposes of
identification within your classroom?

Note the ability of each student to proofread for spelling, capitalization, and
punctuation errors.

Extend Spelling Assessment

Give this in-context assessment of Core Words within the frequencies 1–585 to students who need more practice or challenge.

Teaching Notes, page 342

THE SENTENCE DICTATION TEST

Students do not prestudy the words. Provide students with writing paper and pencil. Have students write the sentences as they are dictated.

For students who are overly challenged by the Sentence Dictation Test, yet who would benefit from the practice, here's a suggestion: Dictate the sentences. Then provide the answer—the written sentences—as a model from which students can proofread and correct their sentences. This, then, is not a spelling achievement test, but proofreading practice that can be graded for proofreading.

1. **Name seven famous people who currently work for the American government.**

2. **Tell whether they're from the north, south, east, or west part of the United States.**

3. **Among those you listed, who began public service late in life and who started early?**

4. **What do you think the yearly pay is for the top job of president?**

Words tested:

the (1), of (2), and (3), in (6), is (7), you (8), for (12), from (23), or (26), what (32), do (45), who (77), people (79), think (118), work (124), part (129), tell (147), name (155), those (182), life (208), began (215), year(ly) (225), top (269), United States (305), American (319), early (324), among (345), list(ed) (372), start(ed) (389), whether (399), job (500), government (558), north (581), seven (582), famous (583), late (584), pay (585), *they're (1010)

*The testing of they're (1010) is included to help students differentiate among the there/their/they're homophones.

Extra words: currently, east, president, public, service, south, west

AFTER THE SENTENCE DICTATION TEST

1. Have students write answers for the sentence requests. Then discuss their answers.

research, writing

2. Have students record the words they missed on the test in their Spelling Notebook (see page 345) for at-school study, and on a copy of the WORDS TO LEARN BLACKLINE MASTER, page 375, for at-home study.

recording words for personal study list

Many abbreviations no longer use periods, especially for numerical units (e.g., doz, ft). Exceptions are numerical abbreviations that, with no period, spell other words (e.g., no, in). No. is an abbreviation with two meanings—number and north. St. is an abbreviation that can stand for three words—street, Saint, and state.
- Have students find abbreviations that stand for more than one word.
- Have students find words that have more than one accepted abbreviation (e.g., tablespoon—T, tbsp).

— Word Test —

Schools Then and Now

(1) _______________ a big (2) _______________ between education in

(3) _______________ America and schools today. In the (4) _______________,

(5) _______________ weren't required to attend school. In fact, in the

(6) _______________, schools (7) _______________ closed during the cold winter

months and all schools (8) _______________ closed for summer. (9) _______________

of school, kids worked from sunup (10) _______________ (11) _______________ at

night helping (12) _______________ families on the farm or in business. Kids who

went to school (13) _______________ to read and write, (14) _______________ with

the (15) _______________ New England Primer that they memorized by

copying each page in perfect penmanship. Students memorized math "timetables"

and (16) _______________ dates in (17) _______________. Elocution, or

(18) _______________ speech and (19) _______________, required students to

recite tongue twisters (20) _______________, such as "(21) _______________

senseless sisters sleep." Indeed, all students had to (22) _______________

attention at school and do a lot of homework. Then schools changed.

(23) _______________ different now. What (24) _______________ contributed

to the changes? Why do you think this turnabout was good or bad?

Skill Test

Write a plural word in each box that follows the rule.

add s				
add es				
change y to i and add es				
change f or fe to v and add es				
change form				
no change				

Proofreading Test

Proofread for one spelling, capitalization, or punctuation error in the underlined parts. Circle errors. Write the corrections in the spaces.

You have <u>learned that writters</u> may use shortcuts   ____________________

for <u>writing some wards</u> or phrases. Occasionally,   ____________________

a writer may <u>use a contraction, blinded</u> word,   ____________________

abbreviation, clipped word, or <u>symbol in they're,</u>   ____________________

<u>writing rather then</u> the longer form. These short-   ____________________

cuts are fine <u>accept for very formal pieces</u> of   ____________________

<u>written work Another</u> communication shortcut   ____________________

is an acronym, a word <u>usually made from the frist</u>   ____________________

<u>letter of a Series of other</u> words. ZIP code is made   ____________________

from <u>zone improvement plann,</u> and the origin of the   ____________________

word radar is radio <u>detecting and ranging. Onse</u> in   ____________________

a while initials <u>are a shortcat, such</u> as BLT for the   ____________________

<u>famus bacon, lettuce, and tomato</u> sandwich.   ____________________

Would the initials of your classmates be an efficient shortcut for purposes of identification within your classroom?

Build Skills and Word Experiences

Use Student Practice Pages 52–53 to follow up instruction for:
Activity 1A • Build Skillful Writers

Build Visual Skills

Do the Word Preview, a visual warm-up activity, with all students.
Use Core Words **sleep** (586), **iron** (587), **trouble** (588), **store** (589), **beside** (590).

Teaching Notes, page 316

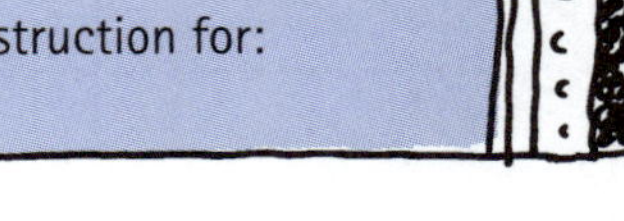

Build Spelling and Language Skills

Choose from among these quick tasks to customize instruction
for all or selected students.

Teaching Notes, page 319

He couldn't sleep.

I stored are food inside the old tree, but than I had troubel going to sleep. I
thought we had ironed out all the possible problems on this camping trip, but
may be a animal would come after dark.

(*our, then, trouble, maybe, an*)

sleepy, trouble, store, history, extra, slim, mystery, introduce, frost, slowly, most, control

(e.g., contains *sl/st/tr*; does/does not contain small word(s) inside; number of syllables)

buy, bought, send, sent, leave, left, ______

(present tense/past tense irregular *t*-ending verbs)

I had trouble finishing the assignment because ______.

Words that begin with the *be* syllable

(e.g., because, beside, become)

Have students write 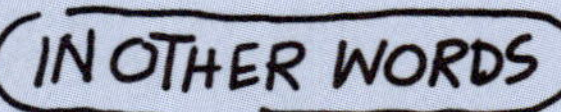: Let sleeping dogs lie.
Opportunity often masquerades as trouble.

Build Basic Concepts

Choose from among these skill-building activities to customize instruction for all or selected students.

Teaching Notes, page 325

concept one	A suffix is a letter or letters added to the end of a word.

1A Review the steps for adding suffixes to words (see Activity 1A, page 38).

Ask students to add suffixes to number words (e.g., seven—seventh, seventy, seventies).
- Note these exceptions to the spelling rule—*forty/fourth* and *ninety/ninth*.
- Have students answer in writing: What does remembering *forty forts* help avoid?

Ask students to write word forms for *store* (e.g., stores, stored, storing, storage, restore).
- Have students write more words with the *age* suffix (note that *mileage* is an exception to the rule).

Ask students to write word forms for *different* (e.g., differ, differs, differed, differing, difference, differences, indifferent).
- Have students write more *ent*-ending words that can become *ence*-ending words (e.g., absent/absence, confident/confidence, evident/evidence, present/presence, excellent/excellence, intelligent/intelligence).
- Help students discover that the *ant/ance* spelling pattern sounds the same as *ent/ence* and behaves the same (e.g., important/importance, brilliant/brilliance, distant/distance, assistant/assistance, ignorant/ignorance, elegant/elegance).
- Have students answer in writing: What's the difference between—*presents* and *presence, assistants* and *assistance*?

Ask students to write word forms for *trouble* (e.g., troubles, troubled, troubling, troublesome).
- Have students write more words to which the some suffix can be added (e.g., adventure/adventuresome, awe/awesome, lone/lonesome, whole/wholesome, bother/bothersome, quarrel/quarrelsome).

suffix practice, vocabulary development, spelling rules, spelling word patterns, making words, homophones

---

The Wordsmith Says

The words *persistence* and *perseverance* both mean "holding fast to a course of action."
- A person's persistence can be positive or negative—
  Positive: Her persistence in studying led to a top grade.
  Negative: Her persistence in getting her own way made her unliked.
- A person's perseverance is always positive because it suggests patience and courage—We admire his perseverance in training for the team.

Have students describe a story character who had persistence and one who had perseverance.

Does our language play tricks on us? The Wordsmith suggests you check these definitions in a dictionary to answer the question—indifferent and indifference.

Teaching Notes, page 328

Build Skillful Writers

Use these interrelated language learnings for all or selected students.

A skillful writer is admired for having proofreading perseverance. Some spellings are easier to remember by using a mnemonic device, such as—

> believe: do not be<u>lie</u>ve a lie
>
> piece: a <u>pie</u>ce of huckleberry pie
>
> forty: <u>fort</u>y forts
>
> principal: princi<u>pal</u> is your pal
>
> friend: fri<u>end</u> to the end
>
> because: <u>b</u>ig <u>e</u>lephants <u>c</u>an <u>a</u>lways <u>u</u>se <u>s</u>crambled <u>e</u>ggs
>
> they: just write <u>the</u>, then add <u>y</u>, it's as easy as eating pie
>
> there: here and <u>there</u>
>
> touch: there's an ouch in t<u>ouch</u>
>
> notice: not + ice = notice

Make a classroom chart of students' personal mnemonic devices for spelling tricky words.

Teaching Notes, page 329

Build Assessment Readiness

Use these at-school and at-home exercises to prepare all students for the Skill Test.

Skill to be tested:
comparisons

at-school Review comparatives/superlatives (Build Skillful Writers, page 102). Organize students into small groups with a large sheet of newsprint folded to make four boxes (two folds). Students number the boxes 2, 3, 4, 5. Post Teaching Poster 2. Tell students the numbers correspond to Rules 2, 3, 4, and 5 on the poster. Next, have students brainstorm *er/est* words to match the criterion for each box. Then have groups present their results to the class.

Skill to be tested:
comparisons

at-home Send home a copy of Take-Home Task 18 Blackline Master, page 157, with each student to encourage parent-child partnerships.

Teaching Notes, page 330

Build Proofreading Skills

Track students' ability to meet a minimum competency for spelling and proofreading within selected samples of their everyday writing.

• Send home papers for proofreading and a copy of the Ideas for Proofreading Blackline Master, page 373.

Have students redefine in rhyme: help from afar (distance assistance), wedding buggy (marriage carriage), twice the bother (double trouble).

Dear Parents,

Your child is learning to spell and use words that make comparisons. In this activity, your child adds er, meaning more (or less), to words. These er words are called comparatives. Your child also adds est, meaning most (or least), to words. These est words are called superlatives. The starting words are called positives.

Help your child use these strategies—

To add the er/est suffixes to words, the usual suffix rules apply.

- For most words, the er/est suffix is just added.
    bright   brighter   brightest
- For words that end in consonant-y, change y to i and add er/est.
    sleepy   sleepier   sleepiest
- For words that end in silent e, drop the e before adding er/est.
    strange   stranger   strangest
- For one syllable words (or if the last syllable of the word is stressed) that end in one vowel and one consonant, double the final consonant before adding er/est.
    big   bigger   biggest
- Usually the er/est suffixes are added to short words, while more (or less) and most (or least) are used with longer words.
    faster/fastest   more sorrowful/most sorrowful
- When a word ends in a suffix (including ful, ous, ive, less, able, and usually ly), more (or less) and most (or least) are used.
    more naturally   most naturally
- Some words do not follow the usual comparison patterns.
    good   better   best

Write the missing words in the boxes.

Positive	Comparative	Superlative
colorful		
	later	
northern		
troubled		
		straightest
friendly		
	drier	
		safest
useful		
	flatter	
willing		
early		
hungry		
blue		
		worst
sad		

Assess Words and Skills

- Spelling Words (words missed on tests) are recorded in the Spelling Notebook.
- Use Proof It, Practice Page 54, for proofreading/editing practice.

Teaching Notes, page 336

Assess Spelling Progress

Give this Cloze Story Word Test of Core Words within the frequencies 1–590 to all students. Words students miss are their Spelling Words.

THE CLOZE STORY WORD TEST

Students do not prestudy the words. Provide students with a copy of REVIEW 18 BLACKLINE MASTER, page 161. Tell students that this story is about sparsely populated lands that take up one-third of the earth's land surface.

Read the entire story aloud, including the test words. Then read it again slowly as students write the missing words.

Desert Land—A Wasteland or a Treasure?

A desert is land that (1) <u>does</u> not get much precipitation. Deserts get less than ten inches of precipitation a year! If (2) <u>you're</u> a person (3) <u>whose</u> (4) <u>sleep</u> has been (5) <u>troubled</u> by the rain rattling on (6) <u>your</u> roof, you may be content in the desert! But would you (7) <u>choose</u> to live in extreme heat? The highest temperatures on record are in the desert, (8) <u>although</u> not every desert is hot. (9) <u>It's</u> possible for deserts to be cold and dry. (10) <u>Their</u> only water is in the form of (11) <u>ice</u>. What problems may occur for (12) <u>humans</u> and other (13) <u>animals</u> living in such dry conditions?

Yet, it may be (14) <u>beside</u> the point (15) <u>whether</u> desert (16) <u>weather</u> conditions are dry and (17) <u>either</u> too hot or cold. A desert can be valuable land. In (18) <u>store</u> within (19) <u>its</u> land may be rich deposits of oil, gas, and (20) <u>iron</u> ore. (21) <u>Once</u> a wasteland, the (22) <u>largest</u> of Earth's deserts became a treasure when deposits of these resources were discovered. (23) <u>Which</u> desert is this, where is it, and why would these resources (24) <u>change</u> the importance of this land?

Words tested:
your (40), which (41), their (42), its (76), does (128), large(est) (185), once (206), it's (253), change (264), whether (399), either (409), animals (418), ice (441), although (450), weather (464), whose (520), you're (552), human(s) (575), choose (580), sleep (586), iron (587), trouble(d) (588), store (589), beside (590)

AFTER THE CLOZE STORY WORD TEST

research, hypothesizing, writing

1. Have students write and share their answers to the story questions. Discuss the problems of sustaining life for plants and animals on drastically dry lands that have extreme temperatures. Conclude that the largest desert is the Sahara, stretching across North Africa from the Atlantic Ocean to the Red Sea, and covering an area of over 3.5 million square miles. Discuss the importance of the Sahara's resources to the world economy and students' everyday life.

recording words for personal study list

2. Have students record the words they missed on the test in their Spelling Notebook (see page 338) for at-school study, and on a copy of the WORDS TO LEARN BLACKLINE MASTER, page 375, for at-home study.

Assess Skill Application

Give this assessment of spelling and related skills to all students.
The Review 18 Blackline Master is on page 162.

Teaching Notes, page 339

THE SKILL TEST

Write the missing words in the boxes.

Skill tested: comparisons

Positive	Comparative	Superlative
sleepy	sleepier	sleepiest
fair	fairer	fairest
doubtful	more doubtful	most doubtful
red	redder	reddest
foggy	foggier	foggiest
brave	braver	bravest
slim	slimmer	slimmest
recent	more recent	most recent
moist	moister	moistest

Note the ability of each student to make comparative and superlatives, and to write the positive (base) word from a comparative or superlative.

Assess Proofreading Application

Give this assessment of spelling and related skills to all students.
The Review 18 Blackline Master is on page 162.

Teaching Notes, page 341

THE PROOFREADING TEST

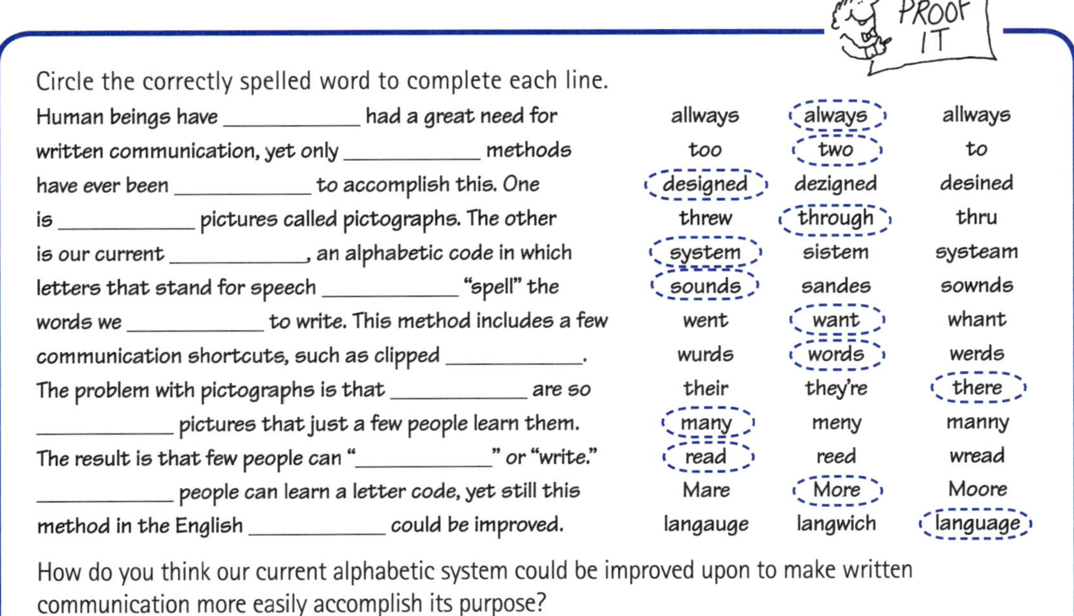

Circle the correctly spelled word to complete each line.

Human beings have ___________ had a great need for	allways	**always**	allways
written communication, yet only ___________ methods	too	**two**	to
have ever been ___________ to accomplish this. One	**designed**	dezigned	desined
is ___________ pictures called pictographs. The other	threw	**through**	thru
is our current ___________, an alphabetic code in which	**system**	sistem	systeam
letters that stand for speech ___________ "spell" the	**sounds**	sandes	sownds
words we ___________ to write. This method includes a few	went	**want**	whant
communication shortcuts, such as clipped ___________.	wurds	**words**	werds
The problem with pictographs is that ___________ are so	their	they're	**there**
___________ pictures that just a few people learn them.	**many**	meny	manny
The result is that few people can "___________" or "write."	**read**	reed	wread
___________ people can learn a letter code, yet still this	Mare	**More**	Moore
method in the English ___________ could be improved.	langauge	langwich	**language**

How do you think our current alphabetic system could be improved upon to make written communication more easily accomplish its purpose?

Note the ability of each student to proofread for spelling and capitalization errors.

Teaching Notes, page 342

Words tested:
of (2), a (4), to (5), in (6), is (7), you (8), that (9), for (12), on (14), are (15), is (16), but (31), there('s) (37), your (40), if (44), will (46), out (51), like(ly) (66), get (101), much (104), good (106), too (112), even (130), school (194), keep (199), sure(ly) (251), it's (253), thing(s) (258), example (261), morning (283), body (285), course (317), nothing (329), certain (353), strong (381), class (391), talk(ing) (398), problem (422), friend(s) (498), caught (527), yourself (534), you're (552), choose (580), late (584), sleep (586), iron (587), trouble (588), store (589), beside (590)

Extra words: cause, fights, sense, sit

making a list

recording words for
personal study list

Extend Spelling Assessment

Give this in-context assessment of Core Words within the frequencies 1–590 to students who need more practice or challenge.

THE SENTENCE DICTATION TEST

Students do not prestudy the words. Provide students with writing paper and pencil. Have students write the sentences as they are dictated.

1. There are certain things that will surely cause you nothing but trouble.

2. For example, there's a problem in store for you if you sleep too late on a school morning.

3. If you choose to sit beside your friends in class, you're likely to get caught talking too much.

4. Of course, it's good sense to keep yourself out of fights even if you're sure your body is as strong as iron.

AFTER THE SENTENCE DICTATION TEST

1. Have students extend this list of things that are sure to cause trouble.

2. Have students record the words they missed on the test in their Spelling Notebook (see page 345) for at-school study, and on a copy of the WORDS TO LEARN BLACKLINE MASTER, page 375, for at-home study.

Have students write (IN OTHER WORDS): Polite words open iron gates.
Serbo-Croatian proverb

— Word Test —

Desert Land—A Wasteland or a Treasure?

A desert is land that (1) _______________ not get much precipitation. Deserts

get less than ten inches of precipitation a year! If (2) _______________ a person

(3) _______________ (4) _______________ has been (5) _______________ by

the rain rattling on (6) _______________ roof, you may be content in the desert!

But would you (7) _______________ to live in extreme heat? The highest temperatures

on record are in the desert, (8) _______________ not every desert is hot.

(9) _______________ possible for deserts to be cold and dry. (10) _______________

only water is in the form of (11) _______________. What problems may occur for

(12) _______________ and other (13) _______________ living in such dry conditions?

Yet, it may be (14) _______________ the point (15) _______________ desert

(16) _______________ conditions are dry and (17) _______________ too hot or cold.

A desert can be valuable land. In (18) _______________ within (19) _______________

land may be rich deposits of oil, gas, and (20) _______________ ore. (21) _______________

a wasteland, the (22) _______________ of Earth's deserts became a treasure when

deposits of these resources were discovered. (23) _______________ desert is this,

where is it, and why would these resources (24) _______________ the importance

of this land?

Name _______________________________

Skill Test

Write the missing words in the boxes.

Positive	Comparative	Superlative
sleepy		
	fairer	fairest
doubtful		
moist		
red		
		foggiest
brave		
	slimmer	
recent		

Proofreading Test

Circle the correctly spelled word to complete each line.

Human beings have _______________ had a great need for   allways   always   allways

written communication, yet only _______________ methods   too   two   to

have ever been _______________ to accomplish this. One   designed   dezigned   desined

is _______________ pictures called pictographs. The other   threw   through   thru

is our current _______________, an alphabetic code in which   system   sistem   systeam

letters that stand for speech _______________ "spell" the   sounds   sandes   sownds

words we _______________ to write. This method includes a few   went   want   whant

communication shortcuts, such as clipped _______________.   wurds   words   werds

The problem with pictographs is that _______________ are so   their   they're   there

_______________ pictures that just a few people learn them.   many   meny   manny

The result is that few people can "_______________" or "write."   read   reed   wread

_______________ people can learn a letter code, yet still this   Mare   More   Moore

method in the English _______________ could be improved.   langauge   langwich   language

How do you think our current alphabetic system could be improved upon to make written communication more easily accomplish its purpose?

Build Skills and Word Experiences

Use Student Practice Pages 55–56 to follow up instruction for:
Activity 1A • Test Ready

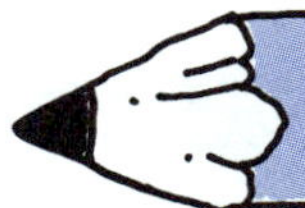

Build Visual Skills

Do the Word Preview, a visual warm-up activity, with all students.
Use Core Words **oil** (591), **modern** (592), **fun** (593), **catch** (594), **business** (595).

Teaching Notes, page 316

Build Spelling and Language Skills

Choose from among these quick tasks to customize instruction
for all or selected students.

Teaching Notes, page 319

No one could catch it.

School's are in the busness to teach. It's true that moderne schools try to teach more then schools of times passed and teachers try to make learning more fun.

(*Schools, business, modern, than, past*)

catch, marching, enriches, chalk, munch, coaching, each, mischief, chapter, much, exchanges

(e.g., position of *ch* in the words; number of syllables; does/doesn't contain small word(s) inside; does/doesn't have suffix)

oil, soil, noise, ______

(/oi/ words spelled *oi*)

The two businesses that I frequent most in my city are ______.

Synonyms for fun

(e.g., amusing, enjoyable)

Have students write 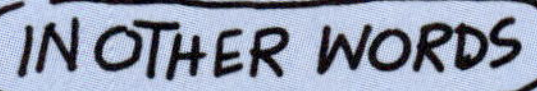

what is meant by *funny business*. Introduce Richard Peck's *A Long Way from Chicago*—the 1999 Newbery Honor Book—and *A Year Down Yonder*—the 2001 Newbery Medal winner. These books illustrate funny business at its best.

Teaching Notes, page 325

Build Basic Concepts

Choose from among these skill-building activities to customize instruction
for all or selected students.

concept one	Some sounds are spelled more than one way.

phonics, spelling word patterns,
hypothesizing, more words

1A Write *catch* and *teach* on the chalkboard. Ask students how the words are alike
(e.g., one syllable, /ch/ ending). Note that /ch/ is spelled *tch* and *ch*. Ask students
to speculate when *tch* is used and when *ch* is used. Have students collect words to
test their hypotheses. Conclude that /ch/ is usually spelled *tch* when a short vowel
immediately precedes the /ch/ ending and spelled *ch* when a consonant or a vowel
other than a short vowel immediately precedes the /ch/ ending (e.g., match; coach).
Exceptions to this usually consistent rule include *rich, much, such, which, watch,* and
sandwich.

Have students write (**IN OTHER WORDS**):   The early bird catches the worm.

Repeat the activity with /k/-ending words. Guide students to discover that most
often the spelling patterns are *ck* or *k/ke*. When students hear a short vowel sound
immediately preceding the /k/ ending, /k/ is usually spelled *ck* (e.g., smack), but if
they hear a consonant or vowel other than a short vowel immediately preceding the /k/
ending, /k/ is usually spelled *k* (e.g., milk). A long vowel usually signals a *ke* spelling
(e.g., stroke). Facilitate the discovery of less frequent ending patterns, such as *nk* (e.g.,
skunk), ic (e.g., basic), and *ch* (e.g., stomach).

Repeat the activity with /j/-ending words (ge/dge). Conclude that /j/ is usually spelled
dge when a short vowel immediately precedes the /j/ ending and spelled *ge* when a
consonant or a vowel other than a short vowel immediately precedes the /j/ ending
(e.g., badge; strange).

Nearly nine out of ten words with the /īz/ suffix are spelled ize, as in
modernize, memorize, organize, criticize. Some /īz/ words are spelled ise,
as in surprise, advertise, exercise, revise. Sometimes the ise does not
spell /īz/, as in promise. The least frequent pattern is yze, as in analyze
and paralyze. Further, /īz/ occurs at the end of /i/-ending words with the
s suffix, as in flies.
• Challenge students to find words for which ise or ize spellings are
   accepted. British spellings are usually ise, while American spellings
   are usually ize, and in some cases both are correct, but one is
   usually preferred (e.g., advertise, criticize).

phonics, suffix practice, spelling
word patterns, more words

1B Write *modern* on the chalkboard. Add the *ize* suffix. Ask students to find and write
more words that end with /īz/ to discover that it can be spelled *ize, ise,* or *yze.*

Build Skillful Writers

Use these interrelated language learnings for all or selected students.

Teaching Notes, page 328

Revisit Teaching Poster 1. Share this jingle with students:

Proofread your writing—it's something expected.

The Proofreading Posse cannot be neglected.

Indeed, careful spellers should take this advice,

And proofread their work—not one time, but twice.

Write the proverb on page 164 in a triangle as it appears here, including repetition of *the*.

Reveal the proverb. Tell students to read the familiar proverb silently. Then have students read it chorally—was one *the* omitted? Ask students to read the proverb again as you touch each word to help them discover the importance of seeing what is really there.

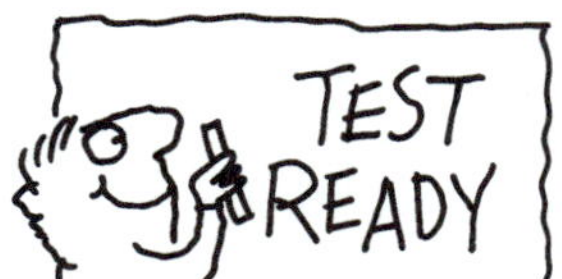

Build Assessment Readiness

Use these at-school and at-home exercises to prepare all students for the Skill Test.

Teaching Notes, page 329

at-school Have students fold paper to make two vertical columns labeled *oi* and *oy*. Then they find and write words for each column. Conclude that *oi* words outnumber *oy* words and that *oy* consistently spells /oi/ at the end of a word. Have student pairs use their /oi/ word banks to play tic-tac-toe. Students take turns asking their partner to spell an /oi/ word. If the word is written correctly, the student can make a mark on the tic-tac-toe game.

Skill to be tested:
/oi/ spelling patterns

at-home Send home a copy of TAKE-HOME TASK 19 BLACKLINE MASTER, page 166, with each student to encourage parent-child partnerships.

Skill to be tested:
/oi/ spelling patterns

Build Proofreading Skills

Track students' ability to meet a minimum competency for spelling and proofreading within selected samples of their everyday writing.

Teaching Notes, page 330

- Send home papers for proofreading and a copy of the IDEAS FOR PROOFREADING BLACKLINE MASTER, page 373.

Name ___________________________

Dear Parents,

One of the challenges of spelling is that many sounds can be spelled in more than one way. We are teaching your child the letters that most frequently spell certain sounds so that spelling can be learned systematically rather than simply memorized.

In this activity you can help your child practice the sound heard at the beginning of oil, spelled oi or oy. The oi spellings outnumber oy, but oy consistently spells the sound at the end of a word.

Have your child read the directions and explain to you what is expected. Then guide your child through the vocabulary-building lesson, letting your child do as much as possible without your help.

Circle words that have similar meanings in each row.

link	join	point	connect
moisten	fasten	dampen	soften
heroic	valiant	ointment	brave
doily	oyster	shellfish	boiling
voyage	journey	excursion	voice
employee	boss	worker	employment
commendable	loyal	faithful	affordable
bothering	annoying	irritating	troublesome
lure	famous	decoy	decay
destroy	destruct	debate	defend
lad	noise	boy	toy
choice	toil	labor	work
adjoining	neighboring	bordering	adjacent
enjoy	cowboy	dodge	avoid
point	poison	royal	noble
loiter	poise	boycott	linger
void	soiled	oily	empty
natural	joy	pleasure	delight

Next, find and write the words with the sound you hear at the beginning of oil. Sort the words by spelling pattern.

Assess Words and Skills

- Spelling Words (words missed on tests) are recorded in the Spelling Notebook.
- Use Proof It, Practice Page 57, for proofreading/editing practice.

Assess Spelling Progress

Give this Cloze Story Word Test of Core Words within the frequencies 1–595 to all students. Words students miss are their Spelling Words.

Teaching Notes, page 336

 **THE CLOZE STORY WORD TEST**

Students do not prestudy the words. Provide students with a copy of REVIEW 19 BLACKLINE MASTER, page 170. Tell students that this story is about the light produced to make the darkness bright.

Read the entire story aloud, including the test words. Then read it again slowly as students write the missing words.

Light at Night

Firelight was the (1) <u>first</u> way to produce light at nighttime to extend (2) <u>natural</u> daylight (3) <u>hours</u>. Sometimes the flame was from a campfire, (4) <u>oil</u> lamp, candle, or gaslight. Then Thomas Edison, an (5) <u>American</u>, invented the (6) <u>modern</u> electric light, but it (7) <u>didn't</u> (8) <u>catch</u> on quickly. People (9) <u>thought</u> of it as a (10) <u>fun</u> novelty (11) <u>instead</u> of a practical item. It was years (12) <u>before</u> electric light (13) <u>became</u> a household and (14) <u>business</u> convenience. Over the years, more (15) <u>energy</u> sources for light were invented. (16) <u>Examples</u> include neon lights, fluorescent tubes, and flashlights. The flashlight (17) <u>began</u> as an "electric flowerpot." It was a spotlight that rose up (18) <u>through</u> a pot to illuminate a houseplant, (19) <u>except</u> it (20) <u>never</u> sold well. With a (21) <u>large</u> overstock of this product, Conrad Hubert used the lights from the pots to make "portable lights." (22) <u>Its</u> success was immediate! The Eveready Flashlight Company was the outcome. Why do you (23) <u>suppose</u> the flashlight was popular, (24) <u>though</u> the electric flowerpot wasn't accepted? What ways are (25) <u>there</u> to make the darkness (26) <u>bright</u> today?

Words tested:
there (37), first (74), its (76), through (102), never (167), thought (179), large (185), began (215), example(s) (261), didn't (281), American (319), though (330), before (332), became (334), instead (408), hour(s) (480), energy (511), bright (541), except (550), suppose (555), natural (556), oil (591), modern (592), fun (593), catch (594), business (595)

 **AFTER THE CLOZE STORY WORD TEST**

1. Have students write and share their answers to the story questions. Discuss the different lights we use today (e.g., headlights, holiday lights, searchlights, candelabras, laser beams, fog beacons, stoplights) and their purposes.

reasoning, writing

2. Have students record the words they missed on the test in their Spelling Notebook (see page 338) for at-school study, and on a copy of the WORDS TO LEARN BLACKLINE MASTER, page 375, for at-home study.

recording words for personal study list

Teaching Notes, page 339

Assess Skill Application

Give this assessment of spelling and related skills to all students.
The REVIEW 19 BLACKLINE MASTER is on page 171.

 **THE SKILL TEST**

Skill tested:
/oi/ spelling patterns

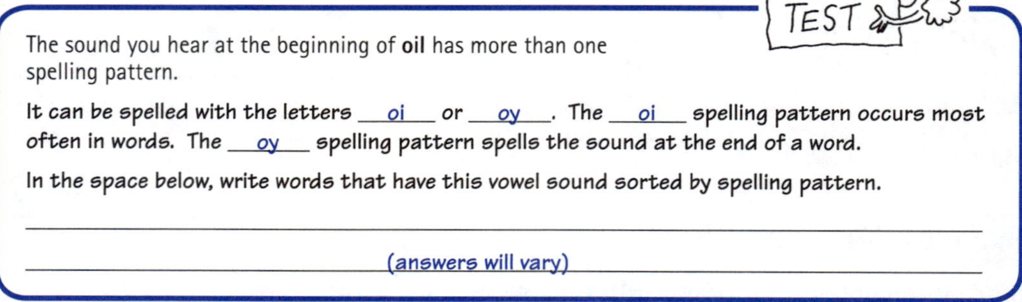

The sound you hear at the beginning of **oil** has more than one spelling pattern.

It can be spelled with the letters ___oi___ or ___oy___. The ___oi___ spelling pattern occurs most often in words. The ___oy___ spelling pattern spells the sound at the end of a word.

In the space below, write words that have this vowel sound sorted by spelling pattern.

(answers will vary)

Note the ability of each student to identify /oi/ spelling patterns and to spell /oi/ words.

Teaching Notes, page 341

Assess Proofreading Application

Give this assessment of spelling and related skills to all students.
The REVIEW 19 BLACKLINE MASTER is on page 171.

 **THE PROOFREADING TEST**

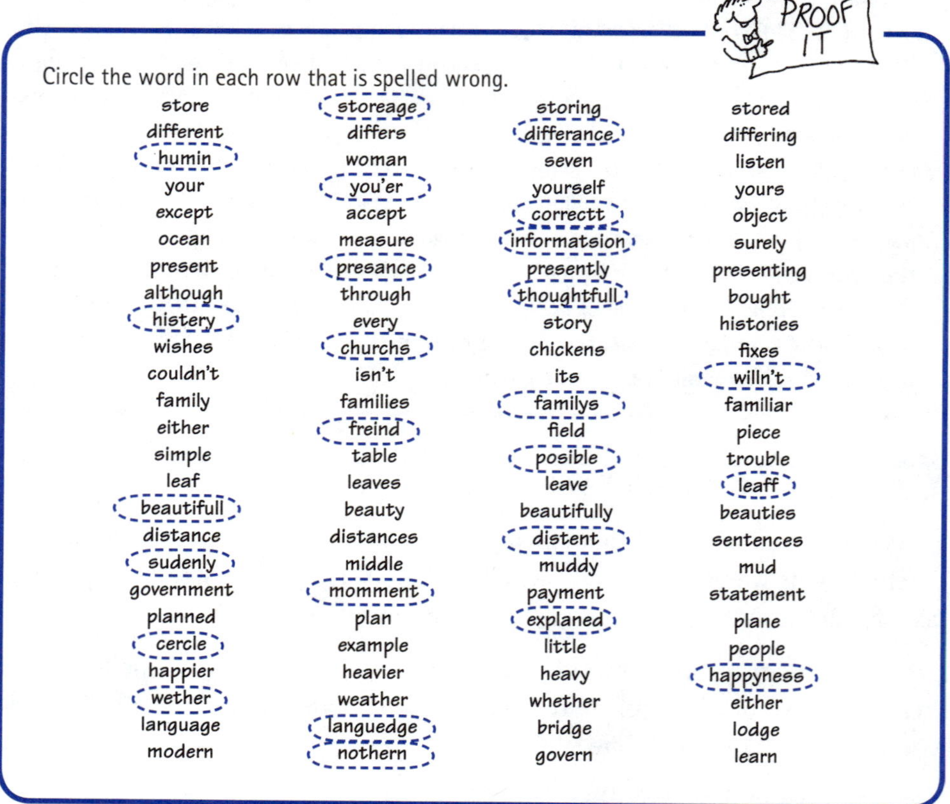

Circle the word in each row that is spelled wrong.

store	storeage	storing	stored
different	differs	differance	differing
humin	woman	seven	listen
your	you'er	yourself	yours
except	accept	correctt	object
ocean	measure	informatsion	surely
present	presance	presently	presenting
although	through	thoughtfull	bought
histery	every	story	histories
wishes	churchs	chickens	fixes
couldn't	isn't	its	willn't
family	families	familys	familiar
either	freind	field	piece
simple	table	posible	trouble
leaf	leaves	leave	leaff
beautifull	beauty	beautifully	beauties
distance	distances	distent	sentences
sudenly	middle	muddy	mud
government	momment	payment	statement
planned	plan	explaned	plane
cercle	example	little	people
happier	heavier	heavy	happyness
wether	weather	whether	either
language	languedge	bridge	lodge
modern	nothern	govern	learn

Note the ability of each student to proofread for spelling errors.

Extend Spelling Assessment

Give this in-context assessment of Core Words within the frequencies
1–595 to students who need more practice or challenge.

Teaching Notes, page 342

THE SENTENCE DICTATION TEST

Students do not prestudy the words. Provide students with writing paper and pencil.
Have students write the sentences as they are dictated.

1. There are several different cooking oils you can buy in a modern supermarket.

2. Vegetable oil is used a lot for making other foods, such as salad dressing.

3. It's fun to catch fish and fry them in hot oil over your campfire.

4. Oil is important in our lives as a common food, but another kind of oil is really big business.

Words tested:

of (2), and (3), a (4), to (5), in (6), is (7), you (8), for (12), are (15), as (16), but (31), there (37), can (38), your (40), them (52), other (60), make(ing) (72), over (82), use(d) (88), our (109), another (121), such (133), different (139), big (158), important (195), food(s) (198), kind (214), live(s) (217), it's (253), several (263), fish (299), really (313), hot (368), common (395), buy (502), oil(s) (591), modern (592), fun (593), catch (594), business (595)

Extra words: campfire, cooking, dressing, fry, lot, salad, supermarket, vegetable

AFTER THE SENTENCE DICTATION TEST

1. Have students identify the "big business" referred to in the last sentence. Oil, fossil fuel, is an important energy source worldwide. Have students explain in writing why this industry would be considered "big business." How does this business influence lives locally?

writing an explanation

2. Have students record the words they missed on the test in their Spelling Notebook (see page 345) for at-school study, and on a copy of the WORDS TO LEARN BLACKLINE MASTER, page 375, for at-home study.

recording words for personal study list

Why did the baker stop baking doughnuts? He got tired of the hole business!

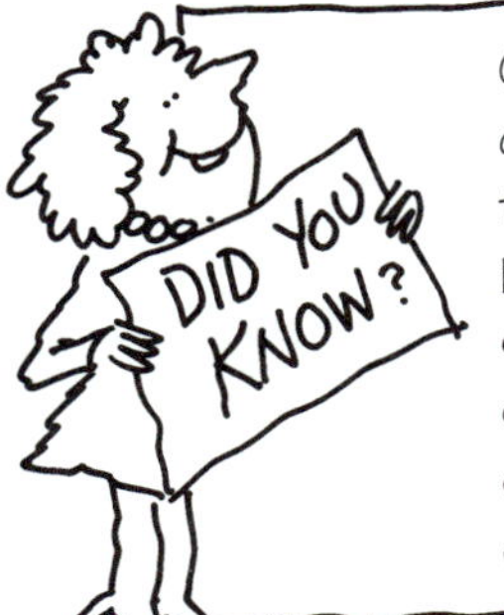

Once students make word banks to illustrate skill lessons, the word collections can be used for multiple skill-building activities. For example, the /ch/, /k/, and /j/-ending words gathered in Activity 1A of this unit could be used to:

- play bingo (Activity 1C, page 20)
- sort by parts of speech
- play a word chain game (Test Ready, page 129)
- make a word-search game (page 391)
- make compound words
- identify antonyms
- identify homophones
- add prefixes/suffixes

Word Test

Light at Night

Firelight was the (1) _______________ way to produce light at nighttime to extend

(2) _______________ daylight (3) _______________. Sometimes the flame was

from a campfire, (4) _______________ lamp, candle, or gaslight. Then Thomas

Edison, an (5) _______________, invented the (6) _______________ electric light, but it

(7) _______________ (8) _______________ on quickly. People (9) _______________ of

it as a (10) _______________ novelty (11) _______________ of a practical item. It

was years (12) _______________ electric light (13) _______________ a household

and (14) _______________ convenience. Over the years, more (15) _______________

sources for light were invented. (16) _______________ include neon lights,

fluorescent tubes, and flashlights. The flashlight (17) _______________ as an

"electric flowerpot." It was a spotlight that rose up (18) _______________ a pot to

illuminate a houseplant, (19) _______________ it (20) _______________ sold well.

With a (21) _______________ overstock of this product, Conrad Hubert used the

lights from the pots to make "portable lights." (22) _______________ success

was immediate! The Eveready Flashlight Company was the outcome. Why do you

(23) _______________ the flashlight was popular, (24) _______________ the

electric flowerpot wasn't accepted? What ways are (25) _______________ to make

the darkness (26) _______________ today?

Skill Test

The sound you hear at the beginning of **oil** has more than one spelling pattern.

It can be spelled with the letters ____________ or ____________.

The ____________ spelling pattern occurs most often in words.

The ____________ spelling pattern spells the sound at the end of a word.

In the space below, write words that have this vowel sound sorted by spelling pattern.

____

____

____

____

Proofreading Test

Circle the word in each row that is spelled wrong.

store	storeage	storing	stored
different	differs	differance	differing
humin	woman	seven	listen
your	you'er	yourself	yours
except	accept	correctt	object
ocean	measure	informatsion	surely
present	presance	presently	presenting
although	through	thoughtfull	bought
histery	every	story	histories
wishes	churchs	chickens	fixes
couldn't	isn't	its	willn't
family	families	familys	familiar
either	freind	field	piece
simple	table	posible	trouble
leaf	leaves	leave	leaff
beautifull	beauty	beautifully	beauties
distance	distances	distent	sentences
sudenly	middle	muddy	mud
government	momment	payment	statement
planned	plan	explaned	plane
cercle	example	little	people
happier	heavier	heavy	happyness
wether	weather	whether	either
language	languedge	bridge	lodge
modern	nothern	govern	learn

Build Skills and Word Experiences

Use Student Practice Pages 58–59 to follow up instruction for:
Activity 1A • Build Skillful Writers

Build Visual Skills

Do the Word Preview, a visual warm-up activity, with all students.
Use Core Words **reach** (596), **lot** (597), **won't** (598), **case** (599), **speak** (600).

Teaching Notes, page 316

Build Spelling and Language Skills

Choose from among these quick tasks to customize instruction
for all or selected students.

Teaching Notes, page 319

He could barely reach it.

Pat is trying to reach her mother. She needs to speak to her, becaus
she lost her case with her glass'es in it. Her mother wont be happy.
pat has alot of trouble keeping track of her things.

(*because, glasses, won't, Pat, a lot*)

speak, happy, doze, talk, nap, glad, sleep, say, rest, utter, merry, voice

(*e.g., words that are synonyms; does/does not have double letters; number of letters*)

distant/distance, assistant/assistance, brilliant/brillance, ______ / ______

(*ant/ance-ending words*)

Another language I would like to learn to speak is ______.

Words that double the final consonant before the addition of a suffix
beginning with a vowel

(*e.g., red, forget*)

Build Basic Concepts

Choose from among these skill-building activities to customize instruction for all or selected students.

Teaching Notes, page 325

| **concept one** | A knowledge of Latin roots unlocks the meaning of many words. |

1A Latin roots are the basis of many English words. Revisit Latin roots explored in Level 4:

vocabulary development, writing an explanation

- the *voc* root means "call" (e.g., vocabulary, vocal)
- the *port* root means "carry" (e.g., transport, portable)
- the *ped* root means "foot" (e.g., pedestrian, pedal)
- the *struct* root means "build" (e.g., construct, structure)

Introduce the *dict* root that comes to us from the Latin verb, dictare, meaning "speak." Ask students how this root influences English vocabulary (e.g., dictionary, diction, dictation, dictator, predict, contradict).

Introduce the *contra* prefix meaning "against" and ask students to explain in writing the meaning of *contradict*.

The literal meanings of words do not always conform to meanings they have acquired. For example, *dictator* has a negative connotation because of the tyrants for which it has been used. *Addict* is a combination of the prefix *ad* (to) and *dict* (speak) which initially was its meaning. Now, the word is associated with drug use. So, a knowledge of word parts and their meanings is useful—to a point, because language use is always changing.

| **concept two** | Some verbs have irregular verb forms. |

2A Ask students how the past tense of most verbs is formed (add *ed*). These are called regular verbs (e.g., reach/reached). Write *speak* on the chalkboard and ask students for its past tense (spoke). Identify it as an irregular verb. Irregular verbs do not form the past tense by adding *ed*, instead a new word is used.

verb forms, irregular verbs, writing words, proofreading, vocabulary development, multiple meanings, writing sentences

Next, dictate present tense verbs for students to write with their past tense forms: *break/broke, draw/drew, drive/drove, feel/felt, grind/ground, leave/left, rise/rose, see/saw.* Write the words on the chalkboard, or have a student do so, for students to self-check. Note that each past tense verb has more than one meaning. Following the dictation, have students use selected past tense verbs in written sentences to illustrate the different meanings.

Teaching Notes, page 328

Build Skillful Writers

Use these interrelated language learnings for all or selected students.

Students know that prefixes, roots, and base words form the foundation for the meaning of words. Note how "spacing" contributes to meaning. Demonstrate with *may be* and *maybe*:

> *Maybe* (perhaps) Beth is sick.   Beth *may be* (could be) sick.

Organize students into small groups. Ask students to explain in writing how the meaning is changed when these words are written as one word and two words:

a way/away	*a long/along*
on to/onto	*in to/into*
every day/everyday	*a part/apart*
all together/altogether	*all ways/always*

Note that *a lot* is never one word. Contrast the two meanings of *a lot*, and then discuss *allot*.

Teaching Notes, page 329

Build Assessment Readiness

Use these at-school and at-home exercises to prepare all students for the Skill Test.

Skill to be tested:
suffixes *s, es, ed, ing, ly, ful*

at-school   Post Teaching Poster 2 to review the process of suffix additions. Have students apply this process to nonsense words to demonstrate understanding. Write these nonsense words randomly on the chalkboard and have students sort them by the rule that states the action necessary to add the *s, ed, ing, ly,* and *ful* suffixes. Then they add the suffixes. Discuss the spellings with the suffix additions and why each rule applies.

Rule 1: *teesp, bray, chell*	**Rule 2:** *mune, whabe, scrime*
Rule 3: *kaf, strim, zib*	**Rule 4:** *brady, shenty, nofy*
Rule 5: *jiss, potch, nish*	

Later, have students reverse the process and return the nonsense words with the suffixes to their base form.

Skill to be tested:
suffixes *s, es, ed, ing, ly, ful*

at-home   Send home a copy of Take-Home Task 20 Blackline Master, **page 175**, with each student to encourage parent-child partnerships.

Teaching Notes, page 330

Build Proofreading Skills

Track students' ability to meet a minimum competency for spelling and proofreading within selected samples of their everyday writing.

- Send home papers for proofreading and a copy of the Ideas for Proofreading Blackline Master, **page 373**.

Name ____

Dear Parents,

In this activity your child will be identifying words with suffixes. Suffixes are word parts your child has learned to add to the end of some words or roots to make more words.

reaches   reached   reaching

Begin by having your child read the directions and explain to you what is expected. Then guide your child through the activity, as well as help your child interpret the proverbs or sayings.

Find words that have a suffix. Underline the suffix.

1. Don't count your chickens before they are hatched.

2. Absolute power corrupts absolutely.

3. Don't cry over spilled milk.

4. Everything's coming up roses.

5. The eyes are bigger than the stomach.

6. Don't jump from the frying pan into the fire.

7. First come, first served.

8. Gone, but not forgotten.

9. A good beginning is half the battle.

10. The handwriting is on the wall.

11. The pen is mightier than the sword.

12. A house divided against itself cannot stand.

13. It is better to travel carefully than to arrive.

14. A liar is not believed when he speaks the truth.

15. A person who makes no mistakes usually does not make anything.

16. Actions speak louder than words.

There's more! Now, have your child write each underlined word without its suffix.
Thanks, parents!

Assess Words and Skills

- Spelling Words (words missed on tests) are recorded in the Spelling Notebook.
- Use Proof It, Practice Page 60, for proofreading/editing practice.

Teaching Notes, page 336

Assess Spelling Progress

Give this Cloze Story Word Test of Core Words within the frequencies 1–600 to all students. Words students miss are their Spelling Words.

THE CLOZE STORY WORD TEST

Students do not prestudy the words. Provide students with a copy of REVIEW 20 BLACKLINE MASTER, page 179. Tell students that this story is about a few of the difficulties in using our language correctly that they will surely be able to relate to!

Read the entire story aloud, including the test words. Then read it again slowly as students write the missing words.

Words tested:
a (4), there (37), their (42), different(ly) (139), often (186), almost (216), let('s) (230), example(s) (261), several (263), matter(s) (386), piece (392), understand (416), language (499), single (509), explain (513), straight (524), except (550), figure (551), you're (552), woman (577), business (595), reach (596), lot (597), won't (598), case (599), speak (600), *they're (1010)

*The testing of they're (1010) is included to help students differentiate among the there/their/they're homophones.

In Plain English

Do you (1) <u>speak</u> and (2) <u>understand</u> English? (3) <u>Let's</u> see. If a (4) <u>woman</u> said, "I bought (5) <u>a lot</u> today," what conclusion would you (6) <u>reach</u>? You might (7) <u>figure</u> that she'd been on a shopping trip and made (8) <u>several</u> purchases. Good guess, (9) <u>except</u> (10) <u>you're</u> wrong! She bought a (11) <u>piece</u> of property! As you know, words (12) <u>often</u> have more than one meaning. Now, to make (13) <u>matters</u> worse, consider the word allot. Look it up in the dictionary so in (14) <u>case</u> you see or hear it, it (15) <u>won't</u> confuse you further. Wow! Watch out for just plain old English! It's tricky (16) <u>business</u>. Our (17) <u>language</u> is confusing! Words with many meanings and homophones are two (18) <u>examples</u>. Homophones sound the same but are spelled (19) <u>differently</u>. For (20) <u>almost</u> everyone, the (21) <u>single</u> most difficult set is there, their, and they're. Then, just when you've learned (22) <u>their</u> differences, (23) <u>there</u> are there's and theirs to keep (24) <u>straight</u>! List words that are the hardest for you to use and spell correctly and (25) <u>explain</u> why (26) <u>they're</u> so annoying.

AFTER THE CLOZE STORY WORD TEST

writing

1. Have students share their written answers to the story requests. Review the challenges the English language poses and the importance of using and spelling words correctly.

recording words for personal study list

2. Have students record the words they missed on the test in their Spelling Notebook (see page 338) for at-school study, and on a copy of the WORDS TO LEARN BLACKLINE MASTER, page 375, for at-home study.

Assess Skill Application

Give this assessment of spelling and related skills to all students.
The Review 20 Blackline Master is on page 180.

Teaching Notes, page 339

THE SKILL TEST

Add the **s** or **es** suffix.

| choose | chooses | reach | reaches | lot | lots |

Add the **ed** suffix.

| travel | traveled | cry | cried | trip | tripped |

Add the **ing** suffix.

| catch | catching | correct | correcting | store | storing |

Add the **ly** suffix.

| happy | happily | strange | strangely | colorful | colorfully |

Add the **ful** suffix.

| wish | wishful | pain | painful | use | useful |

Skill tested:
suffixes *s, es, ed, ing, ly, ful*

Note the ability of each student to add the *s, es, ed, ing, ly,* and *ful* suffixes to base words.

Assess Proofreading Application

Give this assessment of spelling and related skills to all students.
The Review 20 Blackline Master is on page 180.

Teaching Notes, page 341

THE PROOFREADING TEST

If any of the underlined words in each line are incorrect for spelling or grammar, write the correction in the space.

Our <u>Englesh language</u> developed over time from   English
<u>seviral different</u> languages. It is somewhat like   several
an old patchwork quilt that <u>alot of people</u> had a   a lot
hand in making. Not all <u>peices are sewed together</u>   pieces
evenly, the edges have <u>became worn over</u> time,   become
and some additional <u>patchs have been</u> stitched   patches
onto it, as needed. Nonetheless, <u>no one conseders</u>   considers
<u>startting all over</u> to create a new quilt. The old one   starting
<u>isno't perfect, but</u> it's used anyway. It's what we   isn't
are <u>used to using.</u> <u>That's</u> the way it is with many
things. <u>Sometimes what we have is</u> far from ideal,
yet <u>we pach it up the best</u> we can and tolerate the   patch
inconveniences <u>rather then beginning</u> anew.   than

What changes do you think would need to be made to make our language work more efficiently?

Note the ability of each student to proofread for errors.

Teaching Notes, page 342

Extend Spelling Assessment

Give this in-context assessment of Core Words within the frequencies
1–600 to students who need more practice or challenge.

Words tested:
the (1), of (2), a (4), to (5), in (6), is (7), it (10), are (15), as (16), they('re) (19), be (21), this (22), not (30), there (37), an (39), about (48), them (52), make(s) (72), who (77), people (79), just (97), think(ing) (118), because (127), number (145), large (185), often (186), don't (190), going (192), point (272), group (295), front (318), before (332), able (346), dog (347), feel(ing) (355), talk (398), listen(ers) (507), except (550), you're (552), natural (556), reach (596), lot (597), won't (598), case (599), speak(ing) (600)

Extra words: convince, emergency, sick, simply

THE SENTENCE DICTATION TEST

Students do not prestudy the words. Provide students with writing paper and pencil.
Have students write the sentences as they are dictated.

1. There are a lot of people who simply won't speak in front of a large group.

2. Except in the case of an emergency, you're not going to be able to convince them to talk.

3. This is because they're people who don't feel natural speaking before a large number of listeners.

4. Just thinking about it often makes them reach the point of feeling as sick as a dog.

AFTER THE SENTENCE DICTATION TEST

writing a description, writing an explanation

1. Have students describe in writing how they feel about speaking in front of others and why they either like it or don't like it. Then explain how practice can help people learn to do something they initially were uncomfortable doing.

similes, writing

2. Note with students that the last sentence dictation sentences employs a simile—*as sick as a dog*. Review similes and their use with the words *as/like*. Then have students write more similes.

recording words for personal study list

3. Have students record the words they missed on the test in their Spelling Notebook (see page 345) for at-school study, and on a copy of the WORDS TO LEARN BLACKLINE MASTER, page 375, for at-home study.

Our language began in Britain, its vocabulary the result of many influences. When different cultures forced their rule on the island, parts of their language were also forced upon the people—German dialects, the Roman language of Julius Caesar, the French language when William of Normandy conquered the island. Priests and scholars influenced the language with Latin, the language they spoke and wrote. Doctors and scientists brought Greek words to the language. Years later, we use the language that became a combination of it all, known as English.

• Have students investigate the first dictionaries (1604, Robert Cowdry; 1775, Samuel Johnson) and explore how our oral language changed, but spellings were "frozen" in print.

— Word Test —

In Plain English

Do you (1) _________________ and (2) _________________ English? (3) _________________ see. If a (4) _________________ said, "I bought (5) _________________ today," what conclusion would you (6) _________________? You might (7) _________________ that she'd been on a shopping trip and made (8) _________________ purchases. Good guess, (9) _________________ (10) _________________ wrong! She bought a (11) _________________ of property! As you know, words (12) _________________ have more than one meaning. Now, to make (13) _________________ worse, consider the word allot. Look it up in the dictionary so in (14) _________________ you see or hear it, it (15) _________________ confuse you further. Wow! Watch out for just plain old English! It's tricky (16) _________________. Our (17) _________________ is confusing! Words with many meanings and homophones are two (18) _________________. Homophones sound the same, but are spelled (19) _________________. For (20) _________________ everyone, the (21) _________________ most difficult set is there, their, and they're. Then, just when you've learned (22) _________________ differences, (23) _________________ are there's and theirs to keep (24) _________________! List words that are the hardest for you to use and spell correctly and (25) _________________ why (26) _________________ so annoying.

Skill Test

Add the **s** or **es** suffix.

choose____________________   reach____________________   lot____________________

Add the **ed** suffix.

travel____________________   cry____________________   trip____________________

Add the **ing** suffix.

catch____________________   correct____________________   store____________________

Add the **ly** suffix.

happy____________________   strange____________________   colorful____________________

Add the **ful** suffix.

wish____________________   pain____________________   use____________________

Proofreading Test

If any of the underlined words in each line are incorrect for spelling or grammar, write the correction in the space.

Our <u>Englesh language</u> developed over time from   ____________________

<u>seviral different</u> languages. It is somewhat like   ____________________

an old patchwork quilt that <u>alot of people</u> had a   ____________________

hand in making. Not all <u>peices are sewed together</u>   ____________________

evenly, the edges have <u>became worn over</u> time,   ____________________

and some additional <u>patchs have been</u> stitched   ____________________

onto it, as needed. Nonetheless, <u>no one conseders</u>   ____________________

<u>startting all over</u> to create a new quilt. The old one   ____________________

<u>isno't perfect, but</u> it's used anyway. It's what we   ____________________

are <u>used to using. That's</u> the way it is with many   ____________________

things. <u>Sometimes what we have is</u> far from ideal,   ____________________

yet <u>we pach it up the best</u> we can and tolerate the   ____________________

inconveniences <u>rather then beginning</u> anew.   ____________________

What changes do you think would need to be made to make our language work more efficiently?

Build Skills and Word Experiences

Use Student Practice Pages 61–62 to follow up instruction for:
Activity 1C • Build Skillful Writers

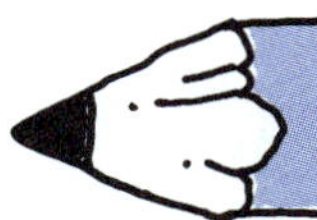

Build Visual Skills

Do the Word Preview, a visual warm-up activity, with all students.
Use Core Words **shape** (601), **eight** (602), **edge** (603), **soft** (604), **village** (605).

Teaching Notes, page 316

Build Spelling and Language Skills

Choose from among these quick tasks to customize instruction
for all or selected students.

Teaching Notes, page 319

We drove right to the edge.

We edged a long the woods near our vilage. In this game, are eight
players where out to get the other players flag. Me and the others walked
softly until we saw the shape of their flag. Would we win after all.

(*along, village, our, were, players', The others and I, ?*)

shape, eight, chain, neighbor, plane, maiden, tale, contain, vein, wait, sale, reign

(e.g., by long *a* spelling pattern; is/isn't homophone; number of syllables)

edge, lodge, fudge, _______

(words ending in *dge*)

Traffic signs have different shapes. For example, _______.

Comparison words

(e.g., er/est)

Teaching Notes, page 325

Build Basic Concepts

Choose from among these skill-building activities to customize instruction for all or selected students.

concept one	A knowledge of Greek and Latin roots unlocks the meaning of many words.

prefix/root/suffix practice, vocabulary development, making words, writing an explanation

1A Review Latin roots (Activity 1A, page 173). Introduce the Latin root *form* that means "shape" or "form." Have students brainstorm words containing *form* (e.g., reform, conformist, information, transform, deformity, formulate, format). Model how the meaning of the word parts shape the meaning of the words, such as:

re (again) + *form* (to shape) + *er* (one who) = reformer
  • What topic might a present-day reformer want to bring to our attention?

con (with/together) + *form* (to shape) + *ist* (one who) = *conformist*
  • What do you think a conformist your age might wear to school?

Add *non* to *conformist*. Ask students to explain in writing how one person's nonconformity could lead to something positive, while another's results in something negative.

vocabulary development, number roots, research, writing questions

1B Write on the chalkboard: *octopus, octet, octagon*. Then ask students to predict the meaning of the root *oct* (eight). Discuss how *eight* relates to the meaning of the words. Review number prefixes (Word Mysteries and Histories, page 16). Then pose questions, such as: How many horns on a triceratops? (tri/three) How many quarts make a gallon? (qua, quad/four) Next ask students to research and write number prefix questions to pose to their classmates.

vocabulary development, reading, phonics, class book

1C Point out the *ei* spelling of *eight*. Have students brainstorm and sort *ie/ei* words (e.g., believe, belief, field, niece, shield, piece, view, thief, mischief, yield, pie, friend, frontier, weird, caffeine, their, either, foreign, weight, neighbor, receive, beige, protein). Write this rhyme on the chalkboard or on a chart for students to read chorally.

The Weirdos

All our friends and our neighbors say it's hard to believe,

That spelling some words is so hard to achieve!

Is it i-e or e-i? Can you seize them relief?

These mischievous weirdos are the height of their grief.

Create a class book of *ie/ei* spellings titled *The Weirdos*. Have students copy the rhyme as their opening page, writing the *ie/ei* letters in color.

WORD MYSTERIES AND HISTORIES

October is the tenth month, yet students learned in this unit that oct means "eight." How can that be? Shouldn't October be named December, the dec root meaning "ten"? It makes sense if you know the Roman year originally began in March, making October the eighth month and December the tenth.

• Challenge students to research the origins for the names of the months. Then have students write the names of the months and their abbreviations.

Build Skillful Writers

Use these interrelated language learnings for all or selected students.

Teaching Notes, page 328

Ask students to brainstorm instances in which capital letters should be used. Then have students sort their examples (e.g., names of people, names of places, titles, months/days, etc.). Next, ask students to ponder questions, such as these:

- Are the names of months always capitalized? (Yes. Discuss *March/march* and *May/may*.)
- Are the names of the days of the week always capitalized? (Yes.)
- Are *mother* and *father* always capitalized? (No, only when they stand for their name—*It's Mom's birthday/It's my mom's birthday*.)
- Is *village* capitalized? (Discuss *a village/Greenwich Village*.)
- Is *ocean* capitalized? (Discuss *Pacific Ocean/an ocean*.)

Then have students write more capitalization questions to pose to the class.

Build Assessment Readiness

Use these at-school and at-home exercises to prepare all students for the Skill Test.

Teaching Notes, page 329

at-school Say *eight ate* and *they're there*. Ask students what you mean. Then write on the chalkboard: *Eight ate. They're there*. The spelling of the homophones provides clarity, if the spellings are correct. Present this written description to students for editing, as well as a chuckle (the passage is on Take-Home Task 21 if you wish to copy the section for this lesson).

> It's Thanksgiving and we can smell Mother's foul cooking. Our ants have joined us for dinner. They brought a nice desert, lovely flours, and a small fur box of current tees. It's really their presents that counts.

Review *there/their/they're/there's/theirs*. Have students write sentences using the homophones, but leaving a blank for the homophone. Then students exchange sentences and fill in the words. Have students proofread together, using their Spell Check card for a reference.

Skill to be tested:
homophones—*there, their, they're, there's, theirs*

at-home Send home a copy of Take-Home Task 21 Blackline Master, page 184, with each student to encourage parent-child partnerships.

Skill to be tested:
homophones—*there, their, they're, there's, theirs*

Build Proofreading Skills

Track students' ability to meet a minimum competency for spelling and proofreading within selected samples of their everyday writing.

Teaching Notes, page 330

- Send home papers for proofreading and a copy of the Ideas for Proofreading Blackline Master, page 373.

Dear Parents,

Earlier in the year, you worked with your child on homophones. Their correct spelling and use is essential. Otherwise, the writer risks being labeled a careless speller, as well as being misunderstood. For example, this should make you and your child grin—

> It's Thanksgiving and we can smell Mother's foul cooking. Our ants have joined us for dinner. They brought a nice desert, lovely flours, and a small fur box of current tees. It's really their presents that counts.

The most frequent homophone errors in writing occur with the homophones below. Escort your child through the exercise using these sentences as a guide.

their	Sam and Ann took <u>their</u> dog to the park.
theirs	Yes, the book is <u>theirs</u>.
there	<u>There</u> is a bird in the nest.
there's	<u>There's</u> no one at home.
they're	<u>They're</u> going to the mall.

Fill in the missing words with there, their, they're, there's or theirs.

_________________ trouble ahead for writers who mix up homophones in

_________________ writing. _________________ sure to look like careless

spellers, but the trouble is not just _________________. _________________

may be problems for the reader, too. _________________ always the

chance that the misuse of a homophone sends a different message than

what the writer meant to say. The writer has mislead the reader! So,

it's important for writers to proofread _________________ homophones.

The responsibility is all _________________, and _________________ alone.

_________________ are many homophones and _________________ all

important to use correctly.

Ahhh, there's more! Have your child find examples of these homophones in print material at home. If possible, cut them out and make a collage of the cutouts by pasting them on heavy art paper.

Assess Words and Skills

- Spelling Words (words missed on tests) are recorded in the Spelling Notebook.
- Use Proof It, Practice Page 63, for proofreading/editing practice.

Assess Spelling Progress

Teaching Notes, page 336

Give this Cloze Story Word Test of Core Words within the frequencies 1–605 to all students. Words students miss are their Spelling Words.

 **THE CLOZE STORY WORD TEST**

Students do not prestudy the words. Provide students with a copy of REVIEW 21 BLACKLINE MASTER, page 188. Tell students that this story is about one of the world's greatest architectural wonders.

Read the entire story aloud, including the test words. Then read it again slowly as students write the missing words.

Great, Greater, Greatest

What is the only man-made structure that people can see from the moon with (1) <u>their</u> naked (2) <u>eye</u>? It took (3) <u>shape</u> solely (4) <u>through</u> the efforts of a million workers laboring over two thousand years. It was made with (5) <u>strong</u> stones compacted tightly with (6) <u>soft</u> soil made into mortar. It is a great, thirty-foot-high structure. The base is (7) <u>almost</u> twenty- (8) <u>eight</u> feet wide. The (9) <u>length</u> is over 3,600 miles long—the longest edifice ever (10) <u>built</u> on the (11) <u>surface</u> of this earth.

Where is this wall-like blockade? What was the (12) <u>reason</u> for (13) <u>its</u> construction? Was (14) <u>its</u> purpose to keep people inside the barrier so that they (15) <u>couldn't</u> escape? Or was it made to keep (16) <u>possible</u> invaders outside to discourage attacks on the land, people, and (17) <u>villages</u>? Are you on the (18) <u>edge</u> of (19) <u>your</u> seat eager for an explanation or do you (20) <u>already</u> know? If not, where might you find this (21) <u>explained</u>? List likely (22) <u>information</u> sources. Now, (23) <u>you're</u> to do the research. Work by yourself or with a (24) <u>group</u> to find and (25) <u>write</u> the (26) <u>right</u> answers.

Words tested:
your (40), their (42), its (76), through (102), write (108), right (116), almost (216), group (295), built (360), strong (381), surface (393), already (411), possible (452), explain(ed) (513), length (546), information (549), you're (552), couldn't (563), reason (564), eye (578), shape (601), eight (602), edge (603), soft (604), village(s) (605)

 **AFTER THE CLOZE STORY WORD TEST**

1. Have students research and write their answers to the story questions. Then have students share their answers. Conclude that this structure is the Great Wall of China that extends across northern and central China from the Yellow Sea east to a point deep in central Asia. It was constructed to keep invaders out, unlike the Berlin wall that was designed to keep people in eastern Germany.

research, writing

2. Have students record the words they missed on the test in their Spelling Notebook (see page 338) for at-school study, and on a copy of the WORDS TO LEARN BLACKLINE MASTER, page 375, for at-home study.

recording words for personal study list

Teaching Notes, page 339

Assess Skill Application

Give this assessment of spelling and related skills to all students.
The REVIEW 21 BLACKLINE MASTER is on page 189.

THE SKILL TEST

Skill tested:
homophones—*there, their, they're, there's, theirs*

> Fill in the missing words with **there**, **their**, **they're**, **there's** or **theirs**.
> _There_ are some homophones that are number words. _They're_ among the numbers 1-10.
> Are _there_ colors that are homophones? Yes, _there_ certainly are!
> _There's_ one color homophone that may be your favorite color. Many people say it's _theirs_ .
> Animal names can be homophones, and _there_ are many of them.
> Parents sometimes name _their_ children homophone names.
> _There_ may be city and state names that you know that are homophones.
> These homophones are all around us, and _they're_ here to stay.

Note the ability of each student to differentiate among *there, their, they're, there's,* **and**
theirs.

Teaching Notes, page 341

Assess Proofreading Application

Give this assessment of spelling and related skills to all students.
The REVIEW 21 BLACKLINE MASTER is on page 189.

THE PROOFREADING TEST

> Circle the word in each row that is spelled right.
>
> | | | | |
> |---|---|---|---|
> | (business) | bussiness | busyness | bisusness |
> | middel | midle | (middle) | middal |
> | differense | (difference) | differennce | diference |
> | supose | seppose | suppoce | (suppose) |
> | goverment | (government) | governmant | govermment |
> | (length) | lingth | leangth | lengtth |
> | montain | monntain | (mountain) | mounteen |
> | singel | scingel | scingal | (single) |
> | fameous | fammous | (famous) | famouss |
> | cought | (caught) | caut | caughte |
> | femilys | famillies | (families) | familie's |
> | (example) | exampple | xample | exampel |
> | peopel | peopple | (people) | pepole |
> | allmost | allmoste | allmast | (almost) |
> | trauble | troubble | (trouble) | troubell |
> | insted | insdead | insteade | (instead) |
> | (through) | troughe | thruogh | threwe |
> | mesure | meissure | (measure) | maysure |
> | usualy | usally | usuallye | (usually) |
> | (enough) | enuf | enuff | enoughf |
> | mashine | (machine) | machinne | machin |
> | (against) | aginst | agains | againstt |
> | themselfs | themself | (themselves) | themsellvs |
> | sentense | sentance | senstence | (sentence) |
> | sudnely | sudennly | (suddenly) | suddenlly |

Note the ability of each student to proofread for spelling errors.

Teaching Notes, page 342

Extend Spelling Assessment

Give this in-context assessment of Core Words within the frequencies 1–605 to students who need more practice or challenge.

THE SENTENCE DICTATION TEST

Students do not prestudy the words. Provide students with writing paper and pencil. Have students write the sentences as they are dictated.

1. There was a pretty skater making wide turns in the shape of a huge figure eight.
2. The bottom edge of her skates made deep marks in the ice as she traveled along.
3. Her soft, straight hair moved with the wind when she began to go faster.
4. There were a few children from the village watching her from outside through the large glass windows.

Words tested:

the (1), of (2), a (4), to (5), in (6), was (13), as (16), with (17), from (23), were (34), when (35), there (37), she (54), her (64), make(ing) (72), made (81), through (102), go (105), along (171), few (181), large (185), children (200), began (215), turn(s) (289), move(d) (290), wind (341), fast(er) (376), outside (420), deep (425), watch(ing) (436), ice (441), wide (477), glass (488), bottom (492), window(s) (503), mark(s) (504), travel(ed) (516), straight (524), hair (528), figure (551), shape (601), eight (602), edge (603), soft (604), village (605)

Extra words: huge, pretty, skater, skates

AFTER THE SENTENCE DICTATION TEST

1. Have students analyze the skills an able ice skater needs and speculate in what other sports these same skills would be necessary.

analyzing, speculating, writing

2. Have students record the words they missed on the test in their Spelling Notebook (see page 345) for at-school study, and on a copy of the WORDS TO LEARN BLACKLINE MASTER, page 375, for at-home study.

recording words for personal study list

> Dictate this homophone sentence for students to write and ponder:
> - The four sails were for sale.
>
> Dictate this tongue-twister for students to write and say:
> - Should she sell shapely socks or should she sell shapeless sashes?

The jingle "*i before e except after c, or when sounded as /ā/ as in neighbor and weigh*" provides misdirection. There is some reliability to the latter part of the rhyme (e.g., eight, beige, freight); however, the exceptions to the jingle are so abundant that it is unwise to suggest it as a spelling aid. Instead, alert students that ie/ei spellings are a strange lot, indeed weird.

- As an ongoing assignment, have students collect ie/ei words for the class book, The Weirdos (Activity 1C, this unit). On occasion, read a word from the book for students to write. Then write the word on the chalkboard for students to self-check.
- Have students make ie/ei word cards using the WORD CARD BLACKLINE MASTER. Partners can play tic-tac-toe spelling (Test Ready, page 165) by drawing a word card from a face-down pile for their partner to read to them to spell.

Name _______________________________

— Word Test —

Great, Greater, Greatest

What is the only man-made structure that people can see from the moon with

(1) _________________ naked (2) _________________? It took (3) _________________

solely (4) _________________ the efforts of a million workers laboring over two

thousand years. It was made with (5) _________________ stones compacted tightly

with (6) _________________ soil made into mortar. It is a great, thirty-foot-high

structure. The base is (7) _________________ twenty- (8) _________________ feet

wide. The (9) _________________ is over 3,600 miles long—the longest edifice ever

(10) _________________ on the (11) _________________ of this earth.

Where is this wall-like blockade? What was the (12) _________________ for

(13) _________________ construction? Was (14) _________________ purpose to keep

people inside the barrier so that they (15) _________________ escape? Or was it

made to keep (16) _________________ invaders outside to discourage attacks on the

land, people, and (17) _________________? Are you on the (18) _________________ of

(19) _________________ seat eager for an explanation or do you (20) _________________

know? If not, where might you find this (21) _________________? List likely

(22) _________________ sources. Now, (23) _________________ to do the research.

Work by yourself or with a (24) _________________ to find and (25) _________________

the (26) _________________ answers.

Skill Test

Fill in the missing words with **there**, **their**, **they're**, **there's** or **theirs**.

______________________ are some homophones that are number words.

______________________ among the numbers 1-10.

Are ______________________ colors that are homophones?

Yes, ______________________ certainly are!

______________________ one color homophone that may be your favorite color.

Many people say it's ______________________.

Animal names can be homophones, and ______________________ are many of them.

Parents sometimes name ______________________ children homophone names.

______________________ may be city and state names that you know that are homophones.

These homophones are all around us, and ______________________ here to stay.

Proofreading Test

Circle the word in each row that is spelled right.

business	bussiness	busyness	bisusness
middel	midle	middle	middal
differense	difference	differennce	diference
supose	seppose	suppoce	suppose
goverment	government	governmant	govermment
length	lingth	leangth	lengtth
montain	monntain	mountain	mounteen
singel	scingel	scingal	single
fameous	fammous	famous	famouss
cought	caught	caut	caughte
femilys	famillies	families	familie's
example	exampple	xample	exampel
peopel	peopple	people	pepole
allmost	allmoste	allmast	almost
trauble	troubble	trouble	troubell
insted	insdead	insteade	instead
through	troughe	thruogh	threwe
mesure	meissure	measure	maysure
usualy	usally	usuallye	usually
enough	enuf	enuff	enoughf
mashine	machine	machinne	machin
against	aginst	agains	againstt
themselfs	themself	themselves	themsellvs
sentense	sentance	senstence	sentence
sudnely	sudennly	suddenly	suddenlly

Build Skills and Word Experiences

Use Student Practice Pages 64–65 to follow up instruction for:
Activity 1A • Test Ready

Build Visual Skills

Do the Word Preview, a visual warm-up activity, with all students.
Use Core Words **object** (606), **age** (607), **minute** (608), **wall** (609), **meet** (610).

Teaching Notes, page 316

Build Spelling and Language Skills

Choose from among these quick tasks to customize instruction
for all or selected students.

Teaching Notes, page 319

It will be ready in a minute.

The object of writing there names on a stone wall was to help us rember those who passed away in one of america's past wars. we stood very still for a few minute with people of all ages rather then hurrying to meet are friends.

(*their, remember, America's, We, minutes, than, our*)

object, weave, agrees, minute, dessert, gone, bass, meet, chews, class, contest, free

(*e.g., homophone/homograph/neither; ends in e/s/t; contains double ee/double ss/no double letters*)

wall, I'll, seashell , ______

(words that end in double *l*)

The object of soccer is to ______.

Words with consonant blends

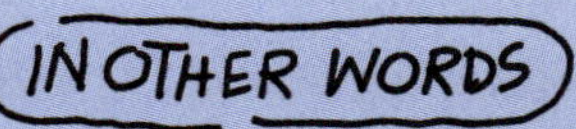

Have students write (IN OTHER WORDS): "If youth only knew; if age only could."
Chinese proverb

Teaching Notes, page 325

Build Basic Concepts

Choose from among these skill-building activities to customize instruction for all or selected students.

| **concept one** | Homographs are words that have the same spelling, different meanings, and may have different pronunciations. |

1A Review the definition of a homograph and revisit Teaching Poster 5. Identify *object* as a homograph. Discuss its different pronunciations and its meaning as a verb and a noun. Repeat with *minute*, *present*, and other homographs students identify.

homographs, parts of speech, visual skill building, writing words, spelling game

Have students create a bingo board (see Activity 1C, page 20) using sixteen homographs from Teaching Poster 5 to play bingo.

| **concept two** | Frequent spelling patterns for /j/ are *j*, *ge*, *dge*, *gi*, and *gy*. |

2A Select students to write *object*, *age*, *edge*, *giant*, and *gym* on the chalkboard. Identify the common sound as /j/. Reestablish *g* spelling /j/ as the soft g sound, as opposed to the hard g sound in *government*. Have students investigate /j/ words spelled with soft g to review when *ge* spells /j/ and when *dge* spells /j/. Conclude that when /j/ follows a short vowel, it is usually spelled *dge*. When /j/ does not follow a short vowel, it is usually spelled *ge*. Have students apply what they know by predicting the *ge/dge* ending of words. Write all but the ending letters on the chalkboard for words, such as *trudge, pledge, camouflage, cartridge, begrudge, submerge, arrange, indulge*. Discuss the meaning of unfamiliar words. (Exceptions include words ending in the unstressed *age* spelling pattern: *village, courage, heritage, manage, wreckage*.)

phonics, word analysis, spelling word patterns, writing words, predicting spelling, vocabulary development

2B Prepare for a letter-card activity (see Activity 2B, page 47) using *a, d, e, e, g, l, r, s, t,* and *u*. Write *age* and *edge* on the chalkboard. Remind students that when /j/ follows a short vowel, it is usually spelled *dge*. When /j/ does not follow a short vowel it is usually spelled *ge*. Together make *age*. Then have students continue making words: *rage—stage—surge— urge—eagle—eager—agree—alert—argue—large—ledge—edge—gesture—deluge— trudge—sludge—sledge—sage—sale—sure—sugar—salute—usage—*and back to *age*.

phonics, visual skills, making words, vocabulary development

WORD MYSTERIES AND HISTORIES

Students are learning that words can be assembled using the prefix-root-suffix formula. Knowing the meaning of word components can often unlock many word mysteries. The *ject* root comes from the Latin verb *jacere*, meaning "to throw." The *ob* prefix means "against." Therefore, students can deduce the meaning of one pronunciation of the homograph *object*—throw against. The American colonists objected to the British tax on tea.

• Have students explore the function of the *ject* root with the prefixes *re* (back/ again), *de* (from/down/away), *inter* (between), *con* (with/together), *in* (to).

Teaching Notes, page 328

Build Skillful Writers

Use these interrelated language learnings for all or selected students.

Demonstrate how writing can be made more interesting by using exciting substitutes for boring, overused, lifeless words—call them "worn out" words. Ask students to define synonyms (words that have similar meanings). Have students brainstorm synonyms for *little* (e.g., minute, tiny, minuscule, microscopic, dainty, miniature). Then prepare for a carousel activity (see Test Ready, page 39) using five charts labeled with "worn out" words. Choices may include: *a lot, happy, eat, said, old, good.* Have students list exciting synonyms for these worn out words. Remind students to use synonyms for these "worn out" words in their writing.

Teaching Notes, page 329

Skill to be tested:
suffixes *s, es, ed, ing, ment, less, ness, able,* and *en*

Build Assessment Readiness

Use these at-school and at-home exercises to prepare all students for the Skill Test.

at-school Post Teaching Poster 2. Position some students at the chalkboard while others write at their desks. Have students write the verb *object.* Then have them add *s, ed,* and *ing.* Next, demonstrate the addition of *tion.* Strictly speaking, the *t* is dropped and *tion* is added (predict/prediction, elect/election).

Have students write *age.* Then they decide which suffixes can be added and write the new words. Provide a model for self-checking. Repeat the activity with *pay, plan, family,* and *soft.* Note the silent *t* when the *en* suffix is added to *soft.* Further, note that the addition of the *less* suffix changes the meaning of the words to which it is added.

Later, organize students into small groups to brainstorm words with the *less, ment, ness, able,* and *en* suffixes. Have groups share their results with the class.

Skill to be tested:
suffixes *s, es, ed, ing, ment, less, ness, able,* and *en*

at-home Send home a copy of TAKE-HOME TASK 22 BLACKLINE MASTER, **page 193,** with each student to encourage parent-child partnerships.

Teaching Notes, page 330

Build Proofreading Skills

Track students' ability to meet a minimum competency for spelling and proofreading within selected samples of their everyday writing.

- Send home papers for proofreading and a copy of the IDEAS FOR PROOFREADING BLACKLINE MASTER, **page 373.**

Name_______________________________

Dear Parents,

We continue to teach your child how to make words through the addition of prefixes and suffixes. In this activity, your child identifies base words to which suffixes can be added and completes each word wheel by writing the words with the suffixes on the "spokes." Guide your child through the activity, discussing the meaning and use of the new words that are made through the addition of the suffixes.

Help your child discover that the addition of a suffix changes the part of speech and use of the word to which it is added—except for the less suffix. The addition of less changes the meaning of the base word.

Identify base words to which these suffixes can be added. Complete each suffix word wheel by writing a word with that suffix on each line.

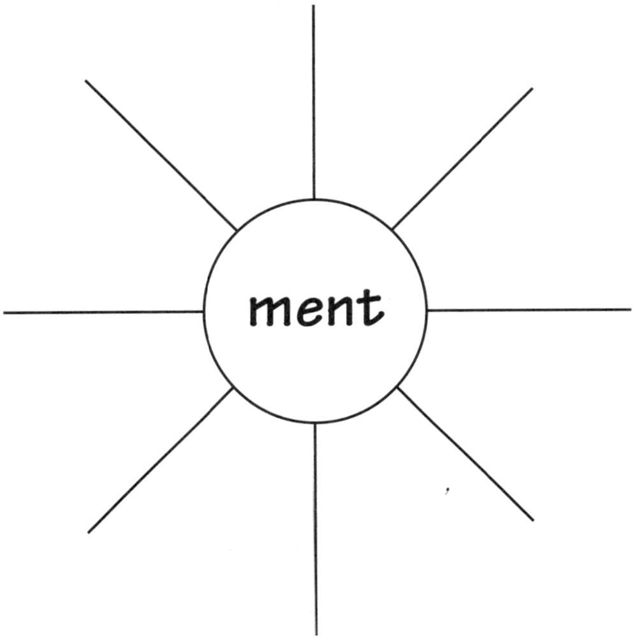

ment

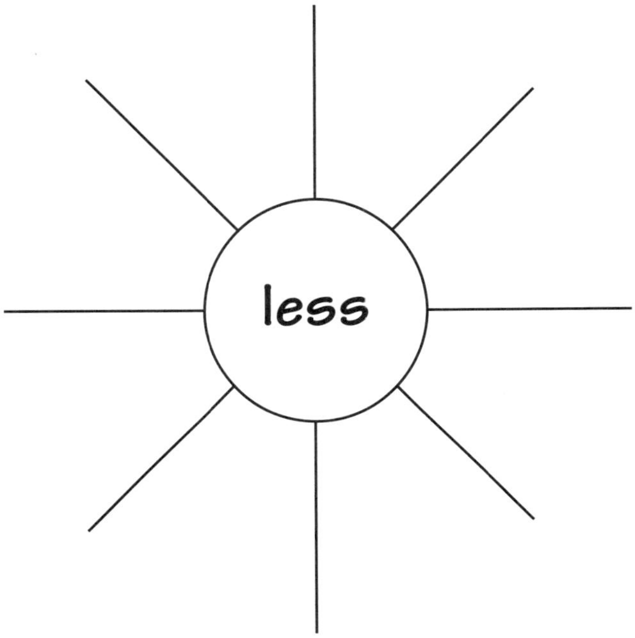

less

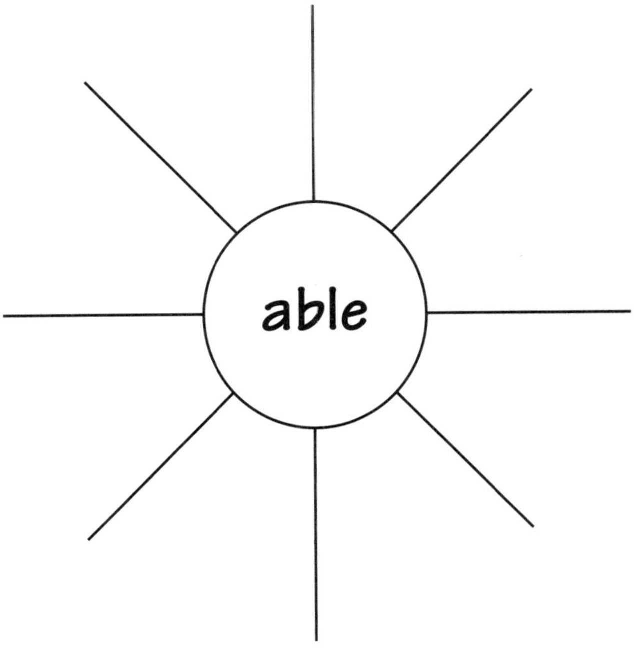

able

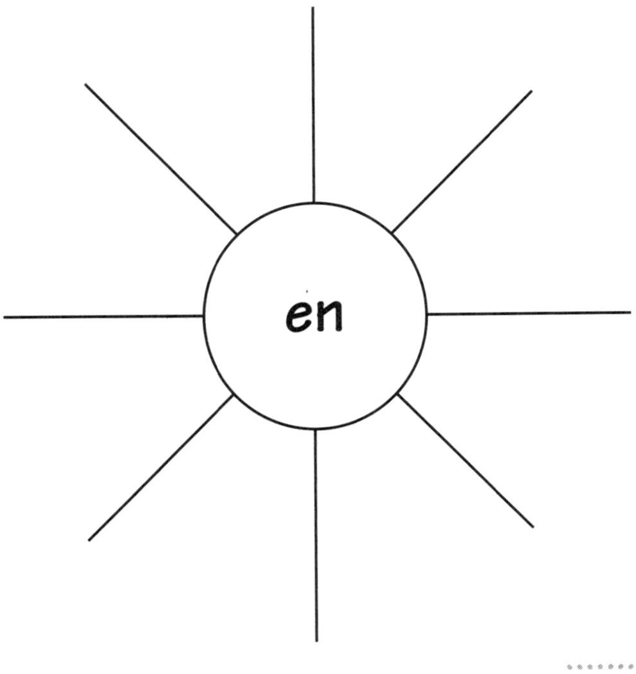

en

- Spelling Words (words missed on tests) are recorded in the Spelling Notebook.
- Use Proof It, Practice Page 66, for proofreading/editing practice.

WORD TEST

Teaching Notes, page 336

Assess Spelling Progress

Give this Cloze Story Word Test of Core Words within the frequencies 1–610 to all students. Words students miss are their Spelling Words.

 **THE CLOZE STORY WORD TEST**

Students do not prestudy the words. Provide students with a copy of REVIEW 22 BLACKLINE MASTER, page 197. Tell students that this story is a fable, and like all fables it has a lesson, or moral.

Read the entire story aloud, including the test words. Then read it again slowly as students write the missing words.

Words tested:

all (33), there (37), water (90), because (127), big(ger) (158), often (186), point (272), table (314), nothing (329), ready (357), piece (392), animals (418), suddenly (458), field (472), friend(s) (498), mouth (568), trouble (588), store (589), catch (594), edge (603), village (605), object (606), age (607), minute (608), wall (609), meet (610), *they're (1010)

*The testing of they're (1010) is included to help students differentiate among the there/their/they're homophones.

> ## Buster, the Butcher, and the Beef
>
> WORD TEST
>
> Old Buster (1) <u>often</u> visited the (2) <u>village</u> butcher who gave him morsels of meat, yet Buster was impatient today and snatched an enormous (3) <u>piece</u> of beef from the butcher's (4) <u>table</u> and darted away. The butcher tossed an (5) <u>object</u> at the old dog and yelled, "(6) <u>Animals</u>! (7) <u>They're</u> nothing but (8) <u>trouble</u>! Don't come back in my (9) <u>store</u>!" But Buster ran free, jumped the (10) <u>wall</u>, and raced through the (11) <u>field</u> to safety at the (12) <u>edge</u> of the pond. He didn't want to (13) <u>meet</u> any of his dog (14) <u>friends</u> (15) <u>because</u> he did not plan to share. Now, Buster was (16) <u>all ready</u> to enjoy his (17) <u>catch</u> when he looked into the (18) <u>water</u>. (19) <u>There</u>, looking up at him, was a dog with a chunk of meat in his (20) <u>mouth</u>! "Wait a (21) <u>minute</u>. I'll have that meat, too!" drooled Buster. "That dog looks the same (22) <u>age</u> as I am, no (23) <u>bigger</u>, and no smarter. I'll scare him! He'll drop his meat and run." So, Buster bared his teeth at the dog in the pond. As he did, his own morsel (24) <u>suddenly</u> dropped from his jaws and sank! Gone! Now, Buster had (25) <u>nothing</u>! What is this fable's (26) <u>point</u>, or moral?

 **AFTER THE CLOZE STORY WORD TEST**

interpreting, writing

1. Have students write and share their answer to the story question. Identify and discuss other fables and the lessons they teach. Then have students write about a real person or a story character with the same attitude as Buster's.

recording words for personal study list

2. Have students record the words they missed on the test in their Spelling Notebook (see page 338) for at-school study, and on a copy of the WORDS TO LEARN BLACKLINE MASTER, page 375, for at-home study.

Assess Skill Application

Give this assessment of spelling and related skills to all students.
The REVIEW 22 BLACKLINE MASTER is on page 198.

Teaching Notes, page 339

 **THE SKILL TEST**

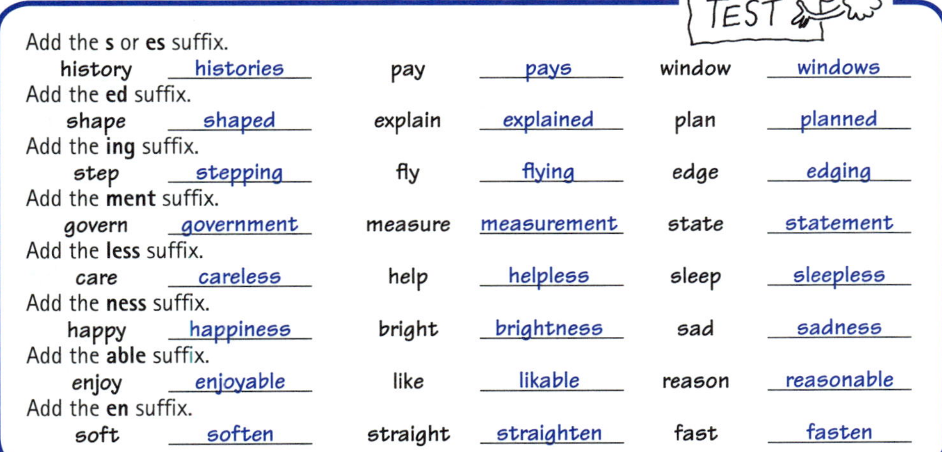

Add the **s** or **es** suffix.

history	histories	pay	pays	window	windows

Add the **ed** suffix.

shape	shaped	explain	explained	plan	planned

Add the **ing** suffix.

step	stepping	fly	flying	edge	edging

Add the **ment** suffix.

govern	government	measure	measurement	state	statement

Add the **less** suffix.

care	careless	help	helpless	sleep	sleepless

Add the **ness** suffix.

happy	happiness	bright	brightness	sad	sadness

Add the **able** suffix.

enjoy	enjoyable	like	likable	reason	reasonable

Add the **en** suffix.

soft	soften	straight	straighten	fast	fasten

Skill tested:
suffixes *s, es, ed, ing, ment, less, ness, able,* and *en*

Note the ability of each student to add the *s, es, ed, ing, ment, less, ness, able,* and *en* suffixes to base words.

Assess Proofreading Application

Give this assessment of spelling and related skills to all students.
The REVIEW 22 BLACKLINE MASTER is on page 198.

Teaching Notes, page 341

 **THE PROOFREADING TEST**

Circle the correctly spelled word to complete each line.

You know that the _____________ of a book is the person
who wrote it. That _____________ name is usually on the
book. Sometimes _____________ the real name of the author,
but occasionally it is a pen name. This is a _____________
name. _____________ word for pen name is pseudonym.
Pseudo _____________ from the Greek word meaning
false. Nym is _____________ from the Greek word that
means name. Samuel Clemens is a _____________ author
who wrote books you may have read or have _____________
about. One of his books is called *The _____________ of
Tom Sawyer.* _____________, he used a pen name. He
didn't _____________ to use his own name. The name that
appears on his books _____________ Samuel Clemens.

auther	**author**	athour
person's	persons	persons'
its	**it's**	its'
made-up	maid-up	mad-up
Annother	**Another**	An other
cames	**comes**	commes
taken	token	tacken
fameous	**famous**	famess
herd	**heard**	hearde
Adventures	Advenchurs	Aventures
Howevver	Howevaer	**However**
choose	chose	chouse
is'nt	**isn't**	isnot'

Who is this author? Identify more authors who use a pseudonym.

Note the ability of each student to proofread for errors.

Teaching Notes, page 342

Extend Spelling Assessment

Give this in-context assessment of Core Words within the frequencies
1–610 to students who need more practice or challenge.

Words tested:
the (1), a (4), to (5), in (6), it (10), on (14), at (20), this (22), I (24), but (31), there('s) (37), she (54), would (59), has (62), her (64), time (69), no (71), its (76), who (77), my (80), work (124), because (127), even (130), why (136), still (153), show(s) (184), large (185), house (189), want(ed) (193), keep (199), live(s) (217), got (219), hand (223), country (228), face (291), age (322), though (330), probably (383), that's (390), piece (392), round (401), quite (447), least (478), hour (480), friend (498), lost (514), correct (521), strange (572), choose (580), object (606), age(s) (607), minute (608), wall (609), meet (610)

Extra words: clock, doesn't, Grandma, grandmother

speculating, writing

recording words for personal study list

 **THE SENTENCE DICTATION TEST**

Students do not prestudy the words. Provide students with writing paper and pencil.
Have students write the sentences as they are dictated.

1. I wanted my friend to meet my grandmother who lives in a house in the country.

2. She has a large clock that's quite strange because there's no minute hand on its round face.

3. It probably got lost ages ago, but at least the timepiece still shows the correct hour.

4. Why would Grandma choose to keep this object on her wall even though it doesn't work?

 **AFTER THE SENTENCE DICTATION TEST**

1. Have students speculate in writing reasons why Grandma continues to keep the old clock on her wall. Then discuss their reasons.

2. Have students record the words they missed on the test in their Spelling Notebook (see page 345) for at-school study, and on a copy of the WORDS TO LEARN BLACKLINE MASTER, page 375, for at-home study.

The Wordsmith Says

Homographs are among the most interesting words in our language and can be a source for challenging the most capable students. Have students ponder the meanings of homographs in these sentences. Then have students write and illustrate their own homograph sentences, using these as a model—one illustrated sentence per page to compile into a class book.

- The **minute** clock on the kitchen wall noted that it was one **minute** to two.
- The farm was used to **produce** fine **produce** for people throughout the valley.
- The landfill was so full that it had to **refuse** more **refuse**.
- She likes to **polish** the **Polish** furniture to a bright shine.
- The bandage was **wound** around the girl's **wound**.
- Do you **object** to this **object** being placed on your desk?
- There is no time like the **present** to **present** this **present** to you.
- A **row** developed among the rafters about how to **row** through the rapids.

Word Test

Buster, the Butcher, and the Beef

Old Buster (1) _______________ visited the (2) _______________ butcher who gave

him morsels of meat, yet Buster was impatient today and snatched an enormous

(3) _______________ of beef from the butcher's (4) _______________ and darted

away. The butcher tossed an (5) _______________ at the old dog and yelled,

"(6) _______________! (7) _______________ nothing but (8) _______________!

Don't come back in my (9) _______________!" But Buster ran free, jumped the

(10) _______________, and raced through the (11) _______________ to safety at the

(12) _______________ of the pond. He didn't want to (13) _______________ any of his

dog (14) _______________ (15) _______________ he did not plan to share. Now, Buster

was (16) _______________ to enjoy his (17) _______________ when he looked into the

(18) _______________. (19) _______________, looking up at him, was a dog with a

chunk of meat in his (20) _______________! "Wait a (21) _______________. I'll have

that meat, too!" drooled Buster. "That dog looks the same (22) _______________ as

I am, no (23) _______________, and no smarter. I'll scare him! He'll drop his meat and

run." So, Buster bared his teeth at the dog in the pond. As he did, his own morsel

(24) _______________ dropped from his jaws and sank! Gone! Now, Buster had

(25) _______________! What is this fable's (26) _______________, or moral?

Skill Test

Add the **s** or **es** suffix.

history_________________   pay_________________   window_________________

Add the **ed** suffix.

shape_________________   explain_________________   plan_________________

Add the **ing** suffix.

step_________________   fly_________________   edge_________________

Add the **ment** suffix.

govern_________________   measure_________________   state_________________

Add the **less** suffix.

care_________________   help_________________   sleep_________________

Add the **ness** suffix.

happy_________________   bright_________________   sad_________________

Add the **able** suffix.

enjoy_________________   like_________________   reason_________________

Add the **en** suffix.

soft_________________   straight_________________   fast_________________

Proofreading Test

Circle the correctly spelled word to complete each line.

You know that the __________ of a book is the person   auther   author   athour

who wrote it. That __________ name is usually on the   person's   persons   persons'

book. Sometimes __________ the real name of the author,   its   it's   its'

but occasionally it is a pen name. This is a __________   made-up   maid-up   mad-up

name. __________ word for pen name is pseudonym.   Annother   Another   An other

Pseudo __________ from the Greek word meaning   cames   comes   commes

false. Nym is __________ from the Greek word that   taken   token   tacken

means name. Samuel Clemens is a __________ author   fameous   famous   famess

who wrote books you may have read or have __________   herd   heard   hearde

about. One of his books is called The __________ of   Adventures   Advenchurs   Aventures

Tom Sawyer. __________, he used a pen name. He   Howevver   Howevaer   However

didn't __________ to use his own name. The name that   choose   chose   chouse

appears on his books __________ Samuel Clemens.   is'nt   isn't   isnot'

Who is this author? Identify more authors who use a pseudonym.

Build Skills and Word Experiences

Use Student Practice Pages 67–68 to follow up instruction for:
Activities 2A and 2B • Test Ready

Build Visual Skills

Do the Word Preview, a visual warm-up activity, with all students.
Use Core Words **record** (611), **copy** (612), **forest** (613), **especially** (614), **necessary** (615).

Teaching Notes, page 316

Build Spelling and Language Skills

Choose from among these quick tasks to customize instruction
for all or selected students.

Teaching Notes, page 319

The forest was dark.

People who work in the forest often record infomation about plant and animals that is expecially important. If necessary, they make copys for others to study.

(*information, plants, especially, copies*)

copy, especially, twenty, already, carefully, probably, usually, busy, necessary, apply, finally, dictionary

(e.g., suffix/no suffix; number of syllables; begins with vowel/consonant; does/doesn't have double letters)

record, use, object, _______

(homographs)

Qualities that I especially like in people are _______.

Words in which *y* is changed to *i* before adding a suffix that begins with a vowel.

Teaching Notes, page 325

Build Basic Concepts

Choose from among these skill-building activities to customize instruction for all or selected students.

| concept one | Synonyms are words that have similar meanings. |

synonyms, vocabulary development, writing words, game

1A Ask students to define *synonyms* (words that have similar meanings). Expand the Build Skillful Writers exercise (page 192) by providing students more vocabulary expansion practice. In this activity, students are given the exciting synonym and they provide the worn-out word.

Divide students into small groups. Each student needs paper/pencil. Call out synonyms for an ordinary word. If additional clues are needed, provide the letter blanks for the answer word. When each member of a group has written the group's answer, members stand. The first group to stand with the correct answer—if all members have accurately written the answer—wins the round. Say, "I'm thinking of the worn-out word for ..."

apprehend, seize (**catch**)	*excursion, venture* (**trip**)
replicate, imitate (**copy**)	*striving, aspiring* (**wishing**)
minute, diminutive (**little**)	*abundant, numerous* (**a lot**)
conversing, discussing (**speaking**)	*construct, create* (**build**)
amusing, entertaining (**fun**)	*inquired, probed* (**asked**)

Then reverse the process and have students create the synonyms for more worn-out words to be used in a subsequent game.

| concept two | Visual skills support spelling and proofreading ability. |

visual skill building, word analysis, chanting/writing a rhyme, more words

2A Write this rhyme on the chalkboard or on a chart for students to chant chorally. Have students write the jingle to reinforce the spelling of *until*, among the top ten most misspelled words. Later, have students chant the rhyme with word substitutes for *until*, such as *careful, travel, natural, oil, special,* and *final*.

One L

Picture "until"—what is it you see?

One l at the end—I'm sure you agree.

One l at the end—alone, straight and tall.

One l at the end—just one and that's all.

writing words, word analysis, visual skills, proofreading

2B Remind students that for words with double letters, only one letter is heard when the word is said, but they must remember to write two letters. Position some students at the chalkboard as others write at their desks. Have students write *especially, necessary, middle, correct,* and *difference*. After each, provide the correct spelling for self-checking. Then ask students what these words have in common (double letters). Write the five words on large sticky notes to attach to the top of the Ten-Box Reusable Chart. Then have students gather and write on small sticky notes words that contain the same double letters.

Build Skillful Writers

Use these interrelated language learnings for all or selected students.

Teaching Notes, page 328

Stretch It encourages students to write more. In this activity, Thomas Jefferson's advice (see In Other Words, below) is demonstrated. Review "double trouble" words that say the same thing (Build Skillful Writers, page 111). Then present students with this exercise:

> *It's unnecessary to repeatedly repeat the exact same thing over again and again.*
> *It's unnecessary to repeatedly repeat the exact same thing over again.*
> *It's unnecessary to repeatedly repeat the exact same thing again.*
> *It's unnecessary to repeatedly repeat the same thing again.*
> *It's unnecessary to repeatedly repeat the same thing.*
> *It's unnecessary to repeatedly repeat.*
> *It's unnecessary to repeat.*

Have students "hitch up" the Proofreading Posse (Teaching Poster 1) to round up and rein in the unnecessary words: *I'll really truly attempt to try to write just the important essentials and I may possibly never revert back to writing more words in number than I really need at any point in time.* (I'll write the essentials.)

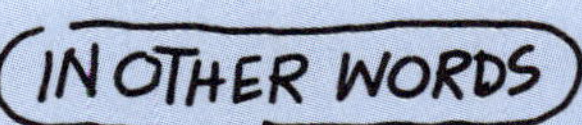

Have students write (**IN OTHER WORDS**): "The most valuable of all talents is never using two words when one will do." Thomas Jefferson

Build Assessment Readiness

Use these at-school and at-home exercises to prepare all students for the Skill Test.

Teaching Notes, page 329

at-school Ask students to define a homograph (words that are spelled the same, have different meanings, and may have different pronunciations). Ask students to list homographs. Post Teaching Poster 5 for students to expand their list and self-check. Choices beyond those on Teaching Poster 5 include *dove, invalid, converse, console, compact, peaked, intimate, conduct, convict,* and *address.* Have students make small posters divided into two sections to illustrate the two meanings of a homograph. Post the vocabulary-building artwork on the bulletin board.

Skill to be tested: homographs

at-home Send home a copy of Take-Home Task 23 Blackline Master, page 202, with each student to encourage parent-child partnerships.

Skill to be tested: homographs

Build Proofreading Skills

Track students' ability to meet a minimum competency for spelling and proofreading within selected samples of their everyday writing.

Teaching Notes, page 330

• Send home papers for proofreading and a copy of the Ideas for Proofreading Blackline Master, page 373.

Dear Parents,

Your child is developing vocabulary skills through the word experiences taught in spelling. In this activity your child works with homographs, words that are spelled the same, have different meanings, and may have different pronunciations. All of these homographs have two pronunciations and at least two meanings. Guide your child through the exercise, letting your child do as much as possible without your help. Then be sure to say the words with your child to demonstrate the two pronunciations. Discuss the meanings of the words and have your child use the words in sentences.

Read each sentence. Circle the set of words that most nearly describes the underlined word.

1. Mary won the creative writing <u>contest</u> with her poem about the forest.

    resist, oppose   competition, tournament

2. George's <u>excuse</u> for being late was weak.

    pardon, forgive   explanation, reason

3. The woman was troubled by an <u>object</u> in her eye.

    thing, item   reject, disapprove

4. The <u>record</u> shows that Matt was absent four days last week.

    report, summary   write down, preserve

5. As a result of the <u>wind</u>, the fir tree was across the middle of the street.

    breeze, gale   twist, turn

6. Holly was chosen to <u>lead</u> the group along the mountain path.

    guide, direct   metal, element

7. The child was <u>content</u> with the toy during the mother's meeting.

    satisfied, pleased   insides, material within

8. The <u>desert</u> reached 110 degrees by noon.

    abandon, leave   dry land, sandy region

9. The <u>minute</u> insect could produce a painful sting.

    tiny, small   unit of time, moment

10. They angled for <u>bass</u>, but came home empty-handed.

    fish, freshwater animal   musical tone, low voice

Here are more homographs for you to explore: bow, conduct, contract, does, perfect, present, read, refuse, sow, subject, tear, use, wound.

Assess Words and Skills

• Spelling Words (words missed on tests) are recorded in the Spelling Notebook.
• Use Proof It, Practice Page 69, for proofreading/editing practice.

Assess Spelling Progress

Give this Cloze Story Word Test of Core Words within the frequencies 1–615 to all students. Words students miss are their Spelling Words.

Teaching Notes, page 336

 **THE CLOZE STORY WORD TEST**

Students do not prestudy the words. Provide students with a copy of REVIEW 23 BLACKLINE MASTER, page 206. Tell students that this story provides some insights into how one of our old, familiar rhymes originated.

Read the entire story aloud, including the test words. Then read it again slowly as students write the missing words.

A Yankee Laughs Last

"Yankee Doodle came to (1) <u>town</u>, riding on a pony, stuck a feather in his cap, and (2) <u>called</u> it macaroni!" We (3) <u>learned</u> this verse as (4) <u>children</u>. (5) <u>Remember</u> how we (6) <u>especially</u> liked the part about the macaroni! Yet, (7) <u>American</u> (8) <u>history</u> shows that this (9) <u>common</u> lyric was an eighteenth century anthem enthusiastically sung by adult colonists to express (10) <u>their</u> patriotism. How so? (11) <u>Early</u> on, according to the (12) <u>record</u>, British soldiers prided (13) <u>themselves</u> on (14) <u>their</u> dapper attire. Colonial soldiers attempted to look spiffy, but (15) <u>usually</u> looked like ragamuffins fresh from the (16) <u>forest</u>. In England, a "macaroni" was a (17) <u>person</u> who tried to (18) <u>copy</u> a stylish outfit, but failed and looked (19) <u>quite</u> foolish (20) <u>instead</u>. So this song was (21) <u>first</u> sung by the British to discredit colonists. But at the British surrender at Yorktown, George Washington's troops struck up the Yankee Doodle chorus making it (22) <u>necessary</u> for the British soldiers to "eat (23) <u>their</u> words!" Why did the colonists love this song from then on and the British (24) <u>government</u> consider it (25) <u>their</u> (26) <u>least</u> favorite tune?

Words tested:
their (42), first (74), called (96), children (200), usually (278), remember (315), American (319), early (324), learned (326), town (364), person (367), common (395), instead (408), themselves (443), quite (447), least (478), government (558), history (567), record (611), copy (612), forest (613), especially (614), necessary (615)

 **AFTER THE CLOZE STORY WORD TEST**

1. Have students write and share their answer to the story question. Ask students to circle and write the phrase "eat their words." Discuss. Add to this discussion "He who laughs last, laughs longest," and relate it to the story title. Ask students to explain in writing another real happening or fictional situation from literature in which these sayings apply.

speculating, writing an explanation

2. Have students record the words they missed on the test in their Spelling Notebook (see page 338) for at-school study, and on a copy of the WORDS TO LEARN BLACKLINE MASTER, page 375, for at-home study.

recording words for personal study list

Teaching Notes, page 339

Assess Skill Application

Give this assessment of spelling and related skills to all students.
The REVIEW 23 BLACKLINE MASTER is on page 207.

 **THE SKILL TEST**

Skill tested:
homographs

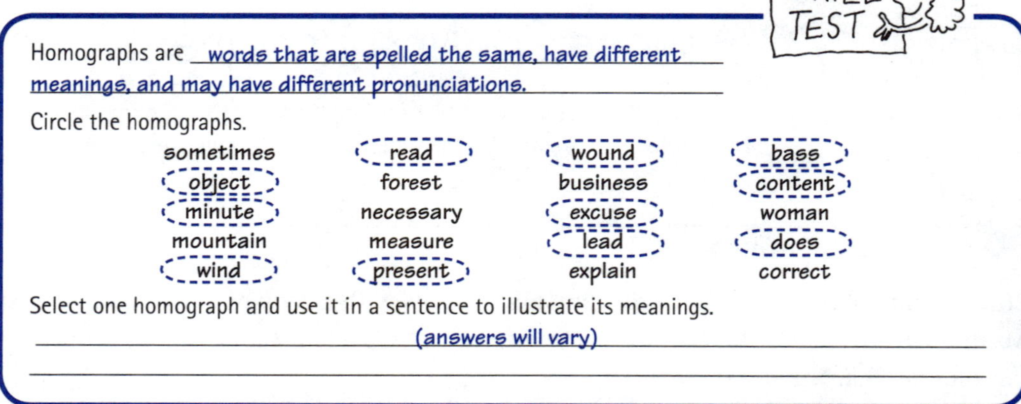

Note the ability of each student to define a homograph, identify homographs, and demonstrate their different meanings.

Teaching Notes, page 341

Assess Proofreading Application

Give this assessment of spelling and related skills to all students.
The REVIEW 23 BLACKLINE MASTER is on page 207.

 **THE PROOFREADING TEST**

If the underlined words in each line are incorrect for spelling or capitalization, write the correction in the space.

Before Samuel <u>clemens began his writing</u> career, he   Clemens
was a steamship <u>pilot who traveled along</u> the great
Mississippi <u>river. In some places</u> the river is quite   River
shallow. A steamship <u>needs fairly deep water,</u> so
it was <u>necesary to journey</u> with much care. It was   necessary
<u>especialy important to</u> avoid the water's edge, but   especially
some areas were rather shallow <u>even in the midlle</u>   middle
of the waterway. <u>Oftten, Samuel would</u> toss out a rope   Often
<u>marked with pointts six feet,</u> or one full fathom, apart   points
<u>to meassure the water's</u> depth. If he called out "mark   measure
twain," that meant <u>the water was a least</u> two fathoms   at
deep, <u>safe for passage. His</u> book, *Life on the Mississippi,*
<u>describes these adventure's</u> as a "cub" pilot.   adventures

Why do you suppose that the personal experiences of an author are often the subject about which he/she writes?

Note the ability of each student to proofread for spelling and capitalization errors.

Extend Spelling Assessment

Give this in-context assessment of Core Words within the frequencies 1–615 to students who need more practice or challenge.

Teaching Notes, page 342

THE SENTENCE DICTATION TEST

Students do not prestudy the words. Provide students with writing paper and pencil. Have students write the sentences as they are dictated.

1. There's some information that's especially important, such as government and business records.

2. If a hard copy is necessary, a printer lets you have one in less than a minute.

3. Rather than keeping it all on paper in files, you're likely to record and store it on computers now.

4. Let's work together to save the trees in the forest by choosing to use this simple method more often.

Words tested:
the (1), and (3), a (4), to (5), in (6), is (7), you (8), it (10), on (14), as (16), this (22), have (25), by (27), one (28), all (33), there('s) (37), if (44), some (56), more (63), than (73), now (78), use (88), work (124), such (133), often (186), together (187), important (195), keep(ing) (199), let(s)('s) (230), paper (241), hard (242), tree(s) (316), less (340), that's (390), simple (455), rather (545), information (549), you're (552), government (558), choose(ing) (580), store (589), business (595), minute (608), record(s) (611), copy (612), forest (613), especially (614), necessary (615)

Extra words: computers, files, likely, method, printer, save

AFTER THE SENTENCE DICTATION TEST

1. Have students state in writing advantages and disadvantages of using a computer to record and store important records. Then ask them to decide which way is better and tell why.

writing

2. Have students record the words they missed on the test in their Spelling Notebook (see page 345) for at-school study, and on a copy of the WORDS TO LEARN BLACKLINE MASTER, page 375, for at-home study.

recording words for personal study list

Have students write (IN OTHER WORDS): Imitation is the sincerest form of flattery.

Research on spelling acquisition strongly supports the development of visual skills. These essential skills are explicitly taught and practiced in the Word Preview that opens each unit. They are applied as students write across the curriculum with stated expectations for meeting a minimum expectation for spelling in everyday writing—their Priority Words. All the while, students are taught skills that form the foundation for understanding English spelling.

• Guide students to see the word *special* inside *especially*. They have learned that when the *ly* suffix is added to words ending in *l*, no *l* is dropped, and the word becomes one with double *l*. Revisit this with *special* + *ly* = *specially*. This should help students remember the double *l* in *especially*. Have students follow up by adding *ly* to *final, equal, natural, careful*.

Name _______________________________

A Yankee Laughs Last

"Yankee Doodle came to (1) _______________, riding on a pony, stuck a feather in his cap, and (2) _______________ it macaroni!" We (3) _______________ this verse as (4) _______________. (5) _______________ how we (6) _______________ liked the part about the macaroni! Yet, (7) _______________ (8) _______________ shows that this (9) _______________ lyric was an eighteenth century anthem enthusiastically sung by adult colonists to express (10) _______________ patriotism. How so? (11) _______________ on, according to the (12) _______________, British soldiers prided (13) _______________ on (14) _______________ dapper attire. Colonial soldiers attempted to look spiffy, but (15) _______________ looked like ragamuffins fresh from the (16) _______________. In England, a "macaroni" was a (17) _______________ who tried to (18) _______________ a stylish outfit, but failed and looked (19) _______________ foolish (20) _______________. So this song was (21) _______________ sung by the British to discredit colonists. But at the British surrender at Yorktown, George Washington's troops struck up the Yankee Doodle chorus making it (22) _______________ for the British soldiers to "eat (23) _______________ words!" Why did the colonists love this song from then on and the British (24) _______________ consider it (25) _______________ (26) _______________ favorite tune?

Skill Test

Homographs are ____
____.

Circle the homographs.

sometimes	read	wound	bass
object	forest	business	content
minute	necessary	excuse	woman
mountain	measure	lead	does
wind	present	explain	correct

Select one homograph and use it in a sentence to illustrate its meanings.

____

____

Proofreading Test

If the underlined word or words in each line are incorrect for spelling or capitalization, write the correction in the space.

Before Samuel <u>clemens began his writing</u> career, he   _______________

was a steamship <u>pilot who traveled along</u> the great   _______________

Mississippi <u>river. In some places</u> the river is quite   _______________

shallow. A steamship <u>needs fairly deep water</u>, so   _______________

it was <u>necesary to journey</u> with much care. It was   _______________

<u>especialy important to avoid</u> the water's edge, but   _______________

some areas were rather shallow <u>even in the midlle</u>   _______________

of the waterway. <u>Oftten, Samuel would</u> toss out a rope   _______________

<u>marked with pointts six feet</u>, or one full fathom, apart   _______________

<u>to meassure the water's</u> depth. If he called out "mark   _______________

twain," that meant <u>the water was a least</u> two fathoms   _______________

deep, <u>safe for passage. His</u> book, *Life on the Mississippi*,   _______________

<u>describes these adventure's</u> as a "cub" pilot.   _______________

Why do you suppose that the personal experiences of an author are often the subject about which he/she writes?

Use Student Practice Pages 70–71 to follow up instruction for:
Activity 1A • Test Ready

Build Visual Skills

Do the Word Preview, a visual warm-up activity, with all students.
Use Core Words **he's** (616), **unit** (617), **flat** (618), **direction** (619), **south** (620).

Teaching Notes, page 316

Build Spelling and Language Skills

Choose from among these quick tasks to customize instruction
for all or selected students.

Teaching Notes, page 319

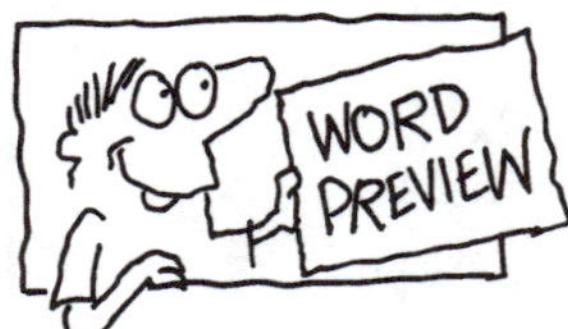

She went the wrong direction.

**From where hes standing, the land changes in every directian. To the
north, the mountain are especially beautiful. Just south of him, the land
is flat. He wishs every one in his unit could see this famous place.**

(*he's, direction, mountains* or *is, wishes, everyone*)

third, south, there's, through, fifth, athlete, bother, they're, fourth, twelfth, weather, that's

(e.g., position of *th*; number of letters; is/isn't a number word; is/isn't a homophone; is/isn't a contraction)

direction, objection, exception, ______

(words that contain *tion*)

Just south of our school you will see ______.

Contractions made with *is* and *has*

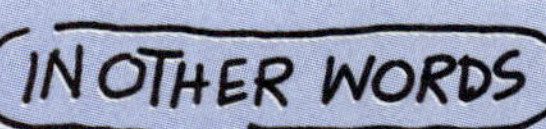
Have students write (*IN OTHER WORDS*) what it means to be flat broke,
or to be flat out of money.

Build Basic Concepts

Choose from among these skill-building activities to customize instruction for all or selected students.

Teaching Notes, page 325

concept one	Antonyms are words with opposite meanings.

1A Review how the prefixes that mean *not/opposite of/wrong* (e.g., un, non, in, im, il, dis, ir, mis, ab) can create antonym pairs (e.g., direct/indirect). Then show how opposite base words can be paired to make antonyms—*north/south*. Have students collect antonym pairs to create a class book with a page for each alphabet letter.

able/unable
abnormal/normal
above/below
acquit/convict
antonym/synonym
actress/actor
addition/subtraction
admit/deny
adult/child
after/before
against/for
agree/disagree

ahead/behind
alike/different
alive/dead
alone/together
always/never
AM/PM
answer/question
appear/disappear
approve/disapprove
arrive/depart
asleep/awake
ask/reply

antonyms, prefix practice, more words, vocabulary development, class book

1B Ask students to write what they can tell you about *north* and *south*. Students' observations may include that the words are:

word analysis, more words

- antonyms
- one syllable
- able to be abbreviated
- end in th
- sometimes used in compounds
- directions
- able to take the ern suffix
- spelled with five letters

Have students springboard from each attribute to more words that meet the criterion.

1C Ask students for the antonyms indicated on a compass that name directions (north/south, east/west). Prepare for a letter-card activity (see Activity 2B, page 47) using *a, d, e, i, l, q, s, t, u,* and *w*. Together make *west*. Then have students continue making words: *quest—quail—equal—detail—dilute—adult—ideal—duel—duet—edit—idle—aisle—ladies—sailed—salted—silt—quilt—quit—quiet—quite—wise—wildest—waited—waste—stew—steal—seal—seat—east*. Later, have students work in pairs to make more words with their letter cards. Have them write the words as they make them.

visual skills, making words, vocabulary development

By far the most frequent spelling for the unstressed syllable /shən/ is *tion* (direction); however, students may be aware of others, such as *sion* (mission), and less frequently *cean* (ocean), *cian* (musician), and *tian* (martian).

- Challenge students to collect and sort /shən/-ending words by spelling pattern.
- Challenge students to sort tion/sion words by sound to discern slight variations, such as among *nation, question, television*.

Teaching Notes, page 328

Build Skillful Writers

Use these interrelated language learnings for all or selected students.

Share these humorous, but actual, product directions with students to illustrate examples to be avoided when writing concise directions.

- On a string of holiday lights: *Use lights for indoor or outdoor use only like regular lights.*
- On a children's cough medicine: *Do not drive car or operate heavy machinery while taking.*
- On an airline nut snack package: *Open packet. Eat nuts. May be harmful to your health. Contains nuts.*

Have students write directions (e.g., how to make a peanut butter sandwich, how to check out a library book). Then have direction evaluations—one student reads another student's directions and follows them to the letter to determine their effectiveness.

Teaching Notes, page 329

Skill to be tested:
singular, singular possessive, plural, plural possessive nouns

Build Assessment Readiness

Use these at-school and at-home exercises to prepare all students for the Skill Test.

at-school Ask students how to show possession (an apostrophe signals possession, use possessive pronouns). Review possession (Activity 1C, page 137).

Play a sorting game with students. Write categories on the chalkboard: *singular, singular possessive, plural, plural possessive*. Say sentences that contain a word that is an example of one of the categories. Have students indicate the category in which the possessive word should be placed. For example:

> The music teacher has a desk. (singular)
> The music teacher's desk is blue. (singular possessive)
> All the fifth grade teachers have desks. (plural)
> The fifth grade teachers' desks are orange. (plural possessive)

Remind students that a plural that does not end in *s* adds *'s* to make the plural possessive (e.g., men's, children's, mice's).

Skill to be tested:
singular, singular possessive, plural, plural possessive nouns

at-home Send home a copy of Take-Home Task 24 Blackline Master, page 211, with each student to encourage parent-child partnerships.

Teaching Notes, page 330

Build Proofreading Skills

Track students' ability to meet a minimum competency for spelling and proofreading within selected samples of their everyday writing.

- Send home papers for proofreading and a copy of the Ideas for Proofreading Blackline Master, page 373.

Dear Parents,

In this activity you can help your child with spelling and usage. Begin by discussing the information in the boxes to help your child differentiate nouns—singular, singular possessive, plural, and plural possessive. Then provide guidance as your child completes the word chart.

See the chicken.   See the chicken's egg.   See the chickens.   See the chickens' eggs.

Write the missing nouns. At the end, fill in your own nouns.

SINGULAR	SINGULAR POSSESSIVE	PLURAL	PLURAL POSSESSIVE
chicken			
owl		owls	owls'
	baby's		babies'
	bird's		
	business's	businesses	businesses'
animal	animal's		animals'
			girls'
family		families	
boy			boys'
	ostrich's	ostriches	ostriches'
		ladies	ladies'
horse			

Assess Words and Skills

- Spelling Words (words missed on tests) are recorded in the Spelling Notebook.
- Use Proof It, Practice Page 72, for proofreading/editing practice.

WORD TEST

Teaching Notes, page 336

Assess Spelling Progress

Give this Cloze Story Word Test of Core Words within the frequencies 1–620 to all students. Words students miss are their Spelling Words.

 **THE CLOZE STORY WORD TEST**

Students do not prestudy the words. Provide students with a copy of REVIEW 24 BLACKLINE MASTER, page 215. Tell students that this story will get them drawing and discovering.

Read the entire story aloud, including the test words. Then read it again slowly as students write the missing words.

Words tested:
a (4), there('s) (37), first (74), once (206), let('s) (230), second (235), it's (253), several (263), point (272), whether (399), follow (428), everyone (430), friend('s) (498), travel (516), measure (523), straight (524), length (546), choose(ing) (580), trouble (588), lot (597), object (606), necessary (615), he's (616), unit (617), flat (618), direction(s) (619), south (620)

WORD TEST

Treasure Tracking

(1) <u>There's</u> a need for (2) <u>everyone</u> to know how to make, read, and (3) <u>follow</u> a map. Have you ever been on a treasure hunt? (4) <u>Let's</u> make a map for a pal to track a treasure! Begin by (5) <u>choosing</u> a place outside to hide an (6) <u>object</u>, the "treasure." Then create a map that takes your buddy along a route to (7) <u>several</u> landmarks to locate this treasure. Indicate the (8) <u>directions</u> north, (9) <u>south</u>, east, and west on your map. Show where to start. Then tell how far to go to the (10) <u>first</u> landmark using some (11) <u>unit</u> of (12) <u>measure</u>, such as the number of steps and the approximate (13) <u>length</u> of each one. Next, tell the treasure hunter what to do to get to the (14) <u>second</u> landmark. Tell him when to go (15) <u>straight</u> and when it is (16) <u>necessary</u> to turn. You'll want to (17) <u>point</u> out (18) <u>whether</u> the land is (19) <u>flat</u> or hilly. Mark some trees, lakes, houses, or streets for this person to be sure (20) <u>he's</u> able to read your map without (21) <u>a lot</u> of (22) <u>trouble</u>. (23) <u>Once</u> the treasure is found, then (24) <u>it's</u> your (25) <u>friend's</u> turn to map a route for you to (26) <u>travel</u> to find his treasure.

 **AFTER THE CLOZE STORY WORD TEST**

writing directions, creating a map, writing a summary

1. Have students work in pairs to create a map for tracking a treasure inside your classroom. Then have students discuss their map-making and treasure-tracking strategies. Help them refine their strategies in preparation for playing this game on a larger scale outside at home. Then have students share their map and report in writing the results of their big treasure hunt. Remind students that written directions must be concise (see Build Skillful Writers, this unit).

recording words for personal study list

2. Have students record the words they missed on the test in their Spelling Notebook (see page 338) for at-school study, and on a copy of the WORDS TO LEARN BLACKLINE MASTER, page 375, for at-home study.

Assess Skill Application

Give this assessment of spelling and related skills to all students.
The REVIEW 24 BLACKLINE MASTER is on page 216.

Teaching Notes, page 339

 **THE SKILL TEST**

Fill in the missing nouns.

singular	singular possessive	plural	plural possessive
baby	baby's	babies	babies'
dog	dog's	dogs	dogs'
cat	cat's	cats	cats'
queen	queen's	queens	queens'

This big, brown ___bear's___ honey tastes sweet.
   bear   (bear's)   bears   bears'
Two big, brown ___bears___ have some honey.
   bear   bear's   (bears)   bears'
These big, brown ___bears'___ honey tastes sweet.
   bear   bear's   bears   (bears')
One big, brown ___bear___ has some honey.
   (bear)   bear's   bears   bears'

Skill tested:
singular, singular possessive,
plural, plural possessive nouns

Note the ability of each student to identify and use singular, singular possessive, plural, and plural possessive nouns.

Assess Proofreading Application

Give this assessment of spelling and related skills to all students.
The REVIEW 24 BLACKLINE MASTER is on page 216.

Teaching Notes, page 341

 **THE PROOFREADING TEST**

Proofread for spelling, capitalization, punctuation, or grammar
errors in the underlined parts. Circle errors. Write corrections in the space.

Mark Twain is a well-known american author. His	American
writing has been popular for many years. It has	
become part of our heritage. Their are several	There
other respected authors who's work has withstood	whose
the test of time. Yet, the author that some poeple	people
think is the finer in the world is an Englishman—a	finest
poet and playwright who lived over four hundrud	hundred
years ago. Still, his writing is ammong the all-time	among
favorites today. This men is William Shakespeare.	man
He rote about all kinds of characters, both good	wrote
and bad, the heroic and selfish the courageous and	,
cowardly. He seemed to understand then all and	them
helped us to understand them, to.	too

Today's authors' writing may also stand the test of time—which authors do you think
they may be?

Note the ability of each student to proofread for errors.

Teaching Notes, page 342

Words tested:
the (1), and (3), to (5), in (6), is (7), he (11), for (12), on (14), as (16), his (18), at (20), be (21), what (32), when (35), their (42), will (46), she (54), him (67), back (103), well (132), home (157), read (165), school (194), enough (209), mother (226), study(ies) (234), it's (253), learn (271), family (287), book (307), American (319), complete(s) (365), understand (416), although (450), possible (452), friend(s) (498), mark('s) (504), listen (507), explain (513), bed (522), teacher (539), happy (540), information (549), especially (614), necessary (615), he's (616), unit (617), flat (618), direction (619), south (620)

Extra words: believes, industry, provide, return, social

writing

recording words for personal study list

Extend Spelling Assessment

Give this in-context assessment of Core Words within the frequencies 1–620 to students who need more practice or challenge.

THE SENTENCE DICTATION TEST

Students do not prestudy the words. Provide students with writing paper and pencil. Have students write the sentences as they are dictated.

1. Mark's teacher will provide direction as he completes the Social Studies unit on South American industry in their Social Studies book.

2. She will explain to him and his mother what she believes is necessary for him to learn.

3. Although he's flat on his back in bed at home, it's possible for him to listen and understand information read to him.

4. His friends and family will be especially happy when Mark is well enough to return to school.

AFTER THE SENTENCE DICTATION TEST

1. Have students write about a time when they were not well and received extra help. Then have them write about how they helped someone who was not well.

2. Have students record the words they missed on the test in their Spelling Notebook (see page 345) for at-school study, and on a copy of the WORDS TO LEARN BLACKLINE MASTER, page 375, for at-home study.

Redefine in rhyme:
axle grease (motion lotion)
work with halves and thirds (fraction action)
church annex (mission addition)
inventor's conference (invention convention)
immunization shot (protection injection)

Two similar expressions mean something different. To come out flat-footed means to be unwilling to compromise. To be caught flat-footed means to be unprepared for action. The latter arose from sports, such as when a ball is thrown to a player who appears unready for play; or when the starting gates for a horse race fly open and the horse is not poised to run.

Word Test

Treasure Tracking

(1) _______________ a need for (2) _______________ to know how to make, read,

and (3) _______________ a map. Have you ever been on a treasure hunt?

(4) _______________ make a map for a pal to track a treasure! Begin by

(5) _______________ a place outside to hide an (6) _______________, the "treasure."

Then create a map that takes your buddy along a route to (7) _______________

landmarks to locate this treasure. Indicate the (8) _______________ north,

(9) _______________, east, and west on your map. Show where to start. Then tell

how far to go to the (10) _______________ landmark using some (11) _______________

of (12) _______________, such as the number of steps and the approximate

(13) _______________ of each one. Next, tell the treasure hunter what to do to get

to the (14) _______________ landmark. Tell him when to go (15) _______________ and

when it is (16) _______________ to turn. You'll want to (17) _______________ out

(18) _______________ the land is (19) _______________ or hilly. Mark some trees,

lakes, houses, or streets for this person to be sure (20) _______________ able to read

your map without (21) _______________ of (22) _______________. (23) _______________

the treasure is found, then (24) _______________ your (25) _______________ turn to

map a route for you to (26) _______________ to find his treasure.

Name ______________________________

Skill Test

Fill in the missing nouns.

singular	singular possessive	plural	plural possessive
baby		babies	
	dog's		dogs'
	cat's		cats'
queen		queens	

This big, brown ____________________ honey tastes sweet.

        bear   bear's   bears   bears'

Two big, brown ____________________ have some honey.

        bear   bear's   bears   bears'

These big, brown ____________________ honey tastes sweet.

        bear   bear's   bears   bears'

One big, brown ____________________ has some honey.

        bear   bear's   bears   bears'

Proofreading Test

Proofread for spelling, capitalization, punctuation, or grammar errors in the underlined parts. Circle errors. Write corrections in the space.

Mark Twain is a well-known american author. His ______________________

writing has been popular for many years. It has ______________________

become part of our heritage. Their are several ______________________

other respected authors who's work has withstood ______________________

the test of time. Yet, the author that some poeple ______________________

think is the finer in the world is an Englishman—a ______________________

poet and playwright who lived over four hundrud ______________________

years ago. Still, his writing is ammong the all-time ______________________

favorites today. This men is William Shakespeare. ______________________

He rote about all kinds of characters, both good ______________________

and bad, the heroic and selfish the courageous and ______________________

cowardly. He seemed to understand then all and ______________________

helped us to understand them, to. ______________________

Today's authors' writing may also stand the test of time—which authors do you think they may be?

Build Skills and Word Experiences

Build Visual Skills

Do the Word Preview, a visual warm-up activity, with all students.
Use Core Words **subject** (621), **skin** (622), **wasn't** (623), **I've** (624), **yellow** (625).

Teaching Notes, page 316

Build Spelling and Language Skills

Choose from among these quick tasks to customize instruction
for all or selected students.

Teaching Notes, page 319

It was yellow.

I wasnt going to subject you to the subject of skin, but I've did it.
Animals people food and even hot dogs have skin. Foods have different
colors of skin. Among the colors are yelow, green, blue, and purple.

(*wasn't*, *done*, comma series, *yellow*)

essays, yellow, recess, baseball, pretty, waitresses, hello, spaghetti, alley, classmates,
motto, hopeless

(e.g., contains *ll/ss/tt*; contains long *a/e/o*; number of syllables)

skin/in, yellow/low, forest/for, _______ /_______
(words inside of words)

The main subject in today's news is _______.

Things in your classroom that are yellow

How do frogs get to Oz? They follow the yellow brick toad!

Teaching Notes, page 325

Build Basic Concepts

Choose from among these skill-building activities to customize instruction
for all or selected students.

concept one	A contraction is a combination of two or more words with an apostrophe replacing a letter or letters.

making words, contractions, apostrophes, writing words, word game, proofreading

1A Discuss why *I've* and *wasn't* are called contractions. Discuss the purpose of using apostrophes in contractions and other words. Write on the chalkboard: *not, shall/will, would/had, have, are, is/has, am, us.* Have students brainstorm contractions made from these words. Time the session (about four minutes). Then students self-check using Personal Poster 4.

Next, have students create a bingo board (see Activity 1C, page 20) using sixteen contractions from Personal Poster 4. Then play bingo. Call out the longer form for students to find the contraction on their bingo board (e.g., *he will* for *he'll*).

concept two	A suffix is a letter or letters added to the end of a word.

suffix practice, writing words, spelling rules, sorting words, word game

2A Ask students to define a suffix. Organize students into small groups, each member with paper/pencil. Post Teaching Poster 2. Assign a different word to each group. Students write the word with all appropriate suffixes. Then have them take turns presenting the word forms to the class—writing them on the chalkboard and explaining the rule on Teaching Poster 2 that applies. (Save the words on the chalkboard.)

Word choices you may wish to assign that reflect each rule include:

Rule 1: subject, record, sleep, reason, straight, pay
Rule 2: minute, measure, edge, store, late, square
Rule 3: skin, flat, refer, begin, plan, trip
Rule 4: rely, baby, history, happy, copy, early
Rule 5: business, furnish, relax, watch, rich, catch

Then have students use the words on the chalkboard for:

- sorting activities, such as by nouns/verbs/adjectives, vowel sound, suffix
- making compound words
- making antonym pairs
- listing words with consonant blends
- listing words with digraphs
- listing words with silent letters
- listing words with double letters
- adding prefixes
- making rhyming word families
- playing spelling games (see page 390)

Remember, students produce quick results when activities are timed.

Build Skillful Writers

Use these interrelated language learnings for all or selected students.

Teaching Notes, page 328

Write on the chalkboard: *Fox said, "I like jelly toast."* Ask students for the names of the punctuation in the sentence (quotation marks, comma, period). Tell students that quotation marks set off a speaker's exact words. The sentence is an example of a direct quotation. However, an indirect quotation is not set off by quotation marks: *Fox said he likes jelly toast.* You may wish to copy the story on Take-Home Task 25 to use for examples of direct quotations and the use of quotation marks. Further, discuss these points regarding quotation marks:

- Punctuation separates a direct quotation from who said it.
- Punctuation is placed inside the quotation marks at the end of a sentence.
- In a broken quotation, do not capitalize the first word of the second part of the quotation, unless it is the beginning of a new sentence.
- When quoting conversations, begin a new paragraph for each speaker.

Have students write a paragraph that uses quotation marks.

Build Assessment Readiness

Use these at-school and at-home exercises to prepare all students for the Skill Test.

Teaching Notes, page 329

at-school Identify *subject* and *object* as homographs and have students use the words in sentences to illustrate their different meanings and pronunciations. Review the *ject* root (Word Mysteries and Histories, page 191). Then ask students to identify the letter spelling /j/ in the words (j). Ask students to identify other spelling patterns for /j/ (ge/dge, gi, gy). Ask students to take turns at the chalkboard, supplying words that illustrate the spelling patterns.

Next, have students strategize when to spell /j/-ending words *ge* and *dge*. If students do not recall, brainstorm words from which to conclude that when /j/ immediately follows a short vowel, *dge* is usually used (edge). Otherwise, *ge* is usually used (age, charge). Ask students to write the strategy and provide word examples to illustrate their explanation.

Skill to be tested:
/j/ spelling patterns

at-home Send home a copy of TAKE-HOME TASK 25 BLACKLINE MASTER, page 220.

Skill to be tested:
/j/ spelling patterns

Build Proofreading Skills

Track students' ability to meet a minimum competency for spelling and proofreading within selected samples of their everyday writing.

Teaching Notes, page 330

- Send home papers for proofreading and a copy of the IDEAS FOR PROOFREADING BLACKLINE MASTER, page 373.

Name _______________________________

Dear Parents,

Enjoy this fable with your child. Then guide your child to find and write all the words in the story that contain the sound heard at the beginning of . This sound is most often spelled with j, gi, gy, ge, and dge. Discuss any unfamiliar words.

Read the fable. Find and write words spelled with the sound at the beginning of . Sort them by spelling pattern.

Here is the legend of the cagey fox and the haughty blue jay. One day the fox spied the blue jay perched on the edge of a limb on the juniper tree. He had a huge morsel of jelly toast wedged in his beak. Fox jealously thought, "There's been a shortage of jelly toast in my diet. I object to that bird's having it and my having none."

So the fox reached for his banjo and began to play a jaunty tune. He called gently to the bird, "Blue jay, I urge you to join me in song, for your voice is majestic." Flattered, the blue jay generously burst into song—and the jelly toast plunged to the ground by the fox's jaw.

"You unintelligent, feathered jerk! Justice reigns, for the jelly toast is now mine!" jeered the joyous fox.

Then a midget-sized mouse emerged from the bushes, her eyes twinkling as she imagined the sweet taste of a smidgen of the jelly toast. Would she have the courage to pursue it?

"Foxy," she smiled as she gestured toward the banjo, "I'm obliged to compliment you on your magical music. Adjectives cannot describe the gorgeous melody you play with such energy! How did you become the agile musician that I judge you to be?"

Fox closed his eyes in cogitation, as all logical thinkers do. "Simple," he acknowledged, "I'm genuinely smarter than..." Just then, the nimble mouse jumped for the jelly toast and lunged into a jungle of leaves to escape danger. Ahh!

- Now who's enjoying jelly toast?
- What do you think is the moral, or lesson, of this fable?
- What would be a good title for this fable?
- What words would describe Fox at the beginning of the story—and at the end?

Assess Words and Skills

- Spelling Words (words missed on tests) are recorded in the Spelling Notebook.
- Use Proof It, Practice Page 75, for proofreading/editing practice.

Assess Spelling Progress

Teaching Notes, page 336

Give this Cloze Story Word Test of Core Words within the frequencies 1–625 to all students. Words students miss are their Spelling Words.

THE CLOZE STORY WORD TEST

Students do not prestudy the words. Provide students with a copy of REVIEW 25 BLACKLINE MASTER, page 224. Tell students that this story will get them thinking in some new ways about a common substance.

Read the entire story aloud, including the test words. Then read it again slowly as students write the missing words.

The Wonders of Water

On the (1) <u>subject</u> of water, (2) <u>I've</u> taken it for granted in the (3) <u>past</u>. That (4) <u>wasn't</u> a good idea (5) <u>because</u> water is truly a (6) <u>natural</u> wonder.

- Water is nature's transformer. (7) <u>It's</u> solid, liquid, or gas. How is water (8) <u>able</u> to transform (9) <u>itself</u> from one state to (10) <u>another</u>?
- Water is nature's dissolver. It makes things disappear as well as any magician can. What (11) <u>could</u> you do with sugar and water to illustrate this (12) <u>simple</u> concept?
- Water is nature's attractor. It can act like glue. Devise an experiment with water and two (13) <u>pieces</u> of plastic wrap to show this.
- Water is nature's mover. How does water move (14) <u>great</u> weights like a big (15) <u>machine</u>?
- Water is nature's climber. It (16) <u>travels</u> from a (17) <u>tree's</u> roots to (18) <u>its</u> leaves (19) <u>through</u> capillary action. (20) <u>Explain</u> how you'd prove this with (21) <u>yellow</u> food coloring, water, and a strip of white paper.
- Water is nature's presser. Why (22) <u>might</u> a scuba diver be (23) <u>especially</u> aware of this?
- Water is nature's lubricator. It smoothly glides a ring over your (24) <u>skin</u> and off your finger.

Wow! (25) <u>There's</u> the possibility that even Wonder Woman or Superman (26) <u>cannot</u> do all this!

Words tested:

there('s) (37), could (70), its (76), through (102), another (121), because (127), great (146), might (173), it's (253), tree('s) (316), cannot (343), able (346), piece(s) (392), past (403), simple (455), itself (474), explain (513), travel(s) (516), machine (548), natural (556), especially (614), subject (621), skin (622), wasn't (623), I've (624), yellow (625)

AFTER THE CLOZE STORY WORD TEST

1. Have students write and share their answers to the story questions. Can students think of other qualities water exhibits besides nature's transformer, dissolver, attractor, mover, climber, presser, and lubricator? What about nature's stretcher? Discuss how water can stretch. For example, have students experiment with blowing soap bubbles.

writing explanations

2. Have students record the words they missed on the test in their Spelling Notebook (see page 338) for at-school study, and on a copy of the WORDS TO LEARN BLACKLINE MASTER, page 375, for at-home study.

recording words for personal study list

Teaching Notes, page 339

Assess Skill Application

Give this assessment of spelling and related skills to all students.
The REVIEW 25 BLACKLINE MASTER is on page 225.

 THE SKILL TEST

Skill tested:
/j/ spelling patterns

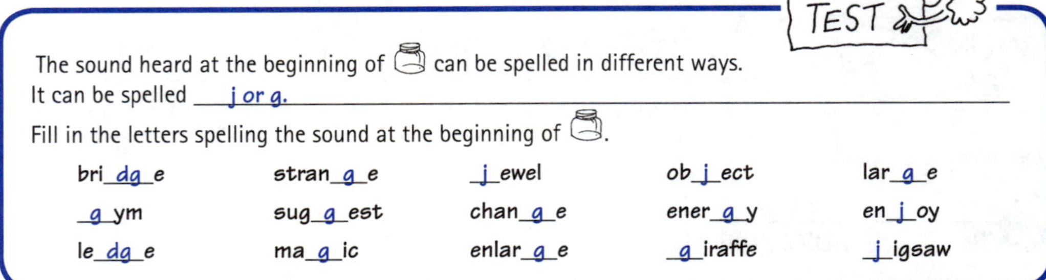

The sound heard at the beginning of 🫙 can be spelled in different ways.
It can be spelled ___*j or g.*___
Fill in the letters spelling the sound at the beginning of 🫙.

bri_dg_e	stran_g_e	_j_ewel	ob_j_ect	lar_g_e
_g_ym	sug_g_est	chan_g_e	ener_g_y	en_j_oy
le_dg_e	ma_g_ic	enlar_g_e	_g_iraffe	_j_igsaw

Note the ability of each student to identify both *j* and *g* as spelling patterns for /j/
and to spell words containing /j/. (Some students may be able to identify the spelling
patterns as *j, ge, dge, gi, gy*).

Teaching Notes, page 341

Assess Proofreading Application

Give this assessment of spelling and related skills to all students.
The REVIEW 25 BLACKLINE MASTER is on page 225.

 THE PROOFREADING TEST

Introduce students to
Shakespeare's life, times,
plays, actors, and words in
Aliki's award-winning picture
book, *William Shakespeare
and the Globe*—the 1999
Boston Globe-Horn Book
Honor for nonfiction.

Circle the correctly spelled word to complete each line.

Shakespeare was __________ fond of using unique	especially	espesially	especialy
words in his writing. He could shape the __________	pickures	pictures	pitchers
in his readers' minds by carefully __________ the	choosing	chooseing	chosing
words he used to __________ things. Sometimes	desribe	deskribe	describe
__________ wasn't a word for precisely what he was	their	there's	there
trying to say. In many __________, he just invented	cases	caces	kases
a new word. __________ of his invented, or "coined,"	Many	Meny	Manny
words are part of our modern __________. It's	langage	languagge	language
likely you __________ use these words when you speak	offen	often	ofen
and write. Words we attribute to him __________	include	enclade	includae
__________, hurry, and suspicious. He had a	lonely	lonly	lonely
__________ effect on our vocabulary than any other	grater	gratter	greater
writer in __________.	hestory	history	histery

Twangling is a word coined by Shakespeare. What do you think he might have meant it
to mean?

Note the ability of each student to proofread for spelling errors.

Extend Spelling Assessment

Give this in-context assessment of Core Words within the frequencies 1–625 to students who need more practice or challenge.

Teaching Notes, page 342

Words tested:

the (1), of (2), and (3), a (4), to (5), is (7), it (10), he (11), for (12), with (17), this (22), I (24), had (29), not (30), there('s) (37), said (43), him (67), my (80), back (103), new (107), me (110), look (117), because (127), again (141), between (154), big (158), asked (188), don't (190), father (229), since (238), change (264), body (285), course (317), already (411), understand (416), fact (445), care (483), explain (513), hair (528), color(ed) (531), bright (541), rather (545), natural (556), reason (564), wish (573), trouble (588), won't (598), especially (614), necessary (615), subject (621), skin (622), wasn't (623), I've (624), yellow (625)

Extra words: decided, discuss, I'd, myself

THE SENTENCE DICTATION TEST

Students do not prestudy the words. Provide students with writing paper and pencil. Have students write the sentences as they are dictated.

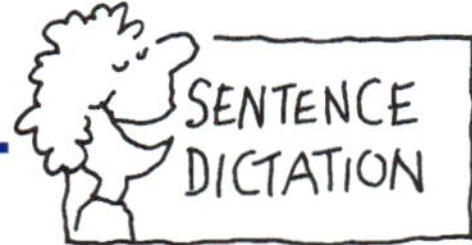

1. Because I colored my hair and skin bright yellow, there's big trouble between my father and me.
2. He said it wasn't necessary and asked me to explain my reason for the color change.
3. Of course, this is a subject I'd rather not discuss with him since I've decided he won't understand.
4. In fact, I don't especially care for this new look myself and already wish I had my natural body color back again.

AFTER THE SENTENCE DICTATION TEST

1. Have students write a dialogue between this child and the father.

writing dialogue

2. Have students record the words they missed on the test in their Spelling Notebook (see page 345) for at-school study, and on a copy of the WORDS TO LEARN BLACKLINE MASTER, page 375, for at-home study.

recording words for personal study list

History, as well as a daily report of the news, often showcases what has come to be known as "soundbites." Here is a soundbite from Abraham Lincoln's speech on March 9, 1832, in Sangamon County, Illinois:

"Upon the subject of education...I can only say that I view it as the most important subject which we, as a people, can be engaged in."

• Have students write soundbites on a subject of current interest across the curriculum.

Have students write (*IN OTHER WORDS*): Beauty is only skin deep.

"You never really understand people until you consider things from their point of view...until you climb into their skin and walk around in it."
Harper Lee, author of *To Kill a Mockingbird*

Name ___________________________

— Word Test —

The Wonders of Water

On the (1) ___________________ of water, (2) ________________ taken it for granted in the

(3) ___________________. That (4) _________________ a good idea (5) ________________

water is truly a (6) ________________ wonder.

- Water is nature's transformer. (7) ________________ solid, liquid, or gas. How

  is water (8) ________________ to transform (9) ________________ from one

  state to (10) ________________?

- Water is nature's dissolver. It makes things disappear as well as any magician can.

  What (11) ________________ you do with sugar and water to illustrate this

  (12) ________________ concept?

- Water is nature's attractor. It can act like glue. Devise an experiment with water

  and two (13) ________________ of plastic wrap to show this.

- Water is nature's mover. How does water move (14) ________________ weights like

  a big (15) ________________?

- Water is nature's climber. It (16) ________________ from a (17) ________________

  roots to (18) ________________ leaves (19) ________________ capillary action.

  (20) ________________ how you'd prove this with (21) ________________ food

  coloring, water, and a strip of white paper.

- Water is nature's presser. Why (22) ________________ a scuba diver be

  (23) ________________ aware of this?

- Water is nature's lubricator. It smoothly glides a ring over your (24) ________________

  and off your finger.

Wow! (25) ________________ the possibility that even Wonder Woman or Superman

(26) ________________ do all this!

Skill Test

The sound heard at the beginning of [jar] can be spelled in different ways. It can be spelled

____

____ .

Fill in the letters spelling the sound at the beginning of [jar] .

bri______e   stran______e   ______ewel   ob______ect   lar______e

______ym   sug______est   chan______e   ener______y   en______oy

le______e   ma______ic   enlar______e   ______iraffe   ______igsaw

Proofreading Test

Circle the correctly spelled word to complete each line.

Shakespeare was __________ fond of using unique	especially	espesially	especialy
words in his writing. He could shape the __________	pickures	pictures	pitchers
in his readers' minds by carefully __________ the	choosing	chooseing	chosing
words he used to __________ things. Sometimes	desribe	deskribe	describe
__________ wasn't a word for precisely what he was	their	there's	there
trying to say. In many __________, he just invented	cases	caces	kases
a new word. __________ of his invented, or "coined,"	Many	Meny	Manny
words are part of our modern __________. It's	langage	languagge	language
likely you __________ use these words when you speak	offen	often	ofen
and write. Words we attribute to him __________	include	enclade	incluade
__________ , hurry, and suspicious. He had a	lonely	lonly	lonelly
__________ effect on our vocabulary than any other	grater	gratter	greater
writer in __________ .	hestory	history	histery

Twangling is a word coined by Shakespeare. What do you think he might have meant it to mean?

Build Skills and Word Experiences

Use Student Practice Pages 76–77 to follow up instruction for:
Activity 1A • Test Ready

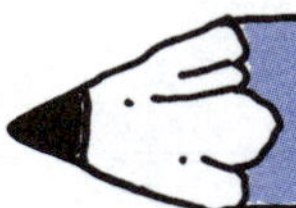

Build Visual Skills

Do the Word Preview, a visual warm-up activity, with all students.
Use Core Words **party** (626), **force** (627), **test** (628), **bad** (629), **temperature** (630).

Teaching Notes, page 316

Build Spelling and Language Skills

Choose from among these quick tasks to customize instruction
for all or selected students.

Teaching Notes, page 319

We have a test today.

Are party was subjected to cold temprature and the strong force of
the winds. Our leader said, "it is not a wise idea to climb the mountain
now." This wether even tested our seven dogs skills.

(*Our, temperature, It, weather, dogs'*)

temperature, wristwatch, bachelor, picture, hitchhiker, stagecoach, furniture,
catcher, schoolchildren, adventure, untouchable, kitchen

(e.g., by spelling of /ch/; number of syllables; is/isn't a compound)

pretest, prerecord, prefix, ______

(words with prefix *pre*)

The search party was called out to ______.

Similes

(e.g., as hot as a firecracker)

Build Basic Concepts

Choose from among these skill-building activities to customize instruction
for all or selected students.

Teaching Notes, page 325

| concept one | Some sounds are spelled more than one way. |

1A Write *party* and *cry* on the chalkboard to point out that /ē/ and /ī/ at the end of
a word are usually spelled *y*. Have students fold paper to make two vertical columns
labeled /ē/-ending words spelled *y* and /ī/-ending words spelled *y*. Have students
briskly write words (about four minutes). Then students share words. Ask students to
note /ē/-ending words spelled *ey*, a fairly frequent spelling pattern (e.g., turkey, honey,
New Jersey).

(phonics, more words, spelling word patterns)

Next, have students brainstorm other ways to spell /ē/ and /ī/ at the end of a word.
Choices may include: *i/ski, ee/tree, ea/flea, ie/prairie; igh/high, ie/pie, ye/dye*. Conclude
that some sounds are spelled more than one way.

1B The soft-syllable /ē/-ending has variants with /ə/, such as the /ərē/-ending words
spelled *ery* (e.g., mystery), *ary* (e.g., summary), *ory* (e.g., history), and *ury* (e.g.,
century). Challenge students to find and write examples sorted by spelling patterns.

(phonics, spelling patterns, more words, sorting words)

1C Ask students what they know about spelling /s/. Statements may include that /s/
can be spelled:

(phonics, word analysis)

> *s* at the beginning, middle, and end of a word (subject, test, units)
>
> *se* at the end of a word (increase)
>
> *ss* in the middle and end of a word (possible, business)
>
> *ce* at the beginning, middle, and end of a word (cent, sincere, force)
>
> *ci* at the beginning, middle, and end of a word (city, decide, Luci)
>
> *cy* at the beginning, middle, and end of a word (cyclone, bicycle, fancy)
>
> *sc* at the beginning and middle of a word (scientist, discipline)
>
> *x*, as in /ks/, in the middle and end of a word (example, box)

Repeat the activity with /ch/ (e.g., ch/choose, t/temperature, tch/catch, te/righteous,
c/cello, cc/cappuccino).

The most frequent spelling for /ch/ is *ch*, as in *children*, which
accounts for over 50% of the spellings. The next most frequent
pattern is *t*, as in the unaccented syllable of *temperature, ture*.
This occurs slightly over 30% of the time.

• Have students find and write words with the *ture* spelling
pattern (e.g., adventure, picture, feature, capture, pasture,
furniture, nature, future, mixture, moisture).

Teaching Notes, page 328

Build Skillful Writers

Use these interrelated language learnings for all or selected students.

Introduce students to an often-confused grammar issue: Is it *bad* or *badly*?

When it's an activity, use *badly*.
    The words are used *badly*.
When it's a condition, use *bad*.
    The writing looks *bad*.
    I feel *bad* about it.

You smell ______________. Have students decide which to use—the right answer depends which is meant!

Expand the lesson to other often misused words:

between/among: Use *between* with two objects. Use *among* with three or more objects.

less/fewer: Use *less* if the items cannot be counted (sand). Use *fewer* with items that can be counted (classrooms).

Teaching Notes, page 329

Skill to be tested:
multiple meanings

Build Assessment Readiness

Use these at-school and at-home exercises to prepare all students for the Skill Test.

at-school Give small groups of students a secret multiple-meaning word (e.g., party, spring, trip, iron, store, lots, mean, state, felt, fine, mind, miss, fall) to use for playing charades. For an additional clue, write letter blanks on the chalkboard for the word being guessed. Later, have students find more multiple-meaning words for subsequent charades.

Skill to be tested:
multiple meanings

at-home Send home a copy of TAKE-HOME TASK 26 BLACKLINE MASTER, page 229.

Teaching Notes, page 330

Build Proofreading Skills

Track students' ability to meet a minimum competency for spelling and proofreading within selected samples of their everyday writing.

• Send home papers for proofreading and a copy of the IDEAS FOR PROOFREADING BLACKLINE MASTER, page 373.

Name________________________________

Dear Parents,

Your child is learning to spell words, as well as learning their meanings and uses in writing. Some words have more than one meaning—examples are in this activity. Ask your child to read the directions and then explain to you what is expected. Guide your child through the activity, taking time to discuss the different meanings of the words.

Cross out the words in each row that cannot be a synonym for the word in the box.

spring	bounce	sprig	jump	pond	May
bright	intelligent	starlight	sunny	generous	silver
mean	cranky	loud	intend	unkind	broken
trip	excursion	accident	stumble	ticket	journey
fall	tumble	decrease	descend	autumn	collapse
party	celebration	streamers	individual	group	slightly
state	city	tell	province	united	declare
store	stockpile	market	groceries	stem	rescue
bill	snout	charge	drain	coast	beak
fair	fresh	new	light	pleasant	carnival
sound	forceful	noise	wrong	strong	section
might	shallow	may	power	bug	meant
last	final	test	endure	level	stair
back	support	suitable	rear	retreat	smooth
just	only	same	fair	complete	difficult
down	ill	gloomy	feathers	lower	swallow
long	yearn	lengthy	seldom	trivial	secure
will	settle	ambition	wish	fence	sell
point	painted	dot	location	aim	top
play	fortune	toddler	compete	act	frolic
run	manage	clever	depart	jog	flee
mind	obey	certain	brain	second	watch

Assess Words and Skills

- Spelling Words (words missed on tests) are recorded in the Spelling Notebook.
- Use Proof It, Practice Page 78, for proofreading/editing practice.

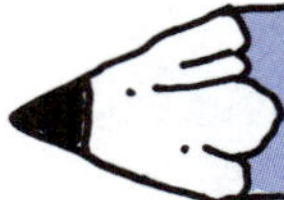

Teaching Notes, page 336

Assess Spelling Progress

Give this Cloze Story Word Test of Core Words within the frequencies 1–630 to all students. Words students miss are their Spelling Words.

THE CLOZE STORY WORD TEST

Students do not prestudy the words. Provide students with a copy of REVIEW 26 BLACKLINE MASTER, page 233. Tell students that this story will get them thinking about minor accidental injuries.

Read the entire story aloud, including the test words. Then read it again slowly as students write the missing words.

Words tested:

a (4), be (21), there (37), their (42), may (89), often (186), half (297), remember (315), perhaps (352), common (395), stop(ping) (396), carefully (427), friend('s) (498), single (509), yourself (534), moment (538), except (550), maybe (566), lot (597), necessary (615), skin (622), party (626), force (627), test (628), bad (629), temperature (630), *they're (1010)

*The testing of they're (1010) is included to help students differentiate among the there/their/they're homophones.

Only Accidental

(1) <u>There</u> are times when you (2) <u>may be</u> thinking about something other than what you're doing. (3) <u>Maybe</u> your mind is on an upcoming (4) <u>test</u> or on a (5) <u>friend's</u> birthday (6) <u>party</u>. Not only are your thoughts occupied, but you're in a hurry. This is when accidents (7) <u>often</u> happen. (8) <u>Remember</u>: Slow down and (9) <u>carefully</u> think about what you're doing. This will avoid more than (10) <u>half</u> the accidents!

A frequent accident is a minor but painful burn. (11) <u>Perhaps</u> you burn the (12) <u>skin</u> on your finger. (13) <u>A lot</u> of people might tell you to put butter on it. This is a (14) <u>common</u> remedy, (15) <u>except</u> (16) <u>their</u> advice is (17) <u>bad</u>. Of course, (18) <u>they're</u> just trying to help. Instead, the (19) <u>moment</u> you're burned, place your burn in ice water. (20) <u>Force</u> (21) <u>yourself</u> to keep it (22) <u>there</u> for at least ten minutes. Aside from the obvious effect the cold (23) <u>temperature</u> has on (24) <u>stopping</u> your burning, you're keeping oxygen from your injury. This is (25) <u>necessary</u> to avoid a blister. Ice water is the (26) <u>single</u> best treatment for slight burns.

Write about an accidental injury you've had. How could it have been avoided?

AFTER THE CLOZE STORY WORD TEST

writing, speculating

1. Have students write about an accidental injury and tell how it could have been avoided. Then have students discuss their answers.

recording words for personal study list

2. Have students record the words they missed on the test in their Spelling Notebook (see page 338) for at-school study, and on a copy of the WORDS TO LEARN BLACKLINE MASTER, page 375, for at-home study.

Assess Skill Application

Give this assessment of spelling and related skills to all students.
The REVIEW 26 BLACKLINE MASTER is on page 234.

Teaching Notes, page 339

THE SKILL TEST

Write four words that can have more than one meaning. Then turn your
paper over and write two sentences for each word that illustrate the
different meanings.

1._______________________   3._______________________

2._______________________   4._______________________

(answers will vary)

Skill tested:
multiple meanings

Note the ability of each student to identify words with more than one meaning and to
use the different meanings in sentences.

Assess Proofreading Application

Give this assessment of spelling and related skills to all students.
The REVIEW 26 BLACKLINE MASTER is on page 234.

Teaching Notes, page 341

THE PROOFREADING TEST

Proofread for spelling, capitalization, punctuation, or grammar
errors in the underlined parts. Circle errors. Write corrections in the space.

Part of growing up is becomeing familiar with   becoming
stories that teach imporetant lifetime lessons.   important
techers and parents seek the finest books for   Teachers
kids to help them learn these lesson. The books   lessons
allso provide good opportunities to practice the   also
skill of reeding, as well as offer pure pleasure.   reading
Writers and illustrators of childrens books are   children's
especialy appreciated. The best books written   especially
and illustrated each yearly receive honors. One   year
award, the Newbery Medal, is gived to an author.   given
The Caldecott Medal is presentted to an illustrator.   presented
The books that have winned these awards can be   won
checked out of any library for you to enjoy.   _______

What do you think it would mean to an author or illustrator to be chosen as the
recipient of the Newbery or Caldecott Medal?

Note the ability of each student to proofread for spelling, capitalization, punctuation, or
grammar errors.

Teaching Notes, page 342

Extend Spelling Assessment

Give this in-context assessment of Core Words within the frequencies 1–630 to students who need more practice or challenge.

Words tested:

the (1), of (2), and (3), a (4), to (5), is (7), for (12), on (14), at (20), I (24), have(ing) (25), all (33), when (35), we('re) (36), can (38), an (39), their (42), than (73), who('s) (77), my (80), get (101), through (102), too (122), work (124), must (126), because (127), house (189), school (194), important (195), keep (199), need (221), study (234), it's (253), hear (260), learn (271), play (274), open (310), English (350), ready (357), can't (380), warm (412), mind (419), outside (420), rock (489), music (501), window (503), rather (545), lot (597), especially (614), party (626), force (627), test (628), bad (629), temperature (630)

Extra words: I'd, myself, tomorrow, tonight, wonder

THE SENTENCE DICTATION TEST

Students do not prestudy the words. Provide students with writing paper and pencil. Have students write the sentences as they are dictated.

1. Tonight I need to get all ready for an important English test we're having tomorrow.

2. I'd rather play than study because the temperature outside is especially warm.

3. I can hear a lot of rock music through my open window and wonder who's having a party at their house.

4. It's too bad when I can't keep my mind on my school work and must force myself to learn.

AFTER THE SENTENCE DICTATION TEST

writing

1. Have students write advice for this student, suggesting ways to study on this warm, noisy night.

recording words for personal study list

2. Have students record the words they missed on the test in their Spelling Notebook (see page 345) for at-school study, and on a copy of the WORDS TO LEARN BLACKLINE MASTER, page 375, for at-home study.

Temperature is measured on the Fahrenheit or Celsius scale. Gabriel Fahrenheit, a German physicist, invented the former and Anders Celsius, a Swedish astronomer, invented the centigrade scale. When something is named for a person or place, it's among a group of words called eponyms.

- Initiate a class book on eponyms. Have students identify eponyms (e.g., Ferris wheel, Graham crackers, Morse code, peach Melba, leotards, frisbee, diesel, braille, sandwich). Then have them write about how the name came to be.
- Have students write a fictional account of how their own name became an eponym.

Word Test

Only Accidental

(1) _______________ are times when you (2) _______________ thinking about something other than what you're doing. (3) _______________ your mind is on an upcoming (4) _______________ or on a (5) _______________ birthday (6) _______________. Not only are your thoughts occupied, but you're in a hurry. This is when accidents (7) _______________ happen. (8) _______________: Slow down and (9) _______________ think about what you're doing. This will avoid more than (10) _______________ the accidents!

A frequent accident is a minor but painful burn. (11) _______________ you burn the (12) _______________ on your finger. (13) _______________ of people might tell you to put butter on it. This is a (14) _______________ remedy, (15) _______________ (16) _______________ advice is (17) _______________. Of course, (18) _______________ just trying to help. Instead, the (19) _______________ you're burned, place your burn in ice water. (20) _______________ (21) _______________ to keep it (22) _______________ for at least ten minutes. Aside from the obvious effect the cold (23) _______________ has on (24) _______________ your burning, you're keeping oxygen from your injury. This is (25) _______________ to avoid a blister. Ice water is the (26) _______________ best treatment for slight burns.

Write about an accidental injury you've had. How could it have been avoided?

Skill Test

Write four words that can have more than one meaning. Then turn your paper over and write two sentences for each word that illustrate the different meanings.

1._______________________   3._______________________

2._______________________   4._______________________

Proofreading Test

Proofread for spelling, capitalization, punctuation, or grammar errors in the underlined parts. Circle errors. Write corrections in the space.

Part of growing <u>up is becomeing</u> familiar with   _______________________

stories <u>that teach imporetant</u> lifetime lessons.   _______________________

<u>techers and parents</u> seek the finest books for   _______________________

kids to help them <u>learn these lesson</u>. The books   _______________________

<u>allso provide good</u> opportunities to practice the   _______________________

<u>skill of reeding, as</u> well as offer pure pleasure.   _______________________

Writers and illustrators <u>of childrens books</u> are   _______________________

<u>especialy appreciated</u>. The best books written   _______________________

and illustrated <u>each yearly</u> receive honors. One   _______________________

award, the Newbery Medal<u>, is gived to an</u> author.   _______________________

The Caldecott Medal <u>is presentted to an</u> illustrator.   _______________________

The <u>books that have winned</u> these awards can be   _______________________

checked out of any <u>library for you to enjoy</u>.   _______________________

What do you think it would mean to an author or illustrator to be chosen as the recipient of the Newbery or Caldecott Medal?

Build Skills and Word Experiences

Use Student Practice Pages 79–80 to follow up instruction for:
Activity 1A • Test Ready

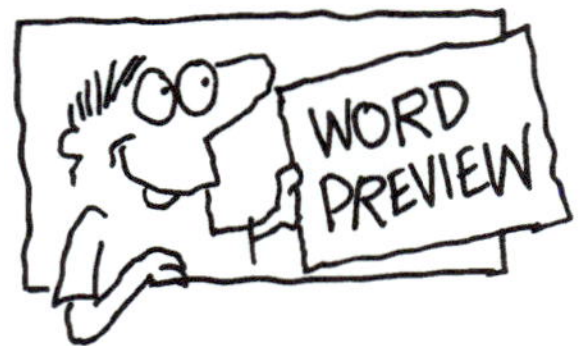

Build Visual Skills

Do the Word Preview, a visual warm-up activity, with all students.
Use Core Words **pair** (631), **ahead** (632), **wrong** (633), **practice** (634), **sand** (635).

Teaching Notes, page 316

Build Spelling and Language Skills

Choose from among these quick tasks to customize instruction
for all or selected students.

Teaching Notes, page 319

It was full of sand.

Its our practice to get up early, move are boat from the sand, and paddle
around the lake. Once we watched a pair of birds circle a head of us
and than dive into the water to catch fish? I feel badly when we can't go.

(*It's*, *our*, *ahead*, *then*, period instead of a question mark, *bad*)

**wrongfully, doorknob, sword, unknown, thumbtack, answered, climb, knapsack,
doubtful, typewriter, knives**

(e.g., contains silent *b/k/w*; number of syllables; is/isn't a compound; does/doesn't contain a suffix)

ahead, amusement, amaze, _______
(words in which the first syllable is /ə/ spelled *a*)

If someone spells a word wrong, they should _______.

Things that come in pairs.

Who did not invent the airplane? The Wrong Brothers!

Teaching Notes, page 325

Build Basic Concepts

Choose from among these skill-building activities to customize instruction for all or selected students.

concept one　　Some words have silent letters.

phonics, more words, writing words, predicting spelling, visual skill building, proofreading

1A Have student pairs brainstorm words with silent *w*, *t*, *b*, *k*, and *l*. Then select students to write word examples on the chalkboard under each heading (e.g., w: wrong, two, answer; t: listen, fasten, whistle; b: thumb, doubt, subtle; k: knee, knit, knew; l: walk, salmon, calves). Expand the lesson to silent *n*, *g*, *h*, and *gh*. Provide clues for students to identify *autumn, column; assign, campaign; honest, graham; straight, daughter*. Write the words on the chalkboard as students predict the spelling. Then conceal the words. Have students write them from memory, underlining silent letters. Next, reveal the words for students to self-check.

Graham crackers, bread, and flour originated with Sylvester Graham about 1830. He said that white flour wasn't nearly as healthful as whole wheat flour. Graham is an eponym (see Word Mysteries and Histories, page 232). Have students add it to their eponym book if they haven't already done so. Challenge students to research and report on why Graham thought whole wheat flours were better than white flours and if that position is still held today among nutritionists.

visual skills, making words, vocabulary development

1B Select a student to write *wrong* on the chalkboard. Ask students to identify the silent letter. Prepare for a letter-card activity (see Activity 2B, page 47) using *a*, *e*, *g*, *i*, *l*, *n*, *o*, *r*, *s*, and *w*. Together make *wrong*. Then have students continue making words: *grown—gown—glow—angle—align—lion—lawn—learn—large—orange—ignore—gnaw—answer—worse—wiser—aisle—rile—reign—resign—ring—single—sign—signal—sling—slang—wrangle—wring*—and back to *wrong*. As words are made, have students identify homophones and words with silent consonants. Later, have students work in small groups to make words. Have them write the words as they make them. Time the session (about four minutes). Then see which group has the most correctly spelled words, the most homophones, and/or the most words with silent consonants.

concept two　　Words are easier to spell when each word part is spelled separately.

word analysis, more words, writing words

2A Demonstrate how words are easier to spell if each word part is spelled separately.

- *a___* words: *ahead, along*
- *be___* words: *because, between*
- compound words: *sandbag, headlight*
- words with suffixes: *wrongful, walking*
- words with prefixes: *repair, pretest*
- multi-syllabic words: *temperature*

Then have students treat each of the above as an Add It lesson in Exercise Express.

Build Skillful Writers

Use these interrelated language learnings for all or selected students.

Teaching Notes, page 328

Skillful writers consider their audience as they select their language and writing style. For example, it is necessary to use more formal language in a report than is used in a personal note. However, both are writing pieces that use correct grammar, punctuation, and spelling. Advertisers consider their audience and often use a very informal style to deliver a quick message to attract attention. Phrases may be used instead of sentences, liberties taken with grammar, and shortcut spellings used, such as *lite*, *quik*, and *E-Z*. Have students find examples to share with the class. Then have the class rewrite the information formally.

Build Assessment Readiness

Use these at-school and at-home exercises to prepare all students for the Skill Test.

Teaching Notes, page 329

at-school Ask students to define *homophones* (words that sound the same but have different spellings and meanings). Ask students to list homophones they can recall (about three minutes). Then post Teaching Poster 5 for students to expand their list and self-check. Reuse Personal Poster 4 with all or some students to revisit homophone contractions.

Skill to be tested: homophones

Next, select troublesome homophone pairs. On a word card (use the Word Card Blackline Master, page 384), have students write a homophone pair, one word to a side. Have student partners play a game in which word cards are placed in a paper bag. The first player draws a card and holds it so s/he sees only the front side and the partner sees only the backside. The first player spells the homophone on the backside as the partner checks the spelling. Then the partner spells the other homophone as the first player checks the spelling. Then another card is drawn and play continues.

at-home Send home a copy of Take-Home Task 27 Blackline Master, page 238.

Skill to be tested: homophones

Build Proofreading Skills

Track students' ability to meet a minimum competency for spelling and proofreading within selected samples of their everyday writing.

Teaching Notes, page 330

- Send home papers for proofreading and a copy of the Ideas for Proofreading Blackline Master, page 373.

Name _______________________________

Dear Parents,

In this activity you can guide your child toward the mastery of homophones, such as bear/bare. Their meaning and spelling is the focus of this activity. Begin by having your child read the directions and then explain to you what is expected. Allow your child to do as much as possible without your help. Then ask your child to explain each response.

Afterward, say one homophone and have your child respond by writing its partner on another piece of paper. Then ask your child to use both homophones in sentences to confirm their meanings.

Underline the word in each row that does not belong because of its meaning. Then circle the homophone partners in each row.

1.	piece	part	peace	fragment
2.	bed	caught	bunk	cot
3.	plane	aircraft	plain	glider
4.	knows	understands	comprehends	nose
5.	battle	wore	war	fight
6.	one	won	single	solitary
7.	sea	gulf	bay	see
8.	elk	deer	dear	moose
9.	pair	pare	duet	twosome
10.	embezzle	steel	swindle	steal
11.	herd	drove	flock	heard
12.	agree	accept	except	approve
13.	roll	rotate	spin	role
14.	principal	principle	rule	law
15.	logo	cymbal	symbol	sign
16.	meet	unite	join	meat
17.	supplement	extension	addition	edition
18.	seem	seam	indicate	appear
19.	authentic	real	reel	actual
20.	vary	diversify	modify	very

Of course, you and your child may wish to reinforce the understanding of the most misunderstood homophones: there—their—they're—there's—theirs.

Thank you for your help. You're on your child's spelling team! Every child a speller!

Assess Words and Skills

- Spelling Words (words missed on tests) are recorded in the Spelling Notebook.
- Use Proof It, Practice Page 81, for proofreading/editing practice.

Assess Spelling Progress

Give this Cloze Story Word Test of Core Words within the frequencies 1–635 to all students. Words students miss are their Spelling Words.

Teaching Notes, page 336

THE CLOZE STORY WORD TEST

Students do not prestudy the words. Provide students with a copy of REVIEW 27 BLACKLINE MASTER, page 242. Tell students that this story is about fashion history.

Read the entire story aloud, including the test words. Then read it again slowly as students write the missing words.

In Style

    Girls, (1) <u>picture</u> yourself running through the (2) <u>sand</u> with your (3) <u>friends</u> at the beach. The (4) <u>temperature</u> is in the (5) <u>eighties</u>. (6) <u>There's</u> an (7) <u>ocean</u> wave roaring (8) <u>toward</u> the shore. Oops! You're wet! Now, (9) <u>let's</u> change this scene. You're not dressed in (10) <u>modern</u> clothing, but in a mid-1800s dress with a (11) <u>beautiful</u> crinoline. A crinoline is a stiff, full-length petticoat. Back then, you'd be in style wearing seven of them! Also, you're laced into a tight corset that gives your (12) <u>figure</u> a tiny waist (13) <u>although</u> it makes your stomach ache. You're (14) <u>probably</u> lucky not to drown!

    Boys, (15) <u>suppose</u> you're at soccer (16) <u>practice</u>. If you're thinking that you're wearing the easy-fitting uniform of shorts and shirt that (17) <u>lets</u> you run freely, you're (18) <u>wrong</u>! It's the 1600s and you're charging down the (19) <u>field</u> in an (20) <u>especially</u> puffy (21) <u>pair</u> of pants tied with a bow below your knee!

    Fashions change. Describe another fashion of the past for (22) <u>either</u> a male or a female. Then (23) <u>explain</u> a fashion you predict will be the hot, new style (24) <u>ahead</u> to make fashion (25) <u>history</u> all (26) <u>across</u> the country.

Words tested:
there('s) (37), let('s)(s) (230), picture (232), across (247), toward (275), probably (383), either (409), beautiful (429), although (450), field (472), friend(s) (498), explain (513), figure (551), suppose (555), ocean (557), history (567), modern (592), eight(ies) (602), especially (614), temperature (630), pair (631), ahead (632), wrong (633), practice (634), sand (635)

AFTER THE CLOZE STORY WORD TEST

1. Have students write about a man's or a woman's fashion of the past and make a written prediction for the next big fashion trend. Then have students share their answers.

speculating, writing a description, writing an explanation

2. Have students record the words they missed on the test in their Spelling Notebook (see page 338) for at-school study, and on a copy of the WORDS TO LEARN BLACKLINE MASTER, page 375, for at-home study.

recording words for personal study list

Teaching Notes, page 339

Assess Skill Application

Give this assessment of spelling and related skills to all students.
The REVIEW 27 BLACKLINE MASTER is on page 243.

🍎 THE SKILL TEST

Skill tested:
homophones

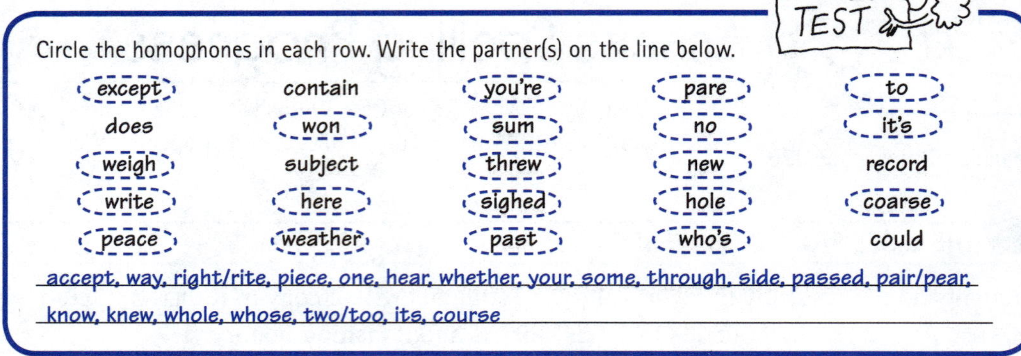

Note the ability of each student to identify and spell homophones.

Teaching Notes, page 341

Assess Proofreading Application

Give this assessment of spelling and related skills to all students.
The REVIEW 27 BLACKLINE MASTER is on page 243.

🍎 THE PROOFREADING TEST

(Both books were noted in IN OTHER WORDS, page 163.) Note the ability of each
student to proofread for spelling, capitalization, punctuation, or grammar errors.

Extend Spelling Assessment

Give this in-context assessment of Core Words within the frequencies 1–635 to students who need more practice or challenge.

Teaching Notes, page 342

Words tested:

the (1), of (2), and (3), a (4), to (5), in (6), it (10), for (12), they (19), at (20), be (21), there (37), their (42), will (46), these (58), would (59), her (64), two (65), first (74), water (90), know (100), get (101), place (131), every (151), last (166), along (171), next (174), try (254), morning (283), body(ies) (285), run(ning) (306), girl(s) (405), field (472), friend (498), plan(ning) (544), maybe (566), shape (601), minute (608), pair (631), ahead (632), wrong (633), practice (634), sand (635), *they're (1010)

*The testing of they're (1010) is included to help students differentiate among the there/their/they're homophones.

Extra words: busy, Jill, month, races, ribbons, track

THE SENTENCE DICTATION TEST

Students do not prestudy the words. Provide students with writing paper and pencil. Have students write the sentences as they are dictated.

1. Jill and her friend practice running every morning in the sand along the water.
2. They're planning ahead for the track and field races next month.
3. They know it would be wrong to try to get their bodies in shape at the last minute.
4. Maybe there will be a pair of first place ribbons for these two busy girls.

AFTER THE SENTENCE DICTATION TEST

1. Have students list sports that require running during the event and those that do not. Then challenge students to determine geographical places where these girls might be training—names of places and bodies of water that might be the setting for this practice. Challenge some students to create a flyer that announces the track and field event.

making lists, compare and contrast, creating a flyer

2. Have students record the words they missed on the test in their Spelling Notebook (see page 345) for at-school study, and on a copy of the WORDS TO LEARN BLACKLINE MASTER, page 375, for at-home study.

recording words for personal study list

Students challenged by the spelling of because may benefit from spelling the word in parts and/or learning this phrase in which the first letter of each word spells because: Big elephants can always use scrambled eggs—because!

Have students write (**IN OTHER WORDS**): Two wrongs do not make one right.

Name _______________________________

— Word Test —

In Style

Girls, (1) _______________ yourself running through the (2) _______________ with your (3) _______________ at the beach. The (4) _______________ is in the (5) _______________. (6) _______________ an (7) _______________ wave roaring (8) _______________ the shore. Oops! You're wet! Now, (9) _______________ change this scene. You're not dressed in (10) _______________ clothing, but in a mid-1800s dress with a (11) _______________ crinoline. A crinoline is a stiff, full-length petticoat. Back then, you'd be in style wearing seven of them! Also, you're laced into a tight corset that gives your (12) _______________ a tiny waist (13) _______________ it makes your stomach ache. You're (14) _______________ lucky not to drown!

Boys, (15) _______________ you're at soccer (16) _______________. If you're thinking that you're wearing the easy-fitting uniform of shorts and shirt that (17) _______________ you run freely, you're (18) _______________! It's the 1600s and you're charging down the (19) _______________ in an (20) _______________ puffy (21) _______________ of pants tied with a bow below your knee!

Fashions change. Describe another fashion of the past for (22) _______________ a male or a female. Then (23) _______________ a fashion you predict will be the hot, new style (24) _______________ to make fashion (25) _______________ all (26) _______________ the country.

Skill Test

Circle the homophones in each row. Write the partner(s) on the line below.

except	contain	you're	pare	to
does	won	sum	no	it's
weigh	subject	threw	new	record
write	here	sighed	hole	coarse
peace	weather	past	who's	could

____

____

Proofreading Test

Proofread for spelling, capitalization, punctuation, or grammar errors in the underlined parts. Circle errors. Write corrections in the space.

Are you familiar with the <u>gand, old lady whos</u> _______________________

<u>called grandma dowdel</u> in Richard Peck's novels _______________________

<u>for yung readers?</u> She seems so authentic in his _______________________

<u>storys that may people</u> ask him if she was really _______________________

his <u>owne grandmother. No,</u> she was not. She is a _______________________

make-believe <u>chariter whose</u> comedy role in _______________________

his award-winning books <u>delivers a very serieous</u> _______________________

message <u>to it's readers. That</u> is, in the long run _______________________

<u>you'll be held responsable</u> for the consequences _______________________

of all your actions. She is <u>full of funny busness</u> as _______________________

the messenger <u>of this principle Enjoy her</u> antics in _______________________

<u>A Long Way from Chicago</u> <u>and in A Year Down Yonder,</u> _______________________

<u>too books credited with</u> notable awards. _______________________

How would you find out the awards bestowed upon Richard Peck's books?

Build Skills and Word Experiences

Use Student Practice Pages 82–83 to follow up instruction for:
Activities 1A and 1B • Test Ready

Build Visual Skills

Do the Word Preview, a visual warm-up activity, with all students.
Use Core Words **tail** (636), **wait** (637), **difficult** (638), **general** (639), **cover** (640).

Teaching Notes, page 316

Build Spelling and Language Skills

Choose from among these quick tasks to customize instruction
for all or selected students.

Teaching Notes, page 319

They had to wait it out.

A generale rule in our house is that my dog dosen't sleep on the
bed covers. It's dificult for him, so he waits untill I'm asleep and
then jumps on the bed. His tail wags the minute I find him their.

(*general, doesn't, difficult, until, there*)

Monday, tail, whale, Maine, way, take, waitress, made, Tuesday, waist, May, wake

(e.g., by long *a* spelling pattern; beginning letter; is/isn't a homophone; is/isn't a proper noun)

general/specific, wait/go, tail/head, ______ / ______

(antonyms)

Something that I find difficult to do is ______.

Words that end in *l* to which you can add the *ly* suffix

Build Basic Concepts

Choose from among these skill-building activities to customize instruction for all or selected students.

Teaching Notes, page 325

concept one | Frequent spelling patterns for words with soft-syllable endings include /əl/ spelled *le*, *al*, and *el*, and /ər/ spelled *er*, *or*, and *ar*.

1A Select students to write on the chalkboard: *cover, director, sugar*. Ask students how the words are alike (end in /ər/). Note that in soft-syllable, or unstressed, endings such as *er*, *or*, and *ar*, the vowel sounds the same, but is spelled with different letters. The most frequent spelling pattern for /ər/ is *er* (e.g., other, after, number), but students will encounter *or* (e.g., author, doctor, motor) and, less frequently, *ar* (e.g., calendar, dollar, singular). Also note the unstressed *ure* spelling (e.g., picture). Few words use the *ur* spelling pattern, so it need not be a focus. Have students write examples sorted by the three spelling patterns.

phonics, spelling word patterns, writing words, sorting words, word analysis

Over two hundred years ago, a tenacious, industrious person was often described by the simile: Works like a beaver. A beaver persistently works to build its dam, only to cause problems with water flow for others. Hence, the term eager beaver originated for people who over-zealously attempt duties that often cause others more work in the end.
• Identify a real person or story character who might be described as an "eager beaver," or someone who "works like a beaver." Explain in writing what the person does to earn this description.

1B Write on the chalkboard: *purple, channel, general, pencil, pistol*. Ask students how the words are alike (end in /əl/). Like the unstressed *er/or/ar* (Activity 1A, this unit), the vowel sound in the unstressed syllable is the same, but spelled with different letters. The *le* is by far the most frequent spelling pattern (e.g., people, circle, trouble), followed by *al* (e.g., oval, natural, central) and *el* (e.g., novel, travel, vowel). Only a few *il* and *ol* spellings are among elementary vocabulary. Students will encounter *ul* spellings as they occur within the *ful* suffix (e.g., colorful).

phonics, spelling word patterns, writing words, sorting words, word analysis

Have students find and write examples of words spelled *le*, *al*, and *el* sorted by spelling pattern. Then have students make /əl/ word couplets:

oval puzzle—triple trouble—metal kettle—local scandal

Later, challenge students to correctly write the couplets when you call them out.

Teaching Notes, page 328

Build Skillful Writers

Use these interrelated language learnings for all or selected students.

Skillful writers know the rules for capitalization. Review capital letters (see Unit 21 Build Skillful Writers, page 183). Ask students if *general* is capitalized (e.g., if it is a person's title; is a word in a title of a written work; is the name of a street, city, river; begins a sentence, is a person's name).

Discuss *general* as a person's title—*General Norman Schwarzkopf*. Ask students to brainstorm more titles for people (e.g., Mr., Mrs., Ms., Miss, Sister, Reverend, Father, Doctor, President, Aunt, Bishop, Senator, Professor, Governor, Lieutenant, Rabbi, Colonel, Major). Write the words on the chalkboard as students suggest them. Then have students determine which have abbreviated forms and research the abbreviated spellings.

WORD MYSTERIES AND HISTORIES

The word *general* is derived from the Latin, *generalis*. It meant "pertaining to the whole." The English adjective has come to mean "nonspecific" (e.g., general store) or "unprecise" (e.g., in general terms). However, the noun *general*, a "military officer," is the specific person that commands over the "whole" army.

Teaching Notes, page 329

Skill to be tested: double letters

Build Assessment Readiness

Use these at-school and at-home exercises to prepare all students for the Skill Test.

at-school Ask students to find and write examples of words that become double-letter words with the addition of a suffix (e.g., forget/forgetting, win/winning). Refer students to Rule 5 on Teaching Poster 2. For these words, students have a strategy for knowing that the word has double letters, but for many words the double letter must simply be remembered (e.g., difficult, yellow, necessary, middle, suppose, correct, difference, business). Have students find and write words with double letters in preparation for a carousel competition. Next, prepare a carousel activity (see Test Ready, page 39) using seven charts labeled: *ff, ll, mm, nn, pp, rr, ss*. Students spend one minute at each chart listing words they can recall with that double letter. Teams earn a point for each correctly spelled word, identified by their color marking pen.

Skill to be tested: double letters

at-home Send home a copy of TAKE-HOME TASK 28 BLACKLINE MASTER, page 247.

Teaching Notes, page 330

Build Proofreading Skills

Track students' ability to meet a minimum competency for spelling and proofreading within selected samples of their everyday writing.

• Send home papers for proofreading and a copy of the IDEAS FOR PROOFREADING BLACKLINE MASTER, page 373.

Name ________________________________

Dear Parents,

Words with double letters can cause a spelling challenge. The writer hears one letter, but must remember to write two letters. Play a double-letter word-find activity with your child by working together to find words to fit the category.

Places	Foods	Animals
Illinois	egg	opossum

Things	People	Games
hammer	drummer	football

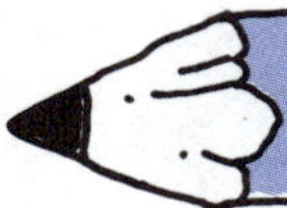

- Spelling Words (words missed on tests) are recorded in the Spelling Notebook.
- Use Proof It, Practice Page 84, for proofreading/editing practice.

Teaching Notes, page 336

Assess Spelling Progress

Give this Cloze Story Word Test of Core Words within the frequencies 1–640 to all students. Words students miss are their Spelling Words.

THE CLOZE STORY WORD TEST

Students do not prestudy the words. Provide students with a copy of REVIEW 28 BLACKLINE MASTER, page 251. Tell students that this story may give them the chills!

Read the entire story aloud, including the test words. Then read it again slowly as students write the missing words.

Words tested:

there (37), their (42), its (76), because (127), always (183), until (196), it's (253), whole (259), course (317), area(s) (384), fact (445), weather (464), information (549), reason(s) (564), difference(s) (565), beside(s) (590), won't (598), temperature(s) (630), tail (636), wait (637), difficult (638), general (639), cover (640), *they're (1010)

*The testing of they're (1010) is included to help students differentiate among the there/their/they're homophones.

How Cold Is It?

Earth's frozen polar (1) <u>areas</u>, the Arctic and the Antarctic, are cold! (2) <u>They're</u> the iciest, windiest, most remote parts of the (3) <u>whole</u> world. (4) <u>Their</u> frigid (5) <u>temperatures</u> are (6) <u>always</u> colder than inside your freezer. Winds make them colder still. Explorers must completely (7) <u>cover</u> up so that (8) <u>their</u> skin (9) <u>won't</u> freeze. (10) <u>Besides</u> the wintry (11) <u>weather</u>, the Arctic and Antarctic may also be dark. As a (12) <u>general</u> rule, (13) <u>it's</u> easier to explore during daylight. Unless explorers (14) <u>wait</u> (15) <u>until</u> summer, they'll find that (16) <u>it's</u> dark both day and night. (17) <u>Because</u> of these (18) <u>reasons</u>, exploration is (19) <u>difficult</u>. We still may have more (20) <u>information</u> about the moon than we do about these regions.

The Arctic and Antarctic are alike in these ways, but (21) <u>there</u> are big (22) <u>differences</u> between the two. Of (23) <u>course</u>, the Arctic is in the north and the Antarctic is in the south. In (24) <u>fact</u>, Antarctic means opposite the Arctic, so (25) <u>its</u> location is sometimes considered to be at the (26) <u>tail</u> end of the earth. What other distinctions can you make between them?

AFTER THE CLOZE STORY WORD TEST

research, writing

1. Have students research and write their answer to the story question. Then have students share their answer. Create a classroom chart that contrasts these remote areas.

recording words for personal study list

2. Have students record the words they missed on the test in their Spelling Notebook (see page 338) for at-school study, and on a copy of the WORDS TO LEARN BLACKLINE MASTER, page 375, for at-home study.

Assess Skill Application

Give this assessment of spelling and related skills to all students.
The REVIEW 28 BLACKLINE MASTER is on page 252.

Teaching Notes, page 339

THE SKILL TEST

Add double letters or a single letter to spell words.

wi_______ing   huma_______   tri_______ed

fo_______ow   fa_______ous   nece_______ary

co_______ect   especia_______y   ch_______se

pla_______ed   ye_______ow   di_______icult

su_______ose   natura_______y   ha_______ened

str_______t   po_______ible   su_______er

di_______erence   fina_______y   reme_______ber

rea_______on   co_______on   vi_______age

(answers will vary)

Skill tested:
double letters

Note the ability of each student to spell double-letter words.

Assess Proofreading Application

Give this assessment of spelling and related skills to all students.
The REVIEW 28 BLACKLINE MASTER is on page 252.

Teaching Notes, page 341

THE PROOFREADING TEST

If the underlined word or words in each line are incorrect
for spelling, capitalization, or grammar, write the correction in the space.

It <u>may be that the picteures</u>, or illustrations, in a book   pictures
are as important as the story. <u>In fact, they usualy</u>   usually
help tell the story. <u>Therefore, the illustrator pays</u>   plays
a special <u>roll in making the book</u> an outstanding   role
<u>one. Sometimes</u> the illustrator and the author of a
book are the same <u>person. For Example</u>, the story   example
and the art in *Snowflake Bentley* <u>we're both created</u>   were
by Mary Azarian. The <u>same goes for david</u> Small in   David
his book *So You Want to Be President?* However,
Richard Egielski illustrated, <u>but did not right</u>, *Hey, Al*.   write
These <u>three books all won a vary</u> meaningful award,   very
the Caldecott Medal, <u>four superb art</u>. Yet, the art in   for
each <u>book is quite diffrent</u>.   different

Select a favorite Caldecott Medal award-winning book and tell why you think
the art makes the book an outstanding one.

Note the ability of each student to proofread for spelling, capitalization, punctuation, or
grammar errors.

Teaching Notes, page 342

Words tested:
the (1), of (2), a (4), to (5), as (16), at (20), I (24), or (26), when (35), your (40), then (53), would (59), first (74), find (87), long (91), look (117), help(ed) (137), line (161), end (170), few (181), often (186), it's (253), turn (289), front (318), become (336), able (346), person (367), probably (383), stand (387), within (439), check (493), straight (524), moment(s) (538), you're (552), step (570), famous (583), pay (585), store (589), I've (624), ahead (632), tail (636), wait(ing) (637), difficult (638), general(s) (639), cover(s) (640), they're (1010)

Extra words: difficult, grocery, magazine, president

Extend Spelling Assessment

Give this in-context assessment of Core Words within the frequencies 1–640 to students who need more practice or challenge.

 **THE SENTENCE DICTATION TEST**

Students do not prestudy the words. Provide students with writing paper and pencil. Have students write the sentences as they are dictated.

1. It's often difficult to wait your turn when you're at the tail end of a long line.

2. Presidents or famous generals would probably find they're able to step ahead straight to the front of the line.

3. At the grocery store, I often look at the magazine covers as I wait at the check stand to pay.

4. Then within a few moments, I've become the first person waiting to be helped.

 **AFTER THE SENTENCE DICTATION TEST**

writing, hyperbole

1. Have students describe in writing a time they had to wait in line a long time. It may have been "years" before they got to the front! Review hyperbole with students, the figure of speech that employs exaggeration. Ask students for other instances of hyperbole, a technique that is often used in tall tales, comics, and children's stories. Often similes and metaphors use hyperbole. Then have students write their descriptions using these techniques.

recording words for personal study list

2. Have students record the words they missed on the test in their Spelling Notebook (see page 345) for at-school study, and on a copy of the WORDS TO LEARN BLACKLINE MASTER, page 375, for at-home study.

Coins have heads and they have tails,
So do mice and big blue whales.
You'll find both on Irish Setters,
Can you spell that with just four letters?
(t-h-a-t)

Have students write (IN OTHER WORDS): Time waits for no one.
Danish Proverb

Word Test

How Cold Is It?

Earth's frozen polar (1) ________________, the Arctic and the Antarctic, are cold!

(2) ________________ the iciest, windiest, most remote parts of the (3) ________________

world. (4) ________________ frigid (5) ________________ are (6) ________________

colder than inside your freezer. Winds make them colder still. Explorers must completely

(7) ________________ up so that (8) ________________ skin (9) ________________

freeze. (10) ________________ the wintry (11) ________________, the Arctic and

Antarctic may also be dark. As a (12) ________________ rule, (13) ________________

easier to explore during daylight. Unless explorers (14) ________________

(15) ________________ summer, they'll find that (16) ________________ dark both

day and night. (17) ________________ of these (18) ________________, exploration

is (19) ________________. We still may have more (20) ________________ about the

moon than we do about these regions.

The Arctic and Antarctic are alike in these ways, but (21) ________________ are big

(22) ________________ between the two. Of (23) ________________, the Arctic is in the

north and the Antarctic is in the south. In (24) ________________, Antarctic means

opposite the Arctic, so (25) ________________ location is sometimes considered to be

at the (26) ________________ end of the earth. What other distinctions can you make

between them?

Name _______________________________

Skill Test

Add double letters or a single letter to spell words.

wi_______ing	huma_______	tri_______ed
fo_______ow	fa_______ous	nece_______ary
co_______ect	especia_______y	ch_______se
pla_______ed	ye_______ow	di_______icult
su_______ose	natura_______y	ha_______ened
str_______t	po_______ible	su_______er
di_______erence	fina_______y	reme_______ber
rea_______on	co_______on	vi_______age

Proofreading Test

If the underlined word or words in each line are incorrect for spelling, capitalization, or grammar, write the correction in the space.

It <u>may be that the picteures</u>, or illustrations, in a book ___________________

are as important as the story. <u>In fact, they usualy</u> ___________________

help tell the story. <u>Therefore, the illustrator pays</u> ___________________

a special <u>roll in making the book</u> an outstanding ___________________

<u>one. Sometimes the</u> illustrator and the author of a ___________________

book are the same <u>person. For Example</u>, the story ___________________

and the art in *Snowflake Bentley* <u>we're both created</u> ___________________

by Mary Azarian. The <u>same goes for david</u> Small in ___________________

<u>his book So You</u> *Want to Be President?* However, ___________________

Richard Egielski illustrated, <u>but did not right</u>, *Hey, Al.* ___________________

These <u>three books all won a vary</u> meaningful award, ___________________

the Caldecott Medal, <u>four superb art</u>. Yet, the art in ___________________

each <u>book is quite diffrent</u>. ___________________

Select a favorite Caldecott Medal award-winning book and tell why you think the art makes the book an outstanding one.

Build Skills and Word Experiences

Use Student Practice Pages 85–86 to follow up instruction for:
Word Mysteries and Histories • Test Ready

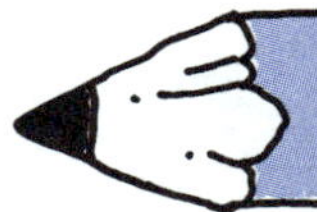

Build Visual Skills

Do the Word Preview, a visual warm-up activity, with all students.
Use Core Words **material** (641), **isn't** (642), **thousand** (643), **sign** (644), **guess** (645).

Teaching Notes, page 316

Build Spelling and Language Skills

Choose from among these quick tasks to customize instruction
for all or selected students.

Teaching Notes, page 319

The sign isn't there.

We have an thousand children in our school. Each student is to draw a pitcher on a piece of materiall and then sign his or her name. Then mrs. Case will sew them together. We can't even gues when it'll be complete.

(*a, picture, material, Mrs., guess*)

isn't, sugar, let's, easy, he's, least, it's, sure, sign, wasn't

(e.g., by the sound *s* spells; number of letters; is/isn't a contraction)

guess, guest, guide, _______

(words with silent *u*)

These are the materials I need for my project: _______.

Words that end with *al* or *le*

Teaching Notes, page 325

Build Basic Concepts

Choose from among these skill-building activities to customize instruction for all or selected students.

concept one Some words are spelled the way they sound while others are not.

phonics, word analysis, chanting a rhyme, more words, explaining

1A Select students to write on the chalkboard: *guess, one, woman, does, said, of.* Ask students to explain why they are unexpected spellings. Introduce the Surprise Word rhyme. Then have students brainstorm more words with unexpected spellings that could be substituted in the rhyme (e.g., laugh, group, freight, beauty, garage, brought) and explain why the spellings are unexpected.

phonics, vocabulary development, word analysis, writing sentences, relating to literature

1B Write on the chalkboard: *signal, signature, signify, significant.* Discuss their pronunciations and meanings and tell students that these words originate from the Latin *signum* meaning "mark." Then select a student to write *sign* on the chalkboard. Note the silent *g* and point out that spelling may make sense when a word's other forms or origin is known. Have students use the words in written sentences.

Introduce the classic Newbery Honor Book *Sign of the Beaver*, by Elizabeth Speare. Create a chart for students to "sign with their signature" after having read the book. Have students note why they think the book was given special recognition.

phonics, word analysis, word games

1C Review the word collections: "The Rough Toughies" (ou spellings, Activity 2A, page 47) and "The Weirdos" (ie/ei spellings, Activity 1C, page 182).

Select from these activities to rekindle attention on these word groups that often cause spelling challenges. Have students—

- play bingo
- make a crossword game
- make a word-search game
- make word cards for partners to flash/spell

Have students use the letters in *material* to make words. Keep students challenged until over 75 words are identified!

Build Skillful Writers

Use these interrelated language learnings for all or selected students.

Teaching Notes, page 328

Ask students for examples of road signs (e.g., stop sign, yield, slow, merge). Road signs manage traffic, just as punctuation manages the use of words in context—punctuation marks are road signs for readers. Ask students for examples (e.g., comma, period, exclamation and question mark). Write on the chalkboard: *No.*   *No!   No?*

Next, have students write dialogue that incorporates these single-word sentences (review quotation marks, Build Skillful Writers, page 219). Conclude that the punctuation conveys as much meaning as the word does.

Build Assessment Readiness

Use these at-school and at-home exercises to prepare all students for the Skill Test.

Teaching Notes, page 329

at-school   Ask students the purposes for an apostrophe (contractions/possessives —except possessive pronouns). Have students provide examples of singular and plural possessives. Review that *'s* is added (bear's honey) to make a singular noun possessive, *s'* is added (bears' honey) to make a plural noun possessive, and *'s* is added to plural nouns not ending in *s* (women's). Ask students to write these phrases and explain what is meant: *the boys' guests, the girl's guests, the guests' invitations, the children's party.*

Skill to be tested: apostrophe

at-home   Send home a copy of Take-Home Task 29 Blackline Master, page 256.

Skill to be tested: apostrophe

Build Proofreading Skills

Track students' ability to meet a minimum competency for spelling and proofreading within selected samples of their everyday writing.

Teaching Notes, page 330

• Send home papers for proofreading and a copy of the Ideas for Proofreading Blackline Master, page 373.

Many Greek and Latin prefixes signal number or size (e.g., kilo/milli meaning "thousand" or "thousandth." Expand students' understanding of number prefixes by challenging them to research prefixes that denote number or size. Have students answer these questions:
• How many years is a century? (cent = 100)
• How does milli relate to the meaning of million? (milli = 1,000; a million is a thousand thousands)
• How many babies make quadruplets? quintuplets? (quad = four, quin = five)
Then have students write questions for their classmates to answer.

Name ______________________________

Dear Parents,

Again, you can help your child become comfortable with the use of an apostrophe. Exposure over time ensures mastery of this often difficult concept. As before, tell your child that an apostrophe is a sign with a purpose.

An apostrophe is a sign that can mean—

- a letter (or letters) has been omitted to make a contraction (e.g., I + have = I've).

- possession, or ownership.

Use an apostrophe to write these words as contractions.

will not __________	should not __________	is not __________
they are __________	we are __________	you are __________
we have __________	you have __________	they have __________
she is __________	she has __________	he had __________

Write a sentence that describes the picture, using an apostrophe to show possession.

____

____

____

____

____

____

Assess Words and Skills

- Spelling Words (words missed on tests) are recorded in the Spelling Notebook.
- Use Proof It, Practice Page 87, for proofreading/editing practice.

Assess Spelling Progress

Give this Cloze Story Word Test of Core Words within the frequencies 1–645 to all students. Words students miss are their Spelling Words.

Teaching Notes, page 336

THE CLOZE STORY WORD TEST

Students do not prestudy the words. Provide students with a copy of REVIEW 29 BLACKLINE MASTER, page 260. Tell students that this story will tickle their funny bone, as well as give them spelling practice.

Read the entire story aloud, including the test words. Then read it again slowly as students write the missing words.

Laughing Allowed (Aloud)

(1) <u>It's</u> joke time! Get (2) <u>all ready</u> for a (3) <u>thousand</u> chuckles! (4) <u>You're</u> probably (5) <u>already</u> laughing just anticipating the fun (6) <u>ahead</u>. (7) <u>Listen</u> up and (8) <u>notice</u> the spellings of the words in these jokes. You'll see that it is (9) <u>necessary</u> to be an (10) <u>able</u> speller of our (11) <u>language</u> to "get" the humor.

- What did the elk call his girlfriend? Deer!
- What (12) <u>material</u> was the rabbit's ring made of? Eighteen carrot gold!
- What does the (13) <u>sign</u> say on the foot doctor's delivery truck? Toe truck!
- Where are the Great Plains? At the (14) <u>biggest</u> airports!
- (15) <u>It's</u> his job to pick up the nails, (16) <u>isn't</u> it? Yes, (17) <u>he's</u> the tacks collector!

Each of these silly jokes uses a homophone in (18) <u>its</u> question or "punch line." Of (19) <u>course</u>, the jokes use the (20) <u>wrong</u> homophone! I (21) <u>guess</u> that's what makes these jokes (22) <u>especially</u> funny! Now, it is (23) <u>your</u> turn to (24) <u>practice</u> writing a homophone joke. Don't object because (25) <u>they're</u> easy to write. You can do it! Then have a joke (26) <u>party</u>!

Words tested:

all (33), your (40), its (76), big(gest) (158), it's (253), course (317), able (346), ready (357), notice (379), already (411), language (499), listen (507), you're (552), especially (614), necessary (615), he's (616), party (626), ahead (632), wrong (633), practice (634), material (641), isn't (642), thousand (643), sign (644), guess (645), *they're (1010)

*The testing of they're (1010) is included to help students differentiate among the there/their/they're homophones.

AFTER THE CLOZE STORY WORD TEST

1. Have students identify homophone "errors" (dear, carat or karat, tow, planes, tax). Ask students to explain the story title. Can they think of another appropriate title for the story? Next, ask students to create homophone jokes for a class book.

writing jokes, explaining, class book

2. Have students record the words they missed on the test in their Spelling Notebook (see page 338) for at-school study, and on a copy of the WORDS TO LEARN BLACKLINE MASTER, page 375, for at-home study.

recording words for personal study list

Teaching Notes, page 339

Assess Skill Application

Give this assessment of spelling and related skills to all students.
The REVIEW 29 BLACKLINE MASTER is on page 261.

 THE SKILL TEST

Skill tested:
apostrophe

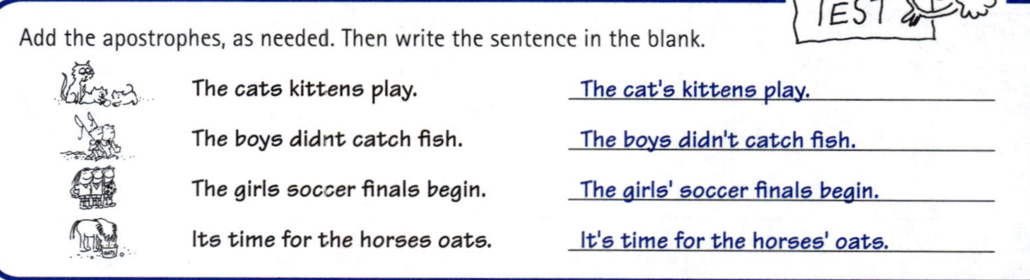

Note the ability of each student to use apostrophes for contractions, singular possessives, and plural possessives.

Teaching Notes, page 341

Assess Proofreading Application

Give this assessment of spelling and related skills to all students.
The REVIEW 29 BLACKLINE MASTER is on page 261.

 THE PROOFREADING TEST

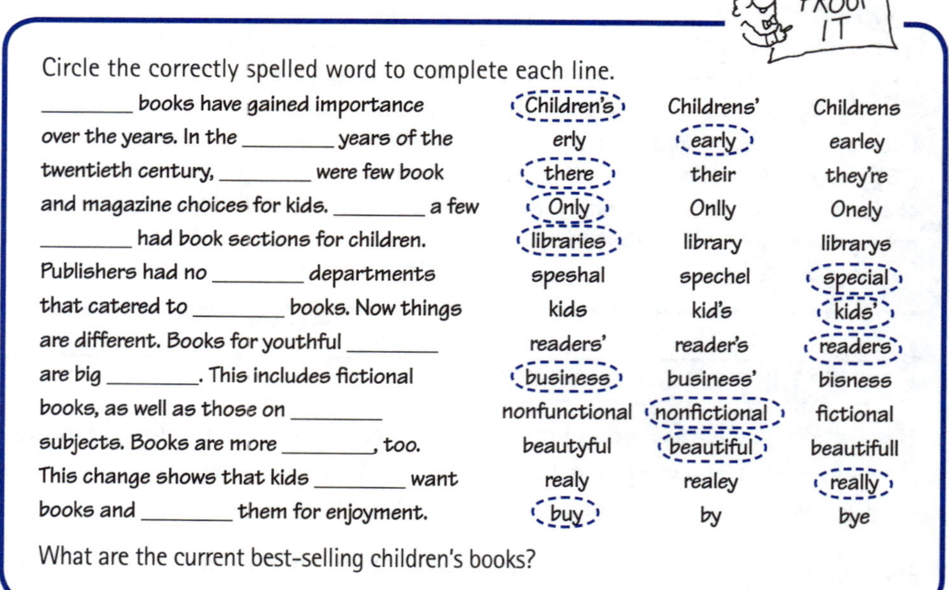

Note the ability of each student to proofread for spelling errors.

Extend Spelling Assessment

Give this in-context assessment of Core Words within the frequencies 1–645 to students who need more practice or challenge.

Teaching Notes, page 342

THE SENTENCE DICTATION TEST

Students do not prestudy the words. Provide students with writing paper and pencil. Have students write the sentences as they are dictated.

1. Our teacher took us on a field trip to the modern city library.
2. There's a lot of reading material there that covers a thousand different subjects.
3. The sign on the wall reminds everyone to be especially quiet.
4. I guess people can talk, but it isn't a good practice to speak in a loud voice.

Words tested:
the (1), of (2), a (4), to (5), in (6), that (9), on (14), be (21), I (24), but (31), there('s) (37), can (38), people (79), good (106), our (109), different (139), us (168), took (210), it's (253), city (273), voice (382), talk (398), everyone (430), field (472), reading (494), teacher (539), trip (576), modern (592), lot (597), speak (600), wall (609), especially (614), subject(s) (621), practice (634), cover(s) (640), material (641), isn't (642), thousand (643), sign (644), guess (645)

Extra words: library, loud, quiet, reminds

AFTER THE SENTENCE DICTATION TEST

1. Have students explain in writing how books are organized in their school library. Then have them evaluate the effectiveness of this system and tell why they think it is a good one or a bad one.

Expand this lesson. Challenge students to identify other instances of organizational techniques enabling people to find items; for example, at the grocery store. Have students describe the organizational method.

2. Have students record the words they missed on the test in their Spelling Notebook (see page 345) for at-school study, and on a copy of the WORDS TO LEARN BLACKLINE MASTER, page 375, for at-home study.

writing an explanation

recording words for personal study list

In old textbooks that taught the alphabet, the "&" followed the alphabet. Children would chant the letters and then say, "and per se, and," meaning "and on its own, and." The Latin *per se* means "on its own" or "by itself." The phrase sounded like "ampersand," hence the sign was named.

Laughing Allowed (Aloud)

(1) _________________ joke time! Get (2) _________________ for a (3) _________________

chuckles! (4) _________________ probably (5) _________________ laughing just

anticipating the fun (6) _________________. (7) _________________ up and

(8) _________________ the spellings of the words in these jokes. You'll see that

it is (9) _________________ to be an (10) _________________ speller of our

(11) _________________ to "get" the humor.

- What did the elk call his girlfriend? Deer!

- What (12) _________________ was the rabbit's ring made of? Eighteen carrot gold!

- What does the (13) _________________ say on the foot doctor's delivery truck?

  Toe truck!

- Where are the Great Plains? At the (14) _________________ airports!

- (15) _________________ his job to pick up the nails, (16) _________________ it?

  Yes, (17) _________________ the tacks collector!

Each of these silly jokes uses a homophone in (18) _________________ question or

"punch line." Of (19) _________________, the jokes use the (20) _________________

homophone! I (21) _________________ that's what makes these jokes (22) _________________

funny! Now, it is (23) _________________ turn to (24) _________________ writing a

homophone joke. Don't object, because (25) _________________ easy to write. You

can do it! Then have a joke (26) _________________!

REVIEW 29

Skill Test

Add apostrophes, as needed. Then write the sentence in the blank.

The cats kittens play. _______________________________

The boys didnt catch fish. _______________________________

The girls soccer finals begin. _______________________________

Its time for the horses oats. _______________________________

Proofreading Test

Circle the correctly spelled word to complete each line.

_____________ books have gained importance	Children's	Childrens'	Childrens
over the years. In the _____________ years of the	erly	early	earley
twentieth century, _____________ were few book	there	their	they're
and magazine choices for kids. _____________ a few	Only	Onlly	Onely
_____________ had book sections for children.	libraries	library	librarys
Publishers had no _____________ departments	speshal	spechel	special
that catered to _____________ books. Now things	kids	kid's	kids'
are different. Books for youthful _____________	readers'	reader's	readers
are big _____________. This includes fictional	business	business'	bisness
books, as well as those on _____________	nonfunctional	nonfictional	fictional
subjects. Books are more _____________, too.	beautyful	beautiful	beautifull
This change shows that kids _____________ want	realy	realey	really
books and _____________ them for enjoyment.	buy	by	bye

What are the current best-selling children's books?

Build Skills and Word Experiences

Use Student Practice Pages 88–89 to follow up instruction for:
Activity 1A • Activity 2A

Build Visual Skills

Do the Word Preview, a visual warm-up activity, with all students.
Use Core Words **forward** (646), **huge** (647), **ride** (648), **region** (649), **nor** (650).

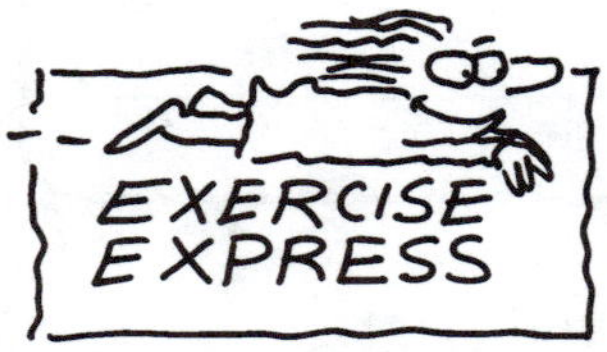

Teaching Notes, page 316

Build Spelling and Language Skills

Choose from among these quick tasks to customize instruction
for all or selected students.

Teaching Notes, page 319

There was a huge one in the road.

Last summer me and my friend worked on a huge farm in the
western rejon of our state. We ride horse's. We learned to ride
foward in are saddles, but we had no idea how sore we would get.

(my friend and I, region, rode, horses, forward, our)

forward, airport, explore, shuffleboard, nor, foretell, hoarse, afford, decorate, seashore,
uproar, horrible, coarse, bookstore

(e.g., by /or/ spelling pattern; number of syllables; does/doesn't have double letters; is/isn't a compound)

ride, aside, pride, decide, ______

(words with *ide*)

Every year I particularly look forward to ______.

Irregular verb forms

Build Basic Concepts

Choose from among these skill-building activities to customize instruction for all or selected students.

Teaching Notes, page 325

| concept one | Homophones are words that sound the same but have different spellings and meanings. |

1A Have students write the word forms of *ride* on the chalkboard (rides, rode, ridden, riding, rider, riders). Discuss *rode* as an irregular verb homophone. Have students find and write more words with this criterion, perhaps using Teaching Poster 5 as a reference (e.g., ate, blew, grown, knew).

word forms, homophones, irregular verbs, more words

Challenge students to hypothesize for which letter of the alphabet most irregular past tense verb forms begin. Have them review irregular verb forms they know, then write their prediction. Next, the Word Find begins! Guide students to discover that the letter *s* outpaces all other letters in this race.

1B Review the homophone contractions on Teaching Poster 4. Then divide students into seven groups, each group with a marker and sheet of chart paper. Assign each group one contraction homophone from Teaching Poster 4. Then students write sentences on their chart that contain the contraction or its partner(s), but placing blanks in the sentences for these words. Next, each group presents their sentences to the class to fill in the blanks.

homophones, contractions, writing sentences

Challenge students to identify homophone triads. How many can they find and write (e.g., road/rode/rowed, cent/scent/sent, aisle/I'll/isle, by/bye/buy, pedal/peddle/petal).

| concept two | Frequent spelling patterns for /j/ are *j, ge, dge, gi,* and *gy*. Frequent spelling patterns for /s/ are *s, ss, sc, ce, ci,* and *cy*. |

2A Ask students to recall the most frequent spelling patterns for /s/ and /j/. Then prepare for a carousel activity (see Test Ready, page 39). Use six charts labeled: *ce, ci, cy, ge, gi, gy*. At the end, tally the number of correctly spelled responses of each group (by their color marker) and note the winning group.

phonics, writing words, visual recall, spelling word patterns, sorting words, proofreading

Later, conceal the charts and have students write words they can recall sorted by spelling pattern. Then post the charts for students to add words and proofread their work.

2B Select a student to write *huge* on the chalkboard. Note the /j/ spelled *ge*. Have students research over-sized animals (e.g., whale, elephant). Then have them use the information to draw and label a size comparison chart.

phonics, research, creating a chart

2C Select a student to write *region* on the chalkboard. Underline *gion* and note /jən/. Then ask students to find and write more words that end in the soft-syllable, unstressed /jən/. Next, students sort the words by spelling pattern. Discuss *gion* (e.g., region), *gin* (e.g., margin), *gine* (e.g., engine), *gen* (e.g., oxygen), *geon* (e.g., dungeon). Help students note that the vowel that follows the *g* (e, i) makes *g* spell /j/.

phonics, spelling word patterns, sorting words

Teaching Notes, page 328

Build Skillful Writers

Use these interrelated language learnings for all or selected students.

Use a coin to demonstrate to students that *either...or* are flip sides of a coin. They must match grammatically. What follows *either* must follow *or*.

- If a subject and verb follow *either*, the same must follow *or—Either Mary likes peas or she doesn't.*

- If a preposition follows *either*, the same must follow *or—Nina is either in school or at home sick.*

- If an adjective follows *either*, the same must follow *or— Luke is either extremely lucky or very smart.*

The same advice can be given for *neither...nor.* Have students write one side of the coin. Then a partner can write the flip side.

Teaching Notes, page 329

Skill to be tested:
synonyms and antonyms

Skill to be tested:
synonyms and antonyms

Build Assessment Readiness

Use these at-school and at-home exercises to prepare all students for the Skill Test.

at-school Have students create synonym and antonym word wheels. For example, on one side of a circle, *huge* is written in the center from which spokes radiate with a synonym for *huge* written on each spoke. On the back, an antonym for *huge* is written in the center, such as *tiny* with synonyms for *tiny* written on each spoke.

at-home Send home a copy of Take-Home Task 30 Blackline Master, **page 265.**

Teaching Notes, page 330

Build Proofreading Skills

Track students' ability to meet a minimum competency for spelling and proofreading within selected samples of their everyday writing.

- Send home papers for proofreading and a copy of the Ideas for Proofreading Blackline Master, **page 373.**

Name______________________________

Dear Parents,

Your child knows that synonyms are words with nearly the same meaning, while antonyms are words with opposite meanings. This synonym/antonym activity targets three important skills—vocabulary development, visual skills, and spelling. Ask your child to read the directions and then explain to you what is expected. As your child completes the activity, discuss words with unfamiliar meanings.

Circle S if the words are synonyms. Circle A if the words are antonyms.

forward	backward	S	A
guess	speculate	S	A
general	specific	S	A
anonymous	nameless	S	A

ahead	behind	S	A
difficult	effortless	S	A
material	fabric	S	A
test	exam	S	A

wrong	accurate	S	A
minute	tiny	S	A
object	agree	S	A
catch	seize	S	A

famous	unknown	S	A
exceptional	remarkable	S	A
explain	clarify	S	A
build	demolish	S	A

natural	abnormal	S	A
middle	halfway	S	A
late	punctual	S	A
base	apex	S	A

sleep	snooze	S	A
trouble	adversity	S	A
sent	received	S	A
modern	dated	S	A

Next, ask your child to look at a set of word pairs for about one minute. Then conceal the words and have your child write as many word pairs as possible on another sheet of paper. Next, reveal the words for your child to review and proofread. Repeat the activity with each set of words. Try this again later, decreasing the time spent looking at the words to 30 seconds. Every child a speller!

Assess Words and Skills

- Spelling Words (words missed on tests) are recorded in the Spelling Notebook.
- Use Proof It, Practice Page 90, for proofreading/editing practice.

Teaching Notes, page 336

Assess Spelling Progress

Give this Cloze Story Word Test of Core Words within the frequencies 1–650 to all students. Words students miss are their Spelling Words.

 **THE CLOZE STORY WORD TEST**

Students do not prestudy the words. Provide students with a copy of REVIEW 30 BLACKLINE MASTER, page 269. Tell students this story asks them to solve a dilemma in Dodge City.

Read the entire story aloud, including the test words. Then read it again slowly as students write the missing words.

Words tested:
there (37), their (42), its (76), again (141), between (154), usually (278), didn't (281), brought (327), whether (399), suddenly (458), else (485), alone (491), single (509), whose (520), except (550), strange(r) (572), famous (583), business (595), object (606), pair (631), ahead (632), forward (646), huge (647), ride (648), region (649), nor (650)

The Dodge City Cowboy Mystery

The cowboy galloped into Dodge City on Sunday, creating a (1) <u>huge</u> cloud of dust. He leaned (2) <u>forward</u> and dismounted his large horse with the white star on (3) <u>its</u> forehead. Every (4) <u>pair</u> of eyes was on him. No one knew this gentleman (5) <u>whose</u> journey (6) <u>brought</u> him to (7) <u>their</u> town. (8) <u>Usually</u> folks knew everyone (9) <u>else</u> from around the (10) <u>region</u>, but he was a (11) <u>stranger</u>. The citizens wondered (12) <u>whether</u> (13) <u>there</u> was big trouble (14) <u>ahead</u>.

Over the next three nights, the cowboy had a (15) <u>single</u> room at the (16) <u>famous</u> Dodge Hotel and spent each daytime reading folklore (17) <u>alone</u> in the lobby. He (18) <u>didn't</u> speak to anyone (19) <u>nor</u> did he (20) <u>ride</u> his horse anyplace. No one could understand the (21) <u>object</u> of his visit. Then he (22) <u>suddenly</u> rode away (23) <u>again</u> on Sunday. Wait! (24) <u>Between</u> his arrival and departure, he never left town and did not spend the night anywhere (25) <u>except</u> the hotel. How could he both come and go on Sunday, yet stay only three nights? Make it your (26) <u>business</u> to solve this mystery.

 **AFTER THE CLOZE STORY WORD TEST**

reasoning, writing an explanation

1. Have students write and share their answer to the Dodge City dilemma. Conclude that the cowboy's horse was named Sunday.

recording words for personal study list

2. Have students record the words they missed on the test in their Spelling Notebook (see page 338) for at-school study, and on a copy of the WORDS TO LEARN BLACKLINE MASTER, page 375, for at-home study.

Assess Skill Application

Give this assessment of spelling and related skills to all students.
The REVIEW 30 BLACKLINE MASTER is on page 270.

Teaching Notes, page 339

THE SKILL TEST

Synonyms are words that _________________________________.
  (mean the same)   sound the same   have the same spelling
Antonyms are words that _________________________________.
    are alike   (have opposite meanings)   are anonymous
Examples of synonyms are:
  _____________________ and _____________________, or
  _____________________ and _____________________.
Examples of antonyms are:
  _____________________ and _____________________, or
  _____________________ and _____________________.

(answers will vary)

Skill tested:
synonyms and antonyms

Note the ability of each student to define and provide examples of synonyms and antonyms.

Assess Proofreading Application

Give this assessment of spelling and related skills to all students.
The REVIEW 30 BLACKLINE MASTER is on page 270.

Teaching Notes, page 341

THE PROOFREADING TEST

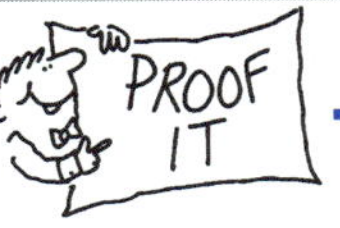

If the underlined word in each line is incorrect, write it correctly in the space.

You <u>know</u> that the Caldecott and Newbery Awards
are distinguished honors, <u>howeaver</u> there are   _____ however _____
many other <u>improtant</u> medals given to remarkable   _____ important _____
children's books each year. One is the <u>faimous</u>   _____ famous _____
Coretta Scott King Award. The finest <u>writters</u> and   _____ writers _____
illustrators deserve recognition. Yet, <u>there</u> are   _______________
<u>hunderds</u> of excellent books that may never be   _____ hundreds _____
<u>singeled</u> out for special acknowledgment. They're   _____ singled _____
good <u>storys</u>, perhaps with outstanding artwork.   _____ stories _____
The reader remembers the characters and <u>picktures</u>   _____ pictures _____
long after <u>its</u> been read. It must be a great pleasure _____ it's _____
to these authors and illustrators that <u>they're</u> work _____ their _____
has <u>bin</u> immensely popular and enjoyed.   _____ been _____

If you could award an honor of your own making to a book you liked, what
would you call the honor and which book would you select? Why?

Note the ability of each student to proofread for spelling errors.

Teaching Notes, page 342

Extend Spelling Assessment

Give this in-context assessment of Core Words within the frequencies
1–650 to students who need more practice or challenge.

Words tested:
the (1), of (2), and (3), a (4), to
(5), that (9), was (13), on (14),
as (16), with (17), they (19), be
(21), were (34), we (36), there
(37), their (42), about (48), them
(52), her (64), two (65), make(ing)
(72), much (104), our (109), too
(112), think (118), around (120),
important (195), until (196),
children (200), began (215),
mother (226), told (255), young
(256), didn't (281), move(d)
(290), voice (382), beautiful
(429), boat (475), listen (507),
energy (511), explain(ed) (513),
travel(ers) (516), mountain (526),
information (549), suppose(d)
(555), history (567), child (571),
woman('s) (577), lot (597),
especially (614), necessary (615),
forward (646), huge (647), ride
(648), region (649), nor (650)

Extra words: lake, loudspeaker,
noise, quiet

writing dialogue

recording words for
personal study list

THE SENTENCE DICTATION TEST

Students do not prestudy the words. Provide students with writing paper and pencil.
Have students write the sentences as they are dictated.

1. The huge boat moved forward as we began our ride around
   the beautiful mountain lake.

2. There was a woman's voice on a loudspeaker that told the
   travelers about important history of the region.

3. Two young children with a lot of energy didn't think her
   information was especially necessary.

4. They were making too much noise until their mother
   explained to them that they were supposed to be quiet
   and listen.

AFTER THE SENTENCE DICTATION TEST

1. Have students write the dialogue for the
woman guide as she tells about the reputation
the lake has for "monster-like" beings lurking
inside it.

2. Have students record the words they missed
on the test in their Spelling Notebook (see page
345) for at-school study, and on a copy of the
WORDS TO LEARN BLACKLINE MASTER, page 375, for
at-home study.

The Cloze Story Word Test and
the Sentence Dictation Test are
group tests, yet the results are
individualized. They identify the
needs of an individual class as
well as each individual student.

Word Test

The Dodge City Cowboy Mystery

The cowboy galloped into Dodge City on Sunday, creating a (1) ______________ cloud of dust. He leaned (2) ______________ and dismounted his large horse with the white star on (3) ______________ forehead. Every (4) ______________ of eyes was on him. No one knew this gentleman (5) ______________ journey (6) ______________ him to (7) ______________ town. (8) ______________ folks knew everyone (9) ______________ from around the (10) ______________, but he was a (11) ______________. The citizens wondered (12) ______________ (13) ______________ was big trouble (14) ______________.

Over the next three nights, the cowboy had a (15) ______________ room at the (16) ______________ Dodge Hotel and spent each daytime reading folklore (17) ______________ in the lobby. He (18) ______________ speak to anyone (19) ______________ did he (20) ______________ his horse anyplace. No one could understand the (21) ______________ of his visit. Then he (22) ______________ rode away (23) ______________ on Sunday. Wait! (24) ______________ his arrival and departure, he never left town and did not spend the night anywhere (25) ______________ the hotel. How could he both come and go on Sunday, yet stay only three nights? Make it your (26) ______________ to solve this mystery.

Name _______________________

Skill Test

Synonyms are words that ____.

mean the same   sound the same   have the same spelling

Antonyms are words that ____.

are alike   have opposite meanings   are anonymous

Examples of synonyms are:

________________________ and ________________________, or

________________________ and ________________________.

Examples of antonyms are:

________________________ and ________________________, or

________________________ and ________________________.

Proofreading Test

If the underlined word in each line is incorrect, write it correctly in the space.

You <u>know</u> that the Caldecott and Newbery Awards _______________________

are distinguished honors, <u>howeaver</u> there are _______________________

many other <u>improtant</u> medals given to remarkable _______________________

children's books each year. One is the <u>faimous</u> _______________________

Coretta Scott King Award. The finest <u>writters</u> and _______________________

illustrators deserve recognition. Yet, <u>there</u> are _______________________

<u>hunderds</u> of excellent books that may never be _______________________

<u>singeled</u> out for special acknowledgment. They're _______________________

good <u>storys</u>, perhaps with outstanding artwork. _______________________

The reader remembers the characters and <u>picktures</u> _______________________

long after <u>its</u> been read. It must be a great pleasure _______________________

to these authors and illustrators that <u>they're</u> work _______________________

has <u>bin</u> immensely popular and enjoyed. _______________________

If you could award an honor of your own making to a book you liked, what would you call the honor and which book would you select? Why?

Build Skills and Word Experiences

Use Student Practice Pages 91–92 to follow up instruction for:
Activity 1B • Activity 1C

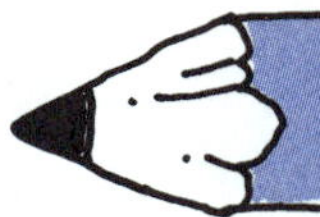

Build Visual Skills

Do the Word Preview, a visual warm-up activity, with all students.
Use Core Words **period** (651), **blood** (652), **rich** (653), **team** (654), **corner** (655).

Teaching Notes, page 316

Build Spelling and Language Skills

Choose from among these quick tasks to customize instruction
for all or selected students.

Teaching Notes, page 319

It was in the corner.

During our first period class, we learned how blood flow thru are
body and feeds our cells. Teams' in each corner of the room was
told to look up more information on the subject to present to the class.

(flows, through, our, Teams, were)

blood, Tennessee, woolly, Minnesota, committee, noodles, Mississippi, embarrassing,
Missouri, sleeplessness, Massachusetts, happier

(e.g., contains 1/2/3 sets of double letters; is/isn't a state name; does/doesn't contain a suffix)

period, question mark, _______

(marks of punctuation)

The long-anticipated game was half over, and our team _______.

Words to which the less suffix can be added

Teaching Notes, page 325

Build Basic Concepts

Choose from among these skill-building activities to customize instruction
for all or selected students.

| concept one | A suffix is a letter or letters added to the end of a word. |

word analysis, plural practice,
suffix practice, writing words,
sorting words, more words

1A Select a student to write *rich* on the chalkboard. Then ask students what they can
tell you about *rich* (e.g., synonym for *wealthy*; antonym of *poor*; an exception to the rule
that *tch* follows a short vowel; becomes plural with the addition of *es*; has more than
one meaning). Focus on the attribute that *es* is added to make *rich* plural. Have students
identify the four other kinds of nouns that meet this criterion (words ending in *s*, *sh*,
x, *z*). Next, ask students to find and write examples that meet this criterion, sorted by
ending letter(s).

suffix practice, plural practice,
writing words, spelling game

1B Review the addition of the *es* suffix to make some nouns plural (Activity 1A, this
unit). Then have students identify other ways nouns are made plural (add *s—teams*,
change *y* to *i* and add *es—parties*, *f/fe* may change to *ves—halves*, no change—*deer*,
new word form—*teeth*). Divide students into teams to find and write examples for each
way nouns are made plural. Ask the class to speculate how many correctly spelled word
examples they can amass for each category. Set the timer (about three minutes) and
begin! Then tally the words and compare the speculated totals to the results.

suffix practice, spelling rules

1C Ask students to identify suffixes that can be added to *rich* (es, er, est, ly, ness).
Focus on *ly*, asking students to find and write more words to which the *ly* suffix can be
added. Then reinforce these spelling generalizations regarding ly:

- usually *ly* is just added to words—*richly* (this includes words ending in *l—really*,
  carefully—Activity 1B, page 56).
- *ally* is added to words ending in *ic—periodically* (Build Skillful Writers, page 3).
- words ending with consonant-soft-syllable *le*, drop the *le* before adding *ly—*
  terrible/terribly, *simple/simply*, *double/doubly*, *able/ably*, *single/singly*, *gentle/*
  gently, *possible/possibly*.

suffix practice, writing words

1D Dictate these words for students to write—after each, write the word on the
chalkboard for students to self-check: *periodically*, *generally*, *practicing*, *flatten*, *partied*,
necessarily, *businesses*, *ably*. Then have students write the words without the suffix.

WORD MYSTERIES AND HISTORIES

Initially, *period*, from the Latin *periodus*, meant a complete
cycle relating to time, such as from dawn back to dark. Then its
meaning expanded to mean the point of completion of the cycle.
Later, it came to include a sentence start to finish. Finally, its
meaning grew to include the actual dot that ends a sentence.

Build Skillful Writers

Use these interrelated language learnings for all or selected students.

Teaching Notes, page 328

Post Teaching Poster 1. Model use of the steps on the poster. Discuss editing marks using the PERSONAL POSTER 1 BLACKLINE MASTER, page 367 (make a copy of the transparency to use on an overhead projector to guide discussion).

After students have written on any topic across the curriculum, organize them into pairs. They use the steps and proofreading/editing marks to mark the papers. Then these papers are handed in for checking. Next, the papers are returned to use the proofreading/editing marks to make the corrections.

Build Assessment Readiness

Use these at-school and at-home exercises to prepare all students for the Skill Test.

Teaching Notes, page 329

at-school   Review the soft-syllable endings *le*, *el*, and *al*. Remind students that *le* is the most prevalent. Then review the soft-syllable endings *er*, *or*, and *ar*. Remind students that *er* is the most prevalent and as a suffix can mean *more* (e.g., richer) or *one who* (e.g., teacher). The suffixes *or* and *ar* can also mean *one who* (e.g., dictator, scholar).

Skill to be tested:
/əl/ and /ər/

Have students fold paper to make four blocks. Ask students to label the boxes *er*, *or*, *ar*, and *?* on the front. On the back they label the boxes *le*, *el*, *al*, and *?* Then dictate words for students to sort by spelling pattern. Words for which the spelling is unfamiliar are written in the *?* box to be checked. Words for dictation may include:

> le: *people, humble, muscle, able, example*
> el: *level, travel, model, camel, vowel*
> al: *general, animal, usual, material, final*
> er: *corner, water, another, cheerleader, daughter*
> or: *color, actor, sailor, doctor, equator*
> ar: *caterpillar, dollar, radar, similar, popular*

at-home   Send home a copy of TAKE-HOME TASK 31 BLACKLINE MASTER, page 274.

Skill to be tested:
/əl/ and /ər/

Build Proofreading Skills

Track students' ability to meet a minimum competency for spelling and proofreading within selected samples of their everyday writing.

Teaching Notes, page 330

- Send home papers for proofreading and a copy of the IDEAS FOR PROOFREADING BLACKLINE MASTER, page 373.

Name ______________________________

Dear Parents,

Here is a crossword puzzle for you and your child that provides practice spelling words with soft-syllable endings le, el, al, er, or, and ar. Words that end in these unstressed syllables are often difficult to spell because the vowel sound is the same when the word is said—

people, camel, animal   corner, doctor, sugar

Fill in vowel letters. Then place the words in the puzzle. Next, sort all the puzzle words on another sheet of paper by the last two letters.

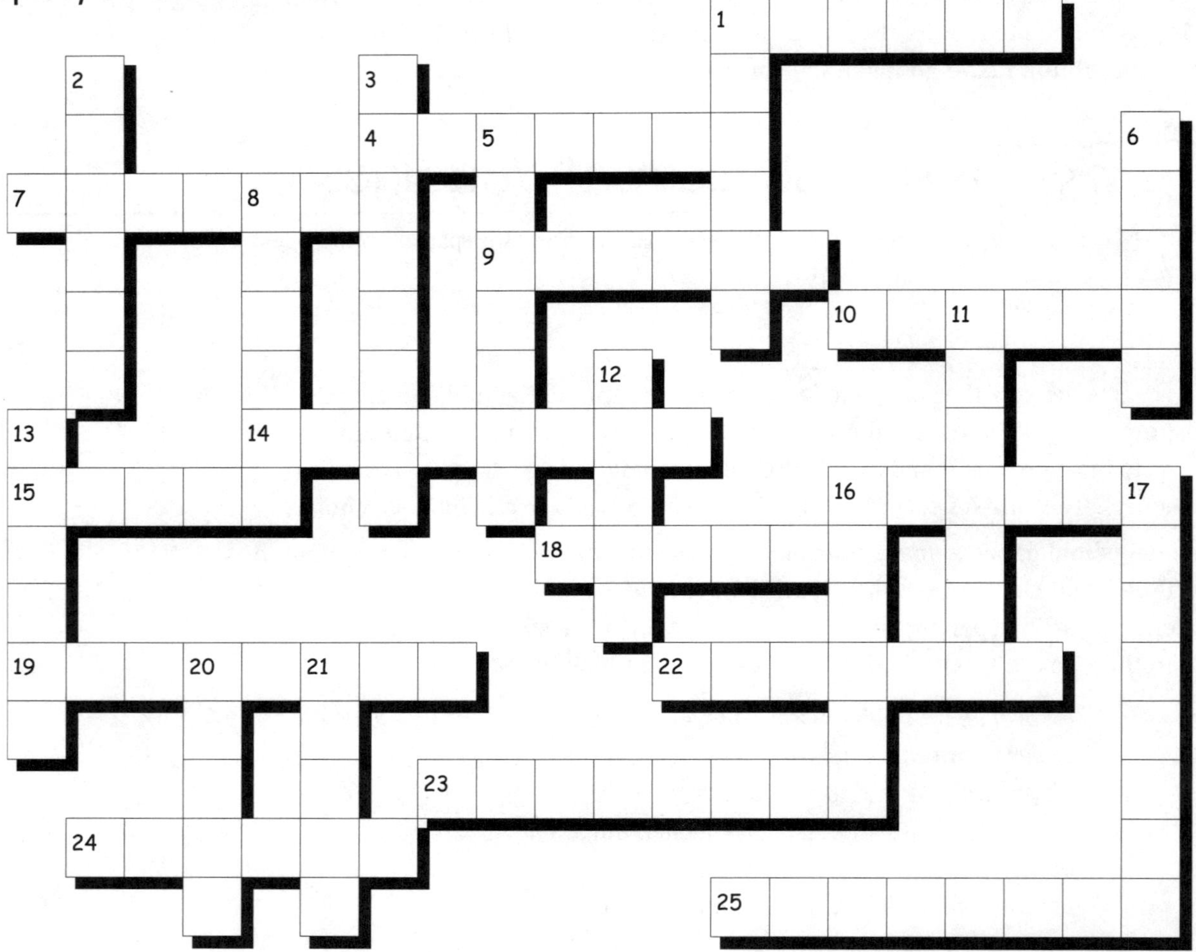

ACROSS

1. p__ckl__
4. tr__ct__r
7. br__th__r
9. m__scl__
10. b__ckl__
14. __l__v__t__r
15. __ng__r
16. k__nd__r
18. c__ndl__
19. l__ft__v__r
22. wr__nkl__
23. sq____rr__l
24. tr__v__l
25. s__rv__v__r

DOWN

1. p__rpl__
2. n__rm__l
3. str__ng__r
5. __dm__r__l
6. c__v__r
8. h__nt__r
11. ch__nn__l
12. r__y__l
13. s__ddl__
16. k__nn__l
17. r__m__nd__r
20. t__t__l
21. v__w__l

Assess Words and Skills

- Spelling Words (words missed on tests) are recorded in the Spelling Notebook.
- Use Proof It, Practice Page 93, for proofreading/editing practice.

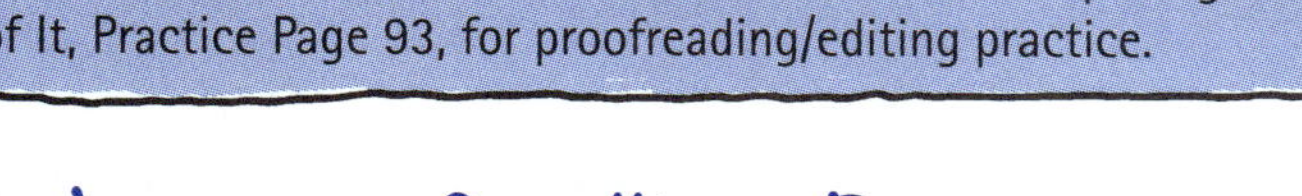

Assess Spelling Progress

Give this Cloze Story Word Test of Core Words within the frequencies 1–655 to all students. Words students miss are their Spelling Words.

Teaching Notes, page 336

 **THE CLOZE STORY WORD TEST**

Students do not prestudy the words. Provide students with a copy of REVIEW 31 BLACKLINE MASTER, page 278. Tell students that this story tells about the origin of one of their favorite snack foods.

Read the entire story aloud, including the test words. Then read it again slowly as students write the missing words.

A Mistake that Made a Hit

George Crum's face grew (1) <u>blood</u> red. This Native American chef was furious! A wealthy diner at the (2) <u>corner</u> table in the elegant cafe where George (3) <u>worked</u> sent his fried potatoes back for the (4) <u>third</u> time that (5) <u>morning</u>—not thin and crisp (6) <u>enough</u>! Well, Crum was (7) <u>through</u> putting up with this (8) <u>rich</u>, picky patron. (9) <u>Period</u>! Crum (10) <u>asked</u> his (11) <u>team</u> of kitchen helpers to step aside (12) <u>because</u> he (13) <u>planned</u> to teach this man a lesson. He began cutting razor-thin potatoes, over-cooking them, and over-salting them. He would (14) <u>teach</u> this customer not to complain! But to (15) <u>everyone's</u> surprise the man was delighted and quickly ordered (16) <u>another</u> helping!

This incident made (17) <u>history</u>. (18) <u>There</u> was immediate demand for these crispy treats. They were called Saratoga chips after the New York town where they were (19) <u>first</u> served in 1853. Now 11% of the potato (20) <u>business</u> in the (21) <u>United States</u> becomes (22) <u>their</u> successor, potato chips. (23) <u>They're</u> even made in (24) <u>several</u> flavors, such as onion. To what (25) <u>reasons</u> do you attribute (26) <u>their</u> long popularity?

Words tested:
there (37), their (42), first (74), through (102), another (121), work(ed) (124), because (127), asked (188), enough (209), several (263), morning (283), United States (305), everyone('s) (430), third (446), teacher (teach) (539), plan(ned) (544), reason(s) (564), history (567), business (595), period (651), blood (652), rich (653), team (654), corner (655), *they're (1010)

*The testing of they're (1010) is included to help students differentiate among the there/their/they're homophones.

 **AFTER THE CLOZE STORY WORD TEST**

1. Have students write their reasons for the lasting popularity of the potato chip. Inform students that people spend over $4 billion every year on potato chips that come from 3,500 billion pounds of potatoes annually. Do students know which state produces the most potatoes? (Idaho, by far!)

speculating, writing reasons

2. Have students record the words they missed on the test in their Spelling Notebook (see page 338) for at-school study, and on a copy of the WORDS TO LEARN BLACKLINE MASTER, page 375, for at-home study.

recording words for personal study list

Teaching Notes, page 339

Assess Skill Application

Give this assessment of spelling and related skills to all students.
The REVIEW 31 BLACKLINE MASTER is on page 279.

 **THE SKILL TEST**

Skill tested:
/əl/ and /ər/

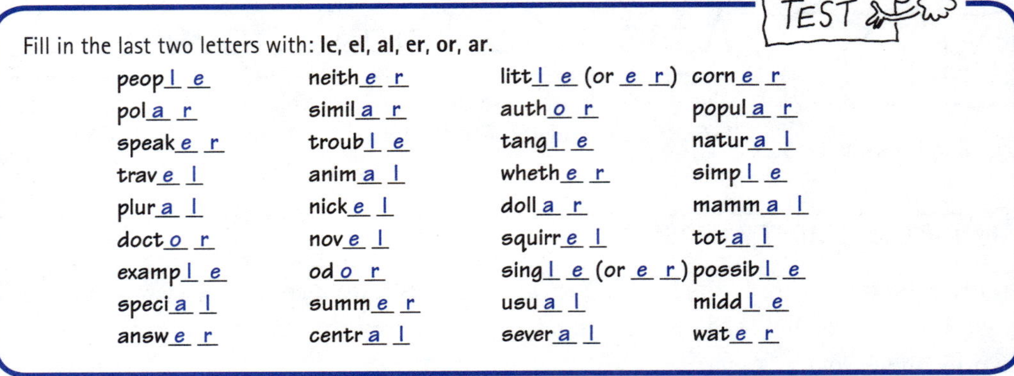

Fill in the last two letters with: **le, el, al, er, or, ar.**

peop**l e**	neith**e r**	litt**l e** (or **e r**)	corn**e r**
pol**a r**	simil**a r**	auth**o r**	popul**a r**
speak**e r**	troub**l e**	tang**l e**	natur**a l**
trav**e l**	anim**a l**	wheth**e r**	simp**l e**
plur**a l**	nick**e l**	doll**a r**	mamm**a l**
doct**o r**	nov**e l**	squirr**e l**	tot**a l**
examp**l e**	od**o r**	sing**l e** (or **e r**)	possib**l e**
speci**a l**	summ**e r**	usu**a l**	midd**l e**
answ**e r**	centr**a l**	sever**a l**	wat**e r**

Note the ability of each student to identify and spell homophones.

Teaching Notes, page 341

Assess Proofreading Application

Give this assessment of spelling and related skills to all students.
The REVIEW 31 BLACKLINE MASTER is on page 279.

 **THE PROOFREADING TEST**

In the underlined parts, there may be errors in spelling,
capitalization, punctuation, or grammar. Circle errors. Write corrections in the space.

All <u>writers do not right stories</u> for our enjoyment.   *write*
Instead, <u>thay write poetry newspaper</u> columns,   *they ,*
<u>technical reporrts, textbook,</u> magazine articles,   *reports textbooks*
movie scripts, plays—<u>there are several different</u>
careers for a <u>writer. Of coarse, frist</u> the basics of   *course first*
writing <u>must be learn. Than thay</u> must decide   *learned Then they*
the kind of <u>writen work thay'd like</u> to create. Each   *written they'd*
kind of <u>writing leeds</u> to a <u>diferent</u> type of work.   *leads different*
For <u>exampel, a reportor who's</u> describes last   *example reporter who*
<u>night's basebal game</u> for the sports page of the   *baseball*
<u>city's newpaper has a live</u> unlike the author whose   *newspaper life*
technical <u>wark is feature</u> in scientific journals.   *work featured*
Indeed, <u>writters have alot</u> of exciting choices.   *writers a lot*

List careers in writing. Which one would be the most appealing to you? Why?

Note the ability of each student to proofread for spelling, capitalization, punctuation, or
grammar errors.

Extend Spelling Assessment

Give this in-context assessment of Core Words within the frequencies 1–655 to students who need more practice or challenge.

Teaching Notes, page 342

THE SENTENCE DICTATION TEST

Students do not prestudy the words. Provide students with writing paper and pencil. Have students write the sentences as they are dictated.

1. During periods of war, we have learned that it's usually necessary for there to be some blood that is shed.

2. Rich lands and beautiful buildings are often hurt, too.

3. Whether you're on the winning team or not, fighting is a difficult way for people and their governments to solve problems.

4. Nearly every corner of the world has been in combat for one reason or another.

Words tested:

the (1), of (2), and (3), a (4), to (5), in (6), is (7), that (9), for (12), on (14), are (15), be (21), have (25), or (26), one (28), not (30), we (36), there (37), their (42), some (56), has (62), been (75), people (79), way (86), too (112), another (121), every (151), often (186), world (191), land(s) (202), near(ly) (243), during (248), it's (253), usually (278), learned (326), whether (399), problem(s) (422), beautiful (429), build(ings) (487), war (532), you're (552), government(s) (558), reason (564), necessary (615), difficult (638), period(s) (651), blood (652), rich (653), team (654), corner (655)

Extra words: combat, fighting, hurt, shed, solve, winning

AFTER THE SENTENCE DICTATION TEST

1. Have students write the major reasons for fighting World War II. Then pair the information they discover with the 2005 Caldecott Honor Book *Coming On Home Soon*, by Jacqueline Woodson and illustrated by E.B. Lewis. This award-winning book tells the story of Ada Ruth, who is left behind with Grandma in Chicago when her mother is called to service for World War II. This story has the timeless quality that appeals to those who wait and hope.

writing reasons, relating to literature

2. Have students record the words they missed on the test in their Spelling Notebook (see page 345) for at-school study, and on a copy of the Words to Learn Blackline Master, page 375, for at-home study.

recording words for personal study list

Have students write (**IN OTHER WORDS**): The greatest of riches is contentment with little.
English Proverb

Word Test

A Mistake that Made a Hit

George Crum's face grew (1) _______________ red. This Native American chef was furious! A wealthy diner at the (2) _______________ table in the elegant cafe where George (3) _______________ sent his fried potatoes back for the (4) _______________ time that (5) _______________—not thin and crisp (6) _______________! Well, Crum was (7) _______________ putting up with this (8) _______________, picky patron.

(9) _______________! Crum (10) _______________ his (11) _______________ of kitchen helpers to step aside (12) _______________ he (13) _______________ to teach this man a lesson. He began cutting razor-thin potatoes, over-cooking them, and over-salting them. He would (14) _______________ this customer not to complain! But to (15) _______________ surprise the man was delighted and quickly ordered (16) _______________ helping!

This incident made (17) _______________. (18) _______________ was immediate demand for these crispy treats. They were called Saratoga chips after the New York town where they were (19) _______________ served in 1853. Now 11% of the potato (20) _______________ in the (21) _______________ becomes (22) _______________ successor, potato chips. (23) _______________ even made in (24) _______________ flavors, such as onion. To what (25) _______________ do you attribute (26) _______________ long popularity?

Skill Test

Fill in the last two letters with: **le, el, al, er, or, ar.**

peop__ __	neith__ __	litt__ __	corn__ __
pol__ __	simil__ __	auth__ __	popul__ __
speak__ __	troub__ __	tang__ __	natur__ __
trav__ __	anim__ __	wheth__ __	simp__ __
plur__ __	nick__ __	doll__ __	mamm__ __
doct__ __	nov__ __	squirr__ __	tot__ __
examp__ __	od__ __	sing__ __	possib__ __
speci__ __	summ__ __	usu__ __	midd__ __
answ__ __	centr__ __	sever__ __	wat__ __

Proofreading Test

In the underlined parts, there may be errors in spelling, capitalization, punctuation, or grammar. Circle errors. Write corrections in the space.

All <u>writers do not right stories</u> for our enjoyment.   _______________________

Instead, <u>thay write poetry newspaper</u> columns,   _______________________

<u>technical reporrts, textbook,</u> magazine articles,   _______________________

movie scripts, plays—<u>there are several different</u>   _______________________

careers for a <u>writer. Of coarse, frist</u> the basics of   _______________________

writing <u>must be learn. Than thay</u> must decide   _______________________

the kind of <u>writen work thay'd like</u> to create. Each   _______________________

kind of <u>writing leeds to a diferent</u> type of work.   _______________________

For <u>exampel, a reportor who's</u> describes last   _______________________

<u>night's basebal game</u> for the sports page of the   _______________________

<u>city's newpaper has a live</u> unlike the author whose   _______________________

technical <u>wark is feature in</u> scientific journals.   _______________________

Indeed, <u>writters have alot of exciting</u> choices.   _______________________

List careers in writing. Which one would be the most appealing to you? Why?

Build Skills and Word Experiences

Use Student Practice Pages 94–95 to follow up instruction for:
Activity 1A • Did You Know?

Build Visual Skills

Do the Word Preview, a visual warm-up activity, with all students.
Use Core Words **cat** (656), **amount** (657), **garden** (658), **led** (659), **note** (660).

Teaching Notes, page 316

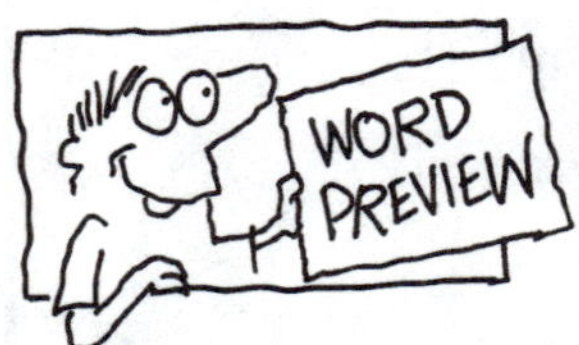

Build Spelling and Language Skills

Choose from among these quick tasks to customize instruction
for all or selected students.

Teaching Notes, page 319

A note was in the book.

We followed the path out of the gardin that led to the area were the
wild cats could walk freely. We arrived while they ate their dinner
I couldn't help but note the huge amount of food the animal's ate.

(*garden*, *where*, period after *dinner*, *animals*)

gardener, cat, graceful, people, cereal, grew, playful, pretending, grassy, caught,
carpenter, piggy

(e.g., noun/verb/adjective; beginning letter; number of syllables)

cat's paw, cats' paws, teacher's desk, teachers' desks, _______, _______

(singular and plural possessives)

If I found a large amount of money, I would _______.

Names of plants that could be grown in a vegetable garden

Build Basic Concepts

Choose from among these skill-building activities to customize instruction
for all or selected students.

Teaching Notes, page 325

| concept one | Frequent spelling patterns for /ou/ are *ou* and *ow*. |

1A Write *amount* and *power* on the chalkboard.
Note the common vowel sound. Have students
write /ou/ words spelled *ou* or *ow* on word cards
(use the WORD CARD BLACKLINE MASTER, page 384).
On the back of the card they write the word,
leaving out the *ou* or *ow* letters. Then they flash
this side of the card to a partner for the partner
to write the word with the missing vowels. If the
word is spelled correctly, the player keeps the
card. Play continues with players reversing roles,
the object being to earn the most word cards.

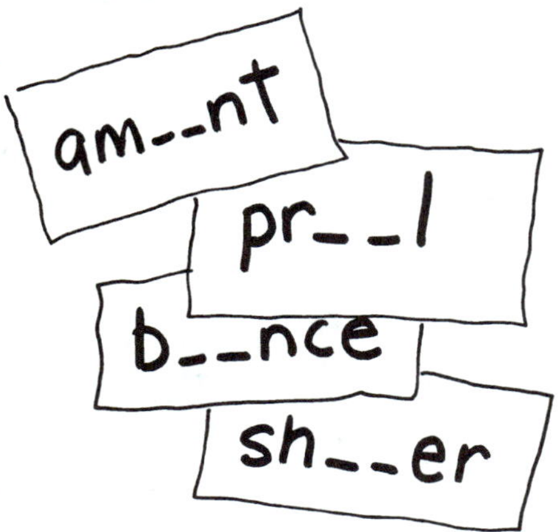

*phonics, writing words, word
game, prefix/suffix practice,
writing sentences*

Later, have students use the words on the word cards to—

- add suffixes and prefixes to the words.
- write the words in sentences containing one of the often-confused words on their
  Spell Check, page 407.

1B Write *amt.* on the chalkboard. Ask students to identify its longer form (amount).
Have students write more abbreviations and their longer forms from memory. Then
review the abbreviation book (Build Skillful Writers, page 147) and the abbreviations on
their Spell Check.

*abbreviations, recall, writing
words*

The letters *ou* and *ow* consistently spell /ou/, but *ou* also spells more sounds than any
other vowel pattern. Some *ou* spellings are further complicated by *gh* that stood for a
German sound that is difficult for us to pronounce, so the sound was abandoned. In some
words the *gh* is now silent. Yet in other words, *gh* can spell /f/, such as in *rough, tough,
laugh,* and *enough*.

Enough! Enough!
We have pour and your and brought and thought,
And soup and group and fought and bought.
We have through and you and would and could,
Of course this group must include should.
We have though and dough and rough and tough,
And cough and trough—enough, enough!

Note the 21 *ou* spellings and the six different sounds the vowel pattern makes in the
rhyme.

Build Skillful Writers

Teaching Notes, page 328

Use these interrelated language learnings for all or selected students.

Review the parts of a letter (e.g., salutation, body, closing, signature). Have students practice writing a thank-you note to someone using the correct form. Students should write legibly, show appreciation, and carefully proofread their note.

Next, discuss the format for addressing an envelope. Have students check abbreviations, including postal abbreviations for states.

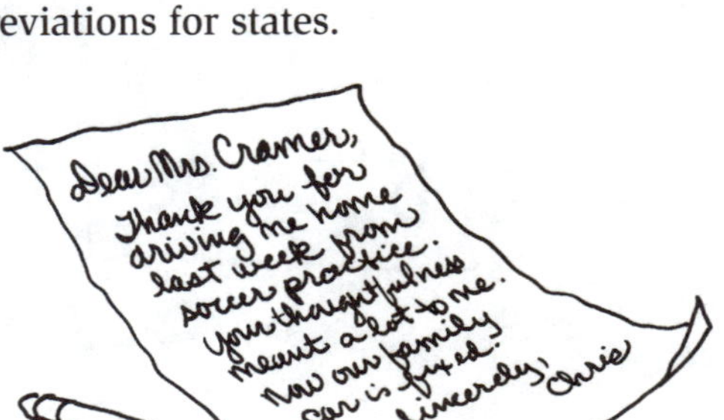

Build Assessment Readiness

Teaching Notes, page 329

Use these at-school and at-home exercises to prepare all students for the Skill Test.

Skill to be tested: irregular verb forms

at-school Ask students how most verbs form their past tense (*ed* suffix). Write *lead* and *led* on the chalkboard. Identify lead as a homograph and *led* as the irregular past tense of *lead* (/lĕd/). Review irregular verb forms with students brainstorming examples. Reinforce the spelling of the irregular verbs with At the Races or the Spelling Bee, page 391, in which students are given the present tense verb and they must identify and spell its irregular past tense form.

Skill to be tested: irregular verb forms

at-home Send home a copy of TAKE-HOME TASK 32 BLACKLINE MASTER, page 283.

Build Proofreading Skills

Teaching Notes, page 330

Track students' ability to meet a minimum competency for spelling and proofreading within selected samples of their everyday writing.

• Send home papers for proofreading and a copy of the IDEAS FOR PROOFREADING BLACKLINE MASTER, page 373.

Name _______________________________

Dear Parents,

In this activity your child practices identifying and spelling irregular verb forms. An irregular verb is one for which the past tense does not add the ed suffix, but forms a new word.

regular verb form: wait/waited   irregular verb form: speak/spoke

Write the irregular past tense verb forms.

begin _______	bite _______	blow _______
break _______	bring _______	build _______
catch _______	choose _______	come _______
dig _______	draw _______	drink _______
drive _______	eat _______	feed _______
feel _______	fight _______	fly _______
forget _______	freeze _______	get _______
give _______	grind _______	grow _______
hear _______	hide _______	hold _______
keep _______	know _______	lead _______
leave _______	lose _______	make _______
ride _______	sell _______	shoot _______
sing _______	sink _______	sit _______
sleep _______	slide _______	spend _______
stand _______	steal _______	stick _______
sting _______	strike _______	sweep _______
take _______	teach _______	tear _______
tell _______	think _______	throw _______
wear _______	weave _______	weep _______
win _______	wind _______	write _______

Discuss the meaning of any unfamiliar words with your child. Next, say the present tense form and ask your child to write the irregular past tense form—or vice versa. Every child a speller!

Assess Words and Skills

- Spelling Words (words missed on tests) are recorded in the Spelling Notebook.
- Use Proof It, Practice Page 96, for proofreading/editing practice.

Teaching Notes, page 336

Assess Spelling Progress

Give this Cloze Story Word Test of Core Words within the frequencies 1–660 to all students. Words students miss are their Spelling Words.

THE CLOZE STORY WORD TEST

Students do not prestudy the words. Provide students with a copy of REVIEW 32 BLACKLINE MASTER, page 287. Tell students that this story introduces them to a game.

Read the entire story aloud, including the test words. Then read it again slowly as students write the missing words.

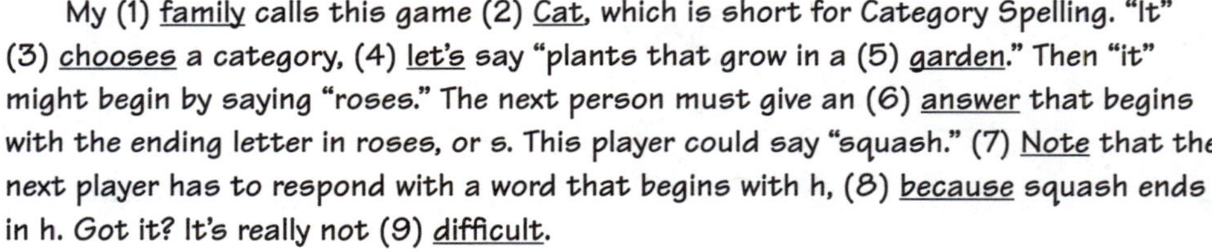

Words tested:
there (37), first (74), because (127), together (187), almost (216), let('s) (230), example (261), answer (265), city(ies) (273), family (287), animals (418), build (487), correct (521), choose(s) (580), necessary (615), subject (621), ahead (632), difficult (638), material(s) (641), thousand(s) (643), team(s) (654), cat (656), amount (657), garden (658), led (659), note (660)

Category Spelling

My (1) <u>family</u> calls this game (2) <u>Cat</u>, which is short for Category Spelling. "It" (3) <u>chooses</u> a category, (4) <u>let's</u> say "plants that grow in a (5) <u>garden</u>." Then "it" might begin by saying "roses." The next person must give an (6) <u>answer</u> that begins with the ending letter in roses, or s. This player could say "squash." (7) <u>Note</u> that the next player has to respond with a word that begins with h, (8) <u>because</u> squash ends in h. Got it? It's really not (9) <u>difficult</u>.

(10) <u>There</u> are (11) <u>thousands</u> of topics, such as ocean (12) <u>animals</u>, European (13) <u>cities</u>, book titles, or (14) <u>materials</u> that are (15) <u>necessary</u> to (16) <u>build</u> a house. A point is earned for every (17) <u>correct</u> response. The more you know about a (18) <u>subject</u>, the easier it is. For (19) <u>example</u>, my dad (20) <u>led</u> the game when the category was car parts, but I was (21) <u>ahead</u> with rock stars. The (22) <u>amount</u> I know on this topic is (23) <u>almost</u> endless! Now, it's your turn. (24) <u>First</u>, play by yourself with names and begin with your own name. Then play in class (25) <u>teams</u>. Decide (26) <u>together</u> which group is "it."

AFTER THE CLOZE STORY WORD TEST

spelling game, writing reasons

1. Have students play "Cat" with categories that reinforce their content subjects. Ask students to prepare a list of possible categories. Then ask them to explain in writing in which category they think they would perform best, giving reasons for their answer.

recording words for personal study list

2. Have students record the words they missed on the test in their Spelling Notebook (see page 338) for at-school study, and on a copy of the WORDS TO LEARN BLACKLINE MASTER, page 375, for at-home study.

Assess Skill Application

Give this assessment of spelling and related skills to all students.
The REVIEW 32 BLACKLINE MASTER is on page 288.

Teaching Notes, page 339

 **THE SKILL TEST**

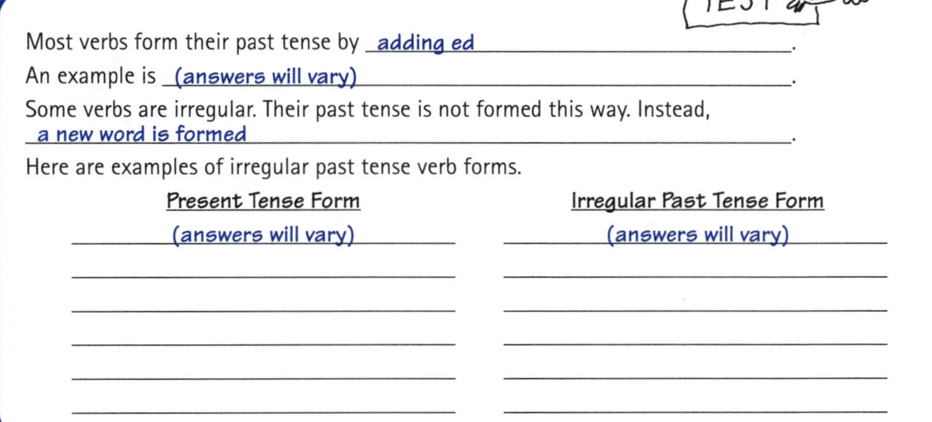

Most verbs form their past tense by _adding ed_ .
An example is _(answers will vary)_ .
Some verbs are irregular. Their past tense is not formed this way. Instead,
 a new word is formed .
Here are examples of irregular past tense verb forms.

Present Tense Form	Irregular Past Tense Form
(answers will vary)	_(answers will vary)_

Skill tested:
irregular verb forms

Note the ability of each student to identify and spell irregular past tense verb forms.

Assess Proofreading Application

Give this assessment of spelling and related skills to all students.
The REVIEW 32 BLACKLINE MASTER is on page 288.

Teaching Notes, page 341

 **THE PROOFREADING TEST**

If the underlined parts are incorrect for spelling, capitalization,
punctuation, or grammar, write the correction(s) in the space.

We <u>our a culture of awards. We</u> reward several
<u>things. Their are awards</u> for performance in
<u>sports. Movie, plays, and</u> television shows that
<u>excel in some way are</u> bestowed awards, as are
the people <u>whose helped make them outsanding.</u>
Citizens who volunteer <u>there time ofen</u> receive
community <u>awards. A students</u> scholarship may
receive <u>recognition, busness organizations</u> may
<u>pressent their top</u> performers with prizes. Mothers
<u>and Fathers are</u> honored on special days of the year
<u>and maybe given a gift</u> of appreciation. Notable
contributions in science <u>and medicine are allways</u>
<u>credited Excellence</u> is definitely applauded!

Tell about an award that you would be proud to win.

are	
There	
Movies	
who outstanding	
their often	
student's	
. Business	
present	
fathers	
may be	
always	
.	

Note the ability of each student to proofread for spelling, capitalization, punctuation,
and grammar errors.

Teaching Notes, page 342

Words tested:
the (1), of (2), and (3), a (4), to (5), you (8), that (9), it (10), he (11), for (12), was (13), with (17), his (18), at (20), this (22), from (23), one (28), not (30), their (42), if (44), them (52), make(ing) (72), made (81), little (92), after (94), know (100), man (111), another (121), such (133), off (142), children('s) (200), animal (207), took (210), high (224), being (233), story (237), it's (253), remember (315), ran (362), start(ed) (389), speed (547), famous (583), trouble (588), direction (619), tail (636), huge (647), corner (655), cat('s) (656), amount (657), garden(er) (658), led (659), note (660)

Extra words: angry, chased, race, rake, vegetable, you'll

Extend Spelling Assessment

Give this in-context assessment of Core Words within the frequencies 1–660 to students who need more practice or challenge.

THE SENTENCE DICTATION TEST

Students do not prestudy the words. Provide students with writing paper and pencil. Have students write the sentences as they are dictated.

1. The angry man made note of the direction the little animal ran and he took off after it with his rake.

2. This started their race that led them at high speed from one corner of the vegetable garden to another.

3. Was it a cat that was making such a huge amount of trouble for the gardener?

4. If you remember this famous children's story, you'll know that it's not a cat's tail being chased.

AFTER THE SENTENCE DICTATION TEST

writing

1. Have students write the name of the tale being described (Peter Rabbit) and ask them to recall the lesson young listeners learn from the tale.

recording words for personal study list

2. Have students record the words they missed on the test in their Spelling Notebook (see page 345) for at-school study, and on a copy of the WORDS TO LEARN BLACKLINE MASTER, page 375, for at-home study.

Have students write IN OTHER WORDS : amount to something, beat around the bush, on all accounts, out and about, one in a thousand, to come around, sound off, on cloud nine, bound and determined, to stand your ground—and the proverb: An ounce of prevention is worth a pound of cure.

(Note the *ou* spellings for /ou/.)

Have students write IN OTHER WORDS : allow for something, ups and downs, frown on something, to knit your brow, till the cows come home, to drown something out, paint the town red, throw in the towel, neither fish nor fowl—and the proverb: April showers bring May flowers.

(Note the *ow* spellings for /ou/.)

Word Test

Category Spelling

My (1) _______________ calls this game (2) _______________, which is short for

Category Spelling. "It" (3) _______________ a category, (4) _______________ say

"plants that grow in a (5) _______________." Then "it" might begin by saying roses."

The next person must give an (6) _______________ that begins with the ending

letter in roses, or s. This player could say "squash." (7) _______________ that the

next player has to respond with a word that begins with h, (8) _______________

squash ends in h. Got it? It's really not (9) _______________.

(10) _______________ are (11) _______________ of topics, such as ocean

(12) _______________, European (13) _______________, book titles, or

(14) _______________ that are (15) _______________ to (16) _______________

a house. A point is earned for every (17) _______________ response. The more you

know about a (18) _______________, the easier it is. For (19) _______________, my

dad (20) _______________ the game when the category was car parts, but I was

(21) _______________ with rock stars. The (22) _______________ I know on this

topic is (23) _______________ endless! Now, it's your turn. (24) _______________,

play by yourself with names and begin with your own name. Then play in class

(25) _______________. Decide (26) _______________ which group is "it."

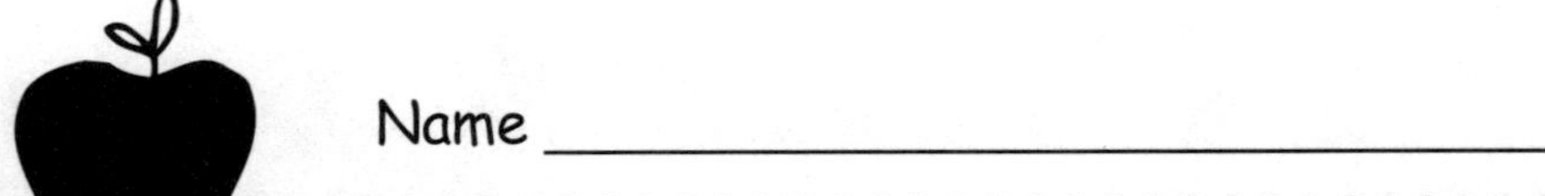

Skill Test

Most verbs form their past tense by _______________________________.

An example is _______________________________.

Some verbs are irregular. Their past tense is not formed this way. Instead, _______________
_______________________________.

Here are examples of irregular past tense verb forms.

Present Tense Form	Irregular Past Tense Form
_______________	_______________
_______________	_______________
_______________	_______________
_______________	_______________
_______________	_______________

Proofreading Test

If the underlined parts are incorrect for spelling, capitalization, punctuation, or grammar, write the correction(s) in the space.

We <u>our a culture of awards. We</u> reward several
<u>things. Their are awards</u> for performance in
<u>sports. Movie, plays, and</u> television shows that
<u>excel in some way are</u> bestowed awards, as are
the people <u>whose helped make them outsanding</u>.
Citizens who volunteer <u>there time ofen</u> receive
community <u>awards. A students</u> scholarship may
receive <u>recognition, busness organizations</u> may
<u>pressent their top</u> performers with prizes. Mothers
<u>and Fathers are</u> honored on special days of the year
<u>and maybe given a gift</u> of appreciation. Notable
contributions in science <u>and medicine are allways</u>
<u>credited Excellence</u> is definitely applauded!

Tell about an award that you would be proud to win.

____
____
____
____
____
____
____
____
____
____
____
____

Build Skills and Word Experiences

Use Student Practice Pages 97–98 to follow up instruction for:
Activity 2A • Test Ready

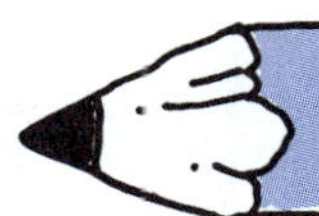

Build Visual Skills

Do the Word Preview, a visual warm-up activity, with all students.
Use Core Words **various** (661), **race** (662), **bit** (663), **result** (664), **brother** (665).

Teaching Notes, page 316

Build Spelling and Language Skills

Choose from among these quick tasks to customize instruction
for all or selected students.

Teaching Notes, page 319

The race will start.

My Brother has variaus interests, but he especially likes to race horse's.
When the horse is cool, he returns it to the stall and takes the bit out of
it's mouth. He thinks good care bring good results.

(*brother, various, horses, its, brings*)

race, sight, cancel, city, dance, listen, facing, once, south, except, cider, else

(e.g., by /s/ spelling pattern; number of letters; does/doesn't have silent letters)

racetrack, quarterback, background, _______

(compounds that contain *ack*)

We thought there were various ways to exit the park, but _______.

Words that begin with the prefix *re*

Teaching Notes, page 325

Build Basic Concepts

Choose from among these skill-building activities to customize instruction
for all or selected students.

concept one	Some words are spelled with consonant digraphs.

phonics, digraphs, consonant
blends, making words

1A Use *brother* to reinforce that when *h* follows *t*, as well
as *c*, *s*, *w*, and *p*, it makes a new sound. Reinforce that
consonant blends, such as *br*, are easier to spell when each
consonant sound is heard. Next, prepare for a letter-card
activity (see Activity 2B, page 47) using *a*, *c*, *e*, *h*, *n*, *o*, *p*, *s*,
t, and *w*. Tell students that all the words they will be making
contain consonant digraphs. Together make *each*. Then have
students continue making words: *cheap—cheat—chat—chant—chase—chews—cashew—
whose—those—oath—phone—shone—shoe—show—shown—shape—phase—poach—
chosen—ashen—when—wheat—peach*—and back to *each*. Later, have students work in
pairs to make more words with their letter cards. Have them write the words as they
make them.

digraphs, relating to literature,
writing a diary

1B Select a student to write *brother* on the chalkboard. Note the *th* digraph. Introduce
Our Only May Amelia, Jennifer Holm's Newbery 2000 Honor Book. Spunky May Amelia
grew up with seven older brothers pioneering in Washington state in the early 1900's.
May Amelia's authentic childhood diary was the basis for the award-winning story.
  • May Amelia was both Jennifer Holm's and Rebecca Sitton's great aunt.
    Contact Rebecca Sitton (see page viii) to obtain a copy of the diary to share with
    your students.
  • Encourage students to initiate a diary to save for a record of their life and times
    to enhance future generations' understanding of life today.

concept two	A suffix is a letter or letters added to the end of a word.

suffix practice, spelling rules,
spelling game, homophones,
vocabulary development, more
words

2A Select a student to write *very* and *vary* on
the chalkboard. Discuss the meanings of the
homophones. Then write on the chalkboard: *vary,
nerve, mystery, fame, mountain, joy, danger, glory.*
Tell students to add the *ous* suffix to the words.

Have students collect more words with the *ous* suffix
to use to play bingo (see Activity 1C, page 20).

To add a suffix to a base word,
begin with the spelling of the
base word. Then decide how to
add the suffix—check Teaching
Poster 2 for assistance.

Build Skillful Writers

Use these interrelated language learnings for all or selected students.

Teaching Notes, page 328

Skillful informational writers are mindful of the organization of their information. Ask students if they were compiling a city telephone book, what information it should contain and how they might organize it. Then check the local phone book. Discuss its organization and the various kinds of information compiled (calling information, alphabetical order of names with address/phone, businesses in yellow pages organized by kind of service). Next, have students provide reasons why they think the information was organized that way.

- Organize students into small groups, each with a telephone book to practice locating information. Ask groups to find information (e.g., the telephone number of the closest cinema to their school or a pet shop in their area).
- Have students brainstorm ways to inform others of a phone number or e-mail address.

Build Assessment Readiness

Use these at-school and at-home exercises to prepare all students for the Skill Test.

Teaching Notes, page 329

at-school Review *there/their/they're/there's/theirs*. Ask students to use print material to find and write a sentence that contains each homophone. Then have students prepare word cards for each homophone—use the TAKE-HOME TASK 33 BLACKLINE MASTER, page 292, or the WORD CARD BLACKLINE MASTER, page 384. Next, organize students into small groups with their sentences and word cards. Students take turns reading their sentences to the group who respond by flashing the correct word card.

Skill to be tested:
there/their/they're/there's/theirs

at-home Send home a copy of TAKE-HOME TASK 33 BLACKLINE MASTER, page 292.

Skill to be tested:
there/their/they're/there's/theirs

Build Proofreading Skills

Track students' ability to meet a minimum competency for spelling and proofreading within selected samples of their everyday writing.

Teaching Notes, page 330

- Send home papers for proofreading and a copy of the IDEAS FOR PROOFREADING BLACKLINE MASTER, page 373.

Have students write 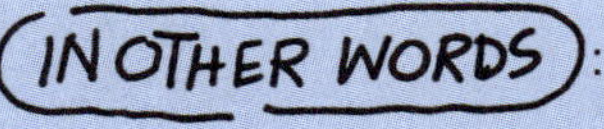: my mother's brothers (my uncles), my brother's brother (my brother/me), my grandmother's child (my mother/father/aunt/uncle), my brother's sibling (me/my brother/sister).

Dear Parents,

Let's make certain that your child can use and spell these homophones—

there   their   they're   there's   theirs

WORD	USE or DEFINITION	EXAMPLE
there	place not <u>here</u>, but <u>there</u>	See the puppies over there.
there	subject	There are five pups.
they're	contraction they are	They're all very small.
their	possessive pronoun belonging to them	They are their pups.
there's	contraction there is	There's only one spotted pup.
theirs	possessive pronoun belonging to them	All the pups are theirs.

Have your child cut out the word cards. Say sentences that contain one of the homophones and ask your child to flash the correct word card.

Continue with short practice sessions until your child confidently selects the correct homophone.

their   there   they're

theirs   there's

Assess Words and Skills

• Spelling Words (words missed on tests) are recorded in the Spelling Notebook.
• Use Proof It, Practice Page 99, for proofreading/editing practice.

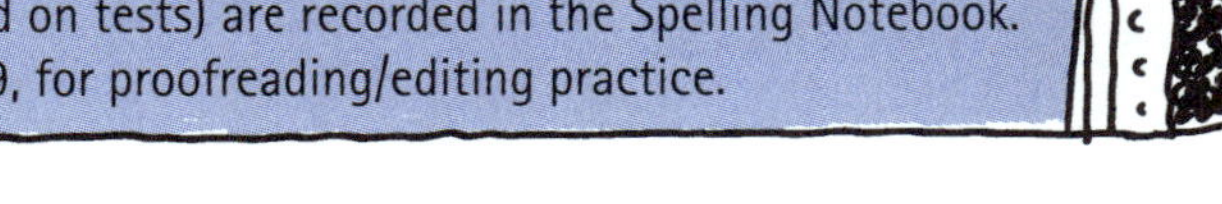

Assess Spelling Progress

Give this Cloze Story Word Test of Core Words within the frequencies 1–665 to all students. Words students miss are their Spelling Words.

Teaching Notes, page 336

THE CLOZE STORY WORD TEST

Students do not prestudy the words. Provide students with a copy of Review 33 Blackline Master, page 296. Tell students that this story shows how advertisements subtly persuade people to think and do certain things.

Read the entire story aloud, including the test words. Then read it again slowly as students write the missing words.

Sales Strategies

   (1) <u>Listen</u> to the man in the commercial: "I had to haul a large (2) <u>amount</u> of sand to fill the (3) <u>children's</u> play box. My new Madison truck passed the test! No (4) <u>trouble</u>! Now my (5) <u>brother</u> wants to borrow it. Wait a minute! I told him, (6) '<u>You're</u> going to need one of (7) <u>your</u> own!' A Madison pickup is (8) <u>necessary</u> for everyone! In-stock trucks are waiting for you in (9) <u>various</u> colors. (10) <u>Yours</u> will be every (11) <u>bit</u> as good as mine! So, (12) <u>race</u> down to the corner showroom, my (13) <u>friends</u>. The (14) <u>result</u> will be a new Madison (15) <u>machine</u> for you! (16) <u>Thousands</u> of Madison (17) <u>owners</u> can't be (18) <u>wrong</u>! For the (19) <u>money</u>, a Madison cannot be beat!"

   This ad is trying to persuade people to buy a (20) <u>certain</u> truck. (21) <u>Because</u> no one can be (22) <u>forced</u> to buy, it's attempting to make them want the truck. (23) <u>There</u> are two strategies used. One is called "bandwagon" that says everyone is buying. Another is "plain folks," a (24) <u>practice</u> that portrays the product as one that (25) <u>common</u>, honest folks use. Tell how this ad uses these techniques. Then find (26) <u>another</u> example of each of these sales methods.

Words tested:
there (37), your(s) (40), another (121), because (127), own(ers) (163), children('s) (200), money (279), certain (353), common (395), friend(s) (498), listen (507), machine (548), you're (552), trouble (588), necessary (615), force(d) (627), wrong (633), practice (634), thousand(s) (643), amount (657), various (661), race (662), bit (663), result (664), brother (665)

AFTER THE CLOZE STORY WORD TEST

1. Have students write and share their answers, identifying ways the story ad uses "bandwagon" and "plain folks" persuasion techniques. Later have students share their advertisement examples of these two common techniques. Discuss with students other propaganda methods, such as testimonials by well-known people, or transfer techniques using something already admired and pairing it with the object(s) to be sold. Discuss how awareness of commonly used ad techniques can help a person be a better consumer.

writing an explanation, identifying persuasion techniques

2. Have students record the words they missed on the test in their Spelling Notebook (see page 338) for at-school study, and on a copy of the Words to Learn Blackline Master, page 375, for at-home study.

recording words for personal study list

Assess Skill Application

Give this assessment of spelling and related skills to all students.
The REVIEW 33 BLACKLINE MASTER is on page 297.

 **THE SKILL TEST**

Teaching Notes, page 339

Skill tested:
there/their/they're/there's/theirs

Write the correct word in the blanks: **there, their, they're, there's,** or **theirs.**

Our neighbors who live over __there__ have five puppies. __Theirs__ is a house full of dogs since __their__ female dog had pups! __There's__ almost no trouble telling three of __their__ pups apart. One of __their__ pups is all black. One is almost all black, but __there's__ a white spot on one leg. One of __their__ pups is almost all white. Then __their__ other two pups look a lot alike. __They're__ spotted black and white, but __there's__ a difference— __they're__ slightly different sizes. Yet, __they're__ all cute! My mom likes __their__ playful nature, but she says she's glad __they're__ __theirs__ and not ours.

Note the ability of each student to discriminate among the *there/their/they're/there's/their* homophones.

Assess Proofreading Application

Give this assessment of spelling and related skills to all students.
The REVIEW 33 BLACKLINE MASTER is on page 297.

 **THE PROOFREADING TEST**

Teaching Notes, page 341

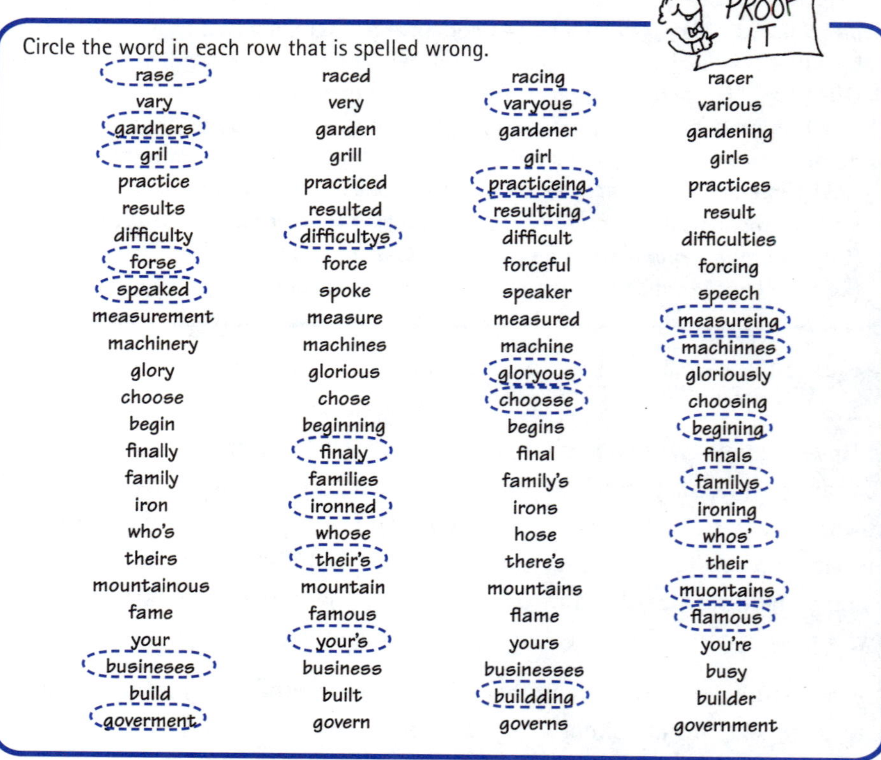

Note the ability of each student to identify misspelled words.

Extend Spelling Assessment

Give this in-context assessment of Core Words within the frequencies 1–665 to students who need more practice or challenge.

Teaching Notes, page 342

THE SENTENCE DICTATION TEST

Students do not prestudy the words. Provide students with writing paper and pencil. Have students write the sentences as they are dictated.

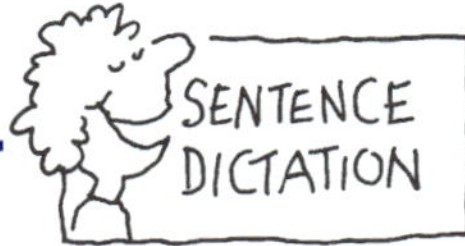

1. My brother and his friends ride their bikes on courses of various difficulties for their group workouts.
2. Every bit of practice makes them a stronger and better racing team.
3. The result could be a new record set in the regional bicycle event later this month.
4. Their bodies are in especially good shape to complete the distance ahead of the others.

Words tested:

the (1), of (2), and (3), a (4), to (5), in (6), for (12), on (14), are (15), his (18), be (21), this (22), their (42), them (52), other(s) (60), could (70), make(s) (72), my (80), good (106), new (107), every (151), set (162), better (245), body(ies) (285), later (288), group (295), course(s) (317), complete (365), strong(er) (381), distance (449), friend(s) (498), shape (601), record (611), especially (614), ahead (632), practice (634), difficult(ies) (638), ride (648), region(al) (649), team (654), various (661), race(ing) (662), bit (663), result (664), brother (665)

Extra words: bicycle, bikes, event, month, workouts

AFTER THE SENTENCE DICTATION TEST

1. Have students list equipment necessary for a bicycle racer, or some other participant in another sport. Then have students research and write about an annual race of some kind in their area. What is its significance and how does it contribute to their community?

research, writing

2. Have students record the words they missed on the test in their Spelling Notebook (see page 345) for at-school study, and on a copy of the WORDS TO LEARN BLACKLINE MASTER, page 375, for at-home study.

recording words for personal study list

WORD MYSTERIES AND HISTORIES

We derive one of our present meanings for *race* from the 13th century Old Norse word meaning "a rush of water" or "a quickly moving stream." By the 14th century its meaning included quickly moving people or animals. Later, it meant rushing or running, particularly in competition.

• Prompt students to recall the many words with more than one meaning, such as *race* (e.g., bit, note, rich, sand, party, flat, turn, point).

Word Test

Sales Strategies

(1) _______________ to the man in the commercial: "I had to haul a large

(2) _______________ of sand to fill the (3) _______________ play box. My new Madison

truck passed the test! No (4) _______________! Now my (5) _______________ wants to

borrow it. Wait a minute! I told him, '(6) _______________ going to need one of

(7) _______________ own!' A Madison pickup is (8) _______________ for everyone! In-

stock trucks are waiting for you in (9) _______________ colors. (10) _______________

will be every (11) _______________ as good as mine! So, (12) _______________ down

to the corner showroom, my (13) _______________. The (14) _______________ will be

a new Madison (15) _______________ for you! (16) _______________ of Madison

(17) _______________ can't be (18) _______________! For the (19) _______________, a

Madison cannot be beat!"

This ad is trying to persuade people to buy a (20) _______________ truck.

(21) _______________ no one can be (22) _______________ to buy, it's attempting

to make them want the truck. (23) _______________ are two strategies used.

One is called "bandwagon" that says everyone is buying. Another is "plain folks," a

(24) _______________ that portrays the product as one that (25) _______________,

honest folks use. Tell how this ad uses these techniques. Then find (26) _______________

example of each of these sales methods.

Name _______________________________   # REVIEW 33

Write the correct word in the blanks: **there**, **their**, **they're**, **there's**, or, **theirs**.

Our neighbors who live over _______________ have five puppies. _______________ is a house full of dogs since _______________ female dog had pups! _______________ almost no trouble telling three of _______________ pups apart. One of _______________ pups is all black. One is almost all black, but _______________ a white spot on one leg. One of _______________ pups is almost all white. Then _______________ other two pups look a lot alike. _______________ spotted black and white, but _______________ a difference—_______________ slightly different sizes. Yet, _______________ all cute! My mom likes _______________ playful nature, but she says she's glad _______________ _______________ and not ours.

Proofreading Test

Circle the word in each row that is spelled wrong.

rase	raced	racing	racer
vary	very	varyous	various
gardners	garden	gardener	gardening
gril	grill	girl	girls
practice	practiced	practiceing	practices
results	resulted	resultting	result
difficulty	difficultys	difficult	difficulties
forse	force	forceful	forcing
speaked	spoke	speaker	speech
measurement	measure	measured	measureing
machinery	machines	machine	machinnes
glory	glorious	gloryous	gloriously
choose	chose	choosse	choosing
begin	beginning	begins	begining
finally	finaly	final	finals
family	families	family's	familys
iron	ironned	irons	ironing
who's	whose	hose	whos'
theirs	their's	there's	their
mountainous	mountain	mountains	muontains
fame	famous	flame	flamous
your	your's	yours	you're
busineses	business	businesses	busy
build	built	buildding	builder
goverment	govern	governs	government

Build Skills and Word Experiences

Use Student Practice Pages 100–101 to follow up instruction for:
Activity 2A • Test Ready

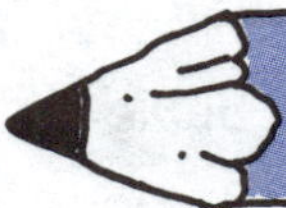

Build Visual Skills

Do the Word Preview, a visual warm-up activity, with all students.
Use Core Words **addition** (666), **doesn't** (667), **dead** (668), **weight** (669), **thin** (670).

Teaching Notes, page 316

Build Spelling and Language Skills

Choose from among these quick tasks to customize instruction
for all or selected students.

Teaching Notes, page 319

It disappeared into thin air.

Our old phone went dead, so we bought a new one. Its small in size,
lightwait, and vary thin. Our plan dosent have call waiting, nor various
other things I was hopping it would have.

(*It's*, omit *in size, lightweight, very, doesn't, hoping*)

weight, dead, thrown, grate, said, stone, eight, alone, fled, trait, red, groan

(e.g., words that rhyme; is/isn't a homophone; does/doesn't contain a consonant blend)

weight, bright, thought, _______

(words with *ght*)

The weight of the present gave me a clue that _______.

Products that are purchased by weight

Teaching Notes, page 325

Build Basic Concepts

Choose from among these skill-building activities to customize instruction for all or selected students.

concept one
An apostrophe is used in a contraction and in some possessives.

1A Ask students to state purposes for an apostrophe (to show possession/to show omission).

Have students fold writing paper lengthwise to make two columns. Students list contractions in the first column. Then they exchange papers and write the longer form of each contraction in the second column.

contractions, writing words

1B Ask students to identify pronouns that show possession without an apostrophe. Then make a cumulative list of the possessive pronouns on the chalkboard (my, mine, your, yours, his, her, hers, our, ours, their, theirs, its). Then have students explain in writing the difference between *there's* and *theirs*.

possessive pronouns, writing words, homophones, writing an explanation

concept two
Homophones are words that sound the same but have different spellings and meanings. Homographs are words that have the same spelling, different meanings, and may have different pronunciations.

2A Have students fold writing paper into four vertical columns. Dictate these words in sentences for students to write in the first column: *weight, knew, whole, hear, very, led, right, theirs, sun.* Ask students to identify the kind of word these illustrate (homophones). Then students write the homophone partner in the second column. In the third/fourth columns, they write a homophone set that rhymes with the set in the first two columns. Next, students self-check using Teaching Poster 5.

homophones, writing words, rhyming awareness, proofreading

2B Write *weight* and *wait* on the chalkboard. Ask students which homophone is a member of "The Weirdos" (Activity 1C, page 182). Have students brainstorm more homophone weirdos (e.g., eight, piece, their, theirs, weigh, reign, die). Ask students to write more weirdos from memory. Then have students self-check using their weirdo collection.

homophones, ie/ei spellings, more words, proofreading, recall

2C Select a student to write *does* and *doesn't* on the chalkboard. Ask students which word is a homograph (does). Have students write a definition for a homograph. Then they list examples. Next, organize students into pairs. Students take turns writing a homograph for their partner. The partner responds by using the homograph in sentences that illustrate its different pronunciations and meanings.

homographs, writing words, pronunciation, usage

Teaching Notes, page 328

Build Skillful Writers

Use these interrelated language learnings for all or selected students.

A double negative is a no-no. It is a sentence that contains two negatives describing words—contractions with *not*; *no, never, not, none, nothing, hardly, scarcely, barely*. Help students avoid double negatives by pointing them out in these sentences. Then have students rewrite the sentences.

> *He doesn't do nothing.*   *You never take me nowhere.*
> *I don't see no pencil.*   *I don't hardly know nobody here.*
> *We don't have none.*   *She can't find nothing.*

Teaching Notes, page 329

Build Assessment Readiness

Use these at-school and at-home exercises to prepare all students
for the Skill Test.

Skill to be tested:
suffixes and prefixes

at-school   Post Teaching Poster 2. Randomly write nonsense words on the board and have students sort them by their endings in preparation for the addition of suffixes:

> *geft, tresk, flear, croy* (**Rule 1**)   *hendry, plasty, lofy, vizy* (**Rule 4**)
> *nobe, grete, kone, chule* (**Rule 2**)   *hesh, jix, nuss, shoch* (**Rule 5**)
> *het, din, strug, prol* (**Rule 3**)

Then call out suffixes and prefixes to add to the nonwords to demonstrate that—
- The addition of a prefix never changes the spelling of the base word or root.
- The addition of a suffix may change the spelling of the base word or root.

Skill to be tested:
suffixes and prefixes

at-home   Send home a copy of TAKE-HOME TASK 34 BLACKLINE MASTER, page 301.

Teaching Notes, page 330

Build Proofreading Skills

Track students' ability to meet a minimum competency for spelling and
proofreading within selected samples of their everyday writing.

- Send home papers for proofreading and a copy of the IDEAS FOR PROOFREADING BLACKLINE MASTER, page 373.

Dear Parents,

Your child's spelling and vocabulary grows through the addition of prefixes and suffixes to base words. Your child is learning the "rules" for adding and subtracting these word parts to/from base words. In this activity, your child practices taking prefixes and suffixes away from a base word.

First, your child should read the clue word. Discuss the meaning of the word and have your child use it in a sentence. Ask your child to identify the base word. Then take the prefix and/or suffix away. If necessary, have your child check the spelling of the base word in a dictionary. Next, your child is ready to write this word in the puzzle.

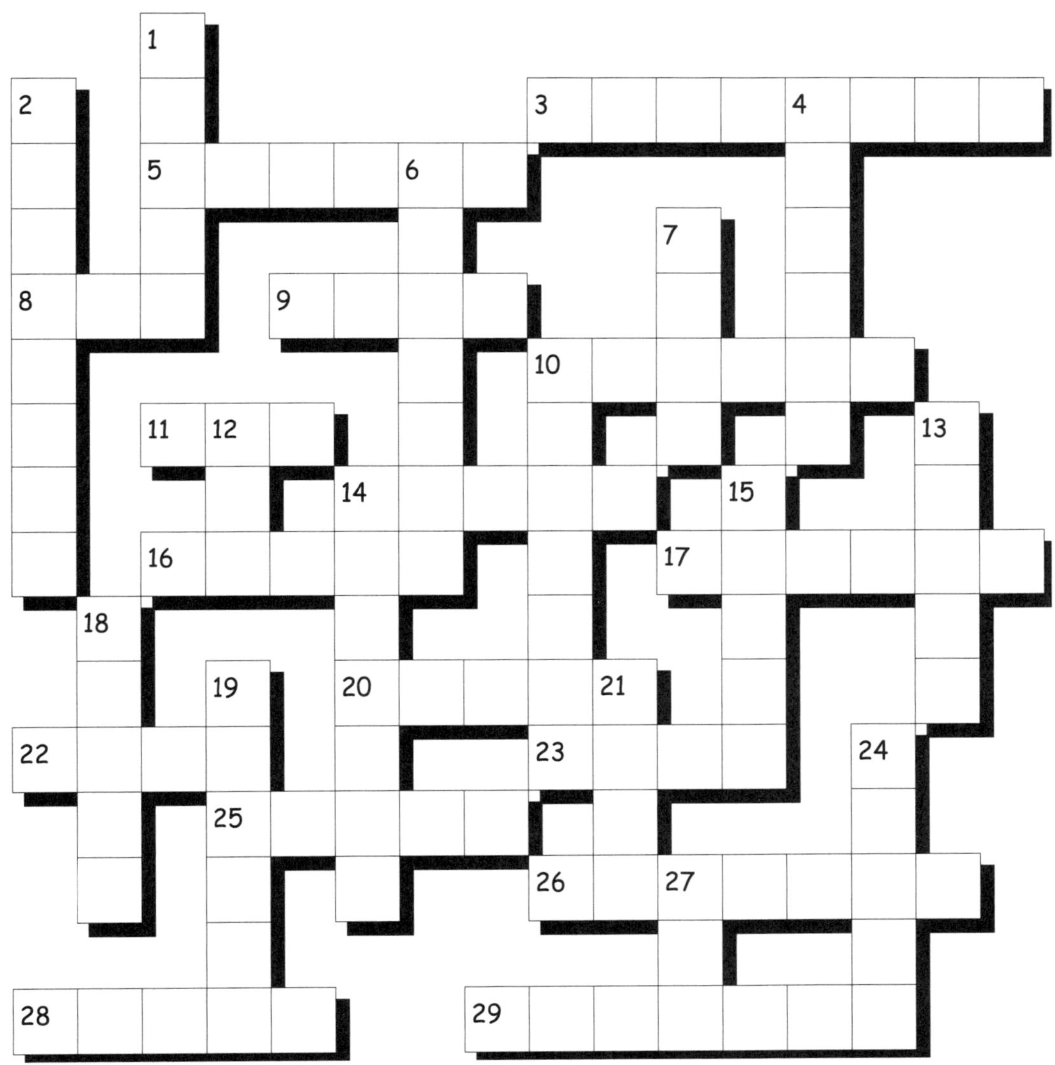

ACROSS

3. impossibility
5. impolitely
8. repaying
9. unstoppable
10. governments
11. funny
14. unthinkable
16. dishearten
17. unfriendly
20. unusually
22. carefully
23. lifeless
25. discolored
26. immeasurable
28. discovering
29. reproducing

DOWN

1. unhappily
2. incompletely
4. misinformation
6. thoughtfulness
7. removable
10. generalize
12. usefulness
13. finally
14. untroubled
15. rewritten
18. replaceable
19. unbecoming
21. reliving
24. enforcement
27. addition

- Spelling Words (words missed on tests) are recorded in the Spelling Notebook.
- Use Proof It, Practice Page 102, for proofreading/editing practice.

Teaching Notes, page 336

Assess Spelling Progress

Give this Cloze Story Word Test of Core Words within the frequencies 1–670 to all students. Words students miss are their Spelling Words.

 **THE CLOZE STORY WORD TEST**

Students do not prestudy the words. Provide students with a copy of REVIEW 34 BLACKLINE MASTER, page 305. Tell students that this story asks them to apply their math skills.

Read the entire story aloud, including the test words. Then read it again slowly as students write the missing words.

Words tested:
they('d) (19), there (37), their (42), every (151), thought (179), asked (188), enough (209), picture (232), body (285), really (313), become(ing) (336), simple (455), explain(ed) (513), correct (521), figure (551), you're (552), necessary (615), wrong (633), practice (634), various (661), brother (665), addition (666), doesn't (667), dead (668), weight(s) (669), thin (670)

The Fence Post Puzzle

"Mike, I (1) <u>really</u> need your help!" yelled Joe. Mike was lifting a pair of (2) <u>weights</u> when his (3) <u>brother</u> beckoned him. Mike had visions of his (4) <u>thin</u> arms (5) <u>becoming</u> huge, muscular ones with the (6) <u>various</u> exercises he was doing. Actually, his (7) <u>body</u> was (8) <u>dead</u> tired from his (9) <u>practice</u>. He'd worked hard (10) <u>enough</u>, so he walked into the next room where Joe was busy with paper and pencil. "What's up?" asked Mike. Joe (11) <u>explained</u> that Aunt Em (12) <u>asked</u> him to help her build a fence to enclose her pet ostriches. It would be 45 yards long and 45 yards wide. Fence posts would be set in concrete (13) <u>every</u> five yards. Joe asked Mike to (14) <u>figure</u> out how many posts (15) <u>they'd</u> need. "That (16) <u>doesn't</u> take much (17) <u>thought</u> Joey. (18) <u>There</u> will be ten posts on each of the four sides! It's (19) <u>simple</u>. It's just (20) <u>addition</u>." Joe smiled and went back to his work. He knew Mike's thinking was (21) <u>wrong</u>. So, what's the (22) <u>correct</u> answer? How many posts are (23) <u>necessary</u> for (24) <u>their</u> project? Draw a (25) <u>picture</u> to prove (26) <u>you're</u> right.

 **AFTER THE CLOZE STORY WORD TEST**

math reasoning, writing an explanation, art

1. Have students write and illustrate their answer to the story question. Then have students share their answer and picture. Conclude that Joe and Aunt Em need 36 posts. Have students reveal why Mike's thinking was incorrect.

recording words for personal study list

2. Have students record the words they missed on the test in their Spelling Notebook (see page 338) for at-school study, and on a copy of the WORDS TO LEARN BLACKLINE MASTER, page 375, for at-home study.

Assess Skill Application

Give this assessment of spelling and related skills to all students.
The REVIEW 34 BLACKLINE MASTER is on page 306.

Teaching Notes, page 339

 **THE SKILL TEST**

The addition of a prefix to a base word or root ___**never**___ changes the spelling of the base word or root.

    never   always   infrequently   often

The addition of a suffix to a base word or root may change the ___**spelling**___ of the base word or root.

    rule   spelling   prefix   plural

Write each word with a prefix. Use each prefix only once.

cover **discover**   possible **impossible**   happy **unhappy**

read **reread**   change **exchange**   spell **misspell**

Write each word twice. Use a different suffix each time.

happy	*(answers will vary)*	
general		
care		
wish		
thin		
fly		
begin		
strange		

Note the ability of each student to understand and apply the process of adding prefixes and suffixes to words.

Assess Proofreading Application

Give this assessment of spelling and related skills to all students.
The REVIEW 34 BLACKLINE MASTER is on page 306.

Teaching Notes, page 341

THE PROOFREADING TEST

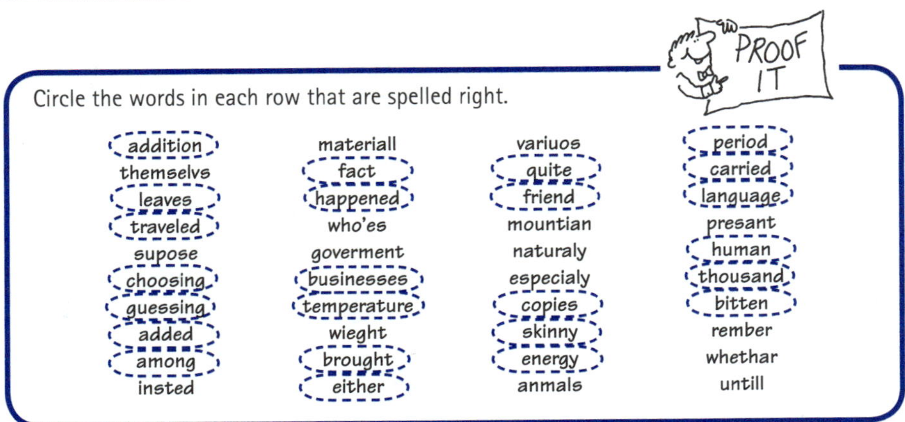

Circle the words in each row that are spelled right.

addition	materiall	variuos	period
themselvs	fact	quite	carried
leaves	happened	friend	language
traveled	who'es	mountian	presant
supose	goverment	naturaly	human
choosing	businesses	especialy	thousand
guessing	temperature	copies	bitten
added	wieght	skinny	rember
among	brought	energy	whethar
insted	either	anmals	untill

Note the ability of each student to identify misspelled words.

Teaching Notes, page 342

Words tested:
the (1), of (2), and (3), a (4), to (5), it (10), for (12), was (13), they('ve) (19), be (21), this (22), their (42), up (50), them (52), many (55), could (70), find (87), water (90), back (103), good (106), our (109), too (112), look (117), because (127), always (183), large (185), almost (216), however (250), young (256), morning (283), plants (300), stand (387), start(ing) (389), already (411), problem (422), heavy (426), dry (438), leaves (460), tall (490), correct (521), straight (524), seem(ed) (535), force (627), amount (657), garden (658), addition (666), doesn't (667), dead (668), weight (669), thin (670)

Extra words: died, health, sometimes, surprise

writing, vocabulary development

recording words for personal study list

Extend Spelling Assessment

Give this in-context assessment of Core Words within the frequencies 1–670 to students who need more practice or challenge.

THE SENTENCE DICTATION TEST

Students do not prestudy the words. Provide students with writing paper and pencil. Have students write the sentences as they are dictated.

1. It was a surprise this morning to find many of our young garden plants starting to look thin and almost dead.
2. The weight of their dry leaves seemed to be too heavy for them to stand up straight and tall.
3. The addition of a large amount of water could force a few of them back to good health.
4. However, this doesn't always correct the problem because sometimes they've already died.

AFTER THE SENTENCE DICTATION TEST

1. Have students write about how they might help a plant back to good health.

The word *leaves* in the sentence dictation is one that has more than one meaning. Have students identify the meanings. Then organize students into cooperative groups to recall words with multiple meanings. Time the session (about three minutes). Then have students from different groups pair and share their words.

2. Have students record the words they missed on the test in their Spelling Notebook (see page 345) for at-school study, and on a copy of the Words to Learn Blackline Master, page 375, for at-home study.

The words on a student's Words to Learn sheet and in the Spelling Notebook are a prescription for word study personalized to each student's spelling needs.

Word Test

The Fence Post Puzzle

"Mike, I (1) _______________ need your help!" yelled Joe. Mike was lifting a pair of

(2) _______________ when his (3) _______________ beckoned him. Mike had visions

of his (4) _______________ arms (5) _______________ huge, muscular ones with

the (6) _______________ exercises he was doing. Actually, his (7) _______________

was (8) _______________ tired from his (9) _______________. He'd worked hard

(10) _______________, so he walked into the next room where Joe was busy with

paper and pencil. "What's up?" asked Mike. Joe (11) _______________ that Aunt Em

(12) _______________ him to help her build a fence to enclose her pet ostriches. It

would be 45 yards long and 45 yards wide. Fence posts would be set in concrete

(13) _______________ five yards. Joe asked Mike to (14) _______________ out how

many posts (15) _______________ need. "That (16) _______________ take much

(17) _______________ Joey. (18) _______________ will be ten posts on each of the

four sides! It's (19) _______________. It's just (20) _______________." Joe smiled

and went back to his work. He knew Mike's thinking was (21) _______________. So,

what's the (22) _______________ answer? How many posts are (23) _______________

for (24) _______________ project? Draw a (25) _______________ to prove

(26) _______________ right.

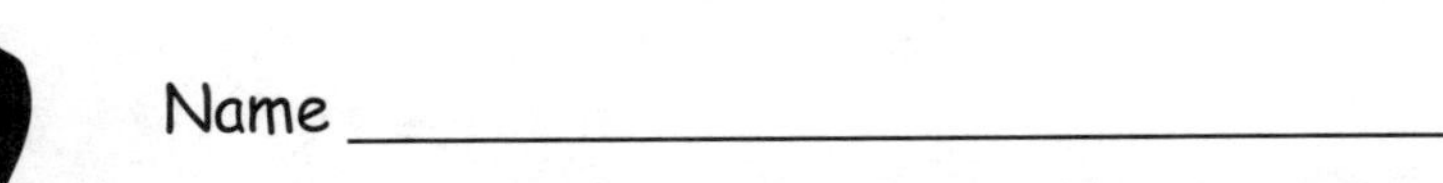

Skill Test

The addition of a prefix to a base word or root _________________ changes the spelling of the base word or root.

never   always   infrequently   often

The addition of a suffix to a base word or root may change the __________ of the base word or root.

rule   spelling   prefix   plural

Write each word with a prefix. Use each prefix only once.

cover _________________   possible _________________   happy _________________

read _________________   change _________________   spell _________________

Write each word twice. Use a different suffix each time.

happy   _________________________   _________________________

general   _________________________   _________________________

care   _________________________   _________________________

wish   _________________________   _________________________

thin   _________________________   _________________________

fly   _________________________   _________________________

begin   _________________________   _________________________

strange   _________________________   _________________________

Proofreading Test

Circle the words in each row that are spelled right.

addition	materiall	variuos	period
themselvs	fact	quite	carried
leaves	happened	friend	language
traveled	who'es	mountian	presant
supose	goverment	naturaly	human
choosing	businesses	especialy	thousand
guessing	temperature	copies	bitten
added	wieght	skinny	rember
among	brought	energy	whethar
insted	either	anmals	untill

Use Student Practice Pages 103–104 to follow up instruction for:
Activity 1B • Test Ready

Build Visual Skills

Do the Word Preview, a visual warm-up activity, with all students.
Use Core Words **stone** (671), **hit** (672), **wife** (673), **island** (674), **we'll** (675).

Teaching Notes, page 316

Build Spelling and Language Skills

Choose from among these quick tasks to customize instruction
for all or selected students.

Teaching Notes, page 319

That record was a hit.

Mr. stone and his wife live on Otter island. There house is just a stones throw away from the the lighthouse. We'll spend time their this summer. Diging for clams is all ways a hit with me, even if I don't get none.

(*Stone*, *Island*, *Their*, *stone's*, delete extra *the*, *there*, *Digging*, *always*, *any*)

stone, hit, race, rock, strike, dash, pebble, run, bang, sprint, boulder, smash

(e.g., words that are synonyms; does/doesn't contain silent letter(s); does/doesn't contain a consonant blend)

wife, half, scarf, ______
(words that end with *f* or *fe*)

Stone has various uses. For example, it is used in ______.

Names of islands

Teaching Notes, page 325

Build Basic Concepts

Choose from among these skill-building activities to customize instruction
for all or selected students.

concept one — Some words have silent letters.

phonics, more words, spelling word patterns, prefix/suffix practice

1A Select a student to write *stone* on the chalkboard. Ask students to identify the silent letter (e). The final silent *e* is the most common silent letter. In these words, the vowel-consonant-silent *e* spelling pattern signals a long vowel. Label columns *a*, *e*, *i*, *o*, and *u* on the chalkboard and have students briskly take turns placing final silent *e* words under each heading. Then use the word bank for students to add prefixes/suffixes to the words.

Have students write 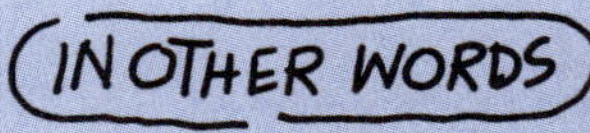 : A rolling stone gathers no moss.

Have students redefine in rhyme—*solitary rock … lone stone!*

silent consonants, spelling game, sorting words

1B Select a student to write *island* on the chalkboard. Ask students to identify the silent consonant. Play "silent consonant word charades." Assign words with silent consonants to small groups to act out their meaning to the class. Word choices may include *fasten, listen, soften, answer, sword, whistle, wrestle, ghost, knot, thumbtack, knee, knight, doubt,* and *half.* Write the words on the chalkboard as they are identified. Then have students sort the words on the chalkboard by silent letter(s).

silent consonants, plural practice, more words, sorting words

1C Write *half* on the chalkboard and ask students to identify the silent consonant (l). Then ask students to make *half* plural (halves). Ask students to identify more words that form their plural by this action (e.g., wife, life, loaf, wolf, calf). Conclude that some words that end in *f* or *fe* are made plural by changing the *f* or *fe* to *v* and adding *es*. Challenge students to identify the other five most common ways of making words plural (see Activity 1A, page 137). Then have students find and write examples of each. Time the session (about five minutes). Then have students make a cumulative list on the chalkboard sorted by the action taken to make the words plural.

Words with silent consonants are often the result of sounds once said, but because the words were difficult to pronounce, their pronunciations were altered—but not their spellings. Words that illustrate this include words spelled with *mb* (lamb), *kn* (know), and *wr* (write). Other words with silent consonants may be the result of their origin. A word that illustrates this is *debt*, from the Latin *debitum*—from which we get *debit*.

• Have students explain the difference between a credit card and a debit card.

Build Skillful Writers

Use these interrelated language learnings for all or selected students.

Teaching Notes, page 328

A skillful writer carefully selects words with exactly the desired meaning. Ask students to define *synonym*. Then suggest that words that are said to be synonyms often have slight differences in meaning or connotation. To illustrate, have students brainstorm synonyms for *stone* (e.g., rock, boulder, pebble, gravel) and *hit* (e.g., slam, punch, knock, strike, wallop, smack, belt, slug). Then assign different generic colors to small groups of students to brainstorm synonyms for color words (e.g., yellow: canary, butterscotch, mustard, lemon, saffron, jasmine, gold, banana). Follow up with students describing in writing another student's article of clothing. Have students creatively identify the color of the article.

Build Assessment Readiness

Use these at-school and at-home exercises to prepare all students for the Skill Test.

Teaching Notes, page 329

at-school   Write often-confused words on the chalkboard, or have students do so, for discussion. Choices may include: *well/we'll, you're/your, there's/theirs, choose/chose, loose/lose, picture/pitcher, are/our, were/where, were/we're, unit/unite, weather/whether, finely/finally, then/than, it's/its, let's/lets, farther/further, dinner/diner, who's/whose.* Divide students into two teams. Select a word on the chalkboard for the first player from one team to use in one sentence. If correctly used, the team earns one point. Alternate players from teams. The winner is the first team to reach a predetermined score.

Skill to be tested: often-confused words

at-home   Send home a copy of Take-Home Task 35 Blackline Master, page 310.

Skill to be tested: often-confused words

Build Proofreading Skills

Track students' ability to meet a minimum competency for spelling and proofreading within selected samples of their everyday writing.

Teaching Notes, page 330

- Send home papers for proofreading and a copy of the Ideas for Proofreading Blackline Master, page 373.

Name ____

Dear Parents,

Your child has learned to spell and understand the use of many words. Some require ongoing attention, such as the often-confused words in this activity. Guide your child through the lesson, letting your child do as much as possible without your help. Then discuss each of the answers together.

Write the missing words.

1. its or it's?

   _____________ time for the cat's dinner. It needs to be fed _____________ dinner.

2. theirs or there's?

   _____________ the book I'd like to read. That one's _____________ .

3. choose or chose?

   I'll _____________ first. You _____________ first at Don's house.

4. your or you're?

   _____________ almost ready. Get _____________ pencils and we'll begin.

5. their, there or they're?

   _____________ over _____________ waiting in line with _____________ tickets.

6. lets or let's?

   _____________ go to Aunt B's. She _____________ us watch TV until we're asleep.

7. whose or who's?

   _____________ lunch bag is this? _____________ without today's lunch?

8. hears or here's?

   Who _____________ that noise? _____________ the cause! What'll we do?

9. wear or where?

   They'll _____________ the blue ones. _____________ are the red ones?

10. we're or were?

    _____________ riding the boys' bikes. The boys _____________ playing inside.

11. lose or loose?

    That button is _____________ . You'll soon _____________ it.

Other often-confused words include these: are/our, dinner/diner, farther/further, finely/finally, picture/pitcher, then/than, unit/unite, weather/whether, well/we'll, were/where. Work with your child to write sentence pairs that use these words.

Assess Words and Skills

- Spelling Words (words missed on tests) are recorded in the Spelling Notebook.
- Use Proof It, Practice Page 105, for proofreading/editing practice.

Assess Spelling Progress

Teaching Notes, page 336

Give this Cloze Story Word Test of Core Words within the frequencies 1–675 to all students. Words students miss are their Spelling Words.

THE CLOZE STORY WORD TEST

Students do not prestudy the words. Provide students with a copy of REVIEW 35 BLACKLINE MASTER, page 314. Tell students that this story's title is an old saying, "on the money." There are many old sayings about money—this story uses two more of these sayings. Tell students to think about the meaning of these phrases.

Read the entire story aloud, including the test words. Then read it again slowly as students write the missing words.

On the Money

(1) <u>There's</u> an old saying, "Money (2) <u>doesn't</u> grow on trees." This is (3) <u>generally</u> true, (4) <u>except</u> tobacco and tea (5) <u>leaves</u> and cacao beans have been used for money in the past. Money can be (6) <u>various</u> things. The (7) <u>heaviest</u> money ever used was (8) <u>stones</u> and the lightest was feathers traded by people on the (9) <u>island</u> of Santa Cruz. Actually, anything can become money in a barter (10) <u>system</u>. Bartering is, for example, if we give some (11) <u>amount</u> of our cow's (12) <u>milk</u> to someone (13) <u>who's</u> in need of it. Then he or she gives us (14) <u>something</u> we need in return. (15) <u>We'll</u> be happy and the other person will be, too. In this case, the bartering (16) <u>business</u> is a big (17) <u>hit</u> with both of us!

Yet, (18) <u>you're</u> (19) <u>probably</u> aware that most money is paper or coins. (20) <u>It's</u> called currency. "Money talks" in many (21) <u>languages</u> around the world. If a husband and (22) <u>wife</u> (23) <u>travel</u> to Germany, (24) <u>their</u> currency is no longer the U.S. dollar. (25) <u>They're</u> using the euro. In Japan, the currency is called a yen. What is the currency in (26) <u>countries</u> such as India, France, Israel, and England?

Words tested:
there('s) (37), their (42), who('s) (77), something (178), country(ies) (228), it's (253), probably (383), heavy(iest) (426), system (434), leaves (460), language(s) (499), travel (516), except (550), you're (552), milk (579), business (595), general(ly) (639), amount (657), various (661), doesn't (667), stone(s) (671), hit (672), wife (673), island (674), we'll (675), *they're (1010)

*The testing of they're (1010) is included to help students differentiate among the there/their/they're homophones.

AFTER THE CLOZE STORY WORD TEST

1. Have students research and write their answer to the story question. Then have students share their answer.

research, writing

2. Have students record the words they missed on the test in their Spelling Notebook (see page 338) for at-school study, and on a copy of the WORDS TO LEARN BLACKLINE MASTER, page 375, for at-home study.

recording words for personal study list

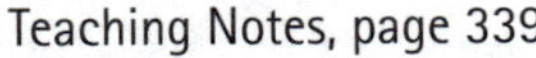

Teaching Notes, page 339

Assess Skill Application

Give this assessment of spelling and related skills to all students.
The REVIEW 35 BLACKLINE MASTER is on page 315.

THE SKILL TEST

Skill tested:
often-confused words

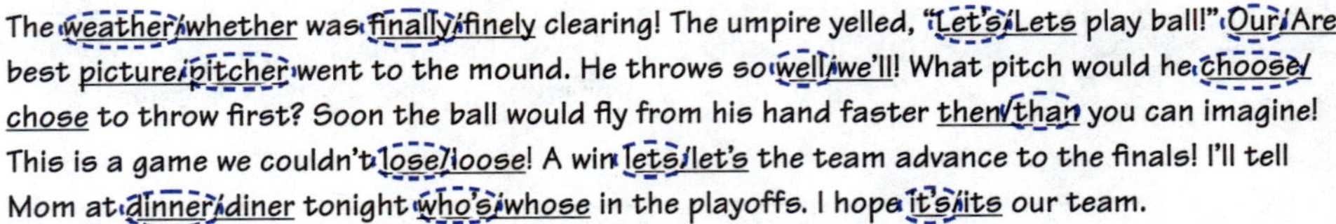

Note the ability of each student to identify the meaning/use of often-confused words.

Teaching Notes, page 341

Assess Proofreading Application

Give this assessment of spelling and related skills to all students.
The REVIEW 35 BLACKLINE MASTER is on page 315.

THE PROOFREADING TEST

weight	wieght	weight
periode	period	period
thousand	thousand	thousand
guess	geuss	guess
generaly	generally	generally
decided	desided	decided
forceing	forcing	forcing
differense	difference	difference
possibly	possibley	possibly
able	abel	able
exception	excepsion	exception
machinery	machinary	machinery
measurable	measurible	measurable
stranger	strainger	stranger
goverment	government	government
allready	already	already
language	langauge	language
throughout	threwout	throughout

Note the ability of each student to proofread for spelling errors.

Extend Spelling Assessment

Give this in-context assessment of Core Words within the frequencies 1–675 to students who need more practice or challenge.

Teaching Notes, page 342

Words tested:

the (1), of (2), and (3), a (4), to (5), in (6), that (9), it (10), was (13), on (14), they (19), be (21), this (22), one (28), all (33), when (35), we('ve) (36), there (37), an (39), their (42), said (43), them (52), then (53), time (69), only (85), use(ing) (88), because (127), such (133), home (157), left (169), house (189), important (195), once (206), told (255), learned (326), built (360), strong (381), stand(ing) (387), heavy (426), beautiful (429), everyone (430), wild (463), build(ing) (487), rock (489), object(ed) (606), (un)necessary (615), subject (621), wasn't (623), material(s) (641), region (649), stone (671), hit (672), wife (673), island (674), we'll (675)

Extra words: husband, lesson, storm

THE SENTENCE DICTATION TEST

Students do not prestudy the words. Provide students with writing paper and pencil. Have students write the sentences as they are dictated.

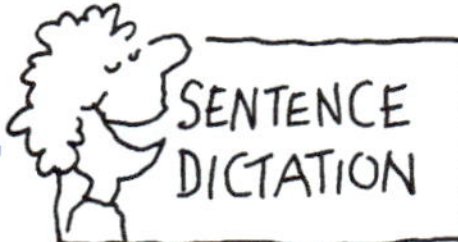

1. Once there was a husband and wife whose beautiful island home was one they built of heavy stone.

2. Everyone objected because they said it was unnecessary to use such strong building materials.

3. Then when the wild storm hit in the region, their house was the only one left standing.

4. "We've learned an important lesson on the subject of building and we'll be using rock this time," they all said.

AFTER THE SENTENCE DICTATION TEST

1. Have students recall an old fairy tale in which three homes were built of materials of differing strengths ("The Three Little Pigs"). Have students ask a librarian for one of the several Three Little Pigs parodies, such as Jon Scieszka's *The True Story of the Three Little Pigs* (as told by Mr. Wolf). This tale provides insights only older readers can appreciate! Then challenge students to rewrite a classic children's tale from a new point of view. For this project, have students work in pairs, proofread and illustrate their stories, and then present them orally to the class.

writing, relating to literature

2. Have students record the words they missed on the test in their Spelling Notebook (see page 345) for at-school study, and on a copy of the WORDS TO LEARN BLACKLINE MASTER, page 375, for at-home study.

recording words for personal study list

For summer vacation practice, consider the Sourcebook student Practice Books if students have not used them throughout the year to reinforce lessons. Every major Level 5 skill is reinforced through the activities in the Practice Books. And each Practice Book contains a list of the Core Words with frequencies 1–675 for summer review.

Name ___________________________

On the Money

(1) _____________ an old saying, "Money (2) _____________ grow on trees."

This is (3) _____________ true, (4) _____________ tobacco and tea

(5) _____________ and cacao beans have been used for money in the past.

Money can be (6) _____________ things. The (7) _____________ money ever

used was (8) _____________ and the lightest was feathers traded by people on the

(9) _____________ of Santa Cruz. Actually, anything can become money in a barter

(10) _____________. Bartering is, for example, if we give some (11) _____________

of our cow's (12) _____________ to someone (13) _____________ in need of it. Then

he or she gives us (14) _____________ we need in return. (15) _____________ be

happy and the other person will be, too. In this case, the bartering (16) _____________

is a big (17) _____________ with both of us!

Yet, (18) _____________ (19) _____________ aware that most money is paper or

coins. (20) _____________ called currency. "Money talks" in many (21) _____________

around the world. If a husband and (22) _____________ (23) _____________ to

Germany, (24) _____________ currency is no longer the U.S. dollar. (25) _____________

using the euro. In Japan, the currency is called a yen. What is the currency in

(26) _____________ such as India, France, Israel, and England?

Skill Test

Circle the right word.

The <u>weather/whether</u> was <u>finally/finely</u> clearing! The umpire yelled, "<u>Let's/Lets</u> play ball!" <u>Our/Are</u> best <u>picture/pitcher</u> went to the mound. He throws so <u>well/we'll</u>! What pitch would he <u>choose/chose</u> to throw first? Soon the ball would fly from his hand faster <u>then/than</u> you can imagine! This is a game we couldn't <u>lose/loose</u>! A win <u>lets/let's</u> the team advance tc the finals! I'll tell Mom at <u>dinner/diner</u> tonight <u>who's/whose</u> in the playoffs. I hope <u>it's/its</u> our team.

Proofreading Test

Circle the word in each pair that is spelled wrong. Then write the word correctly.

weight	wieght	__________________
periode	period	__________________
thousand	thousund	__________________
guess	geuss	__________________
generaly	generally	__________________
decided	desided	__________________
forceing	forcing	__________________
differense	difference	__________________
possibly	possibley	__________________
able	abel	__________________
exception	excepsion	__________________
machinery	machinary	__________________
measurable	measurible	__________________
stranger	strainger	__________________
goverment	government	__________________
allready	already	__________________
language	langauge	__________________
throughout	threwout	__________________

Word Preview

The Word Preview is your source for developing a strategy to see each sequential letter in a word. Research indicates that it is the single, most effective procedure toward this end. It is the first activity in each unit in the Build Visual Skills section. Look for this logo.

In a customary spelling program, often a pretest opens a spelling unit. For this reason, the Word Preview and a pretest may be perceived as the same. They are not. The research indicates that a pretest was never meant to be a test. The researchers did not call it a test, but labeled it a visual procedure. Yet, over the years the procedure has been modified from its original intent.

In most customary programs, a pretest introduces the Spelling Words for the unit. It tests students to identify the words a student already knows so that the student can focus on learning words that were missed. The words on the pretest are sent home for study in preparation for the final test, the Friday Test.

In this program, the original intent of the research-based procedure is reclaimed in the activity called the Word Preview. The Word Preview does not introduce Spelling Words for the unit. It is not a test. The words on the Word Preview are not sent home for study. Instead, the Word Preview is a visual skill-building activity, a prerequisite for good spelling and proofreading. Research indicates that the ability to picture a word and its sequential letters is a skill of able spellers. Further, they have the ability to focus on each letter of a word during the proofreading process, rather than looking at words as they do for reading. The Word Preview provides direct instruction for the development of these skills.

Students who have learned to apply the skills the Word Preview teaches eliminate the careless errors among known words in their everyday writing. Further, they perform with confidence on normed spelling achievement tests, all of which require editing skills.

Therefore, the development of these spelling and proofreading strategies is so essential that the Word Preview is the first activity to open each unit. It delivers a positive, visual warm-up activity—a brisk exercise that becomes a routine, teacher-directed regimen for you and your students as each unit commences. A unit can begin on any day of the week. So, the Word Preview is not limited to Mondays.

Indeed, if this procedure is perceived as a spelling test for the unit's Spelling Words, it yields invalid assessment information that results in false assumptions regarding students' performance. Every teacher's dilemma is the classroom of students who can spell on a customary program's pre/post tests, but forget the spellings after the tests! Valid tests must displace false testing—multiple options for authentic testing in the Sourcebook Series provide ongoing assessment of every student's ability to spell words and to apply spelling skills, see page 350.

The words for this procedure are listed in the Word Preview section of each unit just below the Build Visual Skills heading. These words are called Core Words. Core Words are high-frequency words assigned to each grade level for the purpose of teaching skills. In the Word Preview, the Core Words are used to teach visual skills. There are five Core Words for each Word Preview. They are printed in boldface type accompanied by a number that indicates each word's frequency-of-use in writing.

For the Word Preview, each student needs a pencil and paper. You can use regular writing paper folded lengthwise by the students to produce two columns, a write and a rewrite column. Instead of writing paper, you may prefer to use the WORD PREVIEW BLACKLINE MASTER, page 376. There are six spaces for words on this master, allowing space for a review word of your choice, if you elect to give one.

Students do not prestudy the Core Words for the Word Preview. These are known words that students can read easily and may already know how to spell. In the Word Preview, students practice the ability to call up a familiar word from their long-term memory bank and visualize its letters, they learn to proofread a word letter by letter, and they practice writing a word accurately from a reference. It is not a test of short-term memory of words recently studied.

The research-based steps for administering the Word Preview need to be followed carefully to get the best results in the least amount of time. Tell students exactly what you expect.

Teacher	Students
1. Says the word. Says the word in a sentence. Says the word again.	1. Look at and listen to the teacher.
2. Asks students to write the word.	2. Print the word in the write (left-hand) column of their paper.

After students have written the words, guide them as they check their own paper.

Teacher	Students
3. Spells the word aloud.	3. Proofread the word by touching each letter with the point of their pencil as the letter name is said. Circle errors.
4. Prints the word on the chalkboard, saying the name of each letter as it is printed.	4. Look at the chalkboard and listen to the teacher.
5. Observes students.	5. Rewrite the word in the rewrite (right-hand) column of their paper.

Remind students as they check their words for errors to circle only the part of the word they missed. They should not circle the whole word. This helps students see that only part of the word is wrong.

When do students rewrite the words during the self-correction?

Be certain that students do not write the word in the rewrite column during step 4 while you write the word on the chalkboard and say the name of each letter. This is important. The integrity of the procedure is diminished if students hear your auditory cue as they write the word. Instead, students must watch you write the word. Then they write the word in the rewrite column without the advantage of hearing you say the name of each letter.

Is it necessary to recheck and grade the Word Preview?

After the Word Preview, you or an assistant should examine, but not grade, each student's rewrite column for spelling accuracy. Ask students to place their Word Preview on the side of their desk as they do another task. Then, as soon as is convenient, look at each student's work.

What is the best method to recheck the Word Preview?

Have students fold their first attempt to write the words (the write column) to the back so that it cannot be seen. Do not look at the column of words folded back. Checking these words may encourage some students to erase and fix their first attempt to write the words, making it appear that they spelled them correctly on their first try. If this activity surfaces, ignore it. Boldly praise students for accurate spellings in the rewrite column. With your attention solely focused on this column, it is likely that students will abandon their unproductive "fixing" activity.

If a word is misspelled in the rewrite column, make a small dot next to this word to indicate the mistake. Errors should be corrected by the students, not you. Ask these students to match the word they wrote with your model—letter by letter. This can be done independently or with a partner.

How long does it take to give and correct a Word Preview?

If students are familiar with the precise expectations for the procedure, the Word Preview should take less than five minutes. Maintain a fast but comfortable pace. Students must learn to listen and write the words quickly and confidently. To encourage this, do not repeat words.

What is suggested for students who are absent for the Word Preview?

For students who are absent for the Word Preview, a make-up Word Preview can be given by you or an assistant, such as a teacher's aide, student, or parent volunteer. In lieu of giving a make-up Word Preview, the student who missed the Word Preview could preview the Core Words by using the Word Study Strategy, page 357, and the WORD STUDY BLACKLINE MASTER, page 377.

What is suggested for students who need more visual skill building than the Word Preview provides?

The Word Preview is considered the most effective way to develop visual skills for spelling and proofreading, yet there are other procedures that complement this routine. The Word Study Strategy, page 357, also practices the strategy of visualizing, writing, and proofreading words. In Build Basic Concepts, visual skill-building activities are clearly labeled in the margin. Select these activities for students who need additional visual development.

What is suggested for students who cannot copy a word from the chalkboard to their paper?

Some students may not have developed the ability to copy a word accurately from the chalkboard. This will be learned over time, but to hasten the process, see Students with Spelling Challenges, page 353, for suggestions.

What is suggested for students who cannot read the Core Words to be previewed?

Students with Spelling Challenges also provides readiness ideas for students who are unable to read the Core Words. Included among these suggestions is a modified Word Preview that these students can take with the other students.

Usually, students can meet the expectations for the Word Preview without a challenge. In fact, most students will tell you they can spell the words on the Word Preview with ease. This is true. Remember, the Word Preview provides students with practice visualizing known words and checks their ability to copy and proofread them. It is not a procedure designed to challenge students' spelling ability, so do not add words with the intention of increasing rigor. This would only diminish the effectiveness of this procedure.

If students are able to spell, copy, and proofread each of the Core Words on the Word Preview, this is not confirmation that they have mastered them. The words on the Word Preview are not a student's spelling list. The Word Preview does not test spelling proficiency. Spelling competency is evaluated in students' writing as well as in the testing options of each unit. These assessment options give rise to each student's spelling list, pages 336 and 342.

If the integrity of the Word Preview is maintained, the Core Words used in the procedure function to develop visual skills. After the procedure, the papers need not be saved, nor the activity sent home—remember, the words on the Word Preview are not the unit's Spelling Words. As you proceed into the unit, more skills surface from the unit's Core Words to make *every child a speller*.

What if students can spell all the words on the Word Preview?

After the Word Preview, what is recommended?

Exercise Express

The Exercise Express is your source for six optional, quick practice ideas. It is the second activity in each unit in Build Spelling and Language Skills. Look for this logo.

What is the Exercise Express?

These brisk exercises augment practice at school or at home. The activities teach students processes and strategies for examining and thinking about words and their application in writing. Each unit's Core Words are featured in the activities, but the focus of the learning is on skill development, not on mastering the five Core Words.

What is the purpose of the Exercise Express?

Use Exercise Express activities anytime throughout the unit. In fact, exercises initially bypassed can be revisited as students work in subsequent units.

When should the activities be used?

The activities can be used in several ways to augment student practice. They vary in difficulty and skill focus to meet the needs of diverse learners. This means that practice can be differentiated among students. One or more of the exercises can be used with some or all students.

How should the Exercise Express be used?

Write the activity on the chalkboard as it appears in the unit or use one of the generic blackline masters available for each of the six Exercise Express activities, pages 378–383. These masters can be made specifically for use with the activities in each unit.

The instructional format for the activities is yours to decide. Once students understand the expectations of the activities, use any exercise as homework to enhance parent-child partnerships. The at-school practice options include:

- teacher-directed lesson—students brainstorm possible solutions orally as the teacher records the results on the chalkboard.

- cooperative group lesson—students collaborate in small work groups to produce one written solution. Groups' results can be shared with the class.

- paired student lesson—students work with an assigned partner, each pair producing a written solution. Pairs' results can be shared with the class.

- independent student practice—students work independently to complete the lesson. The results of selected students' work can be shared with the class.

Note that any of these at-school options can be followed up with a second exposure to the same activity for homework. Students who need more reinforcement are good candidates for revisiting an exercise as homework.

How can the Exercise Express activities be initiated with students?

For best results, model each activity prior to using any of the activity formats. Model a deliberate thinking process for completing the activity, as well as an appropriate written response (see modeling examples that follow for specific Exercise Express activities). The modeling can continue into subsequent units, but the goal is for students to do the activity without direction.

Should the exercises be discussed, checked, and graded?

Most of the exercises result in a variety of appropriate responses. For this reason, discussion and self-checking is desirable, because feedback on completed work is helpful to the learning process as students relate their response(s) to those of others.

You may ask students to write their response(s) on the chalkboard to begin the dialogue. Then, during the discussion, an informal assessment of students' performance can be made. Occasionally, student work may be collected for a more thorough evaluation and, if necessary, graded.

Can the Exercise Express be expanded?

Expand the Exercise Express activities by creating more of any of the six exercises. Develop the additional activities for students either by writing them on the chalkboard or by using the appropriate blackline master and providing students with a copy for at-school or at-home completion.

To challenge the most capable students, have them create Exercise Express lessons for their classmates to complete.

What is the purpose of each Exercise Express activity and how should each one be introduced?

Following is an explanation and a purpose statement for each of the six Exercise Express activities with suggestions for modeling each activity prior to students being sufficiently competent to complete it without direction. This information should help you make *every child a speller*.

STRETCH IT

What is the purpose of Stretch It?

The foremost goal of Stretch It is to increase students' level of writing sophistication by providing instruction and practice on sentence expansion. Students learn how to take a "bare bones" sentence and embellish it to make it more informative and interesting. Further, students practice writing, spelling, and proofreading.

To ensure student success, initially model the activity. Write the sentence on the chalkboard as it appears on the page. Then proceed by posing questions, answering them, and expanding the sentence. For example, the Unit 1 Stretch It activity might proceed like this:

> It left a mark on his jacket.
> (**What** is it?)
> The name tag left a mark on his jacket.
> (**What** name tag?)
> The name tag he wore for our field trip left a mark on his jacket.
> (**Which** field trip?)
> The name tag he wore for our field trip to the dairy left a mark on his jacket.
> (**Who**?)
> The name tag our teacher wore for our field trip to the dairy left a mark on his jacket.
> (**When**?)
> The name tag our teacher wore for our field trip to the dairy on Monday left a mark on his jacket.

Stretching could expand to include descriptive information about the mark, the field trip, or the jacket.

Then students can write and illustrate the "stretched" sentence on story paper or on the STRETCH IT BLACKLINE MASTER, page 378.

In subsequent activities, provide assistance as needed until students can complete the activity without direction.

A classroom "Stretch It" chart could guide students during this activity (optional teacher-made chart). Guide words could include: *Who, What, Where, When, Why, How, Size,* and *Color.*

 **FIX IT**

Fix It provides instruction and practice on editing and proofreading. This benefits students' everyday writing. It also prepares students for performance on standardized and/or state spelling tests, which assess editing and proofreading skills. As students have more experience with these tasks, you can expect better performance on the tests.

The errors for revision on Fix It include spelling, usage, capitalization, punctuation, and grammar.

Editing and proofreading success requires visual skills—the ability to see exactly what is written. This is taught and practiced through the Word Preview. Then it is applied in a structured exercise, Fix It. To help students gain confidence with the exercise, begin by modeling the activity. For example, the Unit 1 Fix It activity might proceed like this:

Write the sentences on the chalkboard as they appear on the page: *Window comes from one word that means "wind" and an other that means "eye." We by windows to keep an eye on the wind. We also use them too keep heat in when its cold outside.* Read the sentences aloud. Tell students that these sentences have mistakes. At first, tell students how many mistakes.

How do I model Stretch It?

What is the purpose of Fix It?

How do I model Fix It?

Then demonstrate the skills students have learned and practiced through the Word Preview, touching each letter and spelling every word. If students are not sure of the spelling of a word, ask students to suggest ways to check the spelling (e.g., Spell Check, dictionary, or other classroom references). Demonstrate checking for capitals and punctuation. As errors are identified, circle them. Once the mistakes have been found and circled, fix the errors, or select students to do so.

Then students can write and illustrate the "fixed" sentences on paper or on the FIX IT BLACKLINE MASTER, page 379.

In subsequent activities, provide assistance as needed until students can complete the activity without direction.

A classroom "Fix It" chart could guide students during this activity (optional teacher-made chart). The chart could remind students to check every letter of every word, homophones, capitals, and punctuation.

 **SORT IT**

What is the purpose of Sort It?

Sort It helps students compare and contrast words—to think about their commonalities and differences. This powerful means of exploring words develops skills, including vocabulary, visual, phonemic awareness, structural analysis, and phonetic analysis.

What are a closed sort and an open sort?

The sorting exercises can use a closed or open format. In closed sorts, students are told the categories into which the words are sorted. In open sorts, students examine the words and determine and label their own categories. Suggested categories are noted in the units for each Sort It activity.

At first, use the closed format for the word sorts. In time, use the more difficult open sorts.

How do I model Sort It?

To introduce students to sorting, sort familiar items into two categories, such as sorting students by boys/girls, books by true/make-believe, color chips by dark/light, boxes by large/small. Once students are comfortable with these sorting activities, the Unit 1 Sort It activity might proceed like this:

Write the words for sorting on the chalkboard: *heat, meeting, anything, study, reading, bumblebee, teacher, sheet, suddenly, daydream, energy, weekend, weaver, carefully.* Have students read the words. Then tell students that you are going to sort these words into three groups, or categories. "Let's see," you say. "I see that these words all have a *long e* sound; however, the *long e* is spelled in different ways. It is spelled with *ea* in *heat, reading, teacher, daydream,* and *weaver.* They will go in one group. I see four words in which *long e* is is spelled *ee—meeting, bumblebee, sheet,* and *weekend.* They will go in another group. And I see five words with a *y* spelling the *long e* sound—*anything, study, suddenly, energy,* and *carefully.*" Next sort the appropriate words under headings for each spelling pattern and point out the commonality of the words in each group. Tell students that this is one way the words could be sorted.

Then demonstrate sorting these words by number of syllables.

After a modeled activity, students can write the sorted words on paper or on the SORT IT BLACKLINE MASTER, page 380.

In subsequent activities, provide assistance as needed until students can complete the activity without direction.

A classroom "Sort It" chart could guide students during this activity (optional teacher-made chart). After the first lesson, the chart could list *words with same spelling patterns, number of syllables*. Then the chart could grow as new ways to sort words are discovered in subsequent Sort It lessons.

ADD IT

Add It is an analytical activity to teach students to examine a bank of words to discover a commonality and/or pattern among them. Then students add words to the word bank that reflect the criterion. Add It is one more way for students to work with and think about words.

What is the purpose of Add It?

Begin by modeling the Add It activity. For example, the Unit 1 Add It activity might proceed like this:

How do I model Add It?

Write *care, mark,* and *carve* on the chalkboard. Say, "These words illustrate a sequence." Read the words. Say, "One thing I notice is that these words have the letters *ar* that spell /ar/. Another thing I notice is that each word has one more letter than the word before. So I could add more words that have the letters *ar* that spell /ar/ that increase by one letter. I could add *alarms*, and then *bargain*. What could I add next?" Then see if students can identify an eight-letter word in which *ar* spells /ar/ (e.g., bookmark, carnival, enlarged, particled). Write the words as students suggest them.

Then students can write the Add It bank of words on paper or on the ADD IT BLACKLINE MASTER, page 381.

In subsequent activities, provide assistance as needed until students can complete the activity without direction.

A classroom "Add It" chart could guide students during this activity (optional teacher-made chart). After the first lesson, the chart could list *same spelling pattern*. Then the chart could grow as new commonalities are discovered in subsequent Add It lessons.

FINISH IT

Finish It activities provide practice in thinking, writing, spelling, and proofreading. The activity poses an intriguing, yet incomplete, thought for students to finish. It is an invitation for students to use their imagination to create a conclusion to an open-ended idea. Then they write about it and proofread their work. Sentence and/or story starters are efficient ways to encourage these skills, particularly among reluctant writers.

What is the purpose of Finish It?

Model the Finish It activity to ensure that students are successful. For example, the Unit 1 Finish It activity might proceed like this:

How do I model Finish It?

Begin by writing the story starter on the chalkboard: *I wanted to buy the one in the window, but __________.* Then demonstrate one way the sentence could be finished. For example, say, "When I was shopping for a new winter coat, I saw a red coat in a store window. I wanted it, but I discovered it cost more than I could spend. So, I bought a less expensive one. So, I could finish the sentence with, 'I didn't.'" Write this addition.

"Then I could say, 'I chose another coat that was not as expensive as the red one.'" Write this addition. "Next, I could say, 'I'm happy that I have a new coat that didn't cost me a lot of money.'" Write this addition. Then read the story.

Next, ask students if they can think of another way this story could be finished. Then repeat the activity with students' input.

Students can write the result on paper or on the FINISH IT BLACKLINE MASTER, page 382.

In subsequent activities, provide assistance as needed until students can complete the activity without direction.

A classroom "Finish It" chart could guide students during this activity (optional teacher-made chart). Guide words could include: *Who, What, Where, When, Why, How, Size,* and *Color*. Further, you may want to compile students' finished sentences (or stories) into a class book, perhaps using format 4, page 394.

FIND IT

What is the purpose of Find It?

Find It expands students' word experiences. The activity calls for word observation with a stated criterion, finding and writing more words, and proofreading words.

How do I model Find It?

Begin by modeling the Find It activity. For example, the Unit 1 Find It activity might proceed like this:

Write the word-find criterion on the chalkboard for students: *Words that illustrate types of music.* Then say, "I need to find and write words that name types of music, such as *rock*." Ask students to suggest words. Write the words on the chalkboard (e.g., classical, jazz, pop). Next, demonstrate proofreading the words.

Then students can write the words on paper or they can write them on the FIND IT BLACKLINE MASTER, page 383. On occasion, this activity is appropriate to play as a timed exercise, either independently or in small groups. Then a cumulative list of words can be made on the chalkboard.

In subsequent activities, provide assistance as needed until students can complete the activity without direction.

Seeds for Sowing Skills

Seeds for Sowing Skills is your source for activities that ensure a systematic presentation of spelling skills and concepts. It is in Build Basic Concepts in each unit. Look for this logo.

What is Seeds for Sowing Skills?

For most learners, spelling well doesn't just happen. Instead, it is the result of learning spelling skills and concepts, as well as systematic word study on words not yet mastered. Seeds for Sowing Skills addresses the former—teaching skills and concepts; the assessment options in Assess Words and Skills target the latter.

What is the purpose of Seeds for Sowing Skills?

Seeds for Sowing Skills empowers you to become the Johnny Appleseed for spelling literacy, sowing seeds—the skills and concepts—for your students. As you sow these seeds, you initiate the educational process to grow young, developing writers into able spellers in their writing.

The purpose of the activities is to teach skills and concepts, enabling students to build spelling and related language understandings. These skills are developed through the Core Words. Core Words are high-frequency words assigned to each grade level. They are used to teach skills. Mastering the spelling of the Core Words is not the purpose of these activities. That is the purpose of Assess Words and Skills in each unit.

Do the activities teach the Core Words for the unit?

Each concept is numbered and clearly stated in a band across the page. Under each concept, a menu of skill-building activities supports the growth of the concept. Each activity is labeled with the concept number and a sequential letter of the alphabet. The targeted skills for each activity are listed in the sidenotes.

How are the concepts and skills labeled?

Activities in Seeds for Sowing Skills follow the Word Preview. Note that the Exercise Express activities can be used anytime during the unit. So, after giving the Word Preview and perhaps assigning an Exercise Express activity, attention can be turned to Seeds for Sowing Skills.

When should the activities in Seeds for Sowing Skills be used?

First, note the concepts for the unit. Then survey the menu of activities for each concept and the targeted skills listed in the sidenotes. From this, formulate your own instructional plan. You're in charge!

How are activities chosen?

Begin by selecting the activities. Remember, the activities are your source for teaching skills and concepts—they are not your source for teaching the Core Words for the unit.

The activities selected should support the skill and concept needs of your students. They should provide balance to the total language curriculum, complementing the reading and language programs currently in place. Further, the selections should be made to reflect the instructional guidelines of the school, district, state, or province.

Some teachers may wish to make activity selections as a team with their grade-level colleagues. This would result in greater program unity. Mentor teachers may wish to assist new teachers with their selections.

How many activities should be selected?

There are far too many activities to do them all. You decide the activities you want to do based on the needs of your students and your time frame. At first, you may wish to do just two or three activities in the Seeds for Sowing Skills section—perhaps ones appropriate for whole-group instruction. This modest beginning allows you to familiarize yourself with the program. In subsequent units, you can increase the number of activities, perhaps doing a total of five or six activities. You can also differentiate instruction.

How is differentiated instruction achieved?

Why is differentiated instruction a goal? "One size does not fit all!" This expression reflects the instructional challenge teachers face with the increasing diversity among students in today's classrooms. Differentiated instruction addresses this diversity. A differentiated curriculum specifically targets instructional content and difficulty level to learners' needs.

A simple example of differentiation is to expect capable students to make a greater contribution in a lesson in which all students are engaged. Here, the teacher selects the same concept and activity for the class, but more is expected of able students. For example, they may be asked to follow up the class lesson with an independent activity that is more challenging.

Differentiated instruction can be achieved in another way. Because the menu of skill-based activities varies in content and difficulty in Seeds for Sowing Skills, all students can be engaged in the same concept but be assigned different activities. The more difficult skill-building activities, some of which are projects, can be selected for the most capable students, while easier exercises can be chosen for less able learners.

Yet, the difficulty level of an activity is highly dependent upon the instructional format employed. An activity might be easily understood if the lesson is teacher-directed but be too difficult if it is assigned for independent practice. So, the instructional format for the activities is also flexible to accommodate a range of achievement levels and learning styles among students.

How can the instructional format of the skill-building activities vary to accommodate diverse learners?

All the activities can be used in various instructional formats. The format is yours to decide as you create your instructional plan. Formats include a teacher-directed exercise for the class or select group, a partner or cooperative group activity, or an independent at-school or at-home lesson. In fact, the same activity can be used for some students in one mode, such as for homework, and it can be used with other students in another way, for example as a small-group, teacher-directed lesson. Further, an activity might employ several formats as the lesson progresses.

What is an example of one activity that reflects several instructional formats and provides for differentiated instruction?

Here is one way to develop an activity employing different instructional formats, as well as differentiating for student abilities. Activity 1A, Unit 1, page 2 reinforces the concept "Short vowel sounds are usually spelled with one vowel. Long vowel sounds are usually spelled with two vowels."

Begin by selecting able students to write the suggested long vowel words on the chalkboard. Then pair students to discover that they can make the long vowel words into short vowel words by removing one letter. You may wish to select able student pairs to demonstrate this with their words on the chalkboard (e.g., heat/hat), while less able pairs observe the activity and modify their work accordingly.

Then students write compound words independently. Capable students can be selected again to take turns writing the compounds on the chalkboard for all students to self-check. The sorting activity reinforces the concept with all students. The challenge activity could be a homework assignment in which the number of compounds requested could vary—say, "Everyone must find and write three examples, but I invite you to identify more." This way you offer the opportunity to excel.

The instructional formats used with this activity include direct whole-group instruction, at-home independent study, paired student paper/pencil practice, paired proofreading, and independent study. More able students/student pairs were asked to write spellings on the chalkboard for observation and self-checking by all students. The homework assignment provided a minimum requirement, but invited expansion.

What instructional formats did this activity use, and how were they differentiated to meet the needs of learners?

This activity engages students in a variety of skills as it develops. The targeted skills are listed in the sidenotes next to the activity on page 2 of the unit. The Core Word *heat* is the "seed" for the lesson, but the purpose of this activity, and all other activities in Seeds for Sowing Skills, is to develop the stated concept and cultivate skills. Like the skills and concepts in this activity, all skills and concepts are recycled throughout this level and subsequent levels of the program.

Are the skills and concepts in this activity recycled?

Recycling skills has benefits. First, ongoing exposure and reinforcement aids long-term learning for all students. Even capable students benefit from revisiting important skills and concepts, and for some students, repeated exposure over time is essential for mastery. Without ongoing attention to key skills and concepts, students often do not develop a strong foundation necessary for spelling and language success.

How does ongoing exposure to key skills and concepts aid long-term learning?

Another benefit of recycling important skills and concepts is this: Initially, some skills or concepts may be too difficult to present to all or some students, but later, as students develop, the skills and concepts can be selected for instruction. Over time, these same skills and concepts may become too easy for most students, but be on target for slower students and students deficient in skill and concept development who are new to this program. It follows, then, that this recycling facilitates differentiated instruction.

How does ongoing exposure to key skills and concepts aid differentiated instruction?

Further, this conscientious recycling makes the teaching of each new skill and concept for mastery unnecessary. Mastery grows over time. So, if all or some students have difficulty with a skill or concept, note this, and move on. Do not belabor the activity, because there are multiple opportunities to revisit the same skill and concept.

Is it necessary to teach the skills and concepts in each activity for mastery?

Finally, when skills and concepts recur routinely, they offer ongoing opportunities for informal measurement of students' progress and mastery. Though formal assessment is targeted in Assess Words and Skills in each unit, activities in Seeds for Sowing Skills provide informal but continuous diagnostic information, empowering you to make informed decisions on the selection of subsequent skill-building activities to meet your students' specific needs.

How does the recycling of skills and concepts support assessment and instruction?

A Scope and Sequence of skills is included in the reference section, page 402–403.

Is there a Scope and Sequence of skills?

Information on students' performance on the targeted skills in this section can be gathered and analyzed formally and informally. For some activities, discussion and student self-checking is desirable, because feedback on completed work is helpful to the learning process as students relate their response(s) to those of others. In these instances, you may ask students to write their response(s) on the chalkboard to begin the dialogue. Then during the discussion, students' performance can be noted.

Should the activities be checked and graded?

For a more thorough evaluation, student work may be collected and graded occasionally.

How do the activities extend the Core Words to more words?

The Seeds for Sowing Skills activities are your source for teaching, as well as informally assessing, vital skills and concepts. Concurrently, the Core Words grow to an infinite number of additional word experiences as the activities develop. For example, the description of the representative activity described on page 326 provided word experiences with multiple words that reflect the short vowel to long vowel word concept. An important distinction to note is that students were actively involved in discovering attributes of words in this lesson. The words were not predetermined for them in a programmed list to be memorized for a test.

How do the activities contribute toward total language growth?

Almost as important as providing the crucial skill and concept foundation necessary for students, the activities offer multiple opportunities for total language development —hearing, speaking, reading, writing, and thinking about language. The at-school activities and the at-home extension activities immerse students in learning the language in a motivational, productive context. They learn to be successful language users early on. This formative success with language shapes positive student attitudes that encourage achievement in subsequent grades to make *every child a speller*.

Build Skillful Writers

What is Build Skillful Writers?

Build Skillful Writers is your source for discussion points and practice suggestions to highlight the interrelatedness of language learning—spelling, writing, grammar, usage, mechanics, and vocabulary. Look for this logo.

What is the purpose of Build Skillful Writers?

The purpose of Build Skillful Writers is to provide opportunities for students to learn to spell in concert with the related language skills of a total language program.

When should students be engaged in Build Skillful Writers?

Use the activities anytime throughout the unit. In fact, topics initially bypassed can be revisited as students work in subsequent units.

How should students be engaged in Build Skillful Writers?

The topics range in difficulty and span a variety of language-learning issues. Therefore, they can be targeted for discussion and/or activity to those students who would benefit via a format that meets their needs—teacher-directed lesson, small group exercise, or an independent at-home or at-school activity.

Test Ready

Test Ready is your source for activities that focus on an essential skill that will be assessed in the Skill Test of Assess Words and Skills in each unit. Test Ready has two parts, one labeled *at-school* for classroom practice and one labeled *at-home* for homework practice. It is in the section labeled Build Assessment Readiness. Look for this logo.

What is Test Ready?

Rebecca Sitton's Sourcebook Series teaches spelling within the context of language. Students become better spellers when spelling is not limited to learning words but expanded to learning the language skills and concepts that form the foundation for word study. The purpose of Test Ready is to provide targeted practice for a specific skill prior to testing it on the Skill Test. Students have had previous exposures to each skill prior to this targeted instruction in the Test Ready activities.

What is the purpose of Test Ready?

All skills are recycled, so a skill targeted in Test Ready and tested in the Skill Test does not signal a termination of exposure to that skill. The skill is revisited in Seeds for Sowing Skills and may be recycled in Test Ready for further practice prior to another evaluation of the skill. See the Scope and Sequence of Skills, pages 402–403.

Is the targeted skill recycled in subsequent units?

Unlike the skill-building activities in Exercise Express and Seeds for Sowing Skills that are selected at the discretion of the teacher, Test Ready is intended for all students. This ensures that the skills selected for Test Ready are not incidental in a student's educational program.

Which students should be engaged in Test Ready?

The essential skill targeted in Test Ready is stated in the sidenotes for the at-school and at-home activities.

How is the targeted skill in Test Ready identified?

The instructional format for the at-school activity is yours to decide, such as a teacher-directed class exercise, a partner or cooperative group activity, or an independent lesson. An activity might employ more than one instructional format as the lesson progresses.

How should the at-school activity be used?

As students engage in the activity, make an informal assessment of their competence with the skill. From this you can determine the time and teaching warranted for the skill.

There are answers to the Take-Home Tasks on the Answer Key, pages 398–400.

Where are the answers to the Take-Home Tasks?

The at-home activity supports the at-school activity. Each at-home activity is on a blackline master labeled Take-Home Task. A copy of the Take-Home Task can be sent home with each child to encourage parent-child partnerships.

How should the at-home activity be used?

The at-home activity can be done at school instead of being sent home, or it can be done at school in addition to being sent home. Some students may benefit from two exposures to the skill.

May the at-home activity be done at school?

If the at-home activity is sent home for completion, you may wish to have it returned to school to be checked. However, this is not imperative. Instead, you can suggest that parents keep the completed Take-Home Tasks in a folder to revisit with their child. You see, many Take-Home Tasks have suggestions for activities that extend practice to make *every child a speller*.

Should the at-home activity be returned to school?

Priority Words

What are Priority Words?

Priority Words are high-frequency words. They are the highest frequency words on a frequency-of-use list of writing words. Priority Words are your source for extending proofreading practice to students' daily writing across the curriculum. 

Priority Words, sometimes referred to as "no excuses" words, are words that students are always accountable for in their writing. They designate a minimum competency for spelling accountability. Proofreading for these words is the focus of Build Proofreading Skills in each unit. Look for this logo.

Which words become Priority Words?

The highest-frequency word in English is *the*, so *the* is the first Priority Word. It is introduced early on in first grade. Following *the*, the next sequential words on a researched list of high-frequency writing words are added to the Priority Word list. The number of Priority Words grows over time, from level to level, as students develop as spellers and writers. The list of words is cumulative—once a word is added, it stays. Students are responsible to proofread for their Priority Words to ensure they are written accurately in all their work. They are provided with a list of Priority Words as a reference to aid in this task.

Why is proofreading important?

The acquisition of spelling and proofreading proficiency goes hand in hand. Learning to spell a word is the first step, but the second step—proofreading words for accuracy in writing—is the most authentic test of spelling ability. When students become adults, they will be evaluated by how well they spell in business and personal writing, so it's important for them to develop a lifetime habit of proofreading early on.

What purposes are served by the focus on Priority Words?

The focus on Priority Words contributes toward the achievement of this objective—the development of a proofreading habit. When students are expected to spell their Priority Words correctly every time they write, they not only learn to proofread for these words but for all words.

Another purpose for the emphasis on Priority Words is to diminish spelling errors in students' writing. Priority Words occur often in writing, and their accuracy is essential to the growth of spelling literacy in writing.

Next, a daily Priority Words proofreading requirement for all writing extends spelling practice well beyond the instructional time officially dedicated to spelling. As students write across the curriculum, they apply their spelling and proofreading skills.

Further, the focus on Priority Words helps promote a connection between spelling and writing—a proofreading consciousness. Students will not learn to proofread on their own. They will not appreciate nor expect the look of literacy in writing unless it is cultivated.

How does the focus on Priority Words influence students' achievement test scores.

Students not only learn to spell and proofread proficiently in their writing, but the potential for higher scores on standardized achievement tests increases. The Priority Word focus provides instruction and daily application of proofreading skills—the very skills assessed on standardized achievement and performance-based spelling tests.

Expectations for spelling and proofreading begin with a realistic expectation for which students can be successful. More Priority Words are added in gentle increments so that students are not reluctant to write.

Will students be reluctant to write if they must spell correctly in their writing?

The transition from invented, or temporary, spelling to conventional spelling takes time and practice. The practice is achieved concurrently in several ways. First, the ongoing Word Preview develops visual skills essential for proofreading success. Then skill-building activities help students understand English spelling and the rules that apply. Finally, writing experiences provide opportunities for students to apply their spelling skills. In writing, students learn that spelling counts, and they are accountable to spell words correctly.

How do students learn to be accountable for spelling in writing?

Classroom writing experiences are of two kinds. One writing experience is the writing process. In writing-as-a-process papers, students are taught how to write. Students learn that good writing is a process that consists of steps that lead to a finished, error-free paper.

How do writing experiences develop spelling accountability?

The other writing experience, *everyday writing*, comprises most of students' writing. It does not warrant the commitment necessary to produce a perfect final copy, particularly in the early grades. This writing is written once and proofread.

An example of everyday writing is a written response to a science question: What did dinosaurs eat? Students' answers reveal their command of the information taught. In this example of everyday writing, an error-free paper from developing writers is unrealistic. However, students are expected to proofread for their Priority Words with 100% accuracy.

Students learn accountability as they participate in these two writing experiences.

The requirement for spelling on all writing-as-a-process papers is 100%, while on everyday writing papers, Priority Words are the minimum requirement for spelling accuracy. They are the baseline for spelling accountability below which spelling literacy must not fall. Nonetheless, students are always encouraged to spell more than the Priority Words correctly in their everyday writing, and they should be able to do so.

Are the Priority Words the only words students must spell correctly in their writing?

In addition to the Priority Word requirement, students can be held accountable for topical words. Topical words are those words students need for a particular writing assignment, such as seasonal words, field trip words, or words from a content-subject unit. These words are expected to be spelled correctly on that one assignment, or during the exploration of that one unit.

May words be added to the Priority Words requirement for everyday writing papers?

For example, topical words may include *dinosaurs, carnivores,* and *herbivores* as students answer the question, "What did dinosaurs eat?" For this writing assignment, students must spell their Priority Words correctly. They also are accountable for *dinosaurs, carnivores,* and *herbivores*. These topical words can be listed on the chalkboard while students complete the assignment for which the correct spelling of the words is expected.

You may wish to add words to the Priority Word list permanently. These words may include your name, the name of your school, or the name of your city. Permanent words added to complement the Priority Word list should be words students use often in writing. If you wish to complement the Priority Word list with the addition of permanent words, write them on a chart and post it in the classroom.

What format is suggested for students' Priority Words spelling reference list?

Students should have easy access to their Priority Word reference as they do their everyday writing. Use the PRIORITY WORDS BLACKLINE MASTER, page 366, or provide each student with a durable Spell Check card. Use a colored highlighter pen to mark students' current Priority Words on their reference. More words are highlighted over time as the Priority Word expectation increases.

Should students have a Priority Word list for at-home use?

You may wish students to have a second Priority Word reference for at-home use. Use either an additional copy of the PRIORITY WORDS BLACKLINE MASTER or another Spell Check card for this purpose. Keep parents informed of the Priority Word expectation—those words on the reference that can never be misspelled.

Spell Check and the PRIORITY WORDS BLACKLINE MASTER are alphabetical references. As students use these references, they develop the ability to use an alphabetical reference, a basic study skill. Students should be encouraged to use all the words on these two references as a spelling aid, yet the signaled words are those words for which there is "no excuse" for misspelling or misusing in their everyday writing.

Should Priority Words be posted on a word wall?

In addition to students having their own personal Priority Word list, Priority Words and other words can be posted in the classroom. However, it is best if students do not have access to posted words that occur on tests during the testing (Cloze Story Word Test, page 336–339; Sentence Dictation Test, pages 342–345; Achievement Tests, pages 346–349). Word walls can focus on the words students generate in their word collection activities that occur within every unit.

How many Priority Words are suggested to begin fifth grade?

The number of Priority Words with which to begin depends upon students' current ability to spell in their writing. Examine students' writing at the start of the school year as students reorient themselves after vacation. Informally note the highest-use words missed by many students. Check the frequency of these words. Then either begin with a consecutive Priority Word list up to the first troublesome word on the frequency-of-use list or omit the problem word(s) and begin with a longer list. The difficult words can be added later following instruction and practice to prepare students for their addition.

For example, if students' writing reveals that *many* (word 55) and *would* (word 59) are the highest-use words that are challenging them in their writing, either begin a Priority Word list with words 1–54, or omit these two words and begin with approximately 1–60. This is a judgment you can make, yet it is best to begin with an expectation all students can easily meet.

What pace is suggested for the addition of Priority Words?

Add words to students' Priority Word lists slowly over time. Pacing for the addition of each Priority Word depends on the difficulty of the word and the ability of the students.

If the next word on the frequency-of-use list is one that often challenges students, add only this word. Announce the date of the upcoming addition and tell students they need to ready themselves for this occasion. Help by circling inaccurate spellings of the word in students' writing, without penalty, until the word is added to the list. Also, review strategies for spelling the word correctly.

Pace the addition of Priority Words so that by the end of the year the correct spelling and use of all 100 words is routine with students in their everyday writing.

Remember, Priority Words are a minimum competency for spelling in everyday writing. The goal is to ensure that students spell and use their Priority Words correctly in writing—*all the time.* The goal is not to have an extensive, challenging Priority Word list that students spell and use correctly in writing—*sometimes.*

Priority Word rigor is best achieved by setting a 100% standard for spelling the words, rather than adding more words to the list and reducing the standard for spelling them.

How is Priority Word rigor best achieved?

Priority Words suggested as a minimum requirement for mastery in writing by the end of each grade level are:

How many Priority Words are suggested as a minimum requirement for mastery in writing by the end of each grade?

Level 1:   high-frequency words 1–15 (*Too* of the *to/two/too* homophones can be omitted until second grade.)

Level 2:   high-frequency words 1–35 (Add *too* to the *to/two/too* homophones.)

Level 3:   high-frequency words 1–55 (The *there/their/they're* and *your/you're* homophones can be omitted.)

Level 4:   high-frequency words 1–75 (Add *there/their/they're* and *your/you're.* You can omit *there's/theirs.*)

Level 5:   high-frequency words 1–100 (Add *there's/theirs.*)

Levels 6–8: high-frequency words 1–130

Priority Words for fifth grade are: ***the*** (1), ***of*** (2), ***and*** (3), ***a*** (4), ***to*** (5), ***in*** (6), ***is*** (7), ***you*** (8), ***that*** (9), ***it*** (10), ***he*** (11), ***for*** (12), ***was*** (13), ***on*** (14), ***are*** (15), ***as*** (16), ***with*** (17), ***his*** (18), ***they*** (19), ***at*** (20), ***be*** (21), ***this*** (22), ***from*** (23), ***I*** (24), ***have*** (25), ***or*** (26), ***by*** (27), ***one*** (28), ***had*** (29), ***not*** (30), ***but*** (31), ***what*** (32), ***all*** (33), ***were*** (34), ***when*** (35), ***we*** (36), ***there*** (37), ***can*** (38), ***an*** (39), ***your*** (40), ***which*** (41), ***their*** (42), ***said*** (43), ***if*** (44), ***do*** (45), ***will*** (46), ***each*** (47), ***about*** (48), ***how*** (49), ***up*** (50), ***out*** (51) ***them*** (52), ***then*** (53), ***she*** (54), ***many*** (55), ***some*** (56), ***so*** (57), ***these*** (58), ***would*** (59), ***other*** (60), ***into*** (61), ***has*** (62), ***more*** (63), ***her*** (64), ***two*** (65), ***like*** (66), ***him*** (67), ***see*** (68), ***time*** (69), ***could*** (70), ***no*** (71), ***make*** (72), ***than*** (73), ***first*** (74), ***been*** (75), ***its*** (76), ***who*** (77), ***now*** (78), ***people*** (79), ***my*** (80), ***made*** (81), ***over*** (82), ***did*** (83), ***down*** (84), ***only*** (85), ***way*** (86), ***find*** (87), ***use*** (88), ***may*** (89), ***water*** (90), ***long*** (91), ***little*** (92), ***very*** (93), ***after*** (94), ***words*** (95), ***called*** (96), ***just*** (97), ***where*** (98), ***most*** (99), ***know*** (100).

What are the Priority Words for mastery by the end of fifth grade?

These words are listed and numbered in frequency-of-use order, the order for which words should be learned and mastered in writing. Add words to the Priority Word list in this order.

You may alter the number of Priority Words from the recommended number by making adjustments with participating teachers.

Words are usually added to the Priority Word list in order of frequency-of-use in writing. However, if you prefer to add a word sooner or later than its frequency designates, you may do so.

Most of the students in a classroom have the same Priority Word expectation. The same words are highlighted on their Priority Word list to indicate their Priority Words. Yet, you may wish to have a lower expectation (fewer words) for less able students and a higher expectation (more words) for the most capable students.

Is the Priority Word expectation the same for all students, or should the Priority Word requirement be differentiated?

This deserves a word of caution. Students who cannot read English should not be in a formal spelling program, nor have a Priority Word list (see Students with Spelling Challenges, page 353). Additionally, to challenge able students, a lengthy Priority Word list is not as effective as challenging them through other aspects of the program (see Challenging the Capable Speller, page 351).

Spelling and using all the Priority Words correctly in everyday writing all the time is far more demanding than simply spelling the words in isolation. Further, students are often challenged by homophones and grammatical issues.

Are students responsible for the homophones and grammatical use of Priority Words?

You can determine the level of responsibility required for homophones. Usually when a homophone is added to the Priority Word list, its partner(s) is also added. For example, when *would* becomes a Priority Word, so does *wood*. Yet, students can be responsible for *four* and *for*, but probably not *fore*. Context sentences and/or rhymes on classroom posters for homophones help students learn to differentiate them.

A prerequisite to students' motivation to proofread for their Priority Words, as well as being responsible for homophones and grammatical issues, is having achievable expectations that are clearly stated to students. Students should say, "It's easy. I can do it!"

How can students be motivated to achieve their level of responsibility for proofreading?

Specific time to proofread should accompany each written task so that students can demonstrate they can do it. Encourage students to use their Priority Word list to proofread carefully for their highlighted Priority Words every time they write. They can be prompted to proofread independently or with their classmates. Keep students focused during the proofreading sessions by walking about the classroom giving general proofreading pointers. Be persistent, yet positive.

This ongoing, enthusiastic emphasis on Priority Words helps students make these words a priority *before* their papers are handed in. The goal is to guide students toward their own proofreading success. This success motivates students to develop into able proofreaders.

How is students' accountability for Priority Words evaluated?

Students' ability to spell and use their Priority Words correctly in their everyday writing should be evaluated. Assessment is made by looking at students' writing.

How often is students' accountability for Priority Words evaluated?

About once a week, select a piece of writing from each student. Students should not be told how often a sample will be selected or which piece of writing will be reviewed for Priority Words. They simply know that papers are being selected, unannounced, for evaluation of spelling in writing. Bracket a section of the writing to evaluate—perhaps two to three sentences. This is the sample from which you make your assessment.

Although evaluating all of every student's writing would be more thorough, it is unnecessary. Spelling evaluation should replicate reading evaluation. Judgments are made on students' reading abilities based on samples of oral reading. Hearing the whole book would be more thorough, but it is unnecessary. The same is true for spelling. You can make a sound judgment of students' spelling abilities by evaluating only a section of their writing. Time is limited.

When Priority Words are made a priority, the result is no Priority Word errors. This is as it should be, inasmuch as the Priority Word requirement represents the minimum expectation for spelling in writing.

Note this success on the papers. Then celebrate the success to promote the best motivation for continued, conscientious proofreading.

How are writing samples marked?

If a student does not meet this requirement on the writing sample selected for evaluation, then the error should be noted. Mark the paper so that the student identifies the mistake. For example, place a dot in the margin next to the line of writing in which the error appears. The student should correct the error and return the paper to you.

Save weekly writing samples (or a copy of the paper) in an assessment file folder for each student. This ongoing data documents each student's ability to meet the Priority Word requirement. These folders could be the same ones used for accumulation of students' Word Tests and Skill Tests, Sentence Dictation Tests, and Achievement Tests.

Why should writing samples be filed and saved?

Writing samples do not need to be graded. Students either meet the minimum requirement for spelling in everyday writing, or they do not. This information should contribute to the total spelling evaluation for each student.

How are writing samples graded?

Occasionally, you may wish to judge a piece of students' everyday writing without the use of a spelling reference. This writing is called a no-reference write. Further, Priority Words are among the bank of words tested in Assess Words and Skills, so routine use of the tests in the program automatically assesses Priority Words without the use of references.

Are students ever evaluated on their ability to spell and use the Priority Words without a spelling reference?

Parents can be allies as you develop proofreading skills. In the INTRODUCING SPELLING BLACKLINE MASTER, page 372, parents are invited to assist their child with proofreading. They are told that papers to be proofread will be sent home routinely with suggestions for proofreading them with their child. These suggestions are in another letter to parents, IDEAS FOR PROOFREADING BLACKLINE MASTER, page 373. In these two letters, parents are introduced to Priority Words. Their child's Priority Words and selected written work can be sent home for proofreading. Mark current Priority Words on students' take-home Priority Word reference list—you may wish to use Spell Check or the PRIORITY WORDS BLACKLINE MASTER, page 366—and update the list as words are added to keep parents informed of these important words.

Can parents become their child's proofreading partner?

The goal is for students to spell and proofread their Priority Words effortlessly in all their writing. This has benefits. Even for adults, the words most frequently misspelled and misused are within the 100 highest-frequency writing words. Every teacher's dilemma is how to teach students to eliminate these careless errors from their writing. The ongoing attention to Priority Words not only achieves this objective, but helps students learn to proofread for all words. It raises students' consciousness about proofreading so that they learn to appreciate error-free writing.

What benefits can be expected once students can spell and use their Priority Words correctly in their everyday writing?

Once these high-use words are committed to memory, writing fluidity is significantly increased. Students no longer struggle laboriously with the spelling and use of the most basic words. Now they can mature as writers.

Further, scores on standardized spelling tests and performance-based measurements increase when students learn the skill these tests assess—proofreading. The Priority Word focus of this program provides students with conscientious attention to proofreading—instruction, daily practice, evaluation, and feedback on their performance.

Perhaps the greatest benefit is that students learn they *can* spell words correctly, making each writing experience an easier and more positive one. Success is an ongoing motivator to make *every child a speller*!

Word Test

What is the Word Test?

The Word Test is one of your two sources in Assess Words and Skills of each unit for formal assessment of long-term spelling achievement of all Core Words introduced so far in the program. (Your other source for assessing these words is the Sentence Dictation Test, described on page 342.) The Word Test is the first assessment activity in each unit. Look for this logo.

What purposes does the Word Test serve in the long-term mastery of the Core Words?

Teaching and learning spelling for the purpose of becoming an able writer are most efficient when the words students need for writing that have not been mastered are identified and targeted for study. The Word Test is diagnostic—it identifies the current and all previously introduced Core Words in the program that each student has not mastered. These unmastered words compose an individualized list of *Spelling Words* for each student, all of which are continually recycled in later tests.

In addition to providing a personal study list of *Spelling Words* for each student, the Word Test evaluates spelling progress for a class and for individual students. For example, if on a given Word Test sixteen students in your class miss the same word, you can compare this number with the results of subsequent tests in which the word is recycled. When several Word Tests in which the word is tested reveal that no one misspells the word, measurable progress has been substantiated for this class with respect to that word. Further, each student's progress toward the mastery of the word can be observed.

Another function of the Word Test is to offer ongoing engagement with all current and previously introduced Core Words in the program. This high-density exposure contributes to their long-term mastery.

Which students should take the Word Test?

Administer the Word Test to all students. Some students may be challenged by the Word Test. To help these students participate, see Students with Spelling Challenges, page 353. For students insufficiently challenged by the Word Test, see Challenging the Capable Speller, page 351.

Which words are tested in the Word Test?

All Core Words, beginning with word one—*the*, and including the current unit's Core Words, form the word bank from which test words are drawn for each Word Test. Test words for each Word Test are listed with their frequency number in the sidenotes for the test. The complete bank of test words is listed on the CORE WORDS BLACKLINE MASTER, pages 363–365, which can be sent home to alert parents and students of the body of words that are the focus for mastery.

When is the Word Test administered?

After completing activities in Build Skills and Word Experiences in each unit, begin formal assessment in Assess Words and Skills by giving the Word Test. It can be given on any day of the week.

How are words tested?

The Word Test uses a spelling cloze-story format. Spelling cloze activities are of two kinds. One cloze requires the completion of missing letters to spell a word. The other requires writing words to complete sentences. The Word Test uses the latter—students write the missing words within a story. Each Word Test is on a blackline master called a Review and is labeled with the number of the unit in which it is used.

The story content varies in the Word Test, but each story challenges students to think and respond. Topics include science, math, social studies, and literature. Students learn about these topics while they learn to spell.

What is the story content of the Word Test?

Students do not study the test words in preparation for taking the Word Test. For the Word Test to pinpoint the words a student has not yet mastered long term, test words cannot be practiced before the test. The Word Test assesses long-term mastery rather than short-term memory of words recently studied.

Do students prestudy the words for the Word Test?

For the Word Test, each student needs a pencil and a copy of the Review blackline master specified in Before the Cloze Story Word Test.

What materials do students need to take the Word Test?

The Word Test story is boxed in The Cloze Story Word Test. Test words are underlined and numbered. The test words do not appear on the students' blackline master copy of the Word Test—they are the words students will write in.

How is the Word Test administered?

After following the suggestions in Before the Cloze Story Word Test, read the entire story aloud, including the test words, as students silently follow the story words with their eyes. Then read the story again, perhaps a sentence at a time, providing time for students to fill in the missing story words blank by blank. You may wish to read the story a third time.

Finally, tell students to proofread their work by spelling each word silently or aloud as they touch each letter.

Spelling references are not generally permitted, so the Word Test functions as a test of long-term spelling achievement. Occasionally, you may wish to allow students to use a reference such as Spell Check, the Core Words Blackline Master, and/or classroom charts or word walls. Then the test results reflect a student's ability to use spelling references and to proofread—a valid test criterion, but not a test of long-term spelling achievement. Further, if references are allowed, Spelling Words cannot be accurately identified.

Can students use spelling references during the Word Test?

Tests should be checked. Feedback on completed work is helpful to the learning process.

How is the Word Test checked?

You can check each Word Test, or you may prefer to guide students through the correction procedure with students using a colored pencil to check their own or another student's test words.

You may, on occasion, ask students to work independently or together using spelling references to proofread the spelling of each test word. Suggested references include Spell Check and the Core Words Blackline Master—or the words can be written on a transparency or chalkboard. This method puts less emphasis on formal testing and more emphasis on proofreading.

These options provide ample flexibility to use the Word Test to achieve various objectives. You're in charge!

Save students' Word Tests in individual assessment folders. This provides a record of performance for each student. These folders could be the same ones used for accumulation of students' everyday writing papers marked for Priority Words. If you wish to send the Word Test home, first make a copy for the assessment folder.

Should students' Word Tests be saved or sent home?

How is the Word Test graded?	To grade each Word Test, the number of words right or wrong on each student's test may be recorded in the grade book. This information can contribute to an evaluation of a student's overall spelling performance.
What follow-up is suggested after the Word Test?	After the test, follow the suggestions in After the Cloze Story Word Test. First, initiate the discussion and/or writing activity follow-up related to the story content. The writing can be done independently, in small groups or pairs, or it can be a class response in which you or a student writes on the chalkboard or on a chart with the group's input. Another option is to have students complete this writing follow-up at home.

If this writing activity is done independently at school, it may be used as one source for a writing sample for students' Priority Words writing assessment.

After students' tests are corrected, note if several students missed the same word(s). If so, follow up with a discussion and have students write the word(s) using the Word Study Strategy, page 357, and/or have them write the words in sentences.

What is the Spelling Notebook?	Further, students should record words they missed in their Spelling Notebook and on their WORDS TO LEARN sheet. These words are their *Spelling Words*. Have students check spellings of these words against a copy of the CORE WORDS BLACKLINE MASTER, pages 363–365, to facilitate this process.

The Spelling Notebook provides students with a resource for noting their Spelling Words for at-school study. It provides a personal running record of spelling errors that serves both the teacher and the student. Included in the Practice Book, page 389, is a ready-to-go section, called the Spelling Notebook, for this record. Otherwise, the Spelling Notebook is a pad of lined paper or a student-made booklet of a few sheets of writing paper with a construction paper cover. Check students' Spelling Notebooks to ensure the Spelling Words are spelled correctly and to identify words that recur. Students can routinely practice their Spelling Words independently or with a partner in preparation for their recurrence on subsequent tests.

What is the WORDS TO LEARN sheet?	Students should also record words missed on a copy of the WORDS TO LEARN BLACKLINE MASTER, page 375. This provides them with a personal study list of Spelling Words to take home. Each list is individualized to meet the spelling needs of each student. Send home the lists with a copy of the IDEAS FOR WORD STUDY BLACKLINE MASTER, page 374. Students should study these words in preparation for subsequent Word Tests that retest these words.

You, the student, or a parent may add words to the WORDS TO LEARN sheet in the section, More Words for Super Spellers. The words should have writing relevance for the learner.

Is it necessary to keep class records of spelling errors?	There is no need for you to keep a separate record of students' errors. The Spelling Notebook kept by each student keeps track of these words for at-school review, and their WORDS TO LEARN sheet lists the words for at-home study. The automatic recycling of Core Words is so extensive that by giving the Word Tests and the Sentence Dictation Tests regularly, students systematically revisit all words for ongoing practice to ensure their long-term mastery.
How are the Core Words on a student's Words to Learn sheet and in a student's Spelling Notebook retested?	This conscientious recycling system for all Core Words eliminates the time-consuming task of retesting students individually on their varied spelling lists. Automatically, the Word Tests and Sentence Dictation Tests reassess all words.

The activities in the Cloze Story Skill-Building Extensions provide more word experiences. These activities offer additional practice for words misspelled or misused on the Word Test, or they may be used to challenge some students. They are an optional means of meeting the needs of diverse learners. Consider using these activities for homework to further parent-child partnerships for spelling. The targeted skills for each of the activities are listed in the sidenotes.

What are the Cloze Story Skill-Building Extensions?

Testing in this program differs greatly from that of a customary approach to spelling instruction. Specifically, the Friday Test differs from the Word Test in three significant ways.

How does the Word Test differ from the Friday Test?

Foremost, the objectives of the tests differ. The purpose of the Friday Test is to test the Spelling Words to determine students' grades. It culminates the unit and the study of a predetermined list of Spelling Words. The objective of the Word Test is to make teaching and learning spelling more efficient by identifying the words students have not mastered. These become a student's Spelling Words—targeted for study. The Word Test is diagnostic and initiates the study of individualized lists of Spelling Words for each learner that are automatically retested on subsequent tests.

Second, the Friday Test assesses words from the current spelling unit. The Word Test assesses words from the current spelling unit and recycles all previously introduced words in the program for ongoing mastery checks.

Third, students are encouraged to prestudy the words for the Friday Test; students taking the Word Test do not prestudy the words selected for the test so that long-term, not short-term, knowledge of the spellings can be evaluated.

There are other distinctions. The Friday Test is usually a list test, while the Word Test is always within the context of a story. The Friday Test is given on Friday, but the Word Test can be given on any day. The Friday Test is the totality of the testing, and performance on the test determines students' spelling grades. The Word Test is not the sole test but one of several testing options from which to determine student performance (see Evaluating Spelling, page 350).

Engaging students in spelling assessment that includes the Word Test, instead of a customary Friday Test, is an integral part of making *every child a speller*!

Skill Test

The Skill Test is your source for assessing students' understanding and/or application of selected spelling and language-related skills. The Skill Test follows the Word Test in the Assess Skill Application section of Assess Words and Skills of each unit. Look for this logo.

What is the Skill Test?

Selected skills that form the foundation for spelling growth are tested to assess progress. The specific skill assessed in each unit is identified in the sidenotes.

Which skills are tested?

For further evaluation of an extensive body of skills and concepts, use the ongoing, informal assessment opportunities in the Exercise Express and Seeds for Sowing Skills.

What purpose does the Skill Test serve in the long-term mastery of spelling?	The Sourcebook Series teaches spelling within the context of language. Students become better spellers when spelling is not limited to learning words, but expanded to learning the language skills and concepts that form the foundation for word study. The purpose of the Skill Test is to check the progress students make toward understanding and applying selected language skills and concepts that are critical to their long-term spelling success.
Which students should take the Skill Test?	All students should take the Skill Test unless they are not yet readers and, for this reason, are not in this formal spelling program. Some students in this program may be challenged by the Skill Test. To help them participate, see Students with Spelling Challenges, page 353. Students who appear to know the skills tested on the Skill Test also take the test. For these students, see Challenging the Capable Speller, page 351.
When is the Skill Test administered?	The Skill Test can be administered along with the Proofreading Test or before the Proofreading Test at a later time. It can be administered on any day of the week.
How are skills tested?	Each Skill Test is on a blackline master called a Review. Each Review is labeled with the number of the unit in which it is used. The Skill Test appears at the top of the page followed by the Proofreading Test.
How are students prepared to take the Skill Test successfully?	Students have multiple experiences learning and applying the skill before it is tested on a Skill Test. Previous units focus on the skill, and the preceding at-school and at-home Test Ready activities in Build Assessment Readiness prepare students for the test.
What materials do students need to take the Skill Test?	For the Skill Test, each student needs a pencil and a copy of the Review blackline master specified in Before the Skill Test.
How is the Skill Test administered?	To administer the Skill Test, use the suggestions in Assess Skill Application. The Skill Test is boxed and the answers are indicated. Following the Skill Test, students' responses should be checked, because feedback on completed work is helpful to the learning process.
How is the Skill Test checked?	You may wish to check each Skill Test or have students use a colored pencil to check their own or another student's test. For the latter, you may wish to model the correction process using an overhead projector and a transparency of the Review blackline master.
How is the Skill Test graded?	To grade each Skill Test, the number of items wrong on each student's test may be recorded in the grade book. This information can contribute to an evaluation of a student's overall spelling performance (see Evaluating Spelling, page 350).
What follow-up is suggested after the Skill Test?	After the test is corrected, look at After the Skill Test. Note the ability of the students to perform on the test. Revisit the unit's Test Ready activities with students challenged by the skills. Save students' Skill Tests in an assessment folder for each student. This provides a record of performance. These folders could be the same ones used for accumulation of students' everyday writing papers marked for Priority Words. If you send the Skill Test home, first make a copy for this folder.
Is the targeted skill in the Skill Test recycled?	All skills are recycled, so a skill tested in the Skill Test does not signal a termination of exposure to that skill. The skill is revisited multiple times in Seeds for Sowing Skills and may be recycled in subsequent Test Ready activities and Skill Tests for further practice and/or evaluation of the skill. Ongoing exposure and appraisal of skills helps make *every child a speller*!

Proofreading Test

The Proofreading Test is your source for providing test-taking practice and assessment of following testing directions and performing proofreading and editing tasks. The Proofreading Test follows the Skill Test in the Assess Proofreading Application section of Assess Words and Skills of each unit. Look for this logo. It is on the bottom section of a blackline master for the unit (the Skill Test is on the top of the same blackline master).

What is the Proofreading Test?

Numerous direction and testing formats are used, based on the directions and formats of an extensive bank of actual tests.

What testing format is used?

The Sourcebook Series teaches spelling for writing. Students become better spellers when spelling is not limited to learning specific words, but expanded to include application of spelling in written work across the curriculum. This necessarily engages students in proofreading and editing tasks. The purpose of the Proofreading Test is to ready students for taking wide-range spelling assessments—all of which are proofreading and editing evaluations. Further, the Proofreading Tests reflect a variety of formats and directions to familiarize students with the test-taking process.

What purpose does the Proofreading Test serve for the long-term mastery of spelling, and for performance on state and district spelling tests and/or on standardized spelling achievement batteries?

Not only do the testing formats and directions vary, but the words reflect a range of difficulty. Words and editing skills that are tested on the Proofreading Tests are not limited to the words and skills previously taught in the Sourcebook Series. This is to ensure that the Proofreading Test experience parallels actual testing in which words and skills often extend above the specified grade levels.

Which words and skills are assessed on the Proofreading Test?

All students should take the Proofreading Test. The more knowledgeable students are with a variety of assessments, the better you can expect their performance to be on actual spelling batteries. If students are unfamiliar with typical tests and the testing venue, their performance often reflects deficiency—when perhaps this inadequacy is in test-taking skills rather than spelling and editing ability.

Which students should take the Proofreading Test?

The Proofreading Test can be administered along with the Skill Test or after the Skill Test at a later time. The two tests appear on the same blackline master—the Skill Test at the top of the page and the Proofreading Test at the bottom. The tests can be administered any day of the week.

How is the Proofreading Test administered?

For the Proofreading Test, each student needs a pencil and a copy of the blackline master specified for the unit assessment.

To administer the Proofreading Test, follow the suggestions in Assess Proofreading Application noting the directions for students on the top of their copy of the test page. A reduced Proofreading Test is included in each unit, and answers are indicated.

You may check each test or have students use a colored pencil to check their own or another student's test. For the latter, you may wish to model the correction process

How is the Proofreading Test checked?

using an overhead projector and a transparency of the test blackline master.

How is the Proofreading Test graded?

To grade each Proofreading Test, the number of items wrong on each student's test may be recorded in the grade book. This information can contribute to an evaluation of their overall spelling performance (see Evaluating Spelling, page 350).

What follow-up is suggested after the Proofreading Test?

After the Proofreading Tests are corrected, the tests of students who scored poorly can be examined to determine the reason for the low performance—failure to follow directions, work within the format, edit and/or spell. Then appropriate counsel can be provided. Students who miss words may wish to add these words to their Words To Learn sheet for take-home study and/or record them in their Spelling Notebook for at-school practice.

Save students' Proofreading Tests in an assessment folder for each student. This provides a record of performance. These folders could be the same ones used for accumulation of students' everyday writing papers marked for Priority Words. If you send the Proofreading Test home, first make a copy for this folder.

Are the targeted items for evaluation on the Proofreading Tests recycled?

Words, editing skills, directions, and test formats are recycled. Ongoing exposure and appraisal helps to familiarize students with the testing process to make every child a speller!

Sentence Dictation Test

What is Sentence Dictation?

The Sentence Dictation Test is one of your two sources in Assess Words and Skills of each unit for formal assessment of long-term spelling achievement of all words introduced so far in the program. (Your other source for assessing the Core Words is the Word Test, described on page 336.) Look for this logo.

What purposes does the Sentence Dictation Test serve in the long-term mastery of the Core Words?

Teaching and learning spelling is most efficient when the specific words not mastered are identified and targeted for study. One function of the Sentence Dictation Test is diagnostic—to identify any previously introduced words in the program that each student has not mastered. These unmastered words compose an individualized list of *Spelling Words* for each student, all of which are continually recycled in later tests.

In addition to providing a personal study list for each student, the Sentence Dictation Test evaluates spelling progress for a class and for individual students. For example, if on a given Sentence Dictation Test sixteen students in your class miss the same word, you can compare this number with the results of subsequent tests in which the word is recycled. When several Sentence Dictation Tests in which the word is tested reveal that no one misspells the word, measurable progress has been substantiated for this class with respect to that word. Further, each student's progress toward the mastery of the word can be observed.

Another function of the Sentence Dictation Test is to offer ongoing engagement with all current and previously introduced Core Words in the program. This high-density exposure to the Core Words contributes to their long-term mastery.

Unlike the Word Test that is given to all students, the Sentence Dictation Test is for students who need more practice or challenge. It provides another option for a spelling and language-related experience as well as another opportunity for appraisal of spelling mastery.

Which students should take the Sentence Dictation Test?

The Sentence Dictation Test fully challenges students. Students write complete sentences that form a short story, while in the Word Test students write only selected words. Students' listening skills are challenged as well as their ability to use capitalization and punctuation properly.

How does the Sentence Dictation Test differ from the Word Test?

Because many more words are surveyed in a Sentence Dictation Test than in a Word Test, more assessment information is gained. Yet, more time is involved in extracting this data. A Sentence Dictation Test takes longer to administer and to check than a Word Test.

All Core Words, beginning with word one—*the,* and including the current unit's Core Words, form the word bank from which test words are drawn for each Sentence Dictation Test. Test words for each Sentence Dictation Test are listed with their frequency number in the sidenotes for the test. The complete bank of test words is listed on the CORE WORDS BLACKLINE MASTER, pages 363–365, which can be sent home to alert parents and students of the body of words that are the focus for mastery.

Which words are tested in the Sentence Dictation Test?

The Extra Words in the Sentence Dictation Test are necessary at early levels to create complete sentences. Yet, these words serve other purposes.

What purposes do the Extra Words serve?

The Extra Words can be written on the chalkboard to be used by students as a spelling reference during testing. This reinforces visual and proofreading skills and can provide evaluative information on students' command of these skills.

If a reference is not provided, the Extra Words can be used to provide an informal diagnostic and evaluative tool on students' ability to apply word skills to spell new words. Further, they offer a spelling challenge to more capable students.

All test words are recycled extensively so that students are exposed to them multiple times. The Extra Words may reappear sporadically in the sentences, but they are not systematically recycled like the test words.

Are words tested more than one time in the Sentence Dictation Tests?

After completing the Word Test and the Skill Test, you may give all or some students the Sentence Dictation Test. It can be given on any day of the week.

When is the Sentence Dictation Test administered?

Sentences that form a complete idea or short story make up the format of the Sentence Dictation Tests. There are never more than four sentences. Students write the sentences as they are dictated.

How are the words tested?

Students do not study the test words in preparation for taking the Sentence Dictation Test. For the Sentence Dictation Test to pinpoint the Core Words a student has not yet mastered long term, test words cannot be practiced before the test. For the Extra Words to serve their purpose, they, too, cannot be prestudied for the test. The Sentence Dictation Test assesses long-term mastery rather than short-term memory of words recently studied.

Do students prestudy the words for the Sentence Dictation Test?

What materials do students need to take the Sentence Dictation Test?

For the Sentence Dictation Test, each student needs a pencil and a sheet of writing paper.

How is the Sentence Dictation Test administered?

The test sentences are boxed in The Sentence Dictation Test. After following the suggestions in Before the Sentence Dictation Test, read these sentences aloud to students. Then read the first sentence and ask students to repeat it on signal. After students repeat the sentence aloud in unison, tell them to write the sentence. Wait for students to write the sentence. Then repeat the sentence after saying, "Now, touch each word as I say the sentence again."

Follow this sequence with the remaining sentence(s). At the end, you may wish to read the sentences one more time. Finally, tell students to reread their sentences silently or aloud as they proofread their work.

The testing should be structured and concise. Requests for repetitions should be denied so that students learn to listen carefully and write expeditiously.

Can students use spelling references during the Sentence Dictation Test?

Spelling references are not generally permitted, so the Sentence Dictation Test functions as a test of long-term spelling achievement. Occasionally, you may wish to allow students to use a reference such as Spell Check, the CORE WORDS BLACKLINE MASTER, and/or classroom charts or word walls. Then the test results reflect a student's ability to use spelling references and to proofread—a valid test criterion, but not a test of long-term spelling achievement. Further, if references are allowed, Spelling Words cannot be accurately identified.

How is the Sentence Dictation Test checked?

Tests should be checked. Feedback on completed work is helpful to the learning process. You can check each Sentence Dictation Test, or you may prefer to guide students through the correction procedure with students using a colored pencil to check their own or another student's test words.

You may, on occasion, ask students to work independently or together using references to proofread the spelling of each word in the sentences. Suggested references include Spell Check and the CORE WORDS BLACKLINE MASTER—or the sentences can be written on a transparency or on the chalkboard. This method puts less emphasis on formal testing and more emphasis on proofreading.

These options provide ample flexibility to use the Sentence Dictation Test to achieve various objectives. You're in charge!

Should students' Sentence Dictation Tests be saved or sent home?

Save students' Sentence Dictation Tests in individual assessment folders. This provides a record of performance for each student. These folders could be the same ones used for accumulation of students' everyday writing papers marked for Priority Words. If you wish to send the Sentence Dictation Test home, first make a copy for the assessment folder.

How is the Sentence Dictation Test graded?

To grade each Sentence Dictation Test, the number of Core Words wrong on each student's test may be recorded in the grade book. This information can contribute to an evaluation of a student's overall spelling performance. Further, you may wish to grade errors other than spelling errors, such as capitalization and punctuation.

What follow-up is suggested after the Sentence Dictation Test?

After the test, follow the suggestions in After the Sentence Dictation Test. First, initiate the discussion and/or writing activity follow-up related to the sentence content. The writing can be done independently, in small groups or pairs, or it can be a class response in which you or a student writes on the chalkboard or on a chart with the group's input. Another option is to have students complete this writing follow-up at home.

If this writing activity is done independently, it may be used as one source for a writing sample for students' Priority Words writing assessment, page 334.

After students' tests are corrected, note if several students missed the same word(s). If so, follow up with a discussion and have students write the word(s) using the Word Study Strategy, page 357, and/or have them write the words in sentences.

Further, students should record words they missed in their Spelling Notebook and on their WORDS TO LEARN sheet. These words are their *Spelling Words*.

The Spelling Notebook provides students with a resource for noting their Spelling Words for at-school study. It provides a personal running record of spelling errors that serves both the teacher and the student. Included in the Practice Book, page 389, is a ready-to-go section, called the Spelling Notebook, for this record. Otherwise, the Spelling Notebook is a pad of lined paper or a student-made booklet of a few sheets of writing paper with a construction paper cover. Check students' Spelling Notebooks to ensure the Spelling Words are spelled correctly and to identify words that recur. Students can routinely practice their Spelling Words independently or with a partner in preparation for their recurrence on subsequent tests.

What is the Spelling Notebook?

Students should also record words missed on a copy of the WORDS TO LEARN BLACKLINE MASTER, page 375. This provides them with a personal study list of Spelling Words to take home. Each list is individualized to meet the spelling needs of each student. Send home the lists with a copy of the IDEAS FOR WORD STUDY BLACKLINE MASTER, page 374. Students should study these words in preparation for subsequent Word Tests and Sentence Dictation Tests that retest these words.

What is the WORDS TO LEARN sheet?

You, the student, or a parent may add words to the WORDS TO LEARN sheet in the section, *More Words for Super Spellers*. The words should have writing relevance for the learner.

There is no need for you to keep a separate record of students' errors. The Spelling Notebook kept by each student keeps track of these words for at-school review and their WORDS TO LEARN sheet lists the words for at-home study. The automatic recycling of Core Words is so extensive that by giving the Word Tests and the Sentence Dictation Tests regularly, students systematically revisit all words for ongoing practice to ensure their long-term mastery.

Is it necessary to keep class records of spelling errors?

This conscientious recycling system for all Core Words eliminates the time-consuming task of retesting students individually on their varied spelling lists. The Word Tests and Sentence Dictation Tests automatically reassess all words and provide ongoing exposure to these important words.

How are the Core Words on a student's WORDS TO LEARN sheet and in a student's Spelling Notebook retested?

Indeed, both the Word Test and the Sentence Dictation Test serve a purpose within your spelling curriculum to make instruction and practice more effective—they gather information to specifically target students' learning needs. This is the most efficient way to ensure progress toward making *every child a speller*.

How do the tests benefit students and teachers?

Achievement Battery of Tests

What is the Achievement Battery of Tests?

The Achievement Battery of Tests is your source for assessing students' yearly spelling growth. This battery of three optional tests complements the ongoing Word Test, Sentence Dictation Test, and Priority Word evaluations.

What purpose does this test battery serve?

The Achievement Battery of Tests measures each student's spelling progress from the beginning of the school year to the end. Further comparisons can be made among students and/or classrooms of students.

Which words are tested?

Thirty words are tested on each of the three tests. To maintain integrity for test score comparisons, the same thirty words are tested. The words tested are: *were* (34), *there* (37), *their* (42), *said* (43), *about* (48), *then* (53), *than* (73), *people* (79), *little* (92), *where* (98), *often* (186), *enough* (209), *let's* (230), *it's* (253), *before* (332), *beautiful* (429), *friend* (498), *ask* (508), *whose* (520), *mountain* (526), *information* (549), *except* (550), *you're* (552), *couldn't* (563), *maybe* (566), *middle* (569), *necessary* (615), *direction* (619), *isn't* (642), *they're* (1010).

These words are selected from among all Core Words presented in the program up to and including the Core Words at this level. In each of the tests, three instances for the evaluation of capital letter use are included.

What is the format of the tests?

The three tests use a spelling cloze-story format that mirrors the Word Test in Assess Words and Skills of each unit. Students write the missing test words in the story. The tests are on blackline masters titled, Achievement Test 1, 2, and 3, pages 386–388.

Following each story, three optional questions can be used for writing follow-up. The written responses of the students can also be evaluated for spelling achievement. Following are suggested follow-up questions:

Achievement Test 1
- What are activities people do to prepare for winter?
- If the cricket learned a valuable lesson from the ant, how will his next summer be different from his last summer?
- Do you think the ant's response to the cricket's request for food was justified? Why or why not?

Achievement Test 2
- From what you know about animals' senses, is it possible that animals could predict an earthquake? Why or why not?
- Write the next chapter in this story.
- If you were Jake's mother, how would you have reacted to the boys' warning?

Achievement Test 3
- What advice would you give the young shepherd?
- Do you think the shepherd is suited for his job? Why or why not?
- Were the villagers justified in ignoring the shepherd's third request for help? Why or why not?

Each test can be administered once during the school year. The first test should be given after students have completed Unit 2. This gives students two experiences with the cloze format of the Word Test prior to the first achievement test that uses the same format. This first test sets a baseline score from which to register progress. The final test should be given at the end of the school year. The second test can be given midway between the first and last test to evaluate mid-year progress.

When should the tests be given?

Students do not study the test words in preparation for taking these tests. For the tests to evaluate long-term mastery of the words, they cannot be practiced before the tests. The achievement tests are tests of long-term mastery rather than tests of short-term memory of words recently studied.

Do students prestudy the words for these tests?

To take the tests, each student needs a pencil and a copy of the test blackline master. If the option to have students write a response to one of the follow-up questions is exercised, students also need a sheet of writing paper.

What materials do students need to take the tests?

Each of the three tests are boxed and labeled in this section. Test words are underlined and numbered. The test words do not appear on the students' blackline master copy of the test—they are the words students will write in the blanks.

How should the tests be administered?

Tell students the exercise is like their Word Test. Read the story aloud to students as they silently follow the words with their eyes. Then read the story again, perhaps a sentence at a time, providing ample time for students to write the missing story words in the blanks.

At the end, you may wish to read the story a third time. Finally, tell students to proofread their work by spelling each word silently or aloud as they touch each letter.

Spelling references cannot be permitted. The test results should reflect a student's ability to spell the test words long term, rather than their ability to use spelling references and to proofread. If spelling references are available to students as they take the tests, the tests are not valid assessments of long-term spelling achievement.

Are spelling references allowed during the testing?

Achievement Test 1

The Cricket and the Ant

A story (1) <u>people</u> read long (2) <u>before</u> your grandparents (3) <u>were</u> born was (4) <u>about</u> a cricket and a (5) <u>little</u> ant. On a (6) <u>beautiful</u> summer day, the cricket (7) <u>said</u> to the ant, "My, (8) <u>it's</u> a wonderful day! (9) <u>Let's</u> head over (10) <u>there</u> to the base of the (11) <u>mountain</u>. That's (12) <u>where</u> we can sing and dance." The ant had heard the cricket's appeal (13) <u>often</u>. However, he declined the invitation once again, because he knew it was (14) <u>necessary</u> to gather food in the summer so he would have (15) <u>enough</u> to eat during the long, cold winter.

The cricket, (16) <u>whose</u> goal was to enjoy life, didn't (17) <u>ask</u> his (18) <u>friend</u> again. He (19) <u>couldn't</u> be bothered with work now. He would rather play (20) <u>than</u> gather food. (21) <u>Then</u> the cricket and the ant each went (22) <u>their</u> own way—each proceeding in a different (23) <u>direction</u>. The ant continued to gather food, and the cricket had fun in the sun.

Soon it was the (24) <u>middle</u> of winter, and the cricket's cupboard was empty (25) <u>except</u> for a couple of crumbs. The cricket was very hungry and thought, "(26) <u>Maybe</u> I can borrow food from the ant." He trudged off to visit the ant. "For your (27) <u>information</u>," the wise ant told him, "food (28) <u>isn't</u> available for you in winter unless you spend the summer gathering it. You spent your summer singing, so now (29) <u>you're</u> going to spend your winter with an empty stomach." The ant is not quite sure if the cricket has learned a valuable lesson, but (30) <u>they're</u> still pals anyway.

Achievement Test 2

Can Bears Predict Earthquakes?

Early last spring I visited my (1) <u>friend</u>, Jake, and his family at (2) <u>their</u> vacation cabin in the (3) <u>middle</u> of a forest at the foot of a huge (4) <u>mountain</u>. Jake (5) <u>often</u> sees deer, elk, and even bears when they come out of hibernation late in the spring. We would have more (6) <u>than</u> (7) <u>enough</u> to do to keep us busy.

One morning Jake suggested, "Since (8) <u>it's</u> such a (9) <u>beautiful</u> day, (10) <u>let's</u> take a (11) <u>little</u> hike (12) <u>before</u> breakfast." He didn't have to (13) <u>ask</u> twice. I (14) <u>couldn't</u> wait to get started. We packed some (15) <u>necessary</u> items and headed in the (16) <u>direction</u> of the lake.

"Look over (17) <u>there</u>!" Jake exclaimed. "See the bears across the lake? This time of year (18) <u>they're</u> usually still hibernating. It (19) <u>isn't</u> normal for them to leave the den so soon." (20) <u>Then</u> Jake and I looked at each other and remembered (21) <u>information</u> we studied in school. We learned that in 1974 Alaskan bears came out of hibernation early. (22) <u>People</u> didn't know why. Shortly after, the worst earthquake in the state's history hit Alaska. (23) <u>Maybe</u> an earthquake was (24) <u>about</u> to happen. I'm not sure (25) <u>whose</u> legs (26) <u>were</u> shaking more, mine or Jake's!

We told Jake's mom (27) <u>where</u> we'd seen the bears and what we thought it meant. She (28) <u>said</u>, "Boys, (29) <u>you're</u> not going to convince me that bears can predict an earthquake—(30) <u>except</u>, perhaps, if we have one." We waited.

Achievement Test 3

The Shepherd Boy

Once a young shepherd tended his sheep at the foot of a (1) <u>mountain</u>. He knew that (2) <u>there</u> was (3) <u>enough</u> emerald green grass in every (4) <u>direction</u> to feed his flock. The shepherd liked everything (5) <u>about</u> his work (6) <u>except</u> for being alone. He (7) <u>often</u> wished he had a (8) <u>friend</u> with him. "I think (9) <u>it's</u> lonely up here," he (10) <u>said</u>.

(11) <u>Then</u> in the (12) <u>middle</u> of a (13) <u>beautiful</u> day, he had a brilliant idea. He rushed to the village and shouted, "Wolf, wolf! My sheep are in danger!" The startled (14) <u>people</u> certainly (15) <u>couldn't</u> continue (16) <u>their</u> work when it was (17) <u>necessary</u> to help the boy. By the time they arrived at the pasture (18) <u>where</u> the sheep grazed, the wolf was gone. "Indeed, (19) <u>you're</u> a lucky boy," they stated. "Just to make certain the wolf doesn't return, (20) <u>maybe</u> we should stay a (21) <u>little</u> while."

The shepherd liked the attention. He waited three days and repeated the trick. The villagers cried, "(22) <u>Isn't</u> that the shepherd? (23) <u>Let's</u> hurry to help him." They rushed to the shepherd (24) <u>whose</u> sheep (25) <u>were</u> in danger again, but they didn't see the wolf. Now they suspected that his (26) <u>information</u> was false.

Soon a wolf appeared. The boy cried, "Wolf, wolf!" even louder (27) <u>than</u> (28) <u>before</u>, but the villagers didn't pay attention. "When I need them most, (29) <u>they're</u> not helping," the shepherd lamented. The wolf had a good meal that day. The boy complained to the villagers, "All I did was (30) <u>ask</u> for help, and no one came." A wise man responded, "A liar will not be believed, even when he speaks the truth."

How are the tests checked and scored?

You or a designated adult can check the tests. The score for a test is the number of words misspelled or misused. The test words that require a capital letter should not be marked incorrect if the spelling is accurate, but the first letter is not capitalized. Score capitalization separately. Enter the number wrong in the appropriate boxes at the bottom of each test—spelling errors and capitalization errors.

The scores on these tests can be recorded for each student in a record book. Then file the tests in each student's assessment folder.

An analysis of the scores after giving the second and third tests in the series indicates students' individual achievement, the progress of a classroom, and the improvement of a school toward mastery of important words. Relative comparisons can be made using the results.

The most valid spelling assessment is based on students' writing. Yet, this format has limited use in achievement testing because of time constraints for scoring the tests. Nonetheless, the achievement tests provide legitimate scores on which to base judgments of progress.

A test of spelling in writing can complement the cloze story test. Select a question from among the three options for each test and ask students to write a response to it on another sheet of paper (see "What is the format of the tests?" on page 346).

Students' responses can be checked and scored by you or another adult. Mark any misspelled or misused Core Words identified for the grade level—words 1–675, or evaluate spelling and use of words within a high-frequency range, such as 1–100. Note the number of incorrect words. Then follow up by using the suggestions for the test results of the cloze-story section of the test (see above).

You may wish to use the Achievement Battery of Tests to compare the effectiveness of this program's methodology with another program. Administer the tests to students in both programs. For more thorough results, give students both the cloze-story format and the spelling-in-writing test.

At the end of the school year, compare the scores from the two groups. The results should identify which program is more effective, yet be aware that other factors can influence the scores. For example, the ability of the students in the two test groups may differ significantly enough to invalidate the outcomes. Further, the teachers' influence on spelling achievement, aside from the program used, may also contribute to erroneous results.

Knowing what spelling methods work better than others can help all educators make *every child a speller.*

What follow up is recommended with the test results?

Are the scores a valid test of achievement?

Is there a writing option in the Achievement Battery of Tests?

How are the spelling-in-writing tests checked and scored?

How can the effectiveness of this program's methodology be compared with another program?

Evaluating Spelling

What options are there to evaluate students' spelling growth?

This is your source for an overview of the extensive formal and informal options available to assess students' spelling progress. You can develop an assessment model that meets your evaluative needs from among several testing options in the program.

What purposes are served by evaluation in this program?

The purpose for each evaluation option in the Sourcebook Series is to maximize teaching and learning efficiency. In addition, the evaluations communicate to students that the reason they learn to spell is for writing, not for a single test. These objectives differ significantly from that of a customary spelling program.

What purposes are served by evaluation in a customary spelling program?

In a customary program, the evaluation, limited to a weekly Friday spelling test, culminates a spelling unit. Its primary purpose is to provide a means of grading students. Each unit repeats the process with a new set of words. This process serves to communicate to students that the reason they learn to spell is for a test. They study the words just prior to the test for the purpose of scoring well on the test.

This not only misleads students regarding the purpose for spelling, but results in short-term learning that handicaps students for spelling well in writing—a process that requires long-term mastery of words.

What change is necessary to improve students' spelling in writing?

Therefore, assessment must change. To reverse the short-term learning mind-set that definitively obstructs attaining spelling success in writing, evaluation that delivers long-term learning must replace the cause of the problem—the Friday Test. This program offers that opportunity.

How is a successful assessment model developed?

Develop your assessment model as a group to ensure uniformity. Construct your model from the options this program presents. Your model will build on an evaluation framework already in place in the infrastructure of the program.

What assessments should be administered to all students?

Your model should include three assessments to be administered to all students. First, assess students' writing—their ability to meet the minimum requirement for spelling Priority Words in everyday writing, as well as spelling any topical words identified for a particular assignment, page 331.

The next three assessments are the Word Test, the Skill Test, and the Proofreading Test. These tests are on a Review blackline master in Assess Words and Skills of each unit.

The Word Test, page 336, provides assessment of all previously introduced words in the program. This ongoing information maximizes teaching and learning efficiency, because the test is diagnostic—it identifies the words students have not learned and targets them for study with a personalized list of Spelling Words for every student. All words are recycled continuously so that retesting students' words occurs automatically through subsequent tests. The Skill Test, page 339, assesses essential spelling and language-related skills. The Proofreading Test, page 341, provides assessment and test-taking practice for spelling and editing skills.

What assessments are optional?

In addition to the required evaluation, there is potential for further measures using optional assessments.

First, the Sentence Dictation Test, page 342, in Assess Words and Skills of each unit is for students who need additional practice or challenge. Like the Word Test, it tests all current and previously introduced Core Words and is diagnostic. This test also assesses Extra Words and students' command of capitalization and punctuation.

Second, the Achievement Battery of Tests, page 346, a set of three blackline master tests, measures students' spelling progress three times during the school year.

Third, the no-reference write offers an alternative format for periodically assessing the Priority Words in students' everyday writing. This format disallows spelling references.

Fourth, to complement the Skill Test, students' performance on skill-building activities in Build Skills and Word Experiences of each unit offers insights into students' mastery level of the targeted skills. This continuous diagnostic information expedites the selection of subsequent skill-building activities to meet students' needs.

Your assessment model should specify the relative weight you want to place on the assessments you use. Each of the assessments in your model can contribute toward students' grades (see each assessment section for grading options).

How can the assessments grade student performance?

Once constructed, the evaluation procedures designated in your assessment model should be communicated to students and parents. Tell them what is important to learn and the procedures you'll use to determine the progress being made towards learning it. Tell students and parents what they can do to increase achievement, and provide feedback on that achievement. If grades are given, explain the grading system.

Should the assessment model be communicated to students and parents?

Constructive, ongoing evaluation routinely communicated to students and parents positively impacts spelling growth to help make *every child a speller*.

Challenging the Capable Speller

This is your source for ideas to challenge the most capable spellers—students whose spelling abilities surpass the basic program expectations at their grade level. These students:

Which students need to be challenged in spelling?

- complete skill-building activities successfully,
- always spell and use all of the required Priority Words correctly in their everyday writing,
- spell and use many words correctly in their everyday writing beyond the Priority Word expectation,
- score 100% on the Word Tests (without prestudying the test words),
- apply skills tested on the Skill Tests, and
- use a reference to spell topical words correctly.

Able students can be included in the instructional program with simple modifications to accommodate their needs. Following are suggestions to include students who need to be challenged.

Can able students be challenged in the regular spelling program?

Can able students be challenged with skill-building lessons?

The skill-building lessons in Build Skills and Word Experiences and the Cloze Story Skill Building Extensions in Assess Words and Skills range in difficulty so that students of all ability levels can participate productively. Select the most challenging activities for these able students. They particularly benefit from activities that focus on sorting words, multiple meanings, making hypotheses, and idiomatic usage. These activities occur routinely on your menu of activity choices.

You may wish to direct one part of an activity to the class. Then have the most able students follow up with another part of the activity as homework or as an independent project at school. On occasion, ask them to present their work to the class so that all students can benefit from the activity.

Can able students be challenged with assessments?

All students should take the Word Test in Assess Words and Skills. It is unusual for students to score 100% on the Word Test consistently—remember, students never prestudy the words in preparation for this test.

For students who need challenge beyond the Word Test, use the Sentence Dictation Test. This optional assessment in Assess Words and Skills is more challenging than the Word Test. The Sentence Dictation Test assesses more words; requires more listening and writing; and evaluates mechanics, including capitalization and punctuation. Further, there are Extra Words in every Sentence Dictation Test that may be used to challenge students.

To expedite administering the Sentence Dictation Test to a few students, ask a student to dictate the sentences. Then have students exchange papers and correct the tests using the CORE WORDS BLACKLINE MASTER, pages 363–365, for a spelling reference.

Can able students be challenged with more words for study?

Words students miss on either the Word Test or the Sentence Dictation Test are recorded on a copy of the WORDS TO LEARN BLACKLINE MASTER, page 375. There is also a section labeled *More Words for Super Spellers*. You, the student, or a parent may add words to this section to challenge the able learner. These words should have writing relevance. This individualized list of take-home challenge words goes beyond the basic spelling curriculum for the grade level. Ask parents to test this list of words at home periodically.

An at-school challenge list can be compiled to replicate and/or complement the at-home challenge list. Have students record challenge words in their Spelling Notebook. Students can assess each other on these words periodically.

Can able students be challenged with Priority Words?

The most capable students can be challenged with a Priority Word list that goes beyond the expectations of the class list. As words are added, the standard for spelling the words must not fall below 100%. The Priority Words are a minimum competency for spelling in everyday writing. Students should spell these words correctly in their everyday writing all of the time, not most of the time.

Can able students be challenged with an extended list of topical words?

The words temporarily added to students' Priority Word list for a particular assignment, called *topical words*, can also challenge able spellers. Increase the number of topical words for these students to extend their proofreading practice.

Can able students be challenged with proofreading and writing?

To extend students' proofreading beyond a bolstered Priority Word and topical word expectation, ask able students to assist other students as they proofread and revise their writing-as-a-process papers. Further, they could write and proofread projects that go beyond class assignments. For a motivational writing project, these students could work independently, with a teacher assistant, or with an older student to:

- publish a monthly news bulletin to parents
- write book reviews for a class "Recommended Reading" journal
- create books: jokes, riddles, kids' cooking, sequels to stories
- create a weekly comic strip
- write the lyrics to students' favorite songs
- take notes at class meetings and rewrite the minutes for the class record
- write a play and present it to the class
- make school posters on a timely topic, such as safety
- create spelling crossword or word-search puzzles for their classmates
- create a telephone directory for students
- write the rules to favorite games
- review movies or new TV shows
- develop a school or community *Who's Who?* with mini-biographies
- research and write an extension to a science or social studies lesson
- create an advice column
- make bookmarks, each with a famous saying
- keep an ongoing list of lost-and-found articles for school dissemination
- create a monthly class or school calendar
- compile word collections on a particular topic, such as things you would find on a dairy farm

As students engage in these projects or in writing projects of their own invention, they practice and perfect spelling and proofreading. The best way to improve spelling and proofreading is within writing.

Can able students be challenged with words from their writing?

Guide students in a process by which they accumulate words to learn from their writing. Then students can record these words independently on their WORDS TO LEARN sheet in the section labeled *More Words for Super Spellers* for take-home study and testing and/or record the words for at-school study in their Spelling Notebook. At school, students can review and test their words with a partner.

This process by which able students write extensively and accumulate and review words independently can be beneficial without burdening you. To challenge capable students effectively, provide the framework by which they learn to challenge themselves. You are their coach—coaching to make *every child a speller*.

Students with Spelling Challenges

This is your source for suggestions to meet the needs of students challenged by spelling. These are students who learn to spell more slowly than others, students for whom English is not their native language, and transfer students who initially lack spelling skills.

Who are students with special spelling challenges?

Spelling ability is not related to intelligence—all students can learn to spell. Some students have a greater propensity for spelling than others, but this is true of any ability. The Sourcebook Series offers all students an opportunity to become successful spellers.

Is spelling a skill that only some students can learn?

What are the readiness skills for spelling success?	There are prerequisites to spelling success. The first requirement is some facility with English, because spelling is a language skill. Language skills are learned developmentally. Stated simplistically, speaking the language is the first step in language development. Reading is the next step. Spelling can commence when students have mastered a basic reading vocabulary, have learned the names of the letters of the alphabet, can write each letter, and understand that these letters make words. If these requirements have not been satisfied, attempting to teach a learner to spell is inappropriate.

What are the readiness skills for spelling success?

There are prerequisites to spelling success. The first requirement is some facility with English, because spelling is a language skill. Language skills are learned developmentally. Stated simplistically, speaking the language is the first step in language development. Reading is the next step. Spelling can commence when students have mastered a basic reading vocabulary, have learned the names of the letters of the alphabet, can write each letter, and understand that these letters make words. If these requirements have not been satisfied, attempting to teach a learner to spell is inappropriate.

Which skills does research say are necessary for spelling success?

Basic contributors to spelling success are visual skills, the ability to remember what words look like, the application of phonics generalizations to spell words, and the use of analogous thinking to make words through spelling word patterns and other word forms. Students need to be taught strategies to spell and proofread words. They need many opportunities to work with words to learn about such things as homophones, apostrophes, and the most useful spelling rules—particularly for plurals and suffixes. Research supports a correlation between spelling success and time spent practicing these skills in writing.

These spelling and language-related experiences are the centerpiece of this program. They are experiences that students challenged by spelling need more of than students for whom spelling is easy.

Can students challenged by spelling be included in the regular spelling instruction?

Usually all students can be included in the same instructional program. However, students who cannot read all or some of the Core Words for the grade level should not be expected to perform fully within the formal spelling program. If these students receive spelling assistance, their instructional level can parallel their reading level. For example, the Level 5 Sourcebook would best accommodate students reading on the fifth grade level. Yet, with minor adaptations in instruction, students who read below this level can be included in nearly every aspect of the program.

How can students participate in the Word Preview if they cannot read all or some of the Core Words?

For example, when giving the Word Preview, page 316, prepare an activity sheet for which you use a highlighter to write in the Core Words to be written in the *write* column. Instead of writing the words, they trace the words. Then they rewrite the words in the *rewrite* column using the traced words as a model.

This can be adapted to students' abilities. Use a highlighter to write selected Core Words. They trace these words and spell the others. This serves to include them in the class activity and provides an opportunity to trace and learn to read the words.

How can students participate in the Word Preview if they can read the Core Words, but are challenged by copying a word from the chalkboard?

Modifications can also be made to the Word Preview for students who find it difficult to copy from the chalkboard. One modification is to pair these students with able learners. As these capable students write the words in the *rewrite* column of their paper, they say the name of each letter just audibly enough for their partner to hear. This provides an auditory cue that makes the activity far easier.

Another modification uses cards on which Core Words have been written. When the class is copying the word from the chalkboard, the challenged students copy the word from the word card.

These adjustments to the Word Preview should be accompanied by visual development, such as the activities labeled *visual skill building* in Seeds for Sowing Skills. Over time, modifications to the Word Preview can be phased out.

How can students challenged by spelling participate in the skill-building activities?

Students challenged by spelling benefit from abundant language experiences. The activities in this program are rich in language-integrated learning that contributes extensively toward this end.

Activities in Exercise Express and Seeds for Sowing Skills range in difficulty, and the skills targeted in the activities are recycled extensively. Therefore, select skills and activities that specifically meet the needs of these students.

Some direction or monitoring will be necessary for students who cannot work independently in order for them to benefit from these activities. You, an aide, or another student can provide assistance. In addition, participating in a cooperative group or observing the class discussion of these activities is productive for students challenged by spelling.

The inclusion of these learners in the skill-building activities labeled *relating to literature* should be a priority. A wide body of evidence clearly shows that experiences with literature are basic to the development of measurable growth in students' language skills. This suggests that revisiting the suggested books and follow-up activities, as well as experiences with other literature favorites, would be beneficial. Engage the students' parents, an older student, or an aide to read and reread the books to or with these learners. Make the follow-up activities shared ones between the mentor and the student.

For the Test Ready activity, the at-school activity may require some monitoring. The at-home activity on a Take-Home Task blackline master can be done both at school, with some assistance, and again at home with parental guidance for additional reinforcement.

Students challenged by spelling struggle with writing. To develop their writing and spelling skills, they benefit from both modeled writing (where you are responsible for the content and the actual writing) and guided writing (where you and the students construct the content, but you do the writing with spelling suggestions from students). When students write independently, accept all invented spellings in their writing until they have developed sufficient proficiency that they can participate in the Priority Word proofreading routine on page 331. Begin with only one or two Priority Words, even if the majority of the class is responsible for more.

Can students challenged by spelling participate in the Priority Word proofreading activities?

Writing-as-a-process papers require 100% spelling accuracy on the final copy. Meeting this standard is difficult for students challenged by spelling. You may wish to relax the expectation of a 100% error-free standard to one section of a writing piece. However, this would not result in a paper appropriate for "publishing."

Can students challenged by spelling participate in the writing-as-a-process papers?

Another option is to divide the task into doable portions until the entire paper is error-free. Work with only one small section of the paper at a time in brief work sessions.

Challenged students can participate in the Word Test, page 336, although modifications may be needed. If they cannot read English, use a highlighter to write all the test words in the blanks. Instead of writing the words, they trace the words as the test is given. This serves to include them in the class activity and provides an opportunity to trace and learn to read the words.

How can students challenged by spelling participate in the Word Test?

This modification can be adapted to students' abilities. Use a highlighter to write in selected words on their copy of the Word Test. They trace these words and spell the others. The words they are asked to spell are their test words. Choose the highest frequency words for test words, because they are more useful for writers than words with lower frequencies that occur less often in writing. The word frequencies are listed in the sidenotes next to the Word Test. The lower the number, the higher the frequency of the word.

Words misspelled on the Word Test, as with the other students, become students' Spelling Words for word study. This should not be a lengthy list, perhaps five or six words.

How can students challenged by spelling participate in the Skill Test?

If students need guidance with the Skill Test, provide help with the directions and expectations. If the test is still too challenging, elicit oral answers from them while other students are taking the test independently.

Can students challenged by spelling benefit from the Sentence Dictation Test?

The Sentence Dictation Test is more challenging than the Word Test. If students have difficulty with the Word Test, do not give them the Sentence Dictation Test. However, if their performance on the Word Test is acceptable, the additional practice the Sentence Dictation Test provides is beneficial. The more students are exposed to the words they need to learn, the more expedient the process of mastering them becomes.

Where should instruction begin for challenged spellers who receive special instruction complementary to the regular program?

Even though challenged spellers can benefit from most aspects of the regular spelling instruction, adjunct assistance can be helpful. For the special needs class, begin instruction at the grade level the students read. For example, if a student reads at approximately first grade level, the Sourcebook for Level One would be an appropriate place to begin. Learning on a level commensurate with a student's understanding and development is important for success.

How can motivation to learn to spell be increased among students challenged by spelling?

Some students challenged by spelling have learned "they can't spell." This message is delivered by frequent Friday Test failures in a program that equates spelling proficiency with an ability to memorize words for a test. This "disability" may be reinforced by classmates, parents, and ultimately a low spelling grade on a report card.

Whether students think they can spell, or whether they think they cannot spell—they're right. For this reason, this program offers multiple options to involve students productively in spelling and language-related learning. They learn on their level right along with the rest of the class. When students can participate productively and note their own personal progress and success, the message they receive is, "I can." There is nothing more motivating than success. The goal is to make *every child a speller*!

Suggestions for the Multiage Classrom

Does this methodology complement a multiage learning environment?

Multiage instructional units productively use this methodology because of its flexibility. Students who vary widely in spelling and language-related abilities can be accommodated with only minor modifications.

How can diverse learners be accommodated in the same level of the program?

Multiage students can be instructed in the same unit of the same level of the series, but their learning programs nonetheless reflect extensive diversity. To begin, select a teaching level in which the lowest performers are challenged. Then make modifications to meet all learners' needs.

For example, the Word Preview in the Build Skills and Word Experiences section can be made less challenging for students who have difficulty copying words from the chalkboard. The most sophisticated exercises in the Seeds for Sowing Skills can be selected for students who need a challenge, while the less difficult exercises can be reserved for students who are not yet ready for the most demanding tasks. Each concept is supported by activity options that range widely in difficulty. Because skills are systematically recycled, students who are initially challenged by a task grow with each exposure. This is true for each of the sections.

As these skill-building activities are utilized, students challenged by the level of difficulty usually require more direction. This can be provided by you, but able learners can often mentor students who need assistance—one of the benefits of multiage learning. This support allows you to divide your instructional time more equitably among all learners in the classroom.

In the Assess Words and Skills section of the unit, again the program flexibility allows for diversity. For example, the Word Test can be altered significantly to make it less demanding, while the Sentence Dictation Test can be reserved for students who would benefit from additional practice or more challenge.

As you implement the Priority Words, diversity can exist in the expectation for spelling accuracy, but not the standard set for spelling the words. All students should be afforded a Priority Word list for which 100% accuracy is the standard.

Specific ideas for modification can be gathered from Challenging the Capable Speller, page 351, and Students with Spelling Challenges, page 353. These sections explain the minor alterations necessary to make diverse learners comfortable and productive while learning in the same instructional unit.

What specific modifications are necessary to accommodate all learners in the same instructional unit?

In some cases, such as a three-year spread in the traditional grade levels for students in a multiage environment, you may need to use two levels of the program. Even then, the skills and concepts overlap so that many lessons can productively accommodate all learners.

Is it ever recommended that more than one level of the program be used in a multiage classroom?

This program provides an infrastructure for a spelling curriculum. With this scaffolding, you may build a program that accommodates a teaching and learning format that meets your needs and those of your students. You customize the program your way to make *every child a speller*.

Word Study Strategy

The Word Study Strategy is your source for teaching your students the five research-based steps to visualize a word to learn to spell it. The dominant modality of this procedure is visual, though other study strategies can be included in the procedure.

What is the Word Study Strategy?

It is common for writers to misspell words in writing that they clearly know how to spell. Their challenge is proofreading for these errors—observing the letters to recognize their errors. Therefore, the ability to see the sequential letters in words is essential to the spelling process. The Word Study Strategy strengthens the visual skills and provides a structured opportunity to apply them so that students can proofread their writing more effectively.

Why is the Word Study Strategy effective?

What are the five Word Study Strategy steps?	The five Word Study Strategy steps are:

The five Word Study Strategy steps are:

1. Read the word.
2. Spell the word—touch each letter and say its name.
3. Cover the word.
4. Print the word.
5. Proofread the word—touch each letter and say its name.

Why is it necessary to model the steps for students?

For students to use this Word Study Strategy effectively, the five steps need to be modeled. Demonstrating the process ensures that it is clear to students.

How is step one modeled?

To demonstrate step one, write a word for study on the chalkboard. Read the word aloud. Tell students that when they use the Word Study Strategy they may read the word aloud or silently. Then model how a learner can think about the word. Ask:

- Does this word look like another word I know?
- Does this word sound like another word I know?
- Is this word a homophone?
- Where have I seen this word before?

How is step two modeled?

In step two, spell the word aloud. Touch each letter with the point of the chalk as the letter name is said. Tell students that when they use the Word Study Strategy, they may spell the word aloud or silently. Then direct students' attention to further analyze the word by asking questions, such as:

- How many letters are in this word?
- Are there double letters?
- Is the word spelled the way it sounds?
- Are there silent letters?
- Do I see a spelling pattern in this word?
- Do I see a base word in this word?
- Is there an apostrophe in this word?
- Is this word spelled with a capital letter?
- How many tall letters do I see?
- How many tail letters do I see?
- Is there a jingle that helps to spell the word?
- Is there anything special about this word that would help to remember its spelling?

How is step three modeled?

For step three, demonstrate covering the word. Tell students they can cover the word with their hand or a sheet of paper. Next, ask:

- Can I picture the word in my mind's eye?

How is step four modeled?

Next, model step four. Demonstrate printing the word on the chalkboard. Tell students that you are picturing each letter in your mind's eye as you print the word.

How is step five modeled?

Last, demonstrate how to proofread the word. Uncover the original word. Tell students that to proofread the word, each letter is matched with the same letter in the original word. Show students how to touch each letter of the word and say its name as you match the letters. Point out how your eyes go back and forth from the original word to the word written for practice as the letters are matched.

Is it necessary for students to practice the steps after they are modeled?

Review the five steps. Then tell students it's their turn. Students should immediately practice the study steps to ensure their understanding of the process.

To learn to use this five-step strategy, have students practice the procedure using the WORD STUDY STRATEGY BLACKLINE MASTER, page 377. Make a copy for each student. With your guidance, have students practice the procedure. Your guidance and the framework of the blackline master will aid students as they learn to use this structured process.

Begin by having students write the word for study in the first column. Then have students practice the word in the second column using the five word-study steps listed on their copy of the blackline master. Next, students repeat the five word-study steps in the third column.

When students can use the structured WORD STUDY STRATEGY BLACKLINE MASTER to practice words effectively, the same process can be accomplished using regular writing paper.

Students can employ this strategy on any words needing practice. This includes words misspelled on the Word Test or the Sentence Dictation Test, in writing, or any words students want to learn. The WORD STUDY STRATEGY BLACKLINE MASTER can facilitate this word study practice at home and at school.

The strategy can be used independently, with a partner, or it can be a teacher-directed group activity. Students can use the strategy at home with a parent as a partner. Send home the IDEAS FOR WORD STUDY BLACKLINE MASTER, page 374, a letter to parents that provides suggestions for helping their child use the Word Study Strategy to learn important words.

Occasionally, review the five-step process at the chalkboard with a spelling word that challenges many students. Here you are practicing the spelling of a word, as well as reteaching the technique. Students can follow along by participating on paper at their desk. This is a powerful way to help make *every child a speller*.

Parents as Partners

This is your source for information to cultivate parental support for spelling study. Parents are an important influence on their child's ability to spell well. This program affords many opportunities for them to support your efforts in the spelling process. The potential for their participation in at-home spelling activities to complement the school program is extensive.

To secure support from the parents, two elements must be addressed. First, parents need to be aware of the methodology of the program so that they recognize and appreciate its benefits to their child. Second, parents need to be aware of the potential their involvement has in the spelling and language-related education of their child. To contribute toward this end, send home the parent letter, INTRODUCING SPELLING BLACKLINE MASTER, page 372. Further, invite them to view the Parent Introduction module of the Tutor Me Training CD-ROM series (see page 407).

Ongoing communication is essential to maintain parents' support. The program promotes this in numerous ways, including extensive opportunities for at-home skill-

Can students use regular writing paper to practice the Word Study Strategy?

When should students use the Word Study Strategy?

Is the strategy used independently?

Are there opportunities for parent-child partnerships for spelling?

How can parental support be secured?

How can parental support be maintained?

building and word-study practice supported by take-home blackline masters.

Many parents want to be involved—your obligation and that of the program is to provide opportunities for them to partake in spelling experiences with their child. Following are ideas to achieve this objective.

How can parents support the skills practiced in the Word Preview?

A Word Preview that parallels the at-school procedure can be administered by parents at home. If you wish to have parents work with their child using this procedure, first tell them the purpose of the activity—to help their child develop visual skills to allow them to see sequential letters in familiar words. Explain that these skills are necessary for spelling and proofreading success. Next, guide parents toward the selection of appropriate words for a Word Preview—familiar words with writing relevance that are well established in a child's reading vocabulary. Third, inform parents of the appropriate way to administer the Word Preview.

How can the Exercise Express activities be used for at-home practice?

Selected activities from Exercise Express can be designated for homework. After students have completed several of these tasks at school and are familiar with the expectation, assign selected activities for homework. Each of the six activities is on a blackline master, pages 378–383.

How can Seeds for Sowing Skills activities contribute to parent-child partnerships?

The skill-building activities in Seeds for Sowing Skills develop essential spelling and language-related concepts. All or parts of these activities can be assigned for homework. For example, students may gather words at home to provide examples for an at-school lesson. Often a lesson can be followed up with a homework assignment in which students apply the lesson information.

Seeds for Sowing Skills features Personal Posters on blackline masters, pages 367–371. These can be discussed and completed at school and then sent home.

How can parents be their child's partner with the Test Ready activities?

The Test Ready activities "ready" students for the skill tested in the Skill Test. The at-home activities, called Take-Home Tasks, are on blackline masters with complete instructions. Send these home to inform parents of essential skills their child is learning and to involve them in their child's practice of these skills.

How can the book tie-ins in the activities labeled *relating to literature* be complemented at home?

Many students have access to books in their home or community library. Some parents may wish to read books with their child that are targeted in the activities labeled *relating to literature*. For a complete list of the literature highlighted in the program, see page 397. This book list can be sent home with suggestions for obtaining the books (e.g., school library, community libraries, local bookstores, Internet websites).

Many of the read-aloud books are followed by a thinking/writing activity. This may be assigned for homework.

How can parents support Priority Word practice?

Parents can be allies in proofreading practice at home. Papers not marked for Priority Words at school can be sent home routinely. Send these papers home with a copy of the IDEAS FOR PROOFREADING BLACKLINE MASTER, page 373, that introduces this idea to parents. Also send home a list of the Priority Words. The complete list of Priority Words for this level is on the PRIORITY WORDS BLACKLINE MASTER, page 366. Identify the current Priority Words on this list by marking them before the master is duplicated or by highlighting the words with a colored marker on the copies of the master.

How can parents help their child practice Spelling Words?

The Word Test identifies the Spelling Words. The Spelling Words are the words each student misspells or misuses on the Word Test. Send home a copy of the WORDS TO LEARN

BLACKLINE MASTER, page 375, on which students have written their Spelling Words. You, the student, or a parent may add extra words to the WORDS TO LEARN sheet in the space provided for More Words for Super Spellers. Send it home with a copy of the IDEAS FOR WORD STUDY BLACKLINE MASTER, page 374, a letter to parents that provides suggestions for helping their child use the Word Study Strategy to learn these important words (see Word Study Strategy, page 357).

Test words are not prestudied for a Word Test so that a student's long-term memory of the Core Words can be assessed. Nonetheless, a complete list of the bank of Core Words from which the test words are selected for the Word Tests may be sent home. The CORE WORDS BLACKLINE MASTER, pages 363–365, lists these words in alphabetical order. It serves to inform parents of the words that will recur on their child's spelling tests throughout the school year.

Can parents have access to the words for testing?

Parents can also assist their child in completing the activities that follow the Word Test. Select activities from After the Cloze Story Word Test or the Cloze Story Skill-Building Extensions and send them home with the student's copy of the Review. Parents and child need the cloze story on the Review to do many of the follow-up Word Test activities. Make a copy of the Review for the student's assessment folder before you send it home.

How can parents follow up with the Word Test activities and the Skill Test?

To follow up with their child on the Skill Test, parents can review the test and the answers with their child.

Like the Word Test, the Sentence Dictation Test identifies each student's Spelling Words (see "How can parents help their child practice Spelling Words?" on page 360). The optional Sentence Dictation Test requires more writing than the Word Test, so the potential for more words identified for study is greater. Parents can provide guidance for their child in the study of these important words and assist their child with the Sentence Dictation follow-up writing activities suggested in After the Sentence Dictation Test.

How can parents support the Sentence Dictation Test?

The ongoing communications sent home to parents, such as the blackline master letters, the WORDS TO LEARN sheets, the Take-Home Tasks, and spelling homework assignments keep parents informed of spelling and builds rapport and interest. Yet, most parents usually want more than this. They want to know how their child is "scoring" in spelling. They want evaluation information.

How can parents be kept informed of student spelling performance?

Evaluative information can be shared with parents at conferences, school visits, or in progress reports. If there isn't a formal spelling grade on the progress report, parents often appreciate a written report or checklist indicating their child's spelling progress. This report, which can be developed cooperatively by teachers, sends the message to both parents and students: Spelling is important.

In addition to parents helping their child with spelling at home, parents may help at school. Parent volunteers can support the spelling curriculum in numerous ways. Following are fifteen suggestions.

What volunteer activities can parents do to assist with spelling at school?

- Give the Word Preview to students who were absent.
- Monitor students with their skill-building activities, such as those in Exercise Express, Seeds for Sowing Skills, and Test Ready.
- Check students' Word Tests, Skill Tests, and Sentence Dictation Tests.
- Assist students with their Word Test and Sentence Dictation follow-up activities.

- Assist students who are challenged by spelling as they write or proofread their work.
- Check papers for Priority Words.
- Check the spellings of words students write on their WORDS TO LEARN sheet.
- Check the spellings of words students write in their Spelling Notebook.
- Work with students to make word/letter cards or play spelling games.
- Guide students with the Word Study Strategy.
- Read books featured in activities with the skill labeled *relating to literature*.
- Make copies of spelling blackline masters.
- Practice the spelling and/or use of words with word cards.
- Guide students challenged by spelling with their blackline master Take-Home Task.
- Highlight or mark words to update students' Priority Words on their Spell Check cards or take-home copies of the PRIORITY WORDS BLACKLINE MASTER.

What alternatives are there when parents are not able to be involved?

The spelling program affords ample latitude for parent-child spelling partnerships. Your commitment to ongoing information and opportunities for parents to participate in their child's spelling education is essential whether or not parents exercise interest.

Few parents are simply not interested, but some parents have more time and facility for partaking in these activities.

Parents who are not native English speakers may be unable to offer their child much instructional assistance even though they would like to do so. For these families, communicate the power of an enthusiastic attitude directed toward their child's school program. The skills their child is learning can help all learners, making your school program one that fosters community adult literacy.

For families who do not offer support to their children, the burden falls on you. This means more of the learning and practice must take place in the classroom. Accommodate this responsibility by achieving all that you can within a reasonable time frame. What is not accomplished in one grade is taken on in the next. This program recycles skills and words so that each grade overlaps to reconcile different achievement and ability levels to make *every child a speller*.

Level Five Core Words

Words with Frequencies in Writing 1–675

* Denotes Core Words introduced in Level 5.

a	ask*	boy	come	eat
able	asked	bright*	common	edge*
about	at	bring	complete	eight*
above	away	brother*	copy*	either
across	baby*	brought	corner*	else
add	back	build	correct*	end
addition*	bad*	built	could	energy*
after	ball	business*	couldn't*	English
again	base*	but	country	enough
against	be	buy*	course	especially*
age*	beautiful	by	cover*	even
ago	became	called	cut	ever
ahead*	because	came	dark	every
air	become	can	day	everyone
all	bed*	cannot	dead*	everything
almost	been	can't	deep	example
alone	before	car	did	except*
along	began	care	didn't	explain*
already	begin	carefully	difference*	eye*
also	behind	carry	different	face
although	being	case*	difficult*	fact
always	below	cat*	direction*	fall
am	beside*	catch*	distance	family
American	best	caught*	do	famous*
among	better	center	does	far
amount*	between	certain	doesn't*	farm*
an	big	change	dog	fast
and	bird*	check	done	father
animal	bit*	child*	don't	feel
animals	black	children	door	feet
another	blood*	choose*	down	fell*
answer	blue	circle*	draw	felt
any	boat	city	dry	few
anything	body	class	during	field
are	book	clear*	each	figure*
area	both	close	early	finally
around	bottom	cold	earth	find
as	box	color*	easy	fine

fire	ground	I	length*	miss	on
first	group	ice	less	modern*	once
fish	grow	idea	let	moment*	one
five	guess*	if	letter	money	only
flat*	had	I'll	life	moon	open
floor	hair*	I'm	light	more	or
fly*	half	important	like	morning	order
follow	hand	in	line	most	other
food	happened	information*	list	mother	our
foot	happy*	inside	listen*	mountain*	out
for	hard	instead	little	mouth*	outside
force*	has	into	live	move	over
forest*	have	iron*	lived	much	own
form	he	is	living	music*	page
forward*	head	island*	long	must	pair*
found	hear	isn't*	longer	my	paper
four	heard	it	look	name	part
free*	heart	its	lost*	natural*	party*
friend	heat*	it's	lot*	near	past
from	heavy	itself	low	necessary*	pattern
front	held	I've*	machine*	need	pay*
full	help	job	made	never	people
fun*	her	just	main	new	perhaps
game	here	keep	make	next	period*
garden*	he's*	kept	man	night	person
gave	high	kind	many	no	picture
general*	him	knew	map	nor*	piece
get	himself	know	mark*	north*	place
girl	his	land	material*	not	plan*
give	history*	language	matter	note*	plane*
glass	hit*	large	may	nothing	plants
go	hold	last	maybe*	notice	play
going	home	late*	me	now	point
gold	horse	later	mean	number	poor
gone	hot	lay	measure*	object*	possible
good	hour	learn	meet*	ocean*	power
got	house	learned	men	of	practice*
government*	how	least	middle*	off	present*
grass*	however	leave	might	often	probably
great	huge*	leaves	milk*	oh	problem
green	human*	led*	mind	oil*	put
grew*	hundred	left	minute*	old	question

May be reproduced for classroom use. Sitton Spelling and Word Skills SOURCEBOOK 5 © Educators Publishing Service

quite	set	step*	they	usually	wish*
race*	seven*	still	thin*	various*	with
rain	several	stone*	thing	very	within
ran	shape*	stood	think	village*	without
rather*	she	stop	third	voice	woman*
reach*	shell	store*	this	wait*	won't*
read	ship	story	those	walked	wood*
reading	short	straight*	though	wall*	words
ready	should	strange*	thought	want	work
real	show	street*	thousand*	war*	world
really	shown	strong	three	warm	would
reason*	side	study	through	was	write
record*	sign*	subject*	thus*	wasn't*	wrong*
red	simple	such	time	watch	wrote*
region*	since	suddenly	tiny	water	year
remember	single*	summer	to	way	yellow*
rest	six	sun	today	we	yes
result*	size	suppose*	together	weather	yet
rich*	skin*	sure	told	week*	you
ride*	sky	surface	too	weight*	young
right	sleep*	system	took	well	your
river	small	table	top	we'll*	you're*
road	snow	tail*	toward	went	yourself*
rock	so	take	town	were	
room	soft*	talk	travel*	what	
round	soil*	tall	tree	when	
run	some	teacher*	trip*	where	
sad	someone	team*	trouble*	whether	
said	something	tell	true	which	
same	soon	temperature*	try	while	
sand*	sound	ten	turn	white	
sat	south*	test*	turned	who	
saw	space	than	two	whole	
say	speak*	that	under	whose*	
school	special	that's	understand	why	
sea	speed*	the	unit*	wide	
second	spring*	their	United States	wife*	
see	square*	them	until	wild	
seem*	stand	themselves	up	will	
seen	start	then	upon	wind	
sent*	state	there	us	window*	
sentence	stay	these	use	winter	

Level Five Priority Words

Words with Frequencies in Writing 1–100

A minimum proficiency for accurate spelling in all everyday writing.

a	is	them
about	it	then
after	its	there
all	just	these
an	know	they
and	like	they're
are	little	this
as	long	time
at	made	to
be	make	too
been	many	two
but	may	up
by	more	use
called	most	very
can	my	was
could	no	water
did	not	way
do	now	we
down	of	were
each	on	what
find	one	when
first	only	where
for	or	which
from	other	who
had	out	will
has	over	with
have	people	words
he	said	would
her	see	you
him	she	your
his	so	you're
how	some	
I	than	
if	that	
in	the	
into	their	

Pointers from the Proofreading Posse

1. Slow down, rein in. Whoa!
2. Corral one section of writing at a time to proofread.
3. Read your writing aloud—brand each word with the point of your pencil.
4. Look for—
   Priority Words and topical words—they're the first bunkhouse chore.
   Homophones—they're like barbed wire—watch out!
   Capitals and punctuation—round them up and check them out.
5. Lasso questionable words and look them up.
6. Rustle up a partner and proofread together.
7. Take one last look before you ride off into the sunset!

Proofreading Marks

Mark	Meaning	Example
≡	capitalization	the small turtle was sunning on the road.
↺	turn around	A car was driving down the raod.
/	make a lower case letter	Suddenly, the Turtle knew he was in danger.
∧	add something	He didn't want to leave his warm spot.
		crawl to He began to the other side.
.....	do not make correction	drove Soon the car raced on by.
~~word~~	change word	It He missed the turtle by inches.
⟲	spelling	The turtle breathed a sigh ov relief.
ℛ	take something out	He was relieved is because he was safe.

My "Bad Guys": _______________________________________

____

____

____

Word Popping

Some words are like popcorn—
From one kernel they pop!
They're bigger, they're stronger—
There are a lot!
With a few quick lessons and
Some practice, too,
Your words will explode and
Begin to accrue.
How do you do it?
Listen up and tune in.
A word-popping bonanza
Is about to begin!

I can "pop" words by adding
prefixes to base words.

I can "pop" words by adding
suffixes to base words.

Is a Prefix Unimportant?

Here is something you may not have heard.
In fact, it may be an unheard-of word.
The word is affix, and it means to attach,
Or to join with a word to make a new match.
An affix may join words in front or behind.
It can change what it's called, so keep this in mind.
If it comes at the start, it's a prefix you hear.
A suffix comes at the end, in the rear.
A prefix is little—the size of a flea.
But it's not unimportant, just take it from me.
Adding a prefix can change things a lot.
Just look at these prefixes that can mean not.

happy.....................................unhappy
stop ....nonstop
correct ....incorrect
possible.................................impossible
legal.....................................illegal
appear...................................disappear
regular..................................irregular

un: ____

non: ____

in: ____

im: ____

il: ____

dis: ____

ir: ____

Commonsense Strategies

Save yourself some major stress
By giving proper emphasis
To strategies that help you use
Words that frequently confuse.

· If it makes sense to say it is, use _______________. If not, use _______________.

· If it makes sense to say you are, use _______________. If not, use _______________.

· If it makes sense to say they are, use _______________. If it tells who it belongs to,

use _______________. Otherwise, use _______________.

· If it makes sense to say let us, use _______________. If not, use _______________.

· If it makes sense to say who is, use _______________. If not, use _______________.

The Homophone Challenge

Some words sound a lot alike—just take a look and see,
Write and right, except and accept, it's and its—do you agree?
Good advice for a writer is this—spell them painstakingly!

accept/except	hair/hare	right/rite/write
addition/edition	hear/here	road/rode/rowed
ant/aunt	heard/herd	role/roll
ate/eight	hi/high	sail/sale
bare/bear	him/hymn	scene/seen
base/bass	hole/whole	sea/see
be/bee	hour/our	seam/seem
beat/beet	it's/its	sew/so/sow
billed/build	knead/need	shone/shown
blew/blue	knew/new	side/sighed
brake/break	knight/night	some/sum
buy/by/bye	knot/not	son/sun
caught/cot	know/no	stairs/stares
cell/sell	knows/nose	steal/steel
cent/scent/sent	lead/led	straight/strait
cents/scents/sense	let's/lets	tail/tale
chews/choose	made/maid	their/there/they're
cite/sight/site	main/Maine/mane	theirs/there's
close/clothes	meat/meet	threw/through
coarse/course	might/mite	to/too/two
cymbal/symbol	oar/or/ore	vary/very
dear/deer	one/won	wait/weight
desert/dessert	pair/pare/pear	war/wore
dew/do/due	passed/past	ware/wear/where
die/dye	peace/piece	way/weigh
ewe/yew/you	plain/plane	weak/week
eye/I	principal/principle	weather/whether
find/fined	rain/reign/rein	which/witch
flour/flower	read/red	who's/whose
for/fore/four	read/reed	wood/would
groan/grown	real/reel	you're/your

I can find and write more homophones.

____

____

____

____

Dear Parents,

Your child's spelling program may be different from what you've come to expect as "spelling." Instead of weekly lists of words to memorize, this program emphasizes the learning of important words, not for a Friday Test, but for a lifetime of spelling in the real world—that is, spelling correctly in writing.

This lifelong spelling ability grows over time. It grows through skills instruction (phonics, word origins, spelling rules, usage, etc.), through your child's everyday writing, and through word study on specific words your child has not yet mastered. You can extend this teaching into your home.

Prepare now for your child's at-home spelling experiences by identifying a special place, such as a file folder or box, in which to keep the materials we'll send home for your parent-child partnership opportunities.

To help your child learn and use essential skills:

- **TAKE-HOME TASKS** will be sent home regularly. They are skill-building activity sheets for you and your child to do together. These tasks will complement the skills we're working on at school.

- **SKILL-BUILDING EXERCISES** are homework activities for you and your child to do to prepare for or follow up on our class lessons.

To help your child spell and use essential words:

- **PAPERS FOR PROOFREADING** will come home often. You see, your child will be expected to spell some words correctly all the time to meet the minimum requirement for spelling in everyday writing. These words are called Priority Words. They are the words that occur most frequently in writing. As your child proofreads for these words, s/he will practice the skills for proofreading any word. You and your child will be kept informed of this list of words that will grow throughout the year.

  Along with the first papers for proofreading, we'll send home ideas for you to use as you and your child proofread these papers together.

- **WORDS TO LEARN** is a list of Spelling Words your child has not yet mastered. We'll identify these words and send them home. Help your child study these words every other day or so to master them once and for all. That's our goal.

  With the first Words to Learn sheet, we'll send home ideas for you and your child to do together to learn these words.

Let's make your child's spelling growth a team effort—you, your child, and all of us here at school. We can work together to make your child a speller!

Dear Parents,

Here are papers for proofreading.

Your child is learning to spell and proofread. These two skills go hand in hand. Learning to spell a word is the first step, but a word is not considered mastered unless your child can spell the word correctly in writing. The second step—proofreading—is the real test of spelling ability. You see, in the "real world," spelling is judged by how words are spelled in writing. For this reason, it's important that your child understands that spelling words correctly in writing is a habit needed for a lifetime.

Some of the writing your child does at school is revised until there are no more errors. This is a strenuous task, so not all of your child's writing goes through this revision process. However, to become a good writer and speller, your child needs to write daily. In this everyday writing, approximations of spellings are accepted for a few words. Then, as your child's writing develops over time, these approximated spellings are no longer acceptable.

The words your child is expected to spell correctly all the time are called Priority Words. Sometimes they're referred to as "no excuses" words—there is no excuse for misspelling them! Your child has a list of Priority Words, and time is provided to proofread for them. To see that the Priority Words are spelled accurately, your child's writing is checked routinely.

You can help at home. These papers have not been marked for Priority Words. You and your child can proofread the papers together. Proofread for the Priority Words first. Note your child's current Priority Words on the "No Excuses" list.

Here are tips for making this proofreading activity worthwhile:

- Choose a quiet place to work together.
- Sit next to your child with the paper to be proofread.
- Have your child read the first sentence aloud to you.
- Ask your child to identify the Priority Word(s) in the sentence.
- Have your child match their word, letter by letter, with the word on the Priority Word list.
- Have your child rewrite the word in the sentence, if necessary.
- Continue with the rest of the sentences.
- Remember to compliment your child's efforts!

Here are other proofreading activities to do with your child:

- For misspelled words in your child's writing that are not Priority Words, put a dot in the margin next to a line that has a misspelled word. Put two dots if there are two misspelled words, and so forth. Ask your child to identify the misspelled word(s). Then ask your child to anticipate how each misspelled word should be spelled by attempting to write the word again on scratch paper. If necessary, provide the correct spelling. Then have your child correct the misspelled word.

- Print a word familiar to your child—one your child can read easily. Ask your child if the word is spelled correctly. Occasionally, misspell a word. Then have your child rewrite it correctly.

- Be on the lookout with your child for examples of spelling errors in print material—newspapers, signs, advertising brochures. Gather examples of "commercial spellings," such as *lite* foods and *brite* detergents.

Thank you, parents!

Dear Parents,

Here is your child's Words to Learn list.

These words are basic words your child does not yet
know. They are important words for your child to learn for
everyday writing. Help your child learn these words so that
s/he can spell them, not just for a test, but for a lifetime.
Use the following ideas for word study.

Guide your child through these five word-study steps
recommended by spelling research. Have your child:

- Read the word.
- Spell the word—touch each letter and say its name.
- Cover the word.
- Print the word.
- Proofread the word—touch each letter and say its name.

Make your study sessions brief. Be positive. Praise your child for the effort that is made. Then, during the next
several days, have your child write the words studied. If your child can spell the words each time you ask, you've
made progress! Words misspelled can be restudied using the five word-study steps.

For those words that your child spells correctly, but misuses (e.g., *there*, *their*, and *they're*), work with your child
on their correct use.

At school, we'll revisit the words on your child's Words to Learn list frequently to note the progress your child
is making toward their long-term mastery. Over time, your child will master these and many other words for a
lifetime. Your at-home word study with your child will make it easier for your child to reach this goal.

Thank you for your help.

Every child a speller!

Words to Learn

These are words your child has not yet learned. Use IDEAS FOR WORD STUDY to help your child learn these important words, not just for a test, but forever.

More Words for Super Spellers

These words go beyond the basics. You or your child may wish to add words here.

Name _______________________________

Word Preview

Print the words.   Print the words again.

_________________   _________________

_________________   _________________

_________________   _________________

_________________   _________________

_________________   _________________

Name ____

Word Study Strategy

Write the words for study. Then practice the words for study two times.
Follow these steps.

READ—Look at each letter of the word.
SPELL—Say the name of each letter of the word.
COVER—Cover the word so you cannot see it.
PRINT—Print the word neatly.
PROOFREAD—Check each letter of the word.

Words for Study	Practice	Practice

Stretch It

Add words to make
this sentence longer
and better.

Name _______________________________

Name ___________________________

SORT IT

Sort these words
in some way.

Name

ADD IT

How are these words alike? Add more.

Name ________________________________

FINISH IT

Finish the sentence.
Then tell more.

Name _______________________________

FIND IT

Find and write
the words.

Make Word Cards

Make Letter Cards

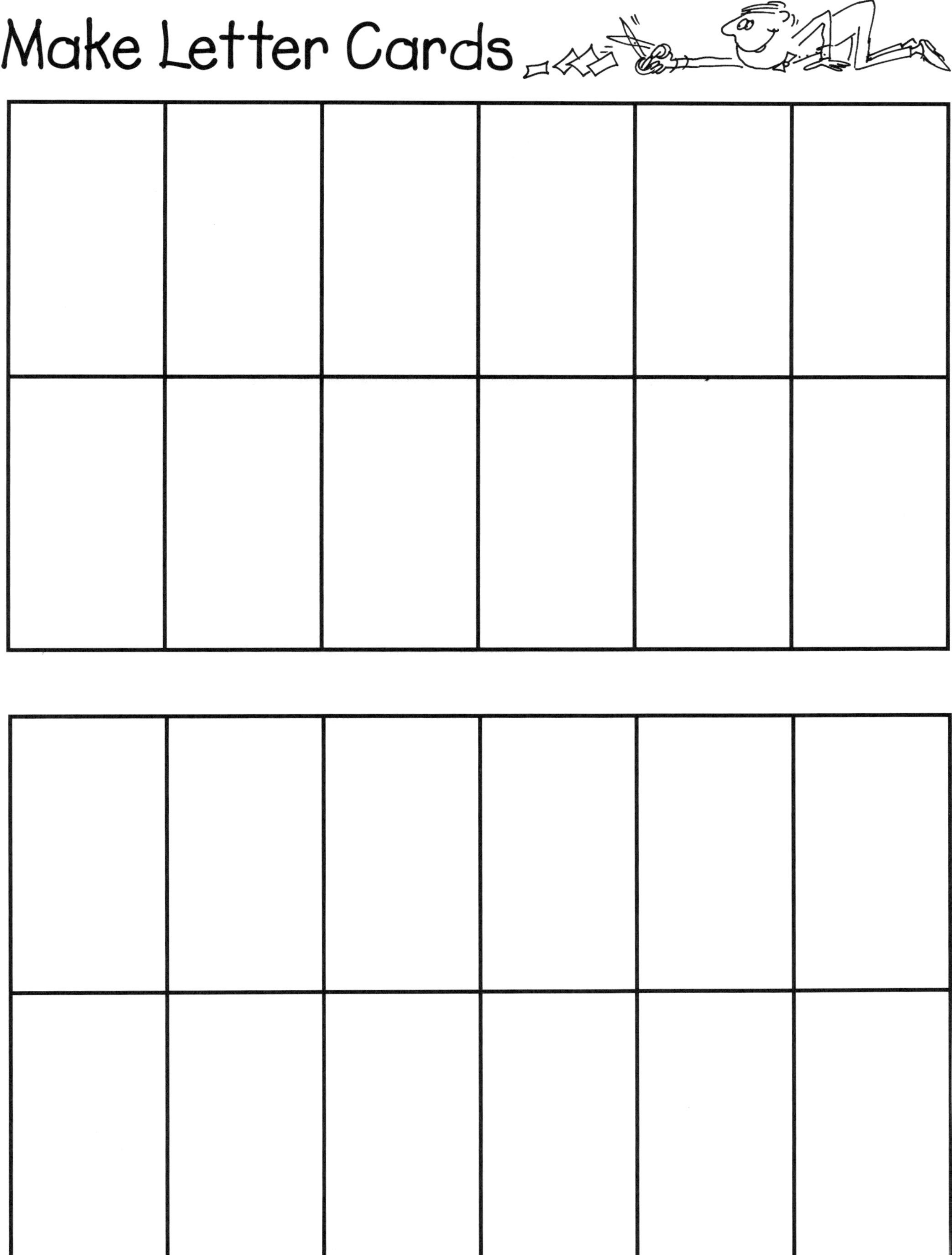

The Cricket and the Ant

A story (1) _______________ read long (2) _______________ your grand-parents

(3) _______________ born was (4) _______________ a cricket and a (5) _______________

___ ant. On a (6) _______________ summer day, the cricket (7) _______________ to

the ant, "My, (8) _______________ a wonderful day! (9) _______________ head over

(10) _______________ to the base of the (11) _______________. That's (12) _______________

we can sing and dance." The ant had heard the cricket's appeal (13) _______________. However,

he declined the invitation once again, because he knew it was (14) _______________ to gather

food in the summer so he would have (15) _______________ to eat during the long, cold winter.

The cricket, (16) _______________ goal was to enjoy life, didn't (17) _______________ his

(18) _______________ again. He (19) _______________ be bothered with work now. He

would rather play (20) _______________ gather food. (21) _______________ the cricket

and the ant each went (22) _______________ own way—each proceeding in a different

(23) _______________. The ant continued to gather food, and the cricket had fun in the sun.

Soon it was the (24) _______________ of winter, and the cricket's cupboard was empty

(25) _______________ for a couple of crumbs. The cricket was very hungry and thought,

"(26) _______________ I can borrow food from the ant." He trudged off to visit the ant.

"For your (27) _______________," the wise ant told him, "food (28) _______________

available for you in winter unless you spend the summer gathering it. You spent your summer

singing, so now (29) _______________ going to spend your winter with an empty stomach."

The ant is not quite sure if the cricket has learned a valuable lesson, but (30) _______________ still

pals anyway.

Spelling errors ☐   Capitalization errors ☐

Name _______________________________________

Can Bears Predict Earthquakes?

Early last spring I visited my (1) _____________________, Jake, and his family at

(2) _____________________ vacation cabin in the (3) _____________________ of a forest at the

foot of a huge (4) _____________________. Jake (5) _____________________ sees deer, elk, and

even bears when they come out of hibernation late in the spring. We would have more

(6) _____________________ (7) _____________________ to do to keep us busy.

One morning Jake suggested, "Since (8) _____________________ such a (9) _____________________

day, (10) _____________________ take a (11) _____________________ hike (12) _____________________

breakfast." He didn't have to (13) _____________________ twice. I (14) _____________________

wait to get started. We packed some (15) _____________________ items and headed in the

(16) _____________________ of the lake.

"Look over (17) _____________________!" Jake exclaimed. "See the bears across the lake?

This time of year (18) _____________________ usually still hibernating. It (19) _____________________

normal for them to leave the den so soon." (20) _____________________ Jake and I looked at

each other and remembered (21) _____________________ we studied in school. We learned that in

1974 Alaskan bears came out of hibernation early. (22) _____________________ didn't know why.

Shortly after, the worst earthquake in the state's history hit Alaska. (23) _____________________

an earthquake was (24) _____________________ to happen. I'm not sure (25) _____________________

legs (26) _____________________ shaking more, mine or Jake's!

We told Jake's mom (27) _____________________ we'd seen the bears and what we thought it

meant. She (28) _____________________, "Boys, (29) _____________________ not going to convince

me that bears can predict an earthquake—(30) _____________________, perhaps, if we have one."

We waited.

Spelling errors ☐   Capitalization errors ☐

Name ____

The Shepherd Boy

Once a young shepherd tended his sheep at the foot of a (1) _________________. He knew that (2) _________________ was (3) _________________ emerald green grass in every (4) _________________ to feed his flock. The shepherd liked everything (5) _________________ his work (6) _________________ for being alone. He (7) _________________ wished he had a (8) _________________ with him. "I think (9) _________________ lonely up here," he (10) _________________.

(11) _________________ in the (12) _________________ of a (13) _________________ day, he had a brilliant idea. He rushed to the village and shouted, "Wolf, wolf! My sheep are in danger!" The startled (14) _________________ certainly (15) _________________ continue (16) _________________ work when it was (17) _________________ to help the boy. By the time they arrived at the pasture (18) _________________ the sheep grazed, the wolf was gone. "Indeed, (19) _________________ a lucky boy," they stated. "Just to make certain the wolf doesn't return, (20) _________________ we should stay a (21) _________________ while."

The shepherd liked the attention. He waited three days and repeated the trick. The villagers cried, "(22) _________________ that the shepherd? (23) _________________ hurry to help him." They rushed to the shepherd (24) _________________ sheep (25) _________________ in danger again, but they didn't see the wolf. Now they suspected that his (26) _________________ was false.

Soon a wolf appeared. The boy cried, "Wolf, wolf!" even louder (27) _________________ (28) _________________, but the villagers didn't pay attention. "When I need them most, (29) _________________ not helping," the shepherd lamented. The wolf had a good meal that day. The boy complained to the villagers, "All I did was (30) _________________ for help, and no one came." A wise man responded, "A liar will not be believed, even when he speaks the truth."

Spelling errors ☐   Capitalization errors ☐

Practice Books

The Practice Books are optional personal student booklets, a practice and word exploration complement to selected Sourcebook lessons. Further, there are pages for students to record words for study, called the Spelling Notebook. The Practice Books can be a Sourcebook accessory used by just some teachers, or by all teachers in a school for regular or Special Education.

The Practice Books can be used with either the Second Edition or this edition, the Third Edition, of the program. They are available for grades 1–6. For this level, Level 5, there are three pages for each unit: two tie-ins to specific unit activities and one proofreading and editing exercise. A teacher resource accompanies the Practice Books that includes answers to all activities.

The Practice Book activities selected for each unit's additional practice and word exploration reflect the essential skills and concepts targeted in that unit. Overall, the Practice Books reflect a focus on every essential skill and concept introduced at that grade. Rules and strategies are highlighted. Coupled with the word collections and language discoveries students make as they complete the activities, a synopsis of important fifth grade information is created by year's end. In the Third Edition, specific activity tie-ins are indicated in each unit on pencils:

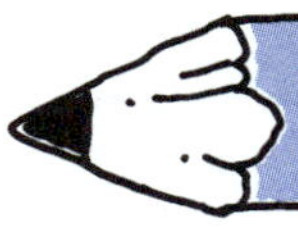

Use Student Practice Pages 1–2 to follow up instruction for:
Activity 1A • Activity 1B

- Spelling Words (words missed on tests) are recorded in the Spelling Notebook.
- Use Proof It, Practice Page 3, for proofreading/editing practice.

For teachers using the Practice Books with the Second Edition of the Sourcebook Series, the teacher resource that accompanies the Practice Books includes a table to indicate each unit's Practice Pages tie-ins.

The Practice Books could be used at home by parents with their children to supplement ongoing in-class work—a homework activity book. Some teachers may find it expedient to indicate on the school/classroom web site which Practice Pages are assigned. If the Practice Books are kept and completed solely at home, later the follow-up answers to the activities could be posted on the web for parent-child self-checking. The Practice Books could be used as summer vacation parent-child activities. This would provide a complete review of all essential skills, strategies, and concepts in preparation for the next school year. Summer school programs would benefit by the organized package of motivational language learnings the Practice Books offer at each grade level. Appropriate Practice Books could be selected for instruction to match the developmental levels of the students in the program. Further, the Practice Books would afford these same benefits for Special Education work.

Games and Productive Practice Ideas

This is your source for enlivening <u>any</u> unit with word experiences.

idea 1 — RESCUE THE RABBIT

Pixie Holbrook, a veteran teacher, says this is her students' all-time favorite spelling game! She calls it "Rescue the Rabbit."

The game begins with Pixie drawing a cartoon rabbit on the chalkboard as students watch. "This," she says, "is my friend Fred." Letter blanks are drawn under the rabbit to represent the letters in the word to be spelled. Students take turns guessing the letters. Pixie reminds her students that every word has at least one vowel to encourage them to begin by selecting vowel letters.

With each incorrect guess, a small part of Fred is erased, such as one floppy ear or one of his two big teeth. Students gasp as Fred slowly disappears, one little bit at a time. Then when the word has been discovered, the winning student steps up to the chalkboard and "rescues" the rabbit by redrawing the missing parts. Students must be careful to remember all the details as Fred is redrawn. Then play continues with another word.

idea 2 — LETTER CARD ACTIVITIES

To complement the Letter Card Lessons in Units 6, 13, 17, 22, 24, 27, and 33, the LETTER CARD BLACKLINE MASTER, page 385, can be used to make a set of letters for your students. Make a copy of the blackline master, print the letters you wish the students to have, then make sufficient copies for your students. Have students cut out the letters. Letter sets can be stored in labeled envelopes.

One way the letter cards can be used is as a class or small-group activity. You may wish to provide students with identical letter sets. Using this option, each child makes the same word. For example, say, "Make the word *friend*." Students respond. Then, write *friend* on the chalkboard for students to self-check.

Next, ask students to make *friendly*, then *unfriendly*. Each time, provide a chalkboard reference for students to self-check.

As an alternative group activity, you may wish to make several letter sets, each different, with enough vowels and consonants to make a variety of words. Using this option, say, "Who

can make the word *beautiful?*" Students assess their letters and respond. Then *beautiful* is written on the chalkboard for students to see.

Letter cards can also be used independently by students. Students manipulate their letters to make words. Then they write each word on a sheet of paper after they make it. The result is a list of words they made from their letters. This format works well with students working cooperatively in small groups to make as many words as they can within a given time. The team with the most words wins.

The letter cards can complement a Language Arts "center"—one activity among several that build language skills.

Encourage students to use letter cards to practice making words at home or at school. A set of letters can be sent home to encourage parent-child learning partnerships.

idea 3 — WORD CARD ACTIVITIES

The WORD CARD BLACKLINE MASTER, page 384, can be used to practice spelling specific words or to make sentences using words. Make a copy of the blackline master, print the words on the word cards that you want the students to have, then make sufficient copies for your students. Have students cut out the word cards. Word card sets can be stored in envelopes that are labeled with the words inside.

Word card sets can be varied. For example, make word card sets that reflect spelling patterns (e.g., fan, man, pan), a single beginning letter (e.g., bat, ball, boy), an ending sound (e.g., last, best, most), frequent spelling patterns for a long vowel sound (e.g., /ā/: day, train, name), or words that together can form a sentence or sentences (e.g., I love you).

Activities with the word cards may include students

- looking at a word, turning it face down, writing the word, and checking it.
- sorting the words and writing the words in the sorted categories.
- alphabetizing the words and writing the alphabetized list.
- choosing two of the words to write in the same sentence.
- making sentences using the words, then writing the sentences.

Students can use word cards for practice at home or at school. Blank word cards can be sent home so parents can help their child make and study words, such as the words that are on their child's WORDS TO LEARN sheet (see page 375).

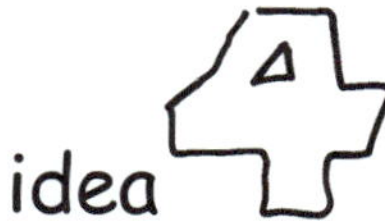

idea 4 — AT THE RACES

Bonnie McClelland's Indiana students like this spelling game. Bonnie makes racetracks by cutting four long construction paper strips of equal length, each a different color. She divides each track into spaces so that each track has fifteen or so spaces of various lengths. The racetracks are placed on a bulletin board.

The class is divided into four teams. Each team is identified by the color of its track. Teams make a paper race car and pin it just outside the first space on their track. Play begins with a "driver" from each team coming forward to sit in a "driver's seat"—desks used for this purpose. Then they are asked to write a word. Bonnie uses small chalkboards or paper for this activity. She also expects each member of the "pit crew"—the other members of each team—to write the word. Then she writes the word on the chalkboard. Students check their work. Each driver who spells the word correctly may advance his or her team's race car one space. The race continues, sometimes over several days. The first team to the finish line-wins!

idea 5 — GRID ACTIVITIES

Use graph paper to build visual skills or to make word games. For visual skill building, write the words for practice on the chalkboard or in a list on a word card provided to students. Students write the words in the boxes with tall letters and tail letters using two vertical spaces. Then they outline the word to accentuate its shape. As an alternative, make word shapes on the chalkboard or on a word card provided to students. Then students write words on their grid sheet that match the shape.

Students can make word games on the grid. To make a word search game, students write words left-to-right or top-to-bottom on their grid sheet. Then they fill the empty boxes with random letters. Some students could be challenged to make crossword puzzles using the grid sheet.

The grid format can be used for Word Stairs. Students begin with a single letter, with each successive word using the letters from the previous word plus on more letter.

idea 6 — MODIFIED SPELLING BEE

Dan Andersen modified the spelling bee so that his students who needed the practice most would not be eliminated from play, as is the case with the customary version. Dan begins by writing words he wants to reinforce on small word cards with a context sentence on the back to confirm the meaning of the words, about twice as many cards as players. Then he

divides his class into two teams of equal spelling ability.

The first player on the starting team selects a card, calls out the word, and reads it in the context sentence. The first player on the opposite team goes to the chalkboard and writes the word. Using the touch-each-letter procedure of the Word Preview, the players check the spelling. If the word is spelled correctly, the word card is eliminated from the game. If the word is misspelled, it is written correctly, erased, and the word card is returned to the pile.

Players are never eliminated from Dan's game, only word cards. The first team to eliminate the opposite team's cards wins!

idea 7 — WORD GAMES

Have students—

Write words that begin and end with the same letter, working through the alphabet (e.g., arena, bomb, comic, depend, edge). Vary the game by requiring that the words be only nouns or only verbs—then students make the nouns plural and add a suffix or prefix to each verb.

Write words that begin and end with consecutive letters (e.g., Arab, basic, compared, describe).

Write words in which the same letter occurs twice, but not together (e.g., bicycle, engage, civil, system, practice).

Write words with five or more letters that use only half the alphabet (e.g., hiked, blade, rusty, worst).

Write sentences that use at least ten words beginning with the same letter (e.g., Eleven enormous elephants enjoy eating extensive edibles every evening, expecting extra energy.)

Write sentences that use consecutive letters (e.g., Like many nice, old places, quaint Roville sells the usual varied ware.)

idea 8 — CATEGORIES

Tom Barsch makes a category game for his students each week. On Friday, students' responses are shared. His categories vary and incorporate current areas of study. The letters along the top can vary, too.

	T	A	B	L	E
animals	tiger	anteater	baboon	lion	elephant
flowers	thistle	aster	bluebell	lupin	edelweiss
authors	Taylor	Aardema	Byars	L'Engle	Emberley
CA cities	Tulare	Aptos	Bakersfield	Los Angeles	Escondido
food	tomato	apple	bread	lettuce	egg

idea 9 — PIGEONHOLE

This game is named for the word that originally was a desk with rectangular compartments that looked like holes in a pigeon roost in which papers were filed. The pigeon-hole desk became an antique, but its name lives on as a verb that means to organize and classify.

To play Pigeonhole, organize students into groups. Each student needs paper and pencil and each group needs a transparency and a pen. Dictate about fifteen words for students to write. Then each group sorts the words in some way on their transparency within the time limit (about three minutes). At the end of the time, words not sorted are automatically in the "pigeonhole." The class checks each group's work by projecting the transparency on the wall or screen with an overhead projector. Words inappropriately sorted or spelled incorrectly also go in the "pigeonhole." Each team's score is the number of words sorted, minus the number of words in the "pigeonhole."

idea 10 — WORDS WITHIN WORDS

Give students a long word. They list all the words they can make using the word's letters. A variation of this game uses a nine-letter word written inside a tic-tac-toe grid. Students make words moving from letter to letter across, up, down, or diagonally, using letters only once. For example, from *generally*, words students may make include

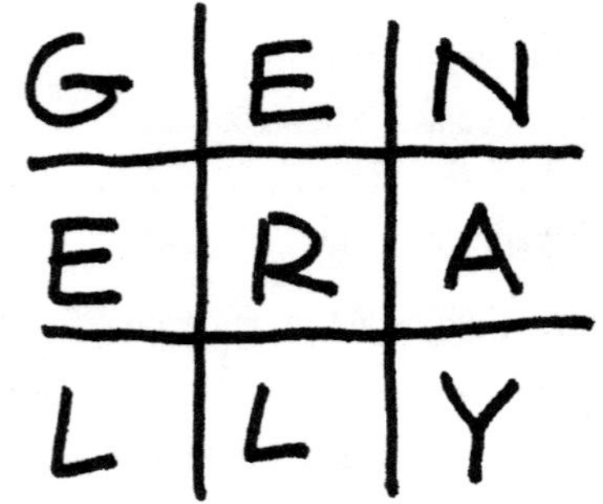

all, are, ear, earl, early, earn, eel, era, gear, green, lane, large, lay, leg, near, nearly, ran, ray, real, yarn.

idea 11 — $10,000.00 WORD GAME

Tracey Yates says this is a favorite in her classroom. First, she makes copies of the WORD CARD BLACKLINE MASTER, page 384, on which she writes about eight words for each of four categories worth the points indicated.

1 point   Priority Words (words expected to be spelled correctly in everyday writing)

2 points   Core Words (any word introduced so far in the program)

3 points   Homophones (any set of homophones)

4 points $10,000.00 Words (challenging words, perhaps from the content areas)

These words are placed in four sacks labeled with the category. She divides her students into two teams. The first player, the Speller, goes to the chalkboard and selects a category. The next player to be the Speller on that team draws a card from the sack and uses it in a sentence for the Speller to spell. If correct, the team earns the point(s). Then the next team sends a Speller to the chalkboard. Play continues until everyone has a turn. The team with the most points wins!

A variation is to omit the word from the sentence as it's said. The speller must guess the word, as well as spell it. Three sentences may be offered to identify the missing word.

On occasion, Tracey has her students write the words for the categories in preparation for play.

idea 12 — SPARKLE

Sometimes this game is called "Typewriter." Whatever its name, students ask to play again and again! The whole class can play at once, small groups can play simultaneously, or one group of students can be selected to play as the class observes. The teacher initiates play by saying a word to be spelled. The first student says the first letter, the second student says the second letter, and so on until the word is spelled. Then the next student says, "Sparkle," and the next student is OUT! Another way to be ousted is to spell the wrong letter. Play continues until one winner remains!

idea 13 — HEADS AND TAILS

The first player writes a word on the chalkboard. Each player in turn writes a word that begins with the ending letter of the previous word. The game continues until someone is unable to think of a word or spells the word incorrectly.

idea 14 — WORD IN YOUR POCKET

Betty Gilla reinforces homophones with this game. She asks her students to wear something with pockets on the day of the game. She makes copies of the Word Card Blackline Master, page 384, has students cut out the cards, and distributes two cards to each student. A homophone set is discussed, such as *least* and *leased*. She asks students to write one homophone on each of their word cards. Then she tells them to place least in their left pocket and leased in their right. Throughout the day—in class, at lunch, at recess—she asks them questions, such as:

- If you "leased" an apartment, in which pocket do you have that word?

- When it's the "least you can do," in which pocket do you have that word?

idea 15 — BE QUICK!

To play this game, students use their Spell Check cards or a copy of the Core Words Blackline Master, page 363. Tell students, or student teams, to find and write words that meet a criterion. For example:

- words to which a suffix can be added—then add it

- nouns—then make them plural

- homophones—then write each word's partner(s)

- seven words to make into one sentence

- words for which the beginning letter or the ending letter can be changed to make a new word (main/gain, easy/east)

To begin, state the criterion. Students look at their words for a moment. Then say, "On your mark, get set, be quick!" Time the session. Then have students share their words with a partner.

idea 16 — CAPTURE

Livingston, Montana, teachers created this game. Teachers divide their class into two teams. A player from each team goes to the "mountain" (desks with paper and pencil). Then the teacher says a word, both players write the word, and they stand when they finish. If the first player to stand has spelled the word correctly s/he "captures" the other player. If the word is spelled incorrectly, the other player's word is checked and, if correct, that player makes the "capture." The object is to capture players to your side.

idea 17 — GO FIGURE

This game of word-making strategies begins by telling students you're thinking of a three-letter mystery word. Students guess the word. If the word guessed contains one letter in the same position as that letter in the mystery word, say "One—go figure!" If it contains two letters in the same position, say "Two—go figure!" And so on until the word is guessed, when you say, "You figured!"

To help students figure out the mystery word, record the words guessed and their number of correct letters on the chalkboard, or have students do so on paper. Later, progress to longer words.

idea 18 — ALL IN THE FAMILY

There are different ways to play this game.

To play one version, organize students into groups, each with a transparency and pen. Call out a word and each group writes all the word's forms they can think of on their transparency within the time limit (about two minutes). Then the class checks each team's work by projecting the transparency on the wall or screen with an overhead projector. Award points to each team for the number of correctly spelled words.

Another version begins with students in groups, as before. The first player writes a form of the word called out on the transparency, then passes it to the next player in the group. Words are added by each player in succession until a player cannot add another. At the end of the time (about two minutes), the class checks the words. One point is awarded for each word form spelled correctly (e.g., help—helps—helped—helping—helper—helpless—helplessly—helpful—helpfully—unhelpful...).

idea 19 — SENTENCE SPELL

Margo Mathis in Cincinnati says this game is full of fun and skills! She organizes her class into teams of five or six students, each group with a transparency and pen. She reads a challenging sentence aloud twice. The first player on each team writes the first word and passes the transparency to the second player who writes the second word, and so on. Words are written without the benefit of references or team assistance. Sentences are checked by the class using an overhead projector. One point is awarded for accuracy for each word, capital, punctuation mark, and for finishing the sentence as dictated.

Class Book Projects

A reading-writing partnership in the classroom can be created through book-making activities. Students experience the full circle of language—thinking, writing, and reading—by creating a class book. Within that circle are varied language-building opportunities, including spelling and proofreading.

Many of the activities in this Sourcebook include suggestions for turning students' work into class books. Here are possible formats for class book projects.

1 Create a series of books on one topic; for example, antonyms. Compile all student-illustrated pages from each antonyms class book writing activity into a new book. Select a student to create a cover; bind the book using staples. Your series will grow during the school year as more antonyms class book activities are completed.

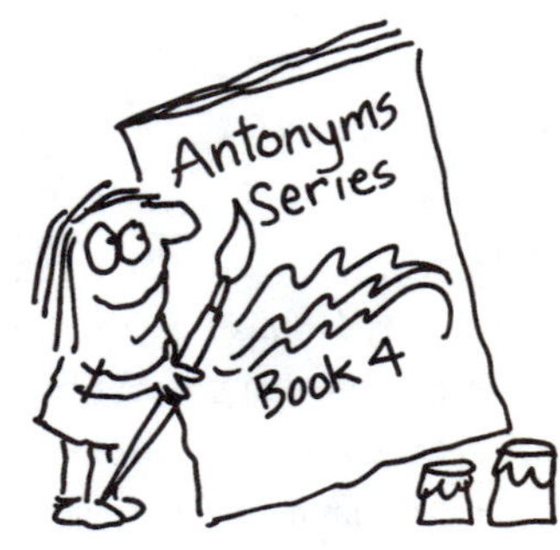

2 Develop an ongoing class book on one topic; for example, homophones. Throughout the year, select one student's illustrated page from the homophones class book writing activities for each homophone set introduced. Use removable fasteners for binding this book so that more pages may be easily added. Select a student to create a cover. During the year, be sure all students have an opportunity to contribute to the class book.

3 Have students create a personal book that comprises their own illustrated work from one writing activity; for example, a book on family members. Have students decorate the cover of their book. Bind each book using staples.

4 Produce a single class book that comprises all students' illustrated pages from one writing activity. Select a student to illustrate the cover of the book. Bind the book using staples.

5 Create novelty books.

Accordion Book: Create an expandable accordion book on one topic; for example, homographs. Have students fold a piece of sturdy art paper. In each section of their paper, have them write and illustrate a sentence using one word from a homograph set. Then tape pages together in accordion-pleated fashion and attach cover paper to the two end pages to create a book that can be folded for storage or displayed accordion style.

Canned Book: Canned books are written on narrow paper, such as cash register tape, wound, and fitted inside a clean soup can that has the title on a decorated paper label.

Shape Book: Shape books have covers and pages cut into a shape appropriate for the book's content. For example, a book about Halloween might be shaped like a jack-o'-lantern.

The Teaching Poster and Personal Poster are introduced in Unit 1, Test Ready, page 3.

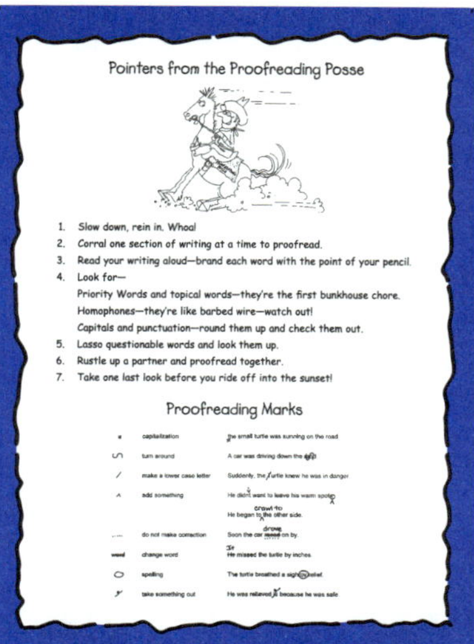

The Teaching Poster and Personal Poster are introduced in Unit 2, Activity 1A, page 11.

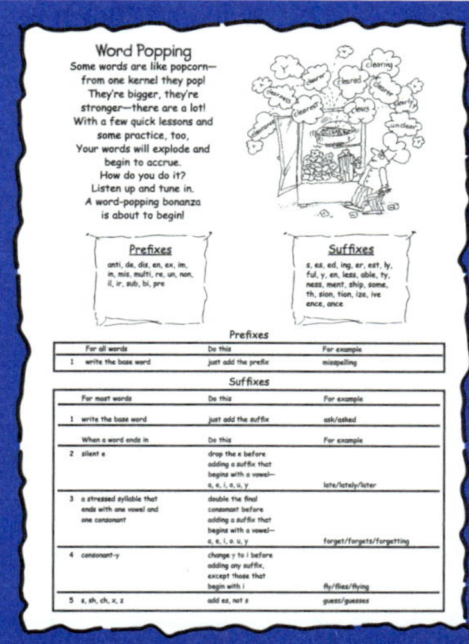

The Teaching Poster and Personal Poster are introduced in Unit 5, Activity 1C, page 38.

The Teaching Poster and Personal Poster are introduced in Unit 11, Activity 1C, page 92.

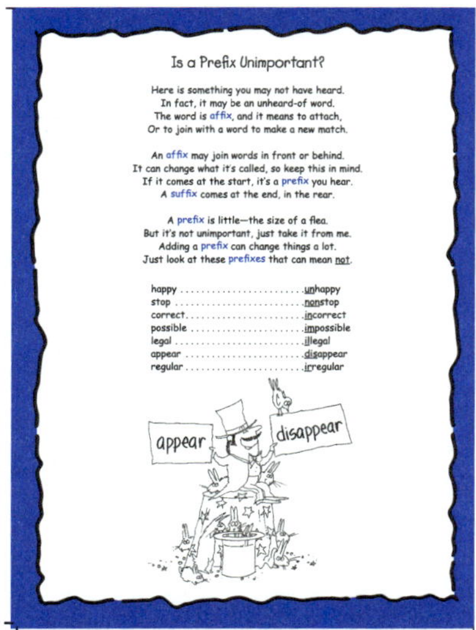

The Teaching Poster and Personal Poster are introduced in Unit 13, Activity 1A, page 110.

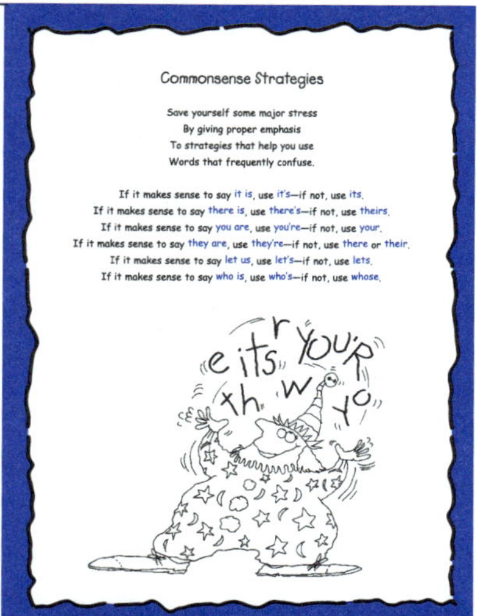

Display the teaching posters in your classroom for a study reference.

Each teaching poster is accompanied by a blackline master personal poster. Completed personal posters may be kept at school and/or sent home for students to share with their family.

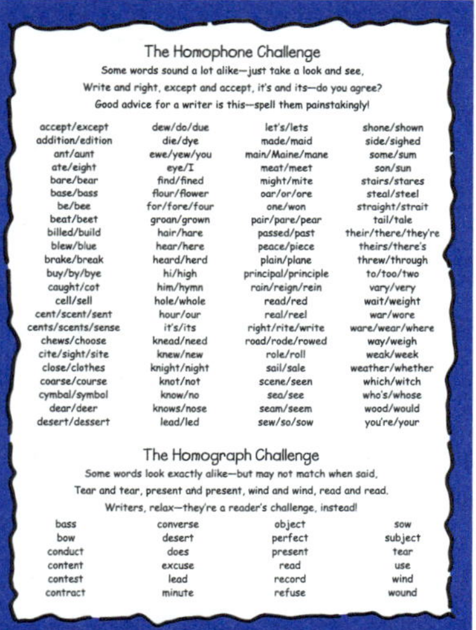

Ten-Box Reusable Chart

The Ten-Box Chart is a teaching aid in several Sourcebook activities. It is a great teaching aid—and not just for spelling. Use it for hands-on learning across the curriculum.

Materials needed: Poster board or oil cloth and colored tape or markers.

1 Cut a piece of poster board or oil cloth so it is 35" wide by 24" tall.

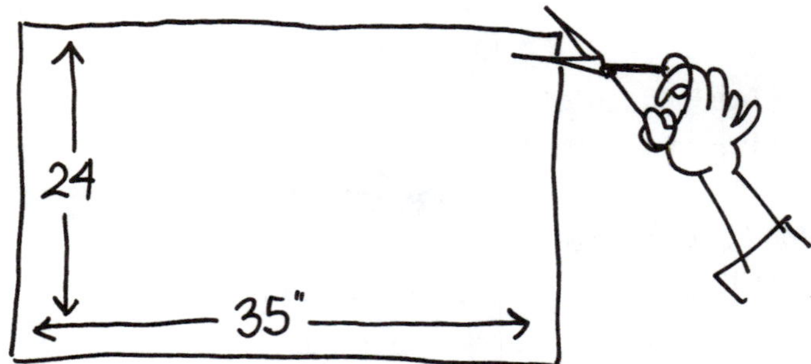

2 Measure and mark 7" increments across the width. Make vertical lines at each mark using colored tape or a marker. This will divide your chart into five equal columns.

3 Measuring 6" from the top, make a horizontal rule using colored tape or a marker. You now have a Ten-Box Reusable Chart. The top five boxes will each hold a large sticky note, and the lower five boxes have room for many small ones.

Level Five Literature List

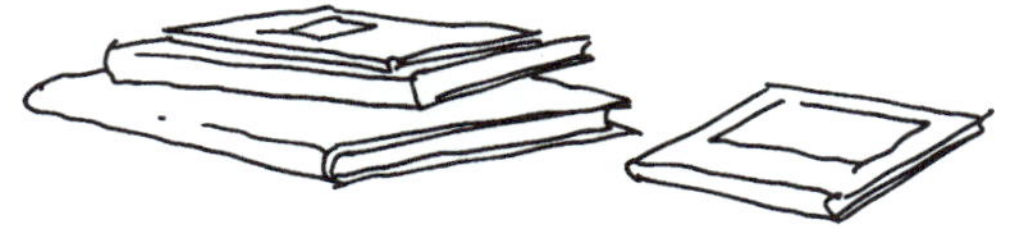

Unit 4	*A Light in the Attic*, Shel Silverstein
	Where the Sidewalk Ends, Shel Silverstein
	Falling Up, Shel Silverstein
Unit 6	*The Top of the World: Climbing Mount Everest*, Steve Jenkins
Unit 7	*Snowflake Bentley*, Jacqueline Briggs Martin
Unit 12	*The Wanderer*, Sharon Creech
Unit 13	*26 Fairmount Avenue*, Tomie de Paola
Unit 15	"Casey at the Bat," Ernest Lawrence Thayer
Unit 19	*A Year Down Yonder*, Richard Peck
	A Long Way From Chicago, Richard Peck
Unit 25	*William Shakespeare and the Globe*, Aliki
Unit 27	*A Year Down Yonder*, Richard Peck
	A Long Way From Chicago, Richard Peck
Unit 29	*The Sign of the Beaver*, Elizabeth Speare
Unit 31	*Coming On Home Soon*, Jacqueline Woodson
Unit 33	*Our Only May Amelia*, Jennifer Holm
Unit 35	*The True Story of the Three Little Pigs*, Jon Scieszka

Level Five Take-Home Task Answer Key

Unit 1
p. 4

music, brought, carefully, anything, ready, thought, beautiful, instead, suddenly, happened

Unit 2
p. 13

grinning/smiling, tacking/nailing, gripping/clasping, hoping/wishing, gabbing/chatting, racing/rushing, dining/eating, sobbing/weeping, dropping/spilling, tapping/knocking

Unit 3
p. 22

bought, blow, wrote, began, talked, thought, found, put, jogged, knelt, wept, fought, explained, caught

Unit 4
p. 31

1. sword; 2. lamb's; 3. Two, wrongs; 4. half; 5. fasten; 6. Knowledge; 7. answer, wrath; 8. Talk; 9. Whose; 10. castles; 11. crawl, walk; 12. half, half; 13. know; 14. often, awry; 15. written

Unit 5
p. 40

pail/bucket, equal/same, superior/excellent, leader/monarch, canoe/kayak, musical/choral, funny/comical, shake/quake, brook/stream, unkind/compassionless, chronological/in order, one-fourth/quarter, sorting/classifying, commandment/rule, beckon/call, curtsy/bow, ruckus/riot, explain/clarify, accurate/correct, quiz/test, battle/combat, quantity/amount, stir/mix, panicked/frightened, four/quad, ache/pain, ask/inquire, add/increase, coat/cloak, copying/mimicking, quarrel/argue, fall/collapse, rest/relax, schooling/training

Unit 6
p. 49

Bess and Tim Chang waited for <u>their</u> bus. The twins were on <u>their</u> way to the snowy mountain to ski with <u>their</u> friends. They were eager to get <u>there</u>. Then they saw Joe and Eric walking to the bus stop with <u>their</u> ski gear. "<u>They're</u> the best skiers on the hill!" said Bess to Tim. "I wish I could ski as well as <u>they're</u> skiing." Tim replied, "<u>They're</u> good skiers, but <u>they're</u> also good in math." The boys were in <u>their</u> older brother Dan's math class. <u>Their</u> math grades were at the top of <u>their</u> class.

Just as the boys got to the bus stop, <u>their</u> bus arrived. The four of them put <u>their</u> equipment in the ski rack and boarded. <u>There</u> were four seats in the back. As they were sitting down, Joe asked the twins, "Are <u>there</u> only two of you going to the mountain today? Will any of your brothers and sisters be <u>there</u>?" Bess told Joe, "The others aren't skiing today because <u>they're</u> doing other things." Then Joe asked, "How many Chang kids are <u>there</u> in the family?" "Well," grinned Tim, "<u>there</u> are several of us. I have as many brothers as sisters." "And I have twice as many brothers as sisters," added Bess. "Are <u>there</u> enough clues for you to figure out how many of us <u>there</u> are?" asked Tim. "Sure, <u>they're</u> great clues!" said Joe. How many kids are in the Chang family?

Unit 7
p. 58

1. springtime, myself, bluebird, newspaper, housefly, basketball, applesauce, anything, yourself; 2. earring, birthday, birdhouse, sailboat, raindrops, skateboard, yardstick, headache, waterfall, afternoon; 3. proofread, footprint, football, birthplace, scorecard, earthquake, touchdown, windshield, wastebasket, basketball, downwind, groundball

Unit 8
p. 67

democracy, city, aunts, circle, success, exclude, piece, surface, niece, actress, boss, complex, colorless, subtraction, princess, summit, myself, spicy, famous, descend, peace, sunset, adults, yolks

Unit 9
p. 76

farmer, whiter, brighter, higher, skinnier, later, teacher, sweeter, tidier, jogger, younger, employer, boxer, baker

Unit 10
p. 85

submarine (m), uncommon (f), rearrange (a), dissatisfied (j), export (q), review (d), expel (r), subnormal (n), exit (p), reconstruct (b), nonfiction (t), excel (s), uncertain (e), discontinue (h), subway (l), unequal (g), reenter (c), disliked (i), exchange (o), disappeared (k)

Unit 11
p. 94

you've, you'll; aren't, won't, isn't; they're, they've; she'll, she's; we're, we've, we'll. The apostrophe signals an omitted letter or letters. mother, mother's, mothers'; boy's, boys, boys'; snake, snake's, snakes'; turtle's, turtles, turtles'. The apostrophe signals ownership or possession. bears' honey, snakes in the grass, team's victory

Unit 12
p. 103

Mr. Bailey didn't solve his problem because the key will be delivered into the mailbox and Millie still won't be able to get in.

Unit 13
p. 112

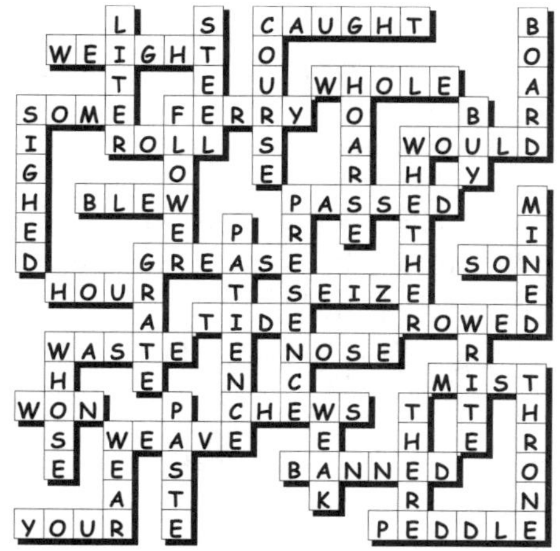

Unit 14
p. 121

journey/trip, mouth/entrance, careful/cautious, boulevard/street, bayou/river, you're/you are, bounce/rebound, town/borough, announce/pronounce, course/route, enough/bountiful, though/however, mountain/mound, young/youthful, pillow/cushion, rough/rigorous, throw/hurl, poultry/chicken, brought/took, throughout/everywhere

Unit 15
p. 130

whisper, phony, fresh, lunch, children, third, launch, paragraph, whistle, wish, fish, through, inch. Spelling is fun!

Unit 16
p. 139

spreader, strength, throw, screen, street, throat, screwdriver, sprinkle, three, screaming, strange, spring, thread, stream, scratch, spruce, straight, through, spry, scrub

Unit 17
p. 148

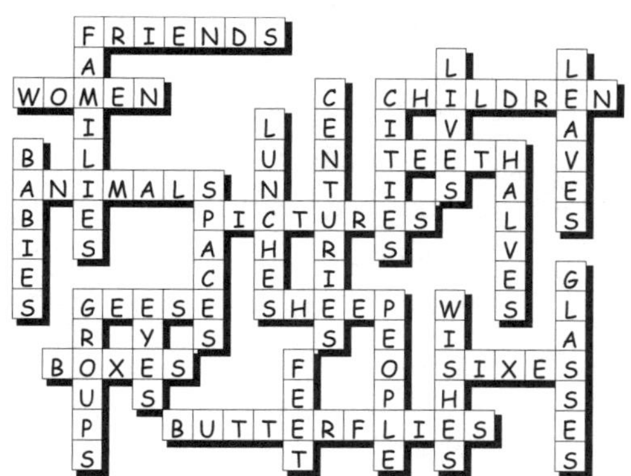

Unit 18
p. 157

more colorful, most colorful; late, latest; more northern, most northern; more troubled, most troubled; straight, straighter; friendlier, friendliest; dry, driest; safe, safer; more useful, most useful; flat, flattest; more willing, most willing; earlier, earliest; hungrier, hungriest; bluer, bluest; bad, worse; sadder, saddest

Unit 19
p. 166

link/join/connect; moisten/dampen; heroic/valiant/brave; oyster/shellfish; voyage/journey/excursion; employee/worker; loyal/faithful; bothering/annoying/irritating/troublesome; lure/decoy; destroy/destruct; lad/boy; toil/labor/work; adjoining/neighboring/bordering/adjacent; dodge/avoid; royal/noble; loiter/linger; void/empty; joy/pleasure/delight

Unit 20
p. 175

1. chickens, hatched; 2. corrupts, absolutely; 3. spilled; 4. coming, roses; 5. eyes, bigger; 6. frying; 7. served; 8. forgotten; 9. beginning; 10. handwriting; 11. mightier; 12. divided; 13. carefully; 14. believed, speaks; 15. makes, mistakes; 16. Actions, louder, words

Unit 21
p. 184

There's trouble ahead for writers who mix up homophones in their writing. They're sure to look like careless spellers, but the trouble is not just theirs. There may be problems for the reader, too. There's always the chance that the misuse of a homophone sends a different message than what the writer meant to say. The writer has mislead the reader! So, it's important for writers to proofread their homophones. The responsibility is all theirs, and theirs alone. There are many homophones and they're all important to use correctly.

Unit 22
p. 193

Answers will vary.

Unit 23
p. 202

competition, tournament; explanation, reason; thing, item; report, summary; breeze, gale; guide, direct; satisfied, pleased; dry land, sandy region; tiny, small; fish, freshwater animal

Unit 24
p. 211

chicken's, chickens, chickens'; owl's; baby, babies; bird, birds, birds'; business; animals; girl, girl's, girls; family's, families'; boy's, boys; ostrich; lady, lady's; horse's, horses, horses'

Unit 25
p. 220

legend, cagey, jay, jay, edge, juniper, huge, jelly, wedged, jealously, shortage, jelly, object, banjo, jaunty, gently, jay, urge, join, majestic, jay, generously, jelly, plunged, jaw, unintelligent, jerk, Justice, jelly, jeered, joyous, midget-sized, emerged, imagined, smidgen, jelly, courage, gestured, banjo, obliged, magical, Adjectives, gorgeous, energy, agile, judge, cogitation, logical, acknowledged, genuinely, Just, jumped, jelly, lunged, jungle, danger

Unit 26
p. 229
Words that cannot be synonyms: spring: sprig, May; bright: starlight, generous, silver; mean: loud, broken; trip: accident, ticket; fall: all can be synonyms; party: streamers, individual, slightly; state: city, united; store: groceries, stem, rescue; bill: drain, coast; fair: fresh, new; sound: forceful, wrong, section; might: shallow, bug, meant; last: test, level, stair; back: suitable, smooth; just: same, complete, difficult; down: ill, swallow; long: seldom, trivial, secure; will: settle, fence, sell; point: painted; play: fortune, toddler; run: clever; mind: certain, second

Unit 27
p. 238
1. peace (piece); 2. caught (cot); 3. plain (plane); 4. nose (knows); 5. wore (war); 6. won (one); 7. see (sea); 8. dear (deer); 9. pare (pair); 10. steel (steal); 11. heard (herd); 12. except (accept); 13. role (roll); 14. principal (principle); 15. cymbal (symbol); 16. meat (meet); 17. edition (addition); 18. seam (seem); 19. reel (real); 20. very (vary)

Unit 28
p. 247
Answers will vary.

Unit 29
p. 256
won't, shouldn't, isn't, they're, we're, you're, we've, you've, they've, she's, she's, he'd.
Answers will vary for sentences.

Unit 30
p. 265
forward/backward—A; guess/speculate—S; general/specific—A; anonymous/nameless—S; ahead/behind—A; difficult/effortless—A; material/fabric—S; test/exam—S; wrong/accurate—A; minute/tiny—S; object/agree—A; catch/seize—S; famous/unknown—A; exceptional/remarkable—S; explain/clarify—S; build/demolish—A; natural/abnormal—A; middle/halfway—S; late/punctual—A; base/apex—A; sleep/snooze—S; trouble/adversity—S; sent/received—A; modern/dated—A

Unit 31
p. 274

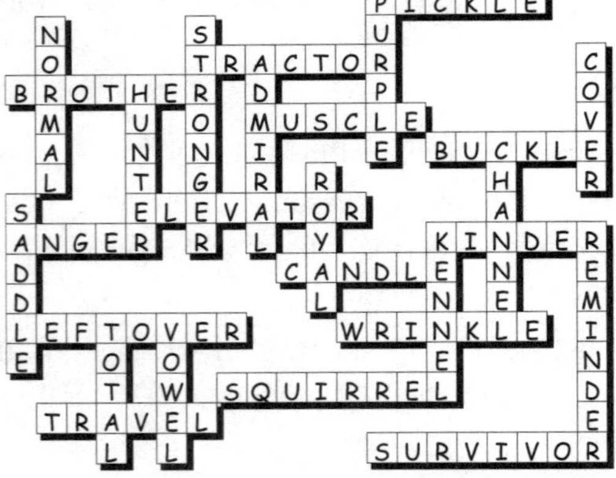

Unit 32
p. 283
began, broke, caught, dug, drove, felt, forgot, gave, heard, kept, left, rode, sang, slept, stood, stung, took, told, wore, won, bit, brought, chose, drew, ate, fought, froze, ground, hid, knew, lost, sold, sunk, slid, stole, struck, taught, thought, wove, wound, blew, built, came, drank, fed, flew, got, grew, held, led, made, shot, sat, spent, stuck, swept, tore, threw, wept, wrote

Unit 33
p. 292
Practice with *there/their/they're/there's/theirs* homophones.

Unit 34
p. 301

Unit 35
p. 310
It's, its; There's, theirs; choose, chose; You're, your; They're, there, their; Let's, lets; Whose, Who's; hears, Here's; wear, Where; We're, were; loose, lose

Word Skills for Becoming a Strategic Writer
Rebecca Sitton's SOURCEBOOK Series

High-Frequency Core Words

Build Skills and Word Experiences

Assess Words and Skills

Basics

Build Visual Skills

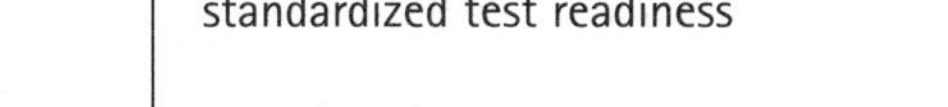

Levels 1–8
Five-minute visual warm-up activity

Build Basic Concepts

Levels 1–8
Selection of activities to develop concepts

Build Assessment Readiness

Levels 1–8
Skill Test preparation activities
•at-home blackline master
•at-school activity

Build Proofreading Skills

Levels 1–8
Everyday accountability for spelling in writing

Electives

Build Spelling and Language Skills

Levels 1–8
"Sponge" activities to use anytime

Build Reading and Writing Connections

Level 1
Literature tie-in activities

Build Skillful Writers

Levels 4–8
Ties spelling to written language conventions

Build Vocabulary

Levels 7–8
Word etymology activities

Basics

Assess Spelling Progress

Levels 1–8
Cloze Story Word Test of all previously introduced Core Words

Assess Skill Application

Levels 1–8
Evaluation of skill utilization

Electives

Extend Spelling Assessment

Levels 1–8
Test of all previously introduced Core Words, plus Extra Words for challenge

Assess Proofreading Application

Levels 5–8
Proofreading/editing tests to provide standardized test readiness

Assess Spelling Achievement

Levels 1–8
Evaluation of student progress using the Achievement Tests

Scope and Sequence for Level 5

Unit No.	1	2	3	4	5	6	7	8	9	10	11	12	13	14	15	16	17	18	19	20	21	22	23	24	25	26	27	28	29	30	31	32	33	34	35
• PHONICS—Exploring the relationship of letters/patterns to sounds for reading and spelling.																																			
short vowel sounds/spellings/patterns/rules	X	X	X			X								X		X			X	X		X			X						X				
long vowel sounds/spellings/patterns/rules	X	X	X		X		X					X				X			X		X	X			X	X		X							X
other vowel sounds/spellings/patterns/rules	X		X						X					X		X			X			X							X		X				
consonant sounds/spellings/patterns/rules	X	X	X	X	X			X	X	X		X				X			X		X	X			X	X				X	X			X	
digraph sounds/spellings/patterns/rules								X	X				X			X							X	X	X								X		
soft-syllable sounds/spellings/patterns/rules				X		X							X	X	X								X	X	X	X	X	X	X						
silent letters		X		X	X		X							X			X		X			X			X		X							X	X
unexpected spellings	X	X			X	X		X				X		X			X	X			X	X						X	X	X		X			
ie/ei or ou spellings						X								X	X		X			X												X		X	
stressed/unstressed syllables				X		X								X	X	X			X				X		X	X	X	X	X		X				
phonological and/or rhyming awareness	X	X	X	X	X	X	X	X		X		X		X	X			X	X	X	X	X		X	X	X			X	X			X	X	X
double letters		X			X	X	X			X		X				X		X			X		X	X		X				X			X	X	
letter-card word-making activities						X							X				X				X		X			X							X		
• PROBLEM SOLVING—Using thinking skills.																																			
logical thinking exercises				X		X		X	X	X			X															X		X			X		
analogies			X						X							X																			
hypothesizing	X	X		X	X	X	X	X	X	X	X	X	X	X	X	X	X	X	X	X	X	X	X	X	X	X	X	X	X	X	X	X	X	X	X
• READING—Participating in reading (e.g., words, sentences, poetry/rhymes, informative/narrative stories, riddles, student-made books).																																			
	X	X	X	X	X	X	X	X	X	X	X	X	X	X	X	X	X	X	X	X	X	X	X	X	X	X	X	X	X	X	X	X	X	X	X
• WRITING OPPORTUNITIES—Participating in modeled, structured, shared, interactive, paired, and independent written communication.																																			
words	X	X	X	X	X	X	X	X	X	X	X	X	X	X	X	X	X	X	X	X	X	X	X	X	X	X	X	X	X	X	X	X	X	X	X
sentences (declarative/exclamatory/interrogative)	X	X	X	X	X	X	X	X	X	X	X	X	X	X	X	X	X	X	X	X	X	X	X	X	X	X	X	X	X	X	X	X	X	X	X
sentence expansion	X	X	X	X	X	X	X	X	X	X	X	X	X	X	X	X	X	X	X	X	X	X	X	X	X	X	X	X	X	X	X	X	X	X	X
dictation	X	X	X	X	X	X	X	X	X	X	X	X	X	X	X	X	X	X	X	X	X	X	X	X	X	X	X	X	X	X	X	X	X	X	X
narrative/descriptive/persuasive		X		X	X				X				X	X	X			X		X	X		X			X		X			X				X
explanatory/informational	X	X	X	X	X	X	X	X	X	X	X	X	X	X	X	X	X	X	X	X	X	X	X	X	X	X	X	X	X	X	X	X	X	X	X
research and writing	X	X	X		X	X	X	X			X	X	X	X					X	X			X	X				X	X	X	X	X		X	X
student-made books						X				X	X			X	X				X	X			X		X				X			X		X	
other (e.g., rhymes/riddles/letters/dialogue/ads)	X					X	X	X				X	X	X					X				X		X	X	X	X	X		X			X	X
• WRITING CONVENTIONS—Understanding and applying the guidelines for writing correctness.																																			
capitalization/punctuation/grammar/usage	X	X	X	X	X	X	X	X	X	X	X	X	X	X	X	X	X	X	X	X	X	X	X	X	X	X	X	X	X	X	X	X	X	X	X
apostrophe	X	X		X			X	X			X	X	X			X			X	X	X	X		X		X	X				X		X	X	X
nouns/verbs/adjectives/adverbs		X					X	X	X			X				X			X	X		X			X			X		X			X		
possessives/possessive pronouns				X	X	X			X			X	X	X		X			X				X	X		X			X			X	X	X	X
plurals (regular/irregular)		X				X		X				X	X			X	X	X		X				X	X				X			X	X		X
comparatives/superlatives (regular/irregular)									X			X							X			X													
irregular verb forms			X																X		X										X		X		
• SPELLING—Mastering the spelling of high-frequency words, and ensuring their long-term application in writing.																																			
	X	X	X	X	X	X	X	X	X	X	X	X	X	X	X	X	X	X	X	X	X	X	X	X	X	X	X	X	X	X	X	X	X	X	X

Scope and Sequence for Level 5

Unit No.	1	2	3	4	5	6	7	8	9	10	11	12	13	14	15	16	17	18	19	20	21	22	23	24	25	26	27	28	29	30	31	32	33	34	35
• PROOFREADING—Mastering editing strategies to increase performance on standardized tests and in everyday writing.																																			
	X	X	X	X	X	X	X	X	X	X	X	X	X	X	X	X	X	X	X	X	X	X	X	X	X	X	X	X	X	X	X	X	X	X	X
• VISUAL SKILLS—Developing strategies to visualize and remember words and their sequential letters.																																			
visualizing letters of known words	X	X	X	X	X	X	X	X	X	X	X	X	X	X	X	X	X	X	X	X	X	X	X	X	X	X	X	X	X	X	X	X	X	X	X
visual skill-building exercises	X		X					X				X															X			X		X		X	
• GENERALIZATIONS FOR AFFIXES—Discovering how to make and use new words by applying the essential rules for the addition of suffixes and prefixes.																																			
suffixes: s/es, ed, ing, er, est, ly, ful, y, en, less, able, ness, ment, ship, some, th, sion, tion, ize, ive, e/ance	X	X				X		X	X	X				X	X	X	X	X	X	X	X			X	X			X				X	X	X	X
prefixes: anti, de, dis, en, ex, im, in, mis, multi, re, un, non, il, ir, sub, bi, pre		X	X		X			X		X		X		X		X		X	X			X	X	X									X	X	X
• WORD GAMES—Participating in motivational activities that build word skills and understandings.																																			
visual		X									X		X	X		X							X	X			X		X			X			
vocabulary/language-related		X	X	X	X		X		X			X		X		X					X	X	X		X	X	X					X		X	X
phonics-based			X	X	X		X		X									X									X		X	X		X			X
palindromes													X																						
spelling			X		X				X			X			X		X	X		X			X				X	X	X			X	X		X
• VOCABULARY—Acquiring words to explore their purpose within our communication system.																																			
word meaning and/or etymologies	X	X	X	X	X	X	X	X	X	X	X	X	X	X	X	X	X	X	X	X	X	X	X	X	X	X	X	X	X	X	X	X	X	X	X
idioms/proverbs/expressions	X	X	X	X	X		X	X	X	X	X		X	X		X	X	X	X	X	X	X	X	X	X		X	X	X	X	X	X	X	X	X
similes, metaphors, onomatopoeia, hyperbole												X			X		X					X		X											
multiple meaning words (e.g., long, just)							X	X	X			X			X		X		X		X	X	X	X							X		X	X	
Latin/Greek word parts	X		X	X	X	X			X	X			X	X	X		X			X	X	X	X		X			X			X			X	X
words from other languages				X				X			X					X				X	X														
eponyms															X									X	X										X
synonyms/antonyms			X	X		X			X		X		X	X	X			X				X	X	X	X	X	X	X			X	X			X
homophones	X	X	X	X	X	X	X	X	X	X	X	X	X	X	X	X	X	X	X	X	X	X	X	X	X	X	X	X	X	X	X	X	X	X	
homographs							X	X	X			X										X	X	X								X			
contractions	X	X			X	X		X	X				X	X				X	X	X					X	X				X			X		
compound words	X		X					X					X	X	X	X		X						X	X	X						X			
often-confused words (e.g., then/than)	X	X	X	X	X		X		X	X			X		X	X	X	X			X	X	X				X	X			X	X			X
numbers/colors/animals/weather/food/names		X				X		X										X				X			X			X			X				
cities/states/geographical words			X			X		X																			X	X					X		
shortcut words (e.g., abbreviations/acronyms)		X				X		X					X					X							X					X	X		X		
• WORD STUDY—Collecting, analyzing, sorting, and contrasting words, and drawing conclusions about their spelling and use.																																			
	X	X	X	X	X	X	X	X	X	X	X	X	X	X	X	X	X	X	X	X	X	X	X	X	X	X	X	X	X	X	X	X	X	X	X
• LITERATURE—Using classic literature as a catalyst for thinking, reading, writing, and speaking (see Level 5 Sourcebook, page 397).																																			
rhymes, poetry, songs				X	X	X	X					X		X	X			X		X		X						X							
folktales/fables/traditional stories		X																					X	X	X								X		X
informational				X	X																						X			X					
narratives									X						X	X					X								X	X	X		X		X

Sitton Spelling and Word Skills™

Overview of Materials

Sitton Spelling and Word Skills™ provides an alternative approach that ensures that students transfer the words th[ey] spell to the words they write by developing essential skills, including proofreading, that they can apply to all word[s].

SOURCEBOOKS • Grades 1–8

SOURCEBOOKS provide the infrastructure to craft a spelling and word skills program your way. One teacher resource book for each level contains everything you need in a unit-by-unit format to create a balanced, differentiated program that's right for your students. Each Sourcebook includes five large teaching posters. Nothing is consumable!

3rd Edition!

In every unit, you will find:
- Differentiated spelling words and activity choices
- Options for all ability learners
- Blackline master assessments and take-home tasks
- Spelling tie-ins—vocabulary, literature, phonics, usage, writing

PRACTICE BOOKS • Grades 1–6

(use with 2nd or 3rd Edition Sourcebooks)

Ideal for both high and low achievers, in-class practice, homework, summer activities, or the Summer School program. Consumable student books extend practice, proofreading, and word exploration for every Sourcebook unit. Each Practice Book includes a Core Words List, a Priority Words List, a running record of Spelling Words, and a Rules for Reference page. Every book creates a synopsis of essentials.

TEACHING POSTERS • Grades 1–8

Five colorful 18" x 24" grade-specific posters come with each Sourcebook, but may be purchased separately—either for replacement or stand-alone use. Visit our web site for a description of each poster.

TUTOR ME Training® • for 2nd or 3rd Edition Sourcebooks

(9 modules: Levels 1–8, plus Parent Introduction)

Learn to use the 2nd or 3rd Edition Sourcebooks either on your own or in a small group. Each module includes an Overview DVD of the Series and grade-specific training on CD-ROM to equip you to begin tomorrow. Invite parents to view the Parent Introduction module to discover how their child will be learning to spell.

100 WORDS CHART (5 posters per package)

This large, colorful poster lists the 100 high-use writing words.

MY SPELL CHECK® K–2 (10 cards per package)

Colorful, durable 8.5" x 11" spelling references list 85 high-use words; plus more words—animals, clothes, numbers, days, months, family, school, food, weather. Teacher resource of 50+ activities to extend students' word experiences is included in each package.

SPELL CHECK® 3–8 (10 cards per package)

Colorful, durable 8.5" x 11" spelling references list 150 high-u[se] words; plus more—months, days, common abbreviations, and [?] context sentences to clarify often-confused words. Teacher resource of 50+ activities to extend students' word experience[s] is included in each package.

CORE WORD ACTIVITY CARDS • Grades 1–3

Springboard from the high-frequency Core Words to more words—and essential language and spelling skills—with colorful 3.5" x 6" word wall activity cards. LEVEL 1 learners have 75 cards—their 35 Core Words, plus 40 onset-rime pattern cards, LEVEL 2 contains the first 170 Core Words, and LEVEL 3 includes the top 335 Core Words—each card with a grade-specific skill-building activity on the back.

WORD SKILLS in RHYTHM and RHYME • Grades 1–3

Extend the Sourcebook language experiences with exciting skill-based, chant-along rhymes introduced to students on a CD-ROM and over 100 blackline-master practice pages at eac[h] level to reinforce essential language concepts.

WORD-WISE SOURCEBOOKS • Grades 1–6

32 language-teaching rhymes and activities on blackline maste[r] Book One—grades 1-2, Book Two—grades 3-4, Book Three—grades 5-6.

SOME WORDS Vocabulary Mini-Course Series

• Grades 4 and above

Use these new mini-courses to give upper grade students the single most research-supported advantage for academic and future success—vocabulary skills! Each 32-page consumable booklet features an on-another-paper extension activity. Wove[n] in are multiple tie-ins to related skills and essential rules to hel[p] students make discoveries about our language and how it work[s]. Absolutely no teacher prep time required—it's ready to go!

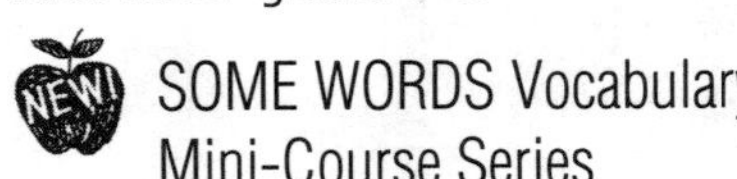

404

A PAGE
FOR NOTES!

A PAGE
FOR NOTES!

A PAGE
FOR NOTES!

A PAGE
FOR NOTES!